A.D. Architectural Design

BRITISH ARCHITECTURE
BRITISH ARCHITECTURE

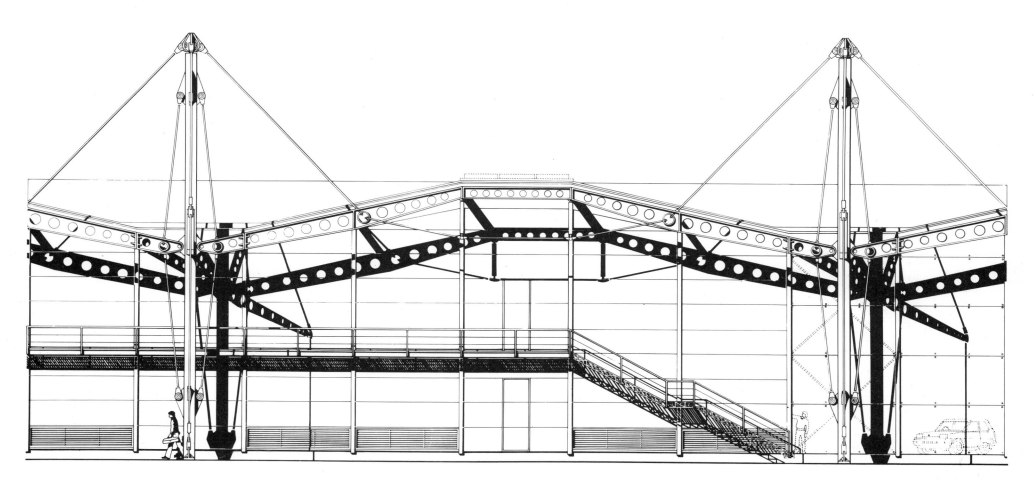

ACADEMY EDITIONS · LONDON   **ST. MARTIN'S PRESS · NEW YORK**

Jeremy Dixon Tate Gallery Cafeteria, London

BRITISH ARCHITECTURE
BRITISH ARCHITECTURE

Editor/Publisher: Dr Andreas C Papadakis
Design conception/coordination: Dennis Crompton
Technical Editor: Ian Latham
Editorial Assistants: Jane Brierley, Louisa Denman
Design Assistant: Bet Ayer

First published in Great Britain in 1982 by
Academy Editions, 7/8 Holland Street, London W8. ISBN (UK): 856-70814-3

Published in the United States of America by St. Martin's Press, 175 Fifth Avenue, New York, NY 10010   ISBN(US): 0-312-10035-3

Printed and bound in Great Britain by Balding & Mansell Ltd., Wisbech.

Front cover: Terry Farrell Partnership, TVAM Headquarters, Camden Lock, model for cover by Bob Kirkman (ph: Graham Challifour)
Back cover: Richard Rogers & Partners, INMOS Microelectronics Factory, section detail
Title page: Foster Associates, Renault Parts Distribution Centre, nr Swindon, elevation detail
Above: Arup Associates, Bab Al Sheikh Development, Baghdad, section through office building

Editorial Note/Acknowledgements

This survey of current British architecture is based on the response to the 1982 Architectural Design Project Awards. The jury's selection of projects is featured in full, together with a number of unpremiated entries. Individual members of the jury were also invited to submit schemes for publication, and *AD* sought particular projects from further practices in an attempt to present a cross-section of today's most interesting work. All featured architects were invited to participate in *AD*'s 'British Architecture 1982' Exhibition held at the RIBA through August receiving both popular and critical acclaim.

We are indebted to the many individuals and organisations who have contributed to the success of this publication. Firstly, for their untiring diligence, the 1982 Project Awards jury under the chairmanship of Derek Walker: Will Alsop, Ted Cullinan, Ted Happold, Denys Lasdun, Frank Newby, Andreas Papadakis, Monica Pidgeon and Elia Zenghelis. The RIBA exhibition would not have been possible without the help of President Owen Luder and the RIBA Events Office; Anna Forbes designed and made the banners hung in the RIBA foyer during the exhibition. Finally we would like to thank Dennis Crompton for the overall design of this publication and, with Ron Herron, for that of the exhibition.

GOLD

Ahrends, Burton & Koralek: Cummins Engine Factory Co Ltd, Shotts, Lanarkshire
Zaha Hadid: Conversion of 59 Eaton Place

SILVER

Colquhoun & Miller: Oldbrook 2, Housing in Milton Keynes
Chris Dawson: Martin Residence, Beverly Hills
Terry Farrell Partnership: Wood Green Northern Industrial Development
Eva Jiricna: Flat for Joseph
Richard Reid: Christmas Steps, Facelift Competition, Bristol
Julyan Wickham: Hospital for the Doubly Handicapped, Boekel, Holland

BRONZE

Mark Fisher: 'The Wall' for Pink Floyd, Earls Court
Campbell, Zogolovitch, Wilkinson, Gough: 'Sir Edwin Lutyens', exhibition design, Hayward Gallery
Keppie Henderson & Partners: Restoration of the Willow Tea Rooms, Glasgow

COMMENDATIONS

Camden Department of Technical Services: Highgate New Stage 2, Site C, London N19
Doug Clelland and Eric Parry Partnership: Headquarters for Solid State Logic Ltd, Stonesfield, Oxon
Darbourne and Darke: Semi-rural Bolzano
Terry Farrell Partnership: Alexandra Pavilion, Alexandra Palace, Haringey
Nicholas Grimshaw & Partners: Industrial Nursery Unit Development, Gillingham
Edward Jones and Margot Griffin: Archives Building for Karl Friedrich Schinkel, Berlin
Rick Mather: Rebuilding and Refurbishment of 4 Eton Villas, London NW3
John Outram: Factories, Kensal Road, London
Richard Reid: 'Learning from the Vernacular', study
Douglas Stephen & Partners: Caergybi (Holyhead) Station and Ferry Terminal
Quinlan Terry: Salute Birdcage

AD STUDENT PROJECT AWARDS

Laurence Bain, Mackintosh School, Glasgow
Vakis Hadjikyriacou, Royal College of Art, London
Amarjit Kalsi, Architectural Association, London
Gregory Penoyre, Sheffield University
Richard Portchmouth, Kingston Polytechnic
Peter St John, Bartlett School, University College, London

Derek Walker
ON BEHALF OF THE ASSESSORS

'A map of the World that does not include Utopia is not worth even glancing at.'

A SIMILAR THOUGHT crossed my mind when the purpose built, ideologically varied jury assessed this year's Project Award submissions. *'Design Awards that do not include idealists, fantasists, fanatics and the fringe are not worth judging ...'*

This year's bumper crop gave the assessors a great deal of pleasure. The inclusion of Monica Pidgeon and Andreas Papadakis added a new dimension to a jury which included two of Britain's greatest engineers—Ted Happold and Frank Newby, looking more than ever like The Brothers Cheeryble. The profession's representatives, Sir Denys Lasdun, Will Alsop, Elia Zenghelis and Ted Cullinan, provided a variety of architectural insight. Only Norman Foster (the perennial absentee) was missing, becalmed in mid air, reflecting on the inconsistencies of Singapore Airlines and purposely doing press-ups in the aisle in preparation for the London Marathon.

The jury buzzed with dissensions, delight and disgust in almost equal quantities. The first rough cut was done by two groups and all entries of interest were put on one side for mutual discussion between the groups.

Last to be judged, but not least in effort and quality, were the submissions of the school entries. Happily the spoils were divided between students of six schools. Richard Portchmouth of Kingston Polytechnic; Peter St John from the Bartlett; Gregory Penoyre from Sheffield University; Laurence Bain from the Mackintosh School; Amarjit Kalsi from the AA and Vakis Hadjikyriacou from the RCA. An extraordinarily interesting collection greatly appreciated by the jury, who were fortunate in the fact that Ted Cullinan seemed to have taught everybody, knew most of the schemes intimately and together with Ted Happold beguiled the Jury with a potted history of almost every entry.

The great difficulty in looking at students' work was the inevitable problem of comparison. Grand schemes, small schemes, wayward schemes and fashionable schemes, tutorial imposition and international smash and grab made judgement in this area something of a lottery. It would have been much more interesting to have confronted all these bright hopes with an identical brief and to have seen comparisons in a more straightforward way.

If the democratic principle ruled in the selection of the assessors and the student winners, the selection of the awards and commendations summarised rather neatly the state of the art. One interpretation could be 'New Directions', another interpretation 'All Directions', and a less charitable view bemoaning the cluttered chaos of current architectural thought. The good, the bad and the mad all seemed to have their supporters and inevitably in this situation only the most interesting and professional solutions surfaced to the second round.

At this point a certain pragmatism took over and the assessors tried first to isolate typologies and effectively choose the best example within each group. The gold, silver and bronze categories proved difficult to isolate and it is true to say that each submission, with the exception of two or three in these categories, had fervent supporters for a gold award.

In the end two schemes seemed to satisfy all the assessors and it was gratifying that the award was shared by a regular prizewinner in Ahrends, Burton and Koralek for their masterly Cummin's Engine Factory at Shotts in Lanarkshire, and to Zaha Hadid, a comparative newcomer, for her elegant and sensitive conversion of 59 Eaton Place.

The Cummin's Factory, like so many good buildings, reflects not only the consistent skills of a highly sophisticated practice but also the singular client who continues to see fine quality architecture as an integral part of company success. Some members of the jury had seen the factory and were unanimous in their judgement of its success as a tailored solution to a particular process—detail that came out of a totally integrated exercise in structure and servicing and a long-demonstrated ability by ABK to tailor any building to its site and contours.

On the other hand, Zaha Hadid's scheme for Eaton Place had a fervent supporter in Elia Zenghelis. His careful interpretation of an extremely beautiful but slightly excessive presentation indicated a rare but idiosyncratic gift for total saturation design. The Zenghelis gift for silent rhetoric headed off a minor revolt to place the project in the silver category. When the final list was prepared I think everyone was unanimous in thinking that the quality of thought and care in what was ostensibly a minor project thoroughly merited its position of pre-eminence in the distinguished group of award winners.

The silver medal winners were much more difficult to determine. This group of seven eventual winners all had minority dissenters for a variety of reasons—ambivalence about the achievement of architecture through public housing, the ambiguities implicit in alteration work, suspicion or research excursions and a marked lack of detail in one premiated submission.

When the dust finally settled and this group became more clearly defined, it became obvious that the typology theory had merit. Colquhoun and Miller's Housing for Oldbrook, Milton Keynes was far and away the best public housing submission. It demonstrated the practice's continuing gift for understatement—quiet, well-organised plans, carefully selected materials and an ability to prosper within the constraints of a very clearly defined Central Area Housing Master Plan.

The two interiors by Eva Jiricna and Chris Dawson offered a contrast in approach that is both cultural and geographical. Jiricna's flat for Joseph offers a very chic London hi-tech look for a man who obviously dines in restaurants. It embodies an approach to restoration which could place Eva in some difficulty if commissioned to renovate the Athenaeum.

Chris Dawson's long stay in Los Angeles is at last being acknowledged in a series of personal essays for exotic clients. His clever alteration of a totally unlovely Beverly Hills 'broiler' is extraordinary in the quality of the space he trawls from a totally undistinguished plan. It is a far cry from Chrysalis and his earlier work, but his exile has produced a remarkable development in his skills. He joins a very select group of young LA architects whose future work will be awaited with keen anticipation.

In contrast, Terry Farrell's current preoccupations are much more fully documented in this country. His pre-eminence as a dogmatic purveyor of Post-Classical forms is not everybody's idea of where architecture should be going. Nevertheless there is no denying the cult is fashionable. However, with a jury equally positive in its views, it was interesting that a much quieter intervention of Terry Farrell's received a silver medal. Wood Green Northern Industrial Estate was unanimously selected over Alexandra Palace, which received a commendation. Irrespective of stylistic diversions, Farrell's ability to plan and to compose within tight spaces is demonstrated to perfection in the Wood Green Project.

Julyan Wickham's Hospital for the Handicapped in Boekel, Holland, was greatly admired by a number of the assessors. It lacked clarity in some aspects of the presentation and this scheme would have been enhanced if the author could have presented his case. Similarly Richard Reid's Christmas Steps for Bristol, though beautifully presented, lacked only the personal poetry that such a project feeds on.

The bronze medal group was very much the province of the lively lads—two ephemeral tableaux and a Charles Rennie Mackintosh revival. The restoration of the Willow Tearooms one felt brought out the best in the jury—not a discussion entirely in accord with the Keppie Henderson intrusion but endearing in its comprehensive generosity on the virtues and design ability of Charles Rennie Mackintosh.

The Piers Gough/Edwin Lutyens affair was obviously a relationship that no credible publisher could resist. A few antis saw the invasion of Lutyens as a personal affront, however the day was saved by the unequivocal realisation that any man who could purposely feature Gertrude Jekyll's gardening boots couldn't be all bad.

Mark Fisher on the other hand got full marks for his submission. His presentation of the Wall for Pink Floyd at Earls Court demonstrated that an event can be architecture and the end of an event can see the end of architecture. His lyrical drawings are so powerful in imagery that a roving commission on the South Bank would perhaps be more to his liking and our delight than a bronze medal.

If anything, the commendations brought into harsh relief the stances preoccupying most architects. To see a list including Quinlan Terry, Darbourne & Darke, Doug Clelland and Eric Parry, Nick Grimshaw, Ed Jones, Rick Mather, Douglas Stephen, John Outram and the Borough of Camden begs the question which fascinated the Jury—where is architecture going? Is it really alive and well and is its fratricidal bigotry, its public dance of death astonishing anybody other than fellow architects? Perhaps its diversions, like the birth of the pointed arch, will discover new virtues, or perhaps it is more useful to finish with Mumford's Utopias: *'With Plato we see the enormous importance of birth and education; we recognise the part good breeding, in every sense of the word, must play in the good community. Sir Thomas More makes us aware of the fact that a community becomes a community to the extent that it has shared possessions and he suggests that the local group might develop such a common life as the old colleges of Oxford have enjoyed. When we turn to Christianopolis, we are reminded that the daily life and work of the community must be infused with the spirit of science, and that an acute practical intelligence such as we find today among the engineers need not be divorced from the practice of the humanities. Even the nineteenth-century utopias have a contribution to make. They remind us by their over emphasis that all the proud and mighty idealisms in the world are so many shadows unless they are supported by the whole economic fabric, so that 'utopia' is not merely a matter of spiritual conversion, as the ancient religions taught, but of economic and geotechnic reconstruction. Finally from James Buckingham and Ebenezer Howard we can learn the importance of converting the Idolum of utopia into plans and layouts and detailed projections, such as a townplanner might utilize: and we may suspect that a utopia which cannot be converted into such specific plans will continue, as the saying is, to remain up in the air.'*

I hope we don't live in the air too long.

Peter Cook
THE ENGLISH ARCHITECTURAL SCENE

INVENTIVENESS AND LYRICISM—that is what English architecture is about.

Waywardness and endless speculative chatter—that is what the London architectural world is about.

It has often been said that London is the best place in which to talk about architecture—but don't expect the fruits of the conversation to be found down the street. It is also a city that genuinely enjoys the presence of foreigners and ecentrics, as well as a special category of person who never seems to *produce* anything but can put in a telling word here and there—and send their more energetic friends once more off in another frantic direction.

So already I am talking about *London* rather than *England*. Unsurprisingly, all the people that I will mention are living in London, for outside is a dreadful (and self-satisfied) provinciality that has no match in Europe. There are better-informed students in Oulu (out there, almost into the Finnish arctic) than in Birmingham or Bristol. There are more thinking architects in sleepy Graz than in bustling Manchester. Back in the village, we have, of course, all the stock characters from folk opera: the sage, the prankster, the wayward sons, the loves and hates, but in a less histrionic way than in New York—the other village from which constant rumours come and go across the bay. To be seen in someone's company is regarded as a demonstrative act in New York, whereas in London it is probably pure companionship or the unexpected sharing of a genuine enthusiasm. To be 'on' or 'off' a list is cause for great concern in New York or Berlin, whereas in London it is shrugged off as the likely result of casual oversight. Such characteristic English nonchalance is a constant puzzle and even cause for irritation amongst other Europeans. 'Why can't you English get *angry* about things?' they implore.

I am sure that the wayward retreat into the territory of ones own imagination, the pursuit of a dream, the deliberate misunderstanding of a great philosophical movement (because it seemed too shrill, too dogmatic and in the end too boring), the preference of the company of a funny character who is an embarrassingly bad designer but has strange thoughts about shadows to the company of an eager young man who is full of the latest angles: this is the true background against which the tradition of inventiveness and lyricism has flourished, and it has served the village well.

At present, the centre stage is occupied by three strong forces: the offices of James Stirling and Michael Wilford, of Norman Foster and of Richard Rogers. Intriguingly, their most discussed projects happen to be sited outside England. Yet in manner, all three offices are atmospherically English. All are highly inventive.

For Stirling, the inevitable development of role was from naughty boy, to rouguish fat man to grand old man, and this could have been predicted twenty years ago: but the amazing trajectory of the work itself could not. It has continued to irritate. First, in the sheer exuberance of the formalism of the Leicester–St Andrews period even his closest friends felt uneasy (and certainly designed uneasily) when they stepped outside the orthodoxy of anglicised Le Corbusier or Bruto-Rationalism. Then there came doors made of bricks, gawky outcrops, cascading glass, naughty pipes, porthole windows and eventually (and inevitably) a caterpillar of moulded plastic in the Olivetti building at Haslemere. What could they say or do? At this point, if his style had frozen the rest of the operatic scenario it would be easy for both Foster and Rogers are the children of technological positivism: and at a certain point one could see the English scene held together, as it were, along a neoprene gaskit.

But then, characteristically, Jim got bored. The debate as to whether his brilliant assistant Leon Krier actually turned the head of the master or heroically retreated into

Foster Associates, Hong Kong and Shanghai Bank
Richard Rogers & Partners, Lloyd's Building, London

Rationalism because his dogmatic European psychology could not lyrically drift in the English way (now *that's* a thought?), will never be resolved. At any rate Jim began to publicly grunt that England was boring and certainly seemed to have more time for Hans Hollein, Richard Meier and Arata Isozaki who collectively display an *élan* that comes from sure-footedness and a certain cosmopolitanism. In recent times the affrontery of the Berlin Scientific Centre plan seems to come out of its sheer sophistication as much as its naughty-boy collisionism and calls the earlier work to mind. Any minute now, Jim is going to get bored again and really launch right into his coloured-building period—or whatever else takes his fancy. In this sense he is still the most exciting architect in London even if he gives little out as a cultural figure; rather prosaic as a lecturer, easily bored by people and something of a gourmand.

Yet neither Foster nor Rogers have so far acheived his personality of style. They come across still as *aspirants*, and by the same token as eager and much, much *younger*. Which is not only delightful but extremely healthy.

Foster is too easily type-cast as the man from the Northern back streets who not only made it to the city, but took a look at the office of Skidmore, Owings and Merrill (when it was still worth the bother) and resolved to do it better. So his office is highly competitive, constantly running on overdrive, and Norman himself sniffs and bites and draws and charges. His ability to project everywhere the almost symbiotic relationship between himself, his helicopter, his buildings and the technology that supports them all is really inspiring, so he has not yet enjoyed the luxury of relaxation. He has never enjoyed that series of drifts: the indulgences and contemplations that couch the bourgeoisie on both sides of the English Channel where spoken witticisms are preferred to the angst of the thorough design, where a good claret is preferred to nightlong hours in pursuit of the perfect joint.

Within the village, there is constant discussion of the pros and cons of the Foster office as against the Rogers office, (Stirling is already elevated to the role of Grand Duke). The clue lies in their personalities. For Richard *is* the child of that bourgeoisie, and is half Italian anyway! He has brought an urbanity to the pursuit of that same technology that allies itself with the culture of full-colour, full-frontal and full three-dimensional; his speech is staccato, the ideas are too fast for the limitations of the English language and the niceties of being a proper architect. His office is a workshop, his buildings wear their Meccano-like quality on their sleeves. A second generation of sheds is beginning to emerge where the structures recall the febrile quality of the 19th-century bridges and railway sheds where the engineering seemed always to be on the edge of the possible. And here we have the first clue as to the continuing dynamic of the London technology-architecture. For a couple of generations of engineers have been closely entwined amongst the architectural avant-garde. Moreover, it is these engineers who have often been more willing to be outrageous.

The role of Frank Newby is critical in the work of Stirling, Cedric Price and the members of Archigram, and that of Anthony Hunt his ex-assistant in that of Norman Foster. Ted Happold and Ian Liddell have eventually broken away from the giant engineering firm of Arup, and Peter Rice is still somehow with them: though he is really a brilliant loner. All these men are much more central to the innovatory discussions than it is convenient to admit. Perhaps one day it will be possible to place them correctly into the history of architecture: for there is the total opposite of the 19th-century conflict between 'architect-as-decorator' and 'engineer-as-conceptualist'. In a way this is the most enduring proof that inventiveness is the thread between today and that other heroic period of English architecture: the 19th century.

The real gurus in England are often hidden from view. Just as they might be engineers then they might also be uncontrollable eccentric figures such as Colin Rowe, who passes through for a few days only each year, but still can tighten the nerve-endings with his 'conversation of the day'. Today it might be the conceptual value of the Pope in Rome, tomorrow it might be the additive nature of North German castles, and so on. A week later it all makes sense on the drawing-board. Such is the essential *lateralism* of English architectural thinking.

Similarly lateral are the roles of Cedric Price and James Gowan. If the total output of their buildings is small and quiet, it belies their importance as the consciences of the last twenty years. It was Cedric who prodded the sixties into considering physical dynamic: the moveability of the bits and pieces as inexorably related to the political and operational dynamic. Most of his drawings have been cartoons about situations rather than carefully poised objects: odd things that float, odd animals that moo rather than chatter, odd things that let in deflected rays of light (or is it sound or is it smell?). Wryness is the underlying characteristic. The implication is that any old bourgeois bore can make pretty walls, but here we are in a complex and civilised world-city and life is to do with justice, strikes and the galvanising of bits of metal. Not for Cedric is the comfortable orthodoxy of Rogers' and Fosters' assistants who almost to a man own French cars (because they're more experimental), Eames chairs (because they're better jointed) and quartz watches (because they're more accurate). His stiff white collar reminds one of a minister in the pre-war government of Baldwin. His assiduous reading of four daily newspapers before most of us have got out of bed, and his immediate recognition of the *least important person* in the room make him a very special person. The consistent logic of his left-wing views alongside the almost studied hedonism of his cigars-and-brandy existence are understandable if you take a lateral view of life, and remember the English tradition, which is often based upon the tactics of studied eccentricity, whereby you watch the discomfiture of those who prefer consistency of appearance as well as behaviour: and immediately have them at a disadvantage. In this way, it is no surprise that Cedric has the most consistent and genuine loathing for Post-Modernism: because he has, in a sense, been there before. The mere, so-called ambiguity that is the fiddling about with pieces of wallboard has nothing on the real ambiguity of a building that might be here today and gone tomorrow, or of an architectural idea that is generated by the patterning of fish-oil distribution.

James Gowan is equally wry, but expresses it less flamboyantly than Cedric, and his lectures, though rare, are the best in London. It is only he that can take a theme like 'details' and by using the acute observation of the odd streetside trinkets, along with a tough morality of thought about motivation in architecture, can make us realise that the high technology of the Foster or Rogers work is part of a two hundred year old tradition. His humour is very dry, but ever present, and behind an almost unhearable voice he intones the virtues of a similarly 'dry' and intense architecture. Amongst the younger architects who use the term 'narrative' to describe their motivation, he has a special place. This is surprising because their own work is to do with atmosphere, suggestion and symbolism and not so much to do with working parts, yet it was Gowan who understood in the early 1970s that ironic and symbolist projects were also in the English tradition and supported them as student works. He even made a flat in Mayfair take on an ironic reference to Robert Adam in exaggerated pastiche manner but the date was 1969 and official Post-Modernism was still some years away: an odd thing for a dry Scotsman?

Traditional English eccentricity: Gatehouse, nr Woodbridge, Suffolk
English Structural Gymnastics: Powell & Moya Architects, the 'Skylon' from the 1951 Festival

By rights, the Smithsons should still be regarded as gurus but they remain very detached from people of one or two generations younger than themselves. Historically, the subsequent audacities of Foster, Rogers, Price and the Archigram Group could not have happened without their own audacity, and the cloying provinciality of the English mainstream could not have been held at bay for so long without their establishment of the first supra-national network: Team Ten. It was the Smithsons who used their combined strengths in order to hit out with four fists: first a project, then an exhibit, then a piece of polemic, then a serious magazine article, and round again with another project. Their buildings have been curious for they certainly lack the verve of Stirling's work, at least as sculptural objects, and the title of one of their books *Without Rhetoric* is illuminating. It is the espousement of such an attitude that continues today. The Arts building at Bath University is punctiliously detailed, and so also have been their more recent unbuilt projects—often recalling the calm and care of some quieter Japanese buildings, yet there is the odd jerk and strangeness: the coalescence of pavilions in the Churchill College project of 1960, the actual condition of the link of the new Bath building with its neighbour.

Their pronouncements have over the years become more and more lyrical and less like strident manifestos and I suppose the give away came several years ago when Alison published a novel. Such a mood has appeared several times since, in their exhibits of structures-as-trees, old trams as prognoses of the future, strange mounds with coiled wool. Once again, a territory has been sighted before the current exploration, for an accompanying narrative is always provided and the range of its references is often wide and strange: history, nature, childhood. It is a contemplative activity.

During the late 1960s and 1970s the Smithsons withdrew from teaching in England, and in general communicated only with a selected coterie, or through magazines. During this period also, Colin Rowe established himself in the United States, and more recently Reyner Banham has done likewise. The village has survived, but its philosophical base has not been explained or developed by written argument: indeed it has returned to the territory of *drawn manifesto*, which perhaps suits the national character. In this way, the individual can legitimately deviate, and as his interpretations become more individual, more expressive, more lyrical, they can finally diffuse the original philosophical ideal. The English cry is often the simple hint: not a cry at all in the histrionic sense.

The Smithsons remain for me an important influence, and the intensity that I have heralded in Norman Foster's investigations into the world at the edge of our physical experience could, and should, be accompanied by a dialogue with those who understand the poetry of substance: as the Smithsons undoubtedly do. Another conversation might exist between them and the young architects who are examining the sensuous nature of experience and then, in Nigel Coates' words 'reassembling it in a form that would attach events to spaces'—even the language of such an idea recalls those early Team Ten pronouncements.

A continuous link with those coming up behind has been instinctive within the Archigram Group, who have all become professional teachers. But it has also characterised the day-to-day world of Cedric Price who has been a continuous critic and inventor of various 'educational' models: lasting anything from one morning to several months, and is finally returning to formal teaching. Even Foster and Rogers themselves project the boiler-suited image of the player-manager, and are constantly in the company of younger architects and the 'team', constantly available, not at all mysterious. The institution of the 'professorial' role does not exist in London, and it is the nature of the place that the elite rapidly ceases to effect the state of play. So I have myself chosen to reinterpret the role of the Smithsons: and heeded the warning of their introvert years. Anyhow, I have been far too interested in the state of the art as it is played out. The Archigram Group looked outward at foreign models at the same time that it looked outward at territories beyond architecture. If we gained sustenance by recognising the same instincts in both Bruno Taut's 'Frulicht' friends and the artists who drew the American space comic cities, we also gained it by recognising the potential of Louis Kahn's Philadelphia megastructures alongside Constant Nieuwenhuys' 'New Babylon'—though the architectural tastes could not be more different. It has also been said many times that we were part of the pop art syndrome. More correctly, I think, we came out of a similar originating culture, which might have been found in the jazz band fringes of the English art schools, where Bucky Fuller was already known along with Thelonius Monk's piano playing, LeRoy Jones' writing and De Kooning's painting.

Archigram was always an essentially *architectural* activity, poking fun at the uptightness of the English mainstream as well as many of the 'art' architects of the time because we feared that their joint sterility would kill the whole thing off before we had had time to get in there. And the continuous teaching ensured that the activity changed itself as the culture changed—especially as most of that teaching took place at the Architectural Association.

I have already hinted at the dreadful things that happen to exciting architectural ideas if they are voiced outside the metropolis. It is worse than that for there are twenty-five thousand architects (at least) in England. Hothouses are needed if the germination of ideas is to be furthered in a hostile climate. In the United States there are several sheltered spots, and maybe one or two hothouses even. In London the extraordinary tradition of the Architectural Association has been subtly metamorphosing as if a wink were being given by lost or dead generations of eccentrics who similarly needed the place. Fresh-faced young men from the Colonies who chose 'modernism' because it was lively from the late 1930s, the Marxist intellectuals and the Marxist optimists of the 1940s (the AA was the repository of the largest Communist cells in London at that time), the American Dreamers of the 1950s and 1960s. Yet it is a far from acquiescent school. Almost every gang has been challenged from within as soon as it has perfected its act: or even before. It symbolises, therefore, the irreverence that the English have for a coercive atmosphere. Yet this atmosphere of irreverence, of challenge, of the expectancy of the next nuance and shift coming at any moment (perhaps even tomorrow) and from any corner: the sleeping man might awake, the absent student suddenly appear with an ace drawing—indecipherable, but ace nonetheless—the upstart suddenly becoming guru again, overnight. And the constant challenge coming from a constant shift of styles, of media, of aesthetics and accents. So it is that the present teachers at the AA were nearly all school kids or very young students when we started Archigram, and since students there can very quickly become teachers, and teachers become heroes, and heroes become yesterday's news, there is an extraordinary dynamic that I have not experienced in the fifty other schools that I have visited.

The Architectural Association School has now become much less English than in former years: the student body is predominantly foreign, and Alvin Boyarsky (the Chairman) is a Canadian of Russian ancestry. So it is as if an aircraft carrier was moored in London with radio messages reaching it from all parts of the globe and landings and take-offs following this world-wide pattern. The crews are competitive fliers and perform acrobatics in the sky immediately

Peter Cook, Gothic Tower
Christine Hawley, 'The Hedonists' Monument'

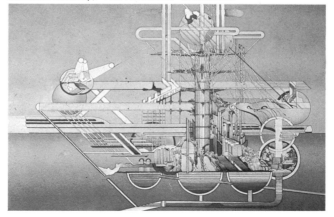

above, though some of them don their goggles carefully and return rather quickly to base. So Boyarsky has invested his amazing energy into a place where the programme of lectures, the programme of exhibitions and the *ambience* (a favourite word of his) are at least equal to the teaching activity. Meanwhile the Royal Institute of British Architects lurches on, essentially provincial in *its* ambience, always puzzled why it is missing the initiative because it is always involved in the conversations of ten years ago against a style of twenty years ago. The AA needn't be bothered with the RIBA, for during the last few years the great upsurge of activity and *style* engendered by Boyarsky has coincided with the great awakening of the architectural drawing. Not only has this been the special territory of the English, the Americans and the Japanese (the French, for instance, remain lousy drawers), but the AA has made deep forays into drawing-as-exotica, drawing-as-erotica and in particular it has perfected the technique of placing pencil shading all over sections and elevations so that even the blandest project looks 'mysterious', 'evocative', 'implicit' or just downright *spooky*. Its only possible rivals are Cooper Union and Cranbrook, both in the United States but lacking the AA's speed of metamorphosis.

The rest of the English scene looks on with distrust and jealousy, but Boyarsky is practised at deflecting this distrust, and is also able to outwit every attempt to unseat him. More importantly, he has the personality to inject his young (and actually quite fragile) teachers with a collective adrenalin, so that they do keep on drawing and teaching, or at least hang on to their absurd thoughts for longer than most others. It will be no surprise to find that everyone whose work is illustrated here (with the exception of James Stirling) has studied or taught at the AA—or both. There it floats, the repository of the inventive, the lyrical, and of course, that endless speculative chatter.

The role of the young teacher-drawer-talker fits the situation today: for there is little new building in England, and for a long time there have been few competions. So the outlets for talent that exist in Germany and Scandanavia are shut, and the self-motivated project has emerged.

Such a project has an interesting history. In the sixties, it was restored to (by groups like Archigram) as a counterbalance to the tightness of building briefs or competition briefs. Such projects were held to be *investigations* so as to give them intellectual credibility. Then they began to be suggested as *alternatives* to currently controversial situations: the third London Airport, the draining of the Wash, and so on. More evocatively, they began to affect the way in which architectural ideas might be expressed: and the medium itself starts to multiply the range of its references. At a certain moment we started to write all over our Archigram drawings, because the statement—the *pitch*—needed to be as incisive as a piece of advertising. Perhaps it needed to shout rather than politely caption. Or there might be the need to carry on a 'discussion' between the visual objects and the different layers of their motivation. Colour became an essential piece of the rhetorical play rather than a means of describing the appearance. Therefore we, and most of the younger architects—whether of 'inventive' or 'narrative' directions—have chosen to use colours of very strange types. And the non-use of colour is a positive step—black and white is gaunt, dogmatic, of the newspaper and the announcement. Acid greens and magenta are of the world of shorthand, of Xerox and colour TV, of video and chemicality. Shadows and the hint of a thin, primary tint are evocative of romanticness: filmy, wispy, gentle. Red and black only announce a strategy. A little red in the midst of carefully drawn grey announces cultural awareness. All this without the New York pastel shades! And beware the English trick of lateral thinking when it gets involved in artworks.

It is intriguing that the founders of the OMA group chose a fundamentally different strategy for the invention of their drawings. It is sequentially intriguing to reflect that as a Greek (Zenghelis) and a Dutchman (Koolhaas) they chose to remain in London, amongst dreamers and inventors who lacked a taste for their own type of enthusiastic scholarship. For how else can you explain the *Delirious New York* book of Rem Koolhaas? An encapsulated world where the reference to *second-hand* architectural imagery in the form of post-cards and modish advertising illustrations is always far more piquant than those of real buildings. The admirable quality of OMA's work is its relish, its enjoyment of fun objects—and I deliberately use a dated phrase to describe a (sadly) dated type of inspiration. In this sense they contrast so greatly with that other unlikely un-Englishman, Leon Krier. It is a pity that he has allowed his later drawings to be coloured: for the true European spirit of dogmatism is stronger in black and white. In the same way, his studied detachment from the day-to-day architectural world of London retains a clarity. It is now as if he were only *conceptually* living in London and, like many pieces of conceptual art, creating an energy in reverse: the minimal presence and the concurrent effect of delayed feedback taking effect.

It is not the result of my own prejudice, but I simply cannot find any good young Rats in London. True, Peter Wilson uses Rationalist formulae for the points of departure of some of his projects: but it is then almost immediately diffused by the *real* stuff of the *place*, the *atmosphere*, the wisps of water, the faintness of the lattices, the trees, and ultimately the effects of an evocative *hint* and an evocative description. Not that Wilson can be described any longer as a 'narrative' designer. Similarly, the early stultifications of Krier influence that might have affected Zaha Hadid's work have all been overthrown: first by Elia Zenghelis and Rem Koolhaas (after all, she was an official member of OMA for more than a year) and, more recently, by her own creative exuberance. How can a Rat explode strange, quivering sticks and twirl strange, quivering spirals into space? It is all far too expressionist, too damned *exciting* for that!

Sadly, the most influential young architect of recent years—certainly around the 'carrier—has left us for New York. His continuing influence comes now from his ex-students, for the succession of Jenny Lowe, Nigel Coates, Rodney Place, John Andrews owe their spirit and their base in the notion of a narrative (or a dramatic) base to Bernard Tschumi. His latest work, as illustrated in *The Manhattan Transcripts* has evolved into a deliberately sparse dia-grammatisation. The staccato registration of events has finally passed over the line between choreography and architecture. Moreover, the delight of it lies in the precision and the economy of the *choice* of these snapshots. They recall the crack of the clapper-board in a filming session, the firing of a shot: they are staged accidents and the architec-tural aspects of these drawings (by which I mean the parts with reference to commonplace architecture, columns, win-dows and so on) are similarly precise. There is no spare information. And here it differs substantially from the work of his London followers. They still find it necessary to *scribble*. In so doing they remain wedded to a stream of evocative description that seems to have started in the 1960s with the work of the Austrian artist, Walter Pichler. In Pichler's drawings, the reiteration of a line is often a deliberate act of coercion, it concentrates more towards the end of its path. The more wayward scribbled lines imply flagrant action and they have all the elements of chance. The imposition of colour is highly erotic: often of a single extra colour used generously. Other Austrians use this dramatic technique, and it reached the AA in the very early 1970s via

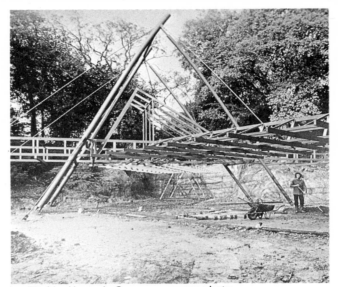

Ian Ritchie, House in Sussex, progress photo
Alsop & Lyall, Pavilion

Raimund Abraham, Freidrich St. Florian and Ugo la Pietra (the Tyrolean Mafia, as it were). Though Tschumi never used the aesthetics himself, his offspring listened to his analysis of architecture—as a recreation of performance art—and scribbled it in. At an imperceptible moment this quite dynamic scribbling became inmeshed with the rediscovery of surface, the creation of patina, the wish for age.

Since then, this instinct has been germinating in London in some mysterious way, and the Germany–France axis has not taken to it easily. At the three corners of Europe, in Italy, Austria and England, you found that the increasing respect-ability of history and of ancient phenomena was essentially a sensuous event. In the more polemical cultures it was essentially an intellectual explosion. No, more vehemently, it had to have the support of both political radicalism and stylistic positivism. No remnant of white Modernism for our Leon. It is as if the ragged, textured surfaces and smoky crevices of Lowe and Wilson and the rest might diffuse the shrillness of the battle cry. As well they might. The tone of the narrativists who hang around the AA, and (incidentally) hang up on walls in small Italian and American galleries is quintessentially soft-voiced and soft-lined and soft-faced and somehow a little too sweet to relate easily to the world of architecture-as-building. It is therefore significant that the most accomplished and most exposed member of this coterie is gradually wandering away in the direction of directness and realism in his projects. And Peter Wilson (for it is he) has begun to work more extensively with his German wife, Julia Bolles who (perhaps to advantage) cannot escape the logical physicality and *operationalism* of a Karlsruhe training.

The English architectural magazines have given very little space to the narrativists, or to the inventors and 'lyrical mechanists', with whom I will end this piece. They have preferred to take the safer path of Post Modern Internation-alism. By deliberately parodying Charles Jencks' predilection for labels I am, I suppose, acknowledging his amazing dynamism. He is hell bent on creating a London branch of the international movement of the day: and in the process he may be missing the point of the best of his chosen protegés. It seems to him (and the magazines) that Jeremy Dixon's houses must be read as primarily to do with paradoxical symbolism—whereas they are almost certainly as much to do with *craft*—but that aspect is more boring, perhaps. Likewise, the true English eccentricity of John Outram's work is swept into a virtual heap of fuel for the iconoclasts. In the days of Archigram Magazine we pub-lished him because he was simply an *original* who gathered in his inspiration from old ironwork, new plasticwork, animal forms, geometric forms and the waywardness of his funny old brain. Moreover, there is the whole philosophy of studying the 'functional tradition' that was written about and talked about when Stirling and Gowan were working to-gether (Outram was a student of them both at this time).

The case of Campbell, Zogolovitch, Wilkinson and Gough is even more parochial for they started their practice as third year students in the early 1970s and have stayed together ever since. They have drawn as much sustenance from the crevices of the London 'rag' trade—a particularly vital mixture of Jewishness and post-art school opportun-ism that means that we need to look as much at the extraordinary dresses designed by Zandra Rhodes and ceramics made by Carol McNicoll as much as the tradition of Lutyens—even if it is a less architecturally respectable line of inspiration. The lyricism is there however, even if it is purely linear for the jobs are all too real: a house for a family, a depot for some furniture, a site that can yield a quick buck. We are in a totally other world from the narrativists.

And nearby is the chosen world of the younger inventors. For underneath the heroic reputations of Foster and Rogers lies a particularly talented circuit of designers. Some, like Mike Davies, choose at this moment to work within the larger umbrella of the Rogers office, and some in a curious secret territory of mysterious projects in France as well as England, as in the case of Alan Stanton and Ian Ritchie. These three constituted the firm of 'Chrysalis' until recently. As such they had emerged from the womb of the Archigram Group (in the case of Davies and Stanton), of Norman Foster (in the case of Ritchie) and variously through the experience of the Centre Pompidou to inevitably start teaching at the AA. During the late 1970s they made a quaint—but active—counterpoint to the pencil painters, and a curious metamorphosis began. Largely at the instigation of Alan Stanton, they began to reinvent the technologically positive monument: it not only softened its edges but it also took on a certain wish to entomb space. This is the only way to describe their best collective project, that for the Trafalgar Square Competition of 1980. It seemed for a short while that the sensitivity of the narrativists and the sheer guts of the inventors might fuse: but since Chrysalis has broken up, I'm not so sure that it will come from that direction.

It might come from the office of Will Alsop and John Lyall. For there is enough of the hard-nosed action in it to seize initiative—and to draw on the interesting personality of Alsop himself. His spiritual attitudes have been fashioned by David Greene, always the most poetic member of Archigram, and by Cedric Price. He remains close to them both. But his intellectual fascination has been with the world of conceptual and minimalist art. The office now has close links with Gareth Jones, the Welsh sculptor, and his influence has caused a virtual act of dismemberment of the tight fabric of parts: the windows jumble, the handrails want to explode, the composition of the buildings is making reference to the mawkish containers of space used by Christo or Barry Flanagan. And there is a curious similarity between the explosiveness of their work and that of Zaha Hadid—a fact that had never occurred to either of them, incidentally. The attenuated character of these things is found in Christine Hawley's work as well, and the explanation may lie in the similarity of age between Alsop, Lyall, Hadid and Hawley, and the fact that they (unlike others of their generation) have never been overwhelmed by the older and more famous personalities with whom they have worked: indeed a close study of the mid 1970s will reveal that Alsop was certainly more than a mere technical assistant to Cedric Price during the development of the Interaction site in Camden Town. It will reveal the instigatory role played by Zaha Hadid in the Dutch Parliament Competition (of OMA). It will also acknowledge the conceptual role played by Christine in our Trondheim Library and Shadow House—she has too often been dismissed by those in search of an easy label as the pretty drawer.

In a sense, a very special difference exists between those young architects who have stepped outside the comfort of the AA, and have enjoyed the process of building as much as (or even more than) drawing and those sweeter, gentler souls who *need* to replace reality with invented narrative.

So it is that the Chrysalis people, Alsop and Lyall, Hawley and two more names, Mark Fisher and Peter Salter, are finding themselves placed in a discernable new current. I call it lyrical mechanism.

It is especially English. These people are very English in origin, as it happens. It is to do with the tradition of inventing and *enjoying* the presence of working parts. So it relates to the inspiration of Stirling, Gowan, Archigram, Foster, Rogers and Outram—which may be no kind of coincidence. It has to do with the deliberate rescrambling of the composition of those parts together. Now *that* is an 'art' instinct, as

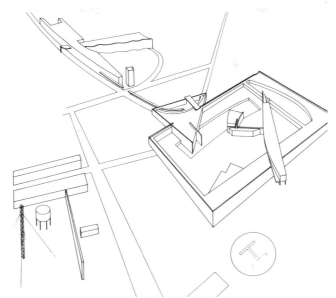

Zaha Hadid
Chrysalis (Alan Stanton, Mike Davies & Ian Ritchie), Trafalgar Square Information Centre

well as being (once more) consistent with the lateral process of associating the unlike with the unlikely, and sometimes inserting the deliberately devient element—just to see what happens. Being very English they are quite amused when nothing happens: which is an almost unexplainable point to a non-English person (but conceptually important). Let me give an instance: the design of our Trondheim Library depended upon the scattering of a series of internal small buildings within a giant cocoon. Each building had its own presence and a shared style. The whole thing was mechanistic, but just where you would expect the parts to be most heroic—towards the central space—they deliberately crumbled away. Just where you expected this crumbliness to create a whole expressionist jungle, the platforms of the building deliberately took on a syncopated rhythm. Just where you expected this contrast to be enough for the composition of the library itself, we introduced a series of meshes: diffusers of space but equally diffusers of the *categories* of 'enclosure', 'furniture', 'horizontal', 'diagonal'. Yet the whole remained sufficiently staccato to have a positive form. So we hid it—or rather held it within a foggy glass cocoon.

The Shadow House is a later and more sophisticated extension of some of these games. In describing the constant series of inversions and decoys I am trying to describe the wayward English mind. This is almost perverse when you remember that the Shadow House has a describable and consistent diagram: semicircle cut by two chords. Every instinct and the scrutiny of so many competition projects tells me that such a strategy would be very difficult for a young German architect to carry through. It is as different as the bittersweet harmonics of Kurt Weil from the deceptive dreaminess of Frederick Delius' tone poems.

Peter Salter's projects take on a deliberate waywardness, as if the thin strands of his little bridges and fragile walls are about to rust away. The exotic inventions of Mark Fisher float into the sky—quite literally—for they have been built for various travelling rock shows: and he has found a legitimate territory for lyrical mechanism to meet real life.

So, it is not too much to hope that Ron Herron's architecture of 'sets'—the meeting place of dream and reality, escapism and the familiar can now take place for, like Fisher, he has found a client who is in the legitimate 'escape' business: in this case, a pleasure park.

For myself, I take the two strands of architecture that appeal to me most and play them against each other: on the one hand monumentalism (which it is now respectable to acknowledge) and on the other the territory of meshes, hints, decoys and shadows. So across the street from the Shadow House in the City of Layers are a series of spiralling pavilions (essentially solid) that are progressively cloaked and veiled and toyed with. The ground is a kind of sea-shore of creeks and bridges and little kiosks that play out their own sweet game of urban structuring without disturbing the big boys.

If Christine Hawley is dissecting the post-Archigram language and replacing it with a lyrical mechanicism of Art Nouveau instincts, I am returning, for the moment, to my old love of urban structuring—but Hilberseimer, Le Corbusier and the figure-ground diagram are of no use to me here.

The English scene is a dance, perhaps?

This article was originally written for the 1982 issue of the Yearbook of the Frankfurt Architecture Museum and was given as a lecture in March, 1982 at the Architectural Association, London and Sci-Arc in Los Angeles.

Charles Jencks
NOTES ON AN ARCHITECTURAL CULTURE

ARCHITECTURAL CULTURE, like culture in general, can be analysed and, to a small degree, consciously influenced if not directed. It would seem obvious that architects, critics and public assume an architectural culture when they act and for each individual this assumption is bound to be different. Is British architecture in decline—an assumption of the public and most of those who took part in the conference 'Why is British Architecture so Lousy'—or is it flourishing in hidden ways?

To generalise about such large and inchoate issues is to invite one-sided polemic. And yet to avoid engaging the debate—in which everyone must have a stake—is to forego conscious action. As is often pointed out culture is the one thing that cannot be created by an act of Parliament. Nevertheless, with high culture and mass culture becoming all the time more influenced by a consumer society, a conscious formulation of the situation appears more and more desirable. The assumption of these notes is that we live in a pluralist mass culture, one in which high standards of excellence have been eroded by the variety and confusion of values. Standards which were kept sharp by an elite, a building tradition and the classical language of architecture—all the things which Christopher Wren could assume as he built up a team—have now become dulled. The same is true of the values of Modernism kept alive by the avant-garde, the last successor to the traditional elite. Both avant-garde and cultivated elite have lost their leadership role in a consumer society. These notes are offered for the creation of that mythical construct, the 'knowing consumer', the self-trained specialist in a fragmented culture of specialists.

World village and cities of the world

A double and opposite movement can be perceived: accompanying the end of national boundaries and ideologies, is the growth of the world architectural village—a result of inexpensive air travel and international magazines. At the same time there is a counter movement: a return to city-based culture. Architectural groups have formed in New York, Chicago and Tokyo, as they did in London in the 60s, and institutions in these cities further architectural culture.

A negative effect of this is the growing asymmetry of influence. Fewer and fewer people have more and more influence over events, or at least the dissemination of ideas and forms. London influences England, Paris dominates France, New York the USA and provincial cities (such as Liverpool) suffer. Post-Modernism, because of the media, has influenced architecture even in socialist countries.

We can see that relatively few individuals and institutions within the major cities have had an inordinate effect: the Smithsons, Cedric Price and Archigram influenced Argentina and Italian architecture in the 60s; in the 70s the Architectural Association and *AD* influenced Europe and USA. While groups may have an important effect on a small elite, there are certain institutions, such as the RIBA, which have not sought to lead. Perhaps this results from a changing leadership within the institute, as well as an uncertain theory and ideology among its leadership.

Triumph of Mid-Cult architecture

Where previous leaders—the avant-garde, groups and institutes—have feared to tread, there lurk well-intentioned amateurs. The mass media has been dominated by professional journalists whose attitude to architecture can be described, loosely as 'mid-cult'. These journalists, one might assume, are as discerning in architectuure as the corporate client and the average practitioner. Altogether they constitute the major cultural milieu for commissioning architecture. They are unlikely to care about architecture either as an art or cultural activity; if they perchance do, they are unlikely to have developed tastes, since such codified perception has to be built up slowly within a taste culture. With the erosion

of classical and modern architecture, and with Post-Modern architecture still in the process of formation, there is little chance for this maturation to occur.

To corroborate this we might adopt the metaphor of a year end stock report. Examine the portfolio of the biggest performers, the largest holdings, the best and worst performances. Compare the ten biggest architectural practices today with the ten 'best' architects; the ten prestige commissions of the last few years with a list of 'leaders' recognised by the profession. Even if we have marginal disputes over the terms 'best' and 'leaders' the comparison will reveal the wide gap between quality and quantity, excellence and business. Colonel Seifert and his values have dominated. He has said, quite accurately: '*I have done more to change the face of London than any architect since Wren*'.

Quite obviously mid-cult has triumphed over both high and avant-garde cultures. The traditional elite, the new 'leaders', have simply failed to lead, partly because they are divided among themselves and disengaged from a commercial society. Very few public buildings of note have been built in ten years: the National Theatre and Clore Gallery symbolise the situation. Minor commissions for two acknowledged architects. Commercial building is dominated by the most pragmatic.

Dynamic balance

An architectural culture consists in an interaction between different taste cultures—high and low, elite and popular, avant-garde and traditional, high brow and kitsch. Probably a culture is best when there is a mixture of tastes expressed in a building, and when no single taste culture dominates. But when a culture lacks cohesion, when it is made up of specialists, tastes are separated, then standards fall.

An indication of specialisation was afforded at the conference on art and architecture at the ICA in February, 1982. It turned out that few artists could identify the 'best' architects and vice-versa. One could conduct similar surveys across the seven 'lively' arts to show the same story. Very few people have developed tastes in more than one or two areas. To admit this is to grant a breakdown in traditional culture, and even the theory of traditional culture which is based on the notion of shared values and tastes. The underlying idea, to simplify somewhat, was of a 'general reader', a well-informed perceiver, who could discern quality in many areas and had a nodding acquaintance with high art in all areas. In an integrated culture standards would be kept high by an elite, and then these standards would 'trickle down' and through a whole culture. To a large extent Georgian architecture bore out this theory.

In terms of this model several surprising things have happened: there has been a levelling down combined with what could be called a bottoming up. That is, mid-cult has levelled down high culture while raising low culture. Elizabeth David has elevated the level of mass taste in food just as much as Habitat has elevated the taste of mass furniture. One benefit of mass culture and the consumer society is the growing sophistication of average tastes. With all the means of reproduction available—film, books, records, video—there has been a trend counter to the general levelling of taste. The 'knowing consumer', although a weak force, is not without its effect.

Yet there is little trickle down of taste from the 'leaders' to the 'followers', that is from the avant-garde, the elite and the best of the professionals to either the man in the street or the average practitioner.

To show this is to point to the collapse of Britain's architectural culture, perhaps an overly dramatic statement. Quite recently James Stirling, Richard Rogers and Norman Foster sent a letter to *The Times* concerning the Palumbo/Mies building. *The Times* didn't print it; one can't imagine three leading figures in industry or politics being disre-

garded in this way. Stirling, Rogers and Foster are more or less unknown by the establishment taste culture, although thanks to the media they are quite well known to the masses. This disparity between cultures —roughly Modernism and Traditionalism—is just one disjunction among many in a pluralist society.

There are ideological and taste divisions created by class, training and personal belief. One can see a fragmentation in British architecture between groups that might be characterised as service-oriented and art-oriented. After that major dichotomy comes a series of further polarities: vernacular and international, technical and intuitive, conceptual and empirical; one can see these are not true opposites. There are all the philosophical disputes between those I would characterise as Late and Post-Modern. In effect, language and a language of architecture divide the elites into 'groupuscules' while commercial practitioners dominate the field with little trouble. Mid-cult has upset the dynamic balance.

Towards a 'rapprochement'

In an integrated culture, or what has often been called an 'organic' community, the notion and practice of imitation plays an important role in disseminating values. Through imitation (or transforming patterns) traditions are passed on, competition ensured and standards kept high. Even if one doesn't achieve the 'progress' that Vitruvius postulated in such a tradition of imitation, there is coherent development. Now, however, imitation tends to be purveyed through the international magazines, forms and solutions are copied without being transformed to their new context.

One can however imagine international communication reaching a certain saturation point, where information is conveyed with enough sharpness that an international culture actually starts working positively. The way the Japanese have responded to Western ideas and inventions, conveyed through the media, is an indication of what can exist. We might postulate that a 'critical mass' is reached in mass culture, when the amount and quality of information is sufficiently high, that the mass media actually sharpen and raise tastes. The 'knowing consumer' is not altogether a fiction; the desideratum is to transform him into the 'pluralist connoisseur'—that is a well educated specialist who can discriminate in many fields.

There are many individuals and groups today who are aware of the general cultural breakdown. The ICA conference showed the general awareness of the problems even if it failed to diagnose a remedy. Artists, craftsmen, patrons and architects professed a desire to unite even while they recognised a disunity of ends, a lack of common goals. One might comment that a culture which does not achieve a balance between these four 'specialisms' (as they are called according to an unfortunate label) is not really a culture at all.

Given the fragmentation of culture, the ascendency of the consumer society and the pluralism of values, it would seem that there is limited scope for improvement. One obvious strategy is a *rapprochement* of the various elites, a pragmatic synthesis of the several institutes, groups and individuals in the form of a collective (if varied) leadership. These elites share a concern for quality, ideas and refinement—in short the values of high culture—whatever their other differing goals; and they also share a mutual distaste for mediocrity. In New York, Chicago and other cities such collective groups have formed and, with the mass media, changed the usual relationship of mass culture to high culture. One can even imagine a critical point being soon reached in these cities where the 'best' architects start getting the most important commissions, a situation which hasn't prevailed since, roughly, the turn of this century. If this happens, it will be a result of conscious effort and it will, no doubt, have a dramatic effect on the culture as a whole.

Anthony McIntyre
REFLECTIONS ON TECHNOLOGY

'... God became angry with Adam, and had him driven, him and his companion, forth out of Paradise, saying to them: "Inasmuch as you have disobeyed the command which God gave you, by your struggle and exertion you shall carry on your lives." And so Adam, recognising the error which he had committed, after being so royally endowed by God as the source, beginning and father of us all, realised theoretically that some means of living by labour had to be found. And so he started with the spade, and Eve with spinning. Man afterward pursued many useful occupations, differing from each other; and some were, and are, more theoretical than others; they could not all be alike, since theory is the most worthy.'
Cennino d'Andrea Cennini, *Il Libro dell'Arte*, 1437

AND SO PLATO CASTS HIS SHADOW across our modern world. But let the quotation stand, for this is an essay of anecdote and exploration, not one of consistent or all-embracing philosophy. Cennini was a Florentine painter, who wrote the *Libro dell'Arte* as a handbook of technical skills for artists. The point of his introduction, quoted in part above, must be that theory and practice are welded together by the very nature of our human condition. Our physical necessity causes us to labour, but by means of that labour we are able to manifest the theoretical ends which are a spiritual necessity. The brick and tile barn on the edge of Lincolnshire, or Paycocke's, a merchant's house at Coggeshall, Essex, might stand as illustrations of the principle. For those who built them, it was a way to make a living, a job, and they did it in such a way that the buildings became more than just a collection of materials. It was materiality embodying ideas, the product of technique. This is the technology of architecture.

Etymologically, 'technology' is a fusion of the Greek for 'art' and 'words', and one of its main English meanings, until quite recently, was a terminology of, or discourse on art. It is not far-fetched to say that technique is of a linguistic nature, whether as terminology itself, or referring to the component parts of a craft. People speak of the 'language' of brickwork, and that is right. There is nothing quaint or simple about brickwork or carpentry. Just as a garden designer would be lost without a good knowledge of plant names, so these crafts have large vocabularies, which are a means of understanding what is seen in existing buildings—analysis—and for objectifying ideas in building new ones, which is synthesis.

One may see this in John Soane's stables at Chelsea Hospital, where the success of the exercise depends upon a high knowledge of brickwork construction.

Only to take a list of manufacturing faults that may be found in bricks is revealing: hearting, bloating, chuffs, crazing, crozzling, efflorescence, grizzling, iron spots, laminations, lime nodule, scumming, shippers. A list like this denotes a wide range of observation and distinction, as indicative of our cultural preoccupations as the 25 Eskimo words for snow are of their's. The fewer means of description or expression at one's command, the less detailed is one's experience, the less readily absorbed. Observation depends upon descriptive power and the ability to manipulate a language. *'A man is a poet'*, said Valéry, *'if the difficulties inherent in his art provide him with ideas; he is not a poet if they deprive him of ideas.'* Such difficulties are turned to advantage in Louis MacNiece's poem 'Reflection', a poem whose technology lies near the surface:

The mirror above my fireplace reflects the reflected
Room in my windows; I look in the mirror at night
And see two rooms, the first where left is right

Paycock's House, Essex

Thomas Tresham, Rushton Triangular Lodge, Northants
Brick barn in Lincolnshire

And the second, beyond the reflected window, corrected
But there I am standing back to my back. The standard
Lamp comes thrice in my mirror, twice in my window,
The fire in the mirror lies two rooms away through the window,
The fire in the window lies one room away down the terrace,
My actual room stands sandwiched between confections
Of night and lights and glass and in both directions
I can see beyond the reflections the street lamps
At home outdoors where my indoors rooms lie stranded,
Where a taxi perhaps will drive in through the bookcase
Whose books are not for reading and past the fire
Which gives no warmth and pull up by my desk
At which I cannot write since I am not lefthanded.'

Returning to Cennini and the art of earning a living, many fine examples can be found in simple designs for clothing. A 19th-century English surplice, or a man's shirt, show instances of what might be called the inventiveness of necessary selection. The cloth width is given by loom dimensions, the material is flat, and there is very little wastage, yet the clothes that are produced are of the most exquisite refinement, the intractable rendered docile. One sees buildings like that, chiefly, but not only, vernacular buildings. Again, the Chelsea stables come to mind. What is so striking is this discrepancy between simplicity of means and complexity of the finished article, promoting mere labour into the realms of theory: art. That technique has its complement. Consider the longbow, an English weapon, but originally a Welsh invention. Edward I in his Welsh campaigns, saw the longbow's potential for refinement, and a hence its increased shooting power. By considering and sophisticating each technical component, he transformed the longbow into medieval England's supreme military weapon. Yew is a particularly good wood for bows because of its capacity to release stored energy very quickly, and the best of it comes from southern countries where it grows with a fine grain and hard texture. (In some periods each cask of Spanish wine had to come to England accompanied by a certain number of yew staves.) For bow strings, however, one went to Flanders, where the best spinning was accomplished with the finest flax. Beeswax was of course English, if one can distinguish amongst bees. The longbow was a simple idea, then, with complex means for its fulfilment: the necessity of inventive selection. Things put together in this way tend towards the mechanical; one thinks of bridges, instruments and so on, where a device's mechanical function sets standards of efficiency. Yet there are more purely theoretical gatherings together. Stonehenge might be a good example, or Avebury's elaborate patterns of construction. You can call these machines if you like, of course. Their workings seem both to observe and to represent nature, their power for us deriving from a contrast between the enormous passive objects and the intricate human rituals we know them to have augmented and sustained.

'That a man can interrogate as well as observe nature', wrote Sir William Osler, *'was a lesson slowly learned in his evolution.'* The progress from the static machine of observation like Stonehenge to the dynamic exploratory devices of modern science has confronted us with a fearsome vision of technology as an independent vital force. During the 1960s and 1970s, a great deal of intellectual energy was spent attempting to prove technology to be an evil thing, and perhaps not quite as much in advocating its ideological rightness. Writers of the first school include Theodore Roszak and Charles A Reich, author of *The Greening of America*; of the second Herman Kahn, whose *The Year 2000* was a best seller, and Buckminster Fuller, are among the better known. But the truth is, as we have seen, that technology is not an independent force or thing, and cannot

legitimately be ascribed a moral character. Like Euclid's demonstrations, the great barns of Essex are strikingly beautiful, but their structural principles as such are devoid of meaning. To identify technology with the ideology of machine culture is a mistake, for we do not suffer from technology but from its disagreeable ends; from the fact that it is poorly understood, narrowly defined and kept inaccessible by those who might have reason to fear its wider application. As a parallel to this one might recall that the medieval Church thought its best interest in power was vested in maintaining illiteracy among the laity, and forbade the clergy to teach reading or writing. Like language, technology cannot be an ideology; it can merely express ideologies. This must be understood if we are successfully to fight the deterministic scientific element in our culture, to deepen our attack by study and broaden the field of battle with knowledge. The attitude of many men of Roszak and Reich's generation is that of the Bellman and his crew in 'The Hunting of the Snark':

'He had bought a large map representing the sea,
Without the least vestige of land:
And the crew were much pleased when they found it to be
A map they could all understand.

"What's the good of Mercator's North Poles and Equators,
Tropics, Zones, and Meridian Lines?"
So the Bellman would cry: and the crew would reply
"They are merely conventional signs!"

"Other maps are such shapes, with their islands and capes!
But we've got our brave Captain to thank"
(So the crew would protest) "that he's brought us the best—
A perfect and absolute blank!"

This was charming, no doubt: but they shortly found out
That the Captain they trusted so well
Had only one notion for crossing the ocean,
And that was to tingle his bell.'

Our real complaint against 'technocracy' is the same as that we have against bureaucracy: unaccountability, capriciousness and a solitary interest in self-preservation. For although the 'expert' is suspect, we hold a place of high regard in our imagination for the craftsman. And who, if not he, could be called a technologist?

The value of technology is in its utility to art in creating deception. There is no value in displaying technique per se, and a skeleton without its covering body is more preposterous than beautiful. Art deceives, and if it is to do this with any success, it must to some extent hide its means. Only plumbers are interested in pipes. 'I have observed', wrote Burke, 'that colonnades and avenues of trees of a moderate length, were without comparison far grander than when they were suffered to run to immense distances. A true artist should put a generous deceit on the spectators, and effect the noblest designs by easy methods. Designs that are vast only by their dimensions are always the sign of a common and low imagination. No work of art can be great but as it deceives; to be otherwise is the prerogative of nature only.'

The comparatively small villa at Chester by James Gowan could have been designed with this passage in mind. Almost all of its architectural effect derives from the use of a steel frame which is completely effaced in itself as an element in the building. Its large spans and overhanging gable are striking just because their means of achievement

are not apparent, and this formal effect sits restlessly in the subconscious beside the beguiling and innocent use of quite traditional materials; oak, stone, slate and hand-made brick.

A great deal of polemic from the 18th century onwards has been directed against what has been thought of as the essentially frivolous nature of this kind of architecture: the mask is deceit, deceit an ethical wrong. As long as the remnants of this attitude last, there will be architects who consider the 'mask' in their art as unserious, no matter how important they claim it to be. The American Post-Modernists—Graves, Eisenman, Moore et al—are the victims of their own cause in this case. Though apparently the deepest care and thought go into external appearances, the buildings they design are generally badly built, and the usual excuse for this is that the exercise was tongue in cheek from the start, ephemeral and certainly not to be taken seriously in its demise. But where is the fun in rain-sodden papier maché? The British partnership of Conell Ward and Lucas found themselves with much the same problem in the 1930s as they built their clean white houses in the International Style. Concentrating all their energies on producing a photogenic building, they took some unwarranted technical liberties, for instance using render on the wrong sort of brick, or steel in contact with antipathetic metals. The result was a fine set of pictures for the architects and daily desolation for the rest of us. The fault, although it may seem paradoxical, is that of not taking the mask sufficiently seriously.

This problem of technical bravado has as a corollary the issue of unprecented design solutions, which, since the last war and the pervasion of plastics, has become crucial, though for the most part unremarked. By now it seems obvious that far too many innovations have been introduced without much thought for their specific consequences. Old techniques are seldom perfect, but our limitless optimism should not deceive us into thinking that purely abstract solutions (those untested over the years) will lead to a higher degree of perfection. The petrochemical industry must bear responsibility for using their enormous influence in advertising to sell unproven goods, lowering the demand for traditional materials and thus making it an easy matter to buy up and shut down traditional manufacturers. Polythene sheet, for example, is now widely used underneath concrete floors as a method of damp proofing, whereas 20 years ago the usual method was to apply an asphaltic paint beneath the floor. It was fairly easy for advertisers to make this traditional method look silly: the paint was black, it was applied with brooms and brushes, it was sticky, and so on. Now polythene was clean, flat, new and shiny: the perfect modern answer. Only today, having for years accepted with credulity the plastics sales pitch, are architects beginning to realise that there may be more problems associated with this material than it is worth. The middle of a polythene sheet presents no difficulty—provided it hasn't been stepped on and punctured—but what about the joints, the edges, the holes where pipes pass through, all the details that are so critical? There is an enormous amount of information about dealing with these matters with sticky tape used in clever ways, but to expect the ordinary builder to succeed in this technique where painting was considered too difficult, is absurd.

The truth is that all building is a compromise. It may be possible to make buildings that don't leak, but it isn't considered to be worth the expense, certainly not by local councils, seldom by private builders. It is more usual to design a building in which small errors, failures and tolerances don't produce disastrous results. If the traditional pitched roof has any advantages over flat roofs, it is not that it is more watertight; it is that any water entering it does not

pass straight into habitable space, but staying in the roof void is able to dissipate in drier weather. The choice between flat and pitched roof types is possibly more political than technical.

Familiarity can often blind us to the arbitrary nature of the artifacts we make and use and the meanings that we give them. Forcing materials into configurations with new meanings is a difficult task—and it is the task of technology. Wittgenstein wrote that 'Every sign by itself seems dead. What gives it life? In use it is alive. Is life breathed into it there? Or is the use its life?' The use of signs, the manipulation of materials: these are matters concerned with forcing familiar objects into new relations, making them suddenly both familiar and newly significant. Man had to wait for Darwin to connect him to the ape: a relationship unwillingly accepted at first, but eventually creating a quite different reality. To generate relationships, architecture often uses metaphor, whose logic can force unlikely elements into conjunction. The cross plan of cathedrals, guarded on the west by city gates and at each corner by a tower: these are clear metaphors which become so conventional to us that they cease being fragments of other ideologies such as city and kingship, and become for us simply 'cathedral', in its turn food for new imaginings. The continuous breaking down and regeneration of meaning is not a progress, but a necessity to establish personal meaning and order in the observed world.

In Northamptonshire stands a small triangular lodge, built by Sir Thomas Tresham in the last decade of the 16th century, a blizzard of metaphors on the Holy Trinity. Each of Rushton Lodge's 3 sides is 33⅓' long; of course there are 3 floors in it and 33 steps connecting them. Even Tresham's name—he was sometimes called 'Tres' by his wife, apparently—is punned upon in the inscriptions. For those who may doubt the serious intention and depth of knowledge of early Renaissance English architects, Tresham's work provides proof to the contrary. Although this is not the place to explain at length the iconography involved, every feature of this building is generated by the idea of the Trinity and the subsequent elaboration and expression of that idea in terms of hermetic and classical reference. Significantly, Tresham was a Roman Catholic, and did not have the Protestant fear and detestation of icons and symbolic meaning. This is a point brought out by the late Dame Frances Yates in her work on artificial memory systems. Using such systems, a person wishing to remember a speech, say, would associate main points in his speech with specific objects (a sword for war, a cornucopia for agriculture etc), in a place that was known to him. Then, when it was desired to recall the speech, he would mentally move through the space, find these images and thus remember what he wanted to say. There appears to have been a tradition of such systems from earliest times until roughly the time of Shakespeare. Clearly architecture takes on a quite different role in this system, as the context for memory, a palimpsest on which various images could be mentally inscribed. Buildings themselves would become redolent with systematic memory images, microcosms of the substantial universe. Yates maintains that the destruction of such systems paralleled the destruction of symbolic architecture in churches and cathedrals by puritanical iconoclasts. Images, within or without, were intolerable, and Wells Cathedral in stone marks the dilapidated condition of our powers of imagination.

Yates indeed claims that Shakespeare's Globe Theatre was built according to the classical Vitruvian description of ancient theatres, themselves designed as microcosms, adapted to the multi-level stage of the English medieval theatre. Though it is commonly thought that Inigo Jones was the first British architect with a knowledge of classicism, he seems merely to have imported the style or appearance in the early 1600s, but the sense and principles had arrived years earlier when parts of Vitruvius were translated, in a book for craftsmen, in 1570. There was a famous and long standing quarrel between Ben Jonson and Jones about who was in charge of the theatre—architect or playwright. Jones in the end won, and his victory was that of the eye over the ear, the spectacle over its meaning. For Vitruvius was clear that a theatre should do all it could technically to help a play be heard and understood in universal moral terms, and the Globe seems to have combined this advice in its symbolic representation of microcosm, theatre of the world. These plays were of course themselves symbolic, and they were acted on three levels of staging: heavens, world and underworld:

'... can this cockpit hold
The vasty fields of France? or may we cram
Within this wooden O the very casques
That did affright the air at Agincourt?
O, pardon! since a crooked figure may
Attest in little place a million;
And let us, ciphers to this great accompt
On your imaginary forces work.'
(Shakespeare, Henry V)

It seems fitting, perhaps inevitable, that Elizabethan drama should have called into being a new architecture, albeit soon abandoned, that could match its language in richness and significance. 'It is in language' to quote Wittgenstein once more, 'that an expectation and its fulfilment make contact.'

After a description of symbolism, to which some people may be apt to react with scepticism, I would like to present an extreme of practicality, Alberti's description of how a house may be rid of 'troublesome vermin'. 'For it is certain to be wished', says he, writing in the mid-15th century, 'that a building could be free of all manner of inconveniencies.' Though we have indoor WCs, refrigerators and fresh water on tap, quite profound elements, consider some of the architectural implications of these: 'The Assyrians, by means of a burnt liver, together with an Onion and a Squirrel hanging over the Transom of the Door, drove away all poisonous Animals ... the Weasle flies from the Smell of a roasted cat ....' Those living on the Isle of Thanet will be interested to learn that their lack of serpents is no accident, for : 'Solinus says, that strewing a Place with some of the Dust of the Isle of Thanet in Britain, will perfectly drive away serpents ... Against Canker-worms we are directed only to stick the Skeleton of a Mare's Head upon a Post in the Garden ... If you sprinkle a Place with Goat's Blood, they will march to it in whole Swarms', and finally: 'Broad flat Vessels full of Water set about the Floor are dangerous Traps for Fleas that take their leaps too daringly.' Not only, I imagine, for fleas.

Technical matters. But a building designed to utilise and take account of these methods would be a strange device indeed; analogous to a cathedral, perhaps. Our own houses accomplish these ends by different means, and those means are so familiar to us as to seem natural. Yet they are not natural, they are creations as arbitrary and as useful as those symbols of which the Triangular Lodge is composed.

So the generation of architectural form and meaning involves many varied techniques. One of the more popular in the days of the Modern Movement, which perhaps culminates the general love of 'movement' begun in the 18th century, has been the tracing of circulation patterns of vehicles and people, making buildings respond to, signify and control these routes and turn their meaning into architecture. Recently, less material, more conceptual methods have been used. For example, purely abstract

Meridian House, Royal Observatory, Greenwich

Foster Associates, Sainsbury Centre, University of East Anglia

lines—that of a vanished street or field, orientation towards some monument near or far, perhaps out of sight. Such methods aren't new, but inasmuch as they attempt to connect buildings with the ideas and images which surround them, and to recognise in built form influences other than the merely physical, they are only recently being re-employed. A church, for example, is traditionally orientated.

Scientifically speaking, there is in England a building that must be considered a type of Jerusalem, for although spaces are not (as far as I know) orientated towards it, time is. This is the Royal Observatory at Greenwich, through which runs the Prime Meridian, an invented line with real power. People stand with one foot on either side of it and have a slightly giddy sensation, unsure if their gesture is profound or trite, while friends snap their photos. Ships, aeroplanes and spacecraft are constantly related to it. And the building from which this potent line is produced, this universal technical hinge, is it a masterpiece of engineering, a celebration of high technology? Not at all. Rather, it is a contraption. Not even an expressively round dome exists to house the fine telescope which traced this line around the globe. Instead we have a building a little like one of the grandfather clocks that hang in the museum collection, a precise mechanism sheltered by an ordinary Georgian building. Well, perhaps not quite as ordinary as it looks. For here one can open a few doors, crank back the roof ridge and peer at the stars. A small technical change that completely alters our understanding of what 'simple' Georgian architecture is and can be. English meiosis, no need to make a big thing of it. Even the Great Equatorial Building is a sort of conversion, its onion dome sprouting to replace a more conventional roof when a larger telescope was installed. Very accommodating, this bricks-and-mortar architecture; even science can't frighten it.

So what are we to make of the High Technology style, with its various manifestations of abstract engineering in recent centuries? What of the Sainsbury Centre for the Visual Arts at the University of East Anglia, where looking at objects would seem to have demanded a technical miracle of a sort considered unnecessary at Greenwich? All one can say is that it too is a style, though whether any more accommodating I wouldn't like to say. The heavy mechanical bits, the heart of the Centre, are buried underground. Only certain pieces of hardware are considered fit for display, so there is no great sincerity about the building, ethical superiority or necessity for it to be as it is. Architectural values must be had from somewhere, and technique as a source has been partly the subject of this chapter. But it could be that here one is being beguiled into a mistaken identification of technique with architecture, being offered a one to one correspondence between what a thing does and what a thing is. An observatory that looks like a house is no less of either, but the confrontation of the two propositions gives a layering of meanings and a source of intellectual speculation that is surrealist.

The most sophisticated technical objects with which most of us are familiar are aeroplanes. But to tour an aircraft factory is to be struck by the fact that they are virtually hand made, and that is their beauty. And when one thinks of the technical demands made on aircraft, it seems foolish for a building to compete on the same level of craft engineering; neither the demands nor the potential for their fulfilment are there. At the Sainsbury Centre we are left with some dusty venetian blinds and a few sheets of aluminium stuck together with rubber seals. The lessons of what architecture can do, its raw materials and potentials, are more fully realised at the Royal Observatory.

This essay forms a chapter in a new guide to British buildings, written by Anthony McIntyre, to be published in the spring of 1983 by David and Charles.

Paul Oliver
ROUND THE HOUSES

IT TAKES ONLY THE MOST CURSORY GLANCE at a batch of international architectural magazines to confirm that what is illustrated between their laminated covers bears only an occasional, glancing resemblance to what most of us experience in the built world around us. Wade into the stream of dreams and schemes that has flowed through *AD* during the past two or three years, for instance. How many of those neatly docketed and documented buildings do you personally *know*; how many encountered, walked through, experienced, lived in? Of course there are diligent critics and enthusiastic students who will tot up a score of such works of architecture visited, the icon-images of the colour plates being matched against a highly selective reality. New 'canonical' buildings are being defined to replace the discarded classics of Modernism coolly appraised in Bonta's book.[1]

That's as it should be, one can argue. After all, publications on art or literature do not have to concern tnemselves with pavement portraits or wire-rack novels—though some of them do. They need only be concerned with what is judged as innovatory or of worth (aesthetic or financial). To say that architecture is different is to state a truism, but for all that it may be banal to repeat it, the fact remains that buildings serve the needs of their users in ways that are far wider in implication than do paintings or fiction, and architecture relates to the adjacent built environment in juxtapositions that have no parallel in other areas of creative endeavour. Lifted out of the pages of the periodical and into the street, buildings are prone to unexpected transformations, sometimes exciting, often disappointing, frequently demanding a perception of the immediate environment that was missing before. Anyone who has ever innocently sought out Rietveld's Schroder house, that canonical De Stijl building, and discovered that it was stuck like a bookend at one extreme of a suburban terrace and overshadowed by a flyover highway, has experienced a shock. It may be, in Lautréamont's words, '*beautiful as the chance meeting on a dissecting table of a sewing machine and an umbrella*'[2], but if so, it's a beautiful encounter that hasn't hit the pages of most esteemed architectural publications.

However, it's my contention that getting to know the environment 'out there' is of far more importance than the serendipitous shoulder-rubbing of selected architecture and anonymous buildings. I believe that we stand to know more about the nature of architecture and the shaping of a humane environment, if we seek to know more about buildings in all their manifestations, uses and meanings. If the study and understanding that this involves has scarcely begun, and if an overall, comprehensive view even of the 'buildings of England' seems virtually impossible (just think what's left after the ecclesiastical buildings, castles, manor houses and town halls have been deleted from Pevsner's work under that title[3]), there's much to be gained by seeking to comprehend at least some of the environment that we share. It's a chip-shop, garden-centre, tractor-store, holiday-chalet, side-street, back-alley, closed-cinema, garden-shed, furniture-warehouse, signal-box, bungalow, cow-byre, double-garage, your-street, my-street, you-name-it, he'll-call-it-something-else mélange we live in; making sense of it isn't easy and most of the time we have no mind to do so.

But if, for the present purposes, we restrict our discussion to houses, the diversity of types, forms, let alone details and plans, is extraordinarily rich in any county in Britain. It's our unwillingness to perceive the distinctions, and our inability to identify unfamiliar characteristics that induce us to dismiss much of the housing we see as monotonous, bourgeois, stock-broker belt, blot on the landscape, or whatever other chosen epithet we employ to screen off the challenge it poses to our entrenched habits of architectural thinking.

One broad category which we are more inclined to acknowledge, if not pursue, is that of 'vernacular architecture'. Quite what the term means is almost as much in doubt as is 'neo-vernacular' (which for some means 'responding to a local tradition' and for others, as at a recent conference in Turkey, means 'illegal settlement'[4]). Regional, frequently anonymous building using indigenous skills and local materials for the use and accommodation of the common populace, generally comes within the compass of building types acknowledged by those engaged in its study. But there are those that contend that there is no vernacular architecture in Britain after the building of the railways; others who acknowledge minor industrial or hand-labour buildings (e.g. chain-making shops) within its broad category; still others who would extend the term to embrace speculative builders' housing in the 1920s and 1930s. Professor RW Brunskill didn't go that far, but his *Illustrated Handbook of Vernacular Architecture*[5] did provide a framework for the identification and classification of vernacular traditions in Britain. Its publication in 1970, though he himself saw it as appearing when systematic study had 'just reached its majority', was certainly a significant landmark in the field.

A dozen years later the *Handbook* has proved its worth to scores of schools, local history groups, WEA classes and the like throughout the country as well as having provided a valuable tool for the identification and recording of building types, forms, materials, structural systems, and so on. The Cordingley-Brunskill system for recording buildings offered coded descriptions and gave examples of their application under the heading 'How to Study Vernacular Architecture'. Unfortunately, the system was a shade too neat, the 'how to study' instructions buttoned up the process. Hundreds of amateur house-hunters have beavered away producing record cards or similar documentation and have got very little nearer to understanding the buildings, why they were built, what needs they met, or how they have been transformed through changing demands over time.

This latter aspect is particularly evident. An obsession to trace the 'original' building, to 'date' its construction and to recapture its nature when it was first built has pervaded much of this work. And it is to be seen in the sanetised, disinfected historic houses that have been herded for their own protection into the reservations of 'museums of folk architecture'. Interest in the minutiae of vernacular architecture has also reached obsessional lengths, with detailed analyses of the distribution of different kinds of scarfed joints, and exhaustive inventories of particular architectural features being common among the members of the Vernacular Architecture Group. Formed in the early 1950s it has undeniably added to the sum of human knowledge on British traditional building, but the plethora of publications and articles on cruck construction, from FWB Charles' 1967 monograph on *Mediaeval Cruck Building and its Derivatives*,[6] to NW Alcock's *A Catalogue of Cruck Buildings*,[7] 1973, and the seemingly unending lists and descriptions of other cruck structures that have been published by the VAG since,[8] suggests that the cruck has metaphorical as well as literal significance.

A number of important books on the subject have been published over the past twenty years or so including MW Barley's *The English Farmhouse and Cottage*,[9] 1961, which

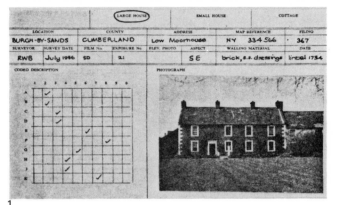

1

BARN AT COURT LODGE, GODMERSHAM

2   3

1 An example of a record card for 'minor domestic architecture' as developed at the School of Architecture, University of Manchester (from R.W. Brunskill, *Illustrated Handbook of Vernacular Architecture*).

2 Barn at Godmersham

3 Cruck construction clearly expressed on the end wall of a house at Didworthy, Gloucestershire (ph Steve Hoare for the 'English Cottages and Small Farmhouses' exhibition).

Co.	Condition	Use	No.	Apex	Roof Form	Type	Blade Curve	Full or Raised	Blade joint	Other Trusses	Wall	Source Publ.	Name	Townland, other distinguishing ref.
Co. Antrim														
J006898	D	D	1	H	G	J	E	R	F	W	S	UF18	AG	Drumderg
D140065	O	A	1	H	G	J	T	F	F	.	S	UF12	EE	Kinbally
J163800	O	D	1	H	G	J	E	F	F	–	S	u	MB	Seacash
Co. Armagh														
H865494	D	D	1	D	G	J	E	F	F	.	C/S	UF18	AG	Allistragh
J014584	C/R	D	1	H	G	C/J	C/E	R	F	.	C/S	UF12	EE	Derrybrugas
H925635	.	D	(1)	D	G	J	T	R	O	.	C/S	IFW	EE	Maghery
J062608	O	D	3	.	G	C	E	F	–	–	C/S	UF8	AG	Turmoyra, Kinnego
Co. Donegal														
C420580	U	D	1	C	G	C	D	R	–	W	S	FL	DM	Ardmalin, Slievebane
C490530	U	D	1	C	G	C	C	R	–	–	S	UF11	DM	Ballynahowna
C540430	U	A	1	C	G	C	S/D	R	–	–	S	UF11	DM	Claggan
C340480	D	D	1	C	G	C	T	R	–	–	S	GW	DM	Crossconnell
C630410	O	D	1	C	G	C	S/T	R	–	W	S	FL	DM	Drumaweer
C500500	U	A	1	C	G	C	S	R	–	–	S	UF11	DM	Faglieran
C420550	O	A	1	C	G	C	D	R	–	–	S	FL	DM	Knockamany
Co. Down														
J140480	.	D	(1)	.	G	J	E	F	F	–	.	UF12	EE	Ballymoney
J095526	U	D	1	H	G	J	E	R	F	T/W	C/S	UF18	AG	Clare, A
J090506	O	D	1	C	G	J	T	F	F	–	C/S	UF18	AG	Clare, B
J084550	R	D	1	.	G	J	E	R	F	–	S	UF18	AG	Corcreeny, A

4

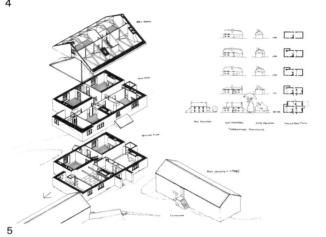

5

6

7

4 Partial list of Northern Irish crucks, compiled by Alan Gailey and Desmond McCourt (from *Vernacular Architecture*, Vol 9, 1978).

5 Change and development of a Devon farmhouse, Narracombe, near Ilsington. The traditional longhouse was reoriented with the addition of a formal extension in the 18th century (drawn by David Ballantyne for the exhibition 'English Cottages and Small Farmhouses, courtesy Arts Council).

6 Spatial organisation in the vernacular environment: the Green at Bledington in the Cotswolds from *The Village Green*, an exhibition by Paul Oliver with students of the Department of Architecture, Oxford Polytechnic, for the Arts Council, ph Paul Oliver, courtesy Arts Council).

7 House at Kingsbury, N.W. London, by E.G. Trobridge (from an exhibition on the work of Trobridge by Graham Paul Smith and students of architecture, Oxford Polytechnic, now in preparation in association with the Grange Museum, London Borough of Brent (ph Ian Davis).

made considerable use of documentary evidence, particularly the '*true and perficte inventories*' of '*all the moveable goods, cattles and chattels*' of a number of 17th-century householders, to create a fuller picture of the relationship of dwelling to society. Among the many regional studies RB Wood-Jones' *Traditional Domestic Architecture of the Banbury Region*,[10] 1963 remains the most comprehensive while Eric Mercer's *English Vernacular Houses*[11] published for the Royal Commission on Historical Monuments, 1975, is monumental in more ways than one. To these must be added the—literally—hundreds of articles which have appeared in *Archaeologia Cantiana*, *Oxoniensia*, *Mediaeval Archaeology* or the *Transactions*, *Notes* or *Newsletters* of numerous county or local historical and archaeological societies. Local publications range from the cyclostyled booklets of the Robertsbridge and District Archaeological Society[12] to the carefully produced booklets of *Traditional Kent Buildings*[13] edited by Jane Wade from work done by students of Canterbury School of Architecture.

These latter publications are among the few that have 'architecture' as their source; for the most part the publications reflect the emphases and the biases of historical and archaeological enquiry. If at first the volume of published material suggests that little remains to be done, in fact this is far from the case. Not only is the recording of traditional building in large areas of Britain still sketchy, but it is also limited in its scope. It would be wrong to suggest that 'the outside view' predominates, but it is arguable how much architectural thinking permeates much of the literature. Of formal or volumetric analysis there is very little; spatial relationships are seldom hinted at. There is much to be done in such areas for the better understanding of the tradition.

Yet this is not, in my view, the principal omission from current studies. Most serious is any real consideration of the changes of use and adaptations that have taken place over time and their bearing on changing values. The meaning of vernacular buildings to their present and recent occupiers is scarcely hinted at; when it is, as in the writings of George Ewart Evans,[14] it is often buried among the wart-cures and hag-stones. A more searching study, which was nonetheless weak on architecture, was hinted at in WJ Turner's immediately post-war *Exmoor Village*[15] backed up by researches made by Mass Observation. But the promise of this start was never realised in later works.

In spite of the changes in philosophy and anthropology which have occurred since then, and which have been reflected to some degree in architectural writing, there hasn't been much evidence of their influence on thoughts concerning the vernacular in Britain. There is for example no work that brings structuralist thinking to vernacular studies in the way that Henry Glassie has combined both structuralism and the analysis of structural innovation in his *Folk*

Housing in Middle Virginia.[16] And we surely can take no pride in the fact that the only work that relates the architecture of a folk community in the British Isles to its historic and present culture in the way in which the dwellings are built, used, lived in, comes from the same author: *Passing the Time in Ballymenone: Culture and History of an Ulster Community*.[17]

There's something cosy about vernacular architecture; it's a sheltered retreat for many who fondle the adze-marks, feel the fit of the ashlar or marvel at the assembly of post, wall-plate and tie-beam. Somehow, there's not the craftsmanship any more; all that honest workmanship with simple tools and muscle—it's gone. What is a comfort for some is a turn-off for others—except, that is, when it comes to buying a house in Devon or Wales to visit with the family at weekends, and get away from the practice and the telephone. Recently sold because the farmer's family wanted a bungalow just up the road—you know the sort of thing.

But *why* did he prefer the bungalow—if he did, that is, which is a moot point—what values does it represent for him? We make our assumptions as we generally do, and are quite ready to back them by designing in accordance with them. Though frankly, we seldom *know*. For the truth of the matter is, the major proportion of housing in Britain is vernacular no longer, unless you happen to belong to the category that does extend the term to spec builders' semis. Half the population of Britain lives in the suburbs of our cities, and a lot more live in housing of a similar kind that clusters round our small towns and villages. Not only semi-detached houses, but terraced houses too. And in the outer suburbs, where land was cheaper and there was room to spread a little, bungalows, chalet bungalows and detached houses ranging in size from three bedrooms to five or six. The latter may be few in number, relatively speaking, but they are at one end of a scale that embraces a wide range of domestic buildings which also includes rows of four, maisonettes, houses over shops and much else.

If the vernacular seems at times to be a comfortable corner of architecture in which to hide, there are not many who have chosen to go out and meet the suburbs. In spite of the fact that the most conspicuous element in the built environment of Britain must surely be the suburbs around the cities, until extremely recently there has been an almost total disregard of them. Compared with the extent of the phenomenon the extent of the writing on it is still miniscule, but nevertheless within the past few years it has continued to grow. Not all of it, rightly, is concerned with the subject of the suburbs alone, but rather with housing generally during the period of population growth and considerable social change. John Burnett's *A Social History of Housing*[18] first appeared in 1978 and on a broad canvas plotted the dramatic developments in domestic accommodation between approximately 1815 and 1970. It's a masterly work within the inevitable limitations, but even here a strange myopia sets in when he discusses the suburbs of the twenties and thirties: with literally millions of examples from which to draw for illustrations for his themes he chose to depict them with five watercolours from John Prizeman's *Your Home: The Outside View*.[19]

Still more recently, *The Design of Suburbia: A Critical Study in Environmental History*[20] by Arthur M Edwards covers much of the same span of time. By 'critical history' he means that he is no lover of the suburbs: '*as the narrow house is the cheapest, commonest and ugliest of detached two-storey houses, so the square-plan bungalow is the cheapest, commonest and ugliest of single-storey dwellings*'. Edwards cannot be accused of being dispassionate. Others more coolly examine an aspect of the housing issue, like Professor John Nelson Tarn, whose *Five Per Cent*

Philanthropy[21] is a scholarly appraisal of the housing of the urban poor over the three-quarters of a century that culminated in World War 1 and the commencement of the Old Oak Estate at Acton. Or a particular building type is documented in a specific area, of which Alan A Jackson's *Semi-Detached London*,[22] published nearly a decade ago in 1973, is an informative example.

All this activity has not promoted, as far as I know, a society to match the Vernacular Architecture Group, though a Suburban Architecture Group would have plenty of work to do. If there is as yet no inventory of vernacular houses and even a comprehensive typology still remains to be compiled, as far as suburban housing is concerned the work has scarcely begun. To which no doubt, the answer comes readily that there is little variety to document and what there is would not merit the effort. But only a few hours spent in Hastings, Harrow or Hull reveal that such is not the case. Though the types of semi-detached house are modest in number they still add up to a sizeable range, while the forms encompassed within the bungalows and chalet-bungalows of the inter-war years extend far beyond the 'cheap and common' square plan. The activities of individual builders of the thirties, the much-maligned spec builders about whom so little is known, also provide an area for research that could be done at local level. In fact there are local studies to match, in type of approach if not in abundance, the studies made by local history groups and the like in the vernacular field, such as *Pinner Streets Yesterday and Today*[23] by Elizabeth Cooper, or James Murphy's *The Semi-Detached House: Its Place In Suburban Housing*,[24] from the School of Architecture, University College, Dublin.

Much of the writing on the suburbs (well, there isn't *much*, but a good proportion of what there *is*) reflects the archaeological and socio-historical emphases that are to be found in the vernacular field. Very little has been considered in essentially architectural or planning terms, if only because the architects and planners have been the bitterest in their attacks on the homes of half of Britain's population. Their spokesman of another era, the *Architectural Review* bestowed 'a name in the hope it will stick—SUBTOPIA'[25]— and unhappily its patronising term and definition ('Philosophically, the idealisation of the Little Man who lives there; from suburb + Utopia') did stick and the mud-slinging has hardly abated. The times seemed to be a-changing when *AD* published at the close of 1981 a Profile on 'The Anglo-American Suburb'.[26] Hearts sank as we padded round the paths of Park Town, sipped again at Bournville and bathed in Port Sunlight. The American bit would not be familiar to many, though it was comfortably conventional. Here was the architect congratulating other architects on their tasteful ventures into the suburbs—which bear only tangentially today on the suburbs of either Britain or the United States. As for occupants they, as usual, hardly came into the picture—or the pictures.

It's all the more surprising because studies of the suburbs have been made in the United States since at least 1925 when Harlan Paul Douglass published *The Suburban Trend*.[27] Thirty years later though, David Riesman was still complaining that '*we know very little about the relatively settled suburbs and ... almost nothing about the suburbs (old and new) surrounding the smaller cities*.[28] His work, and that of Herbert J Gans, William H Whyte, William Dobriner, AC Spectorsky, Stanley Buder and many others have largely repaired the omission. They aren't always in favour of the suburbs, but they do base their conclusions on considered research and not cliché responses about 'monotony' 'soul-destroying environments' or 'Little Men'.

Largely, of course, they remain unread by planners and architects in the US as their few counterparts in Britain are similarly ignored. We might have been spared the débacle

of high-rise housing, for example, if the warnings in Willmott and Young's *Family and Kinship in East London*[29] had been taken seriously. There *are* studies of suburban houses and communities of comparatively recent date, but they are far less well known than those undertaken by the Institute of Community Studies and likely to be even less influential while architects' resistance to, or ignorance of them persists. I have in mind Lynette Carey and Roy Mapes' *The Sociology of Planning*,[30] for instance. The daunting title is not likely to induce architects to respond to their work on social interactions within eight new housing estates of differing configurations. Or again, there is *Mental Health on a New Housing Estate*[31] by EH Hare and GK Shaw which compares the incidence of neuroses in an old and a new housing estate in Croydon. Of course, these are sociological and psychological works, and they use the tools and the methods of those disciplines. Still, their conclusions should surely have some significance for designers, though they may not be the ones they'd expect. '*If an architect is really concerned with the way in which a realised design is used and enjoyed by the people who will have to experience it as part of their lives, then the architect must become something of a sociologist or must at least employ one*' write Carey and Mapes.

Tables and statistics do not seem to express the values of the householders and their families, it's true. How *do* you ascertain what those values are, and how they bear upon house and home? *Voices from the Middle Class*[32] by Jane Deverson and Katherine Lindsay uses free association and the tape recorder to try and get an answer in two South London suburbs, but though some of what they document has design implications the bulk of the book is concerned with other domestic matters. Far more original and more thought-provoking is the work of Stephen Willats with his West London Social Resources Project.[33] Stephen Willats is the editor of *Control Magazine*, and an artist with a concern for the social roles of art. His Social Resources Project was conducted in Greenford, Osterley, Hanwell and Harrow and it involved the participation of local residents not only in the recording of their activities, needs and responses to their own environment, but also in qualitative decision-making after the completed record sheets had been publically displayed. Its purpose was to demonstrate the 'externalisation of art' but it offers lessons in the externalisation of architecture. And by that I mean getting far more feedback from the community for whom architects are theoretically working, and gaining far more of its participation in their design processes.

Even so, the significance of the personally shaped, embellished, planted, wall-hung, done-it-yourself environment of the home, whether it's in the village, the town or the suburbs has not been examined closely in Britain. Not as closely, at any rate, as when Mihaly Csikszentmilhalyi and Eugene Rochberg-Halton sought to uncover the empirical relationships between objects and their owners, or 'people and things', in Rogers Park and Evanston in the northern limits of Chicago. Their exhaustive study of the home as a symbolic environment was concerned mainly with the values attached to objects gathered, kept, owned, nurtured, displayed, from beds to bric-a-brac, potted plants to pin-up photos. But if the significance of domestic symbols in

8

9

10

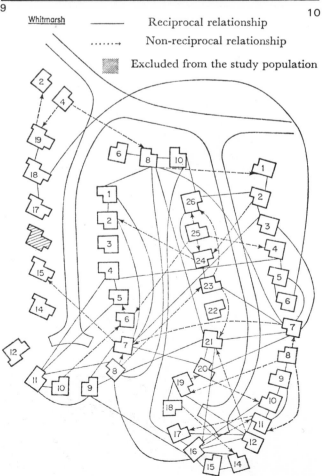

Whitmarsh ——— Reciprocal relationship

......→ Non-reciprocal relationship

▨ Excluded from the study population

8 Housing in Hastings, c. 1935 (from *Dunroamin: the Suburban Semi and its Enemies*, Paul Oliver, Ian Davis and Ian Bentley, 1981, courtesy Barrie & Jenkins Ltd, ph Ian Davis).

9 Local idiom in suburban housing: Edwardian semis at Littlehampton, Sussex where flint walling is traditional (ph Paul Oliver).

10 Social relationships on a North Staffordshire housing estate plotted by Lynette Carey and Roy Mapes (from *The Sociology of Planning*).

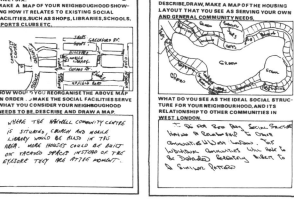

11

12   13

11 Examples of participant returns from the *West London Re-Modelling Book*, part of 'Art and Social Function' project by Stephen Willats.

12 Bay window, shutters and garden furniture proclaim private ownership of former council houses in the Old Oak Estate, Acton (ph Graham Paul Smith).

13 Roughcast and stone veneered walls, new walls and Dutch net curtains on other Old Oak Estate houses (ph Graham Paul Smith).

relation to the self is treated with contempt, as 'good taste' (or whatever guise is worn to distinguish 'our' taste from 'theirs') ensures that it is, there's little likelihood that the message of *The Meaning of Things*[34] is going to get through to the design professions.

Rochberg-Halton and his partner were concentrating on the internal, personally-shaped home and did not extend their work to the houses in which their subjects lived. This Ian Davis, Ian Bentley and myself attempted to do in *Dunroamin: The Suburban Semi and Its Enemies*.[35] But our intention was also to reveal how virulent, biased and irrational were the attacks of the modernist architects on the suburban environment of the inter-war years. It was only the identification of a reasonably defined period that made us end with the outbreak of war; there's massive evidence to show that such attitudes not only persisted throughout the fifties and sixties, but with few exceptions, are flourishing today.

In a way it's hardly surprising. Much Post-Modern is old-style Modernism in a recut suit and the attitudes of formalist designers to the qualities which appeal to those who never hear, let alone learn the language of their formal games are not noticeably different. One of the fascinating aspects of the breaches in the modernist ranks, brought about by the sharp assaults of Brolin and others, is how rapidly and securely have the ranks closed again. If the old attitudes were shaken it wasn't for long: the condescension to the vernacular and the patronising of the suburbs persists where either are considered at all.

Does it matter? Well, obviously I think it does. I believe we should learn by the successes, even if they were not of our making, and we should acknowledge and learn from the mistakes, especially when they were. It is proper that architectural magazines are largely concerned with the schemes of innovatory designers, but only if it is recognised that the entire spectrum of environmental research and thought does not reside within them. Nor is it encompassed by a few photographs of sturdy examples of functional vernacular barns or the games that architects occasionally play with the textures and motifs that they may extract from the mass of houses on the urban periphery. It's not only the values of architects that matter in the design of houses or community buildings; its the values of those that live in them, work in them and adapt, extend or remodel them when they can. And that goes as much for our understanding of the vernacular traditions as it does for the necessary recognition of all the other kinds of building that are overlooked 'out there'.

Rather than select a number of examples to discuss in this article I've chosen to comment on the state of research and writing in vernacular and popular architecture. I've tried to show what kind of emphases there are, to indicate some of the aspects that are little pursued in this country, and to suggest some of the lines along which, in my view, potentially valuable work is being done which can have direct bearing on architectural design for a humane environment. Vernacular architecture in the conventional sense may have come to an end in Britain, though it is still lived in and adapted. But while I write the popular environment is evolving and changing. In the Old Oak Estate at Acton

mentioned above many of those LCC estate council houses are now being sold off and their new owners are intent on expressing their new home ownership by remodelling them. It's not easy of course—as in all council estates where architects were in control, the houses were deliberately designed to inhibit any hints of individualism.

But it's happening, here and in scores of other estates around the country, new messages are being uttered in the vernacular but, as far as I'm aware, no one is devoting much attention to finding out what they mean. But at least, just this once, they've slipped in between these covers.

Notes

1 Juan Pablo Bonta, *Architecture and Its Interpretation*, Lund Humphries, London, 1979.
2 Comte de Lautréamont (Isadore Ducasse), see William S Rubin, *Dada, Surrealism and Their Heritage*, Museum of Modern Art, NY 1968.
3 Nikolaus Pevsner, *The Buildings of England*, Penguin Books, Harmondsworth, 1951 et seq.
4 EAAE Workshop on Vernacular and Neo-Vernacular Architecture, Middle East Technical University, Ankara, May 16–22, 1982.
5 RW Brunskill, *Illustrated Handbook of Vernacular Architecture*, Faber and Faber, London, 1970.
6 FWB Charles, *Medieval Cruck-Building and its Derivatives*, Society for Medieval Archaeology, Monograph Series No 2, 1967.
7 NW Alcock, *A Catalogue of Cruck Buildings*, Phillimore for the Vernacular Architecture Group, Chichester, 1973.
8 *Vernacular Architecture*, Vernacular Architecture Group, York, 1969.
9 MW Barley, *The English Farmhouse and Cottage*, Routledge and Kegan Paul, London, 1961.
10 RB Wood-Jones, *Traditional Domestic Architecture of the Banbury Region*.
11 Eric Mercer, *English Vernacular Houses: A Study of Traditional Farmhouses and Cottages*, Her Majesty's Stationery Office, London, 1975.
12 For example, David Martin, *The Robertsbridge Wealdens*, Robertsbridge and District Archeological Society, nd.
13 Jane Wade (ed) *Traditional Kent Buildings*, 1 & 2, School of Architecture, Canterbury College of Art, Kent County Council, 1981.
14 For example, George Ewart Evans, *The Pattern Under the Plough*, Faber and Faber, London, 1966.
15 WJ Turner, *Exmoor Village*, George C Harrap, London, 1947.
16 Henry Glassie, *Folk Housing in Middle Virginia, A Structural Analysis of Historic Artifacts*, University of Tennessee Press, Knoxville, 1975.
17 Henry Glassie, *Passing the Time in Ballymemone: Culture and History of an Ulster Community* (awaiting publication).
18 John Burnett, *A Social History of Housing 1815–1970*, David and Charles, Newton Abbot, 1978.
19 John Prizeman, *Your Home: The Outside View*, Blue Circle Group, London, 1975.
20 Arthur M Edwards, *The Design of Suburbia: A Critical Study in Environmental History*, Pembridge Press, London, 1981.
21 John Nelson Tarn, *Five Per Cent Philanthropy: An Account of Housing in Urban Areas Between 1840 and 1914*, Cambridge University Press, 1973.
22 Alan A Jackson, *Semi-Detached London*, George Allen and Unwin, London, 1973.
23 Elizabeth Cooper, *Pinner Streets Yesterday and Today*, Pinner and Hatch End Historical and Archaeological Society, Vol V, 1976.
24 James Murphy, *The Semi-Detached House: Its Place in Suburban Housing*, Housing Research Unit, School of Architecture, University College, Dublin, 1977.
25 Ian Nairn, 'Outrage' Special Number, *Architectural Review*, June, 1955.
26 Robert AM Stern and John Montague Massengale, 'The Anglo-American Suburb', *Architectural Design* Profile 37, 10/11, 1981.
27 Harlan Paul Douglass, *The Suburban Trend*, Century Press, NY, 1925.
28 David Riesman, 'The Suburban Dislocation' in *The Annals of the American Academy of Political and Social Science*, Vol I 314, Nov, 1957.
29 Michael Young and Peter Willmott, *Family and Kinship in East London* (1957) Penguin Books, Harmondsworth, 1963.
30 Lynette Carey and Roy Mapes, *The Sociology of Planning: A Study of Social Activity on New Housing Estates*, BT Batsford, London, 1972.
31 EH Hare and GK Shaw, *Mental Health on a New Housing Estate: A Comparative Study of Health in Two Districts of Croydon*, Oxford University Press, London, 1965, Maudsley Monographs No 12.
32 Jane Deverson and Katherine Lindsay, *Voices From the Middle Class: A Study of Families of Two London Suburbs*, Hutchinson, London, 1976.
33 Stephen Willats, *Art and Social Function: Three Projects*, Latimer New Dimensions, London, 1976.
34 Mihaly Csikszentmihalyi and Eugene Rochberg-Halton, *The Meaning of Things: Domestic Symbols and the Self*, Cambridge University Press, 1981.
35 Paul Oliver, Ian Davis and Ian Bentley, *Dunroamin: The Suburban Semi and Its Enemies*, Barrie and Jenkins, London, 1981.

Richard Reid
LEARNING FROM THE VERNACULAR

TO MANY THE WORD ARCHITECTURE is a generic term for any kind of building, good or bad, a misunderstanding arising most likely from the fact that the term architecture, first used in the mid 16th century was derived from the Greek word *architekton* which meant literally chief craftsman or master builder. In the 19th century Ruskin wrote that it is nothing but ornament applied to building. Sir Nikolaus Pevsner in his *An Outline of European Architecture*, sees the cathedral as architecture, the bicycle shed as building—building being any enclosure of sufficient scale for a person to move about in, the term architecture being reserved for only those buildings designed with a view to aesthetic appeal. Scott, in his book *The Architecture of Humanism* goes further when he discussed the romanticism of natural simplicity: the romanticism of Wordsworth and of a 'rustic architecture'. He sees no fault in the domestic type of building in which variety of form is conditioned solely by convenience. He sees repose because the picturesqueness is unstudied, fitting the house to unselfconscious nature, a poetry without rhetoric, its beauty secure from fashion because it is both elementary and genuine. He sees this as the true rival to architecture.

Quite clearly the term Architecture is not a generic term for all building, but is a qualitative term for buildings of a particular excellence. All architecture has to be well built and well planned. If it is bad not only can it not be architecture, but it won't be good building either. But if one accepts the existence of both building and architecture, one has to accept the existence of two distinctly different yet related traditions, one a Regionalist tradition seen in the simple, utilitarian structures of the Mediterranean, the other a more grand design tradition epitomised by Versailles. The Regionalist tradition reflects the life and activities of people directly whereas the other, influenced and concerned with theories of architecture, fashions, impressiveness and the like, reflects the pomp and ceremony of public occasions. The first has a richly modelled fabric and less clearly defined image, whilst the second has a clearly structured and highly defined image. The first is humble and unpretending and a reflection of everyday social life, the second is more ritualistic and acute, with a distinctive outline, a reflection of corporate mindedness. The first is mosaic in form, consisting of an overall design composed of individual elements related to a common ground, the twisting frontage of street or path. The second has an arrangement of elements and manner of organisation which is clearly defined along a predominantly undeviating street or edge. The first is multiform, disordered, non-linear, multi-coloured, non-repetitive and involving. The second is clearly structured, ordered, monochrome, linear, uniform, repetitive, continuous and non-involving. Any example of building and architecture fits somewhere between these two extremes.

The thesis here is about the possibility of making a synthesis between *both* building and architecture for '... *it has come to this*', as Thoreau wrote, '*that the lover of art is one, and the lover of nature another, though true art is but one expression of our love of nature: it is monstrous when one cares but little about trees and much about Corinthian columns, and yet this is exceedingly common*'.

The Context

Rye, Sussex, a member of the confederation of Cinque Ports, and one of the principal bastions of England during the medieval wars with France. She was at the height of her prosperity in the 13th and 14th centuries both as a flourishing market centre and as a thriving port and continued as a prosperous trading town up to the first half of the 16th century.

It is a town with more examples of building than architecture. What is particularly interesting is the way both, especially the former, have been enriched and extended by time. Accepting the context of a typical Wealden town, what are the formal architectural and structural elements that have made this kind of *accretions* possible?

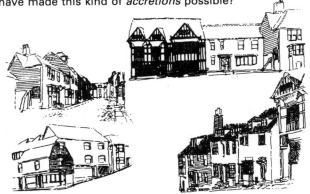

The Additive Fabric

Habraken describes how the old houses left to us from the past have more often than not been transformed—of how each generation, each occupant, changed what he found. He sees DWELLING as the sum of human actions within a certain framework, of how a house or living unit becomes a dwelling the moment the occupant begins to *possess* it by the very act of transforming it. He sees the relationship between the basic fabric or framework and the transformation made within it by the occupant as the *natural relationship*.

Towards a Pattern Language

Habraken asks us to look at the architect in the way he likes to see himself—the artist, the poet in stone, steel and glass; and also look at the building which is his product as a work of art, as materialised poetry. Let us agree that civilisation needs this poetry, indeed that a civilisation can in part be seen as such because of its existence. What then is this special work and the normal everyday buildings which have so far concerned us? Poetry cannot arise without a powerful, living, spontaneously developing language of communication. The poet whose work exceeds the language of everyday conversation is nevertheless in great need of it. The language he hears around him is the source from which he draws. It enriches his work with new images and colours and he gives back what he took from everyday life.'

He goes on to blame the monstrosities around as a product of architects little motivated by a society of which they are a part. Of how architects are in *need* of ideas. But these ideas, because of the context in which they are so often taken and used, will gradually force him to repeat himself. '*The poet who no longer hears everyday conversation will exhaust himself in increasingly artificial syntax. He will call forth every sound he can think of, for he hears no echo.*' Clearly the problem is not one of looking, and describing, but of seeing and observing.

The Elements

If the style of an architecture was dead, the principles were still very much alive.

The Dynamic of Time

People require more time to *grow* into a community, and it is exactly this that Habraken's natural relationship will give us. *'The formation of a community may be encouraged, but it should never be forced. Undoubtedly more than one generation is required to enable a society to become one with its environment, and to allow the environment in turn to grow into harmony with its people'*. But he sees the most weighty argument for re-introducing the natural relationship is the need to come to terms with the future.

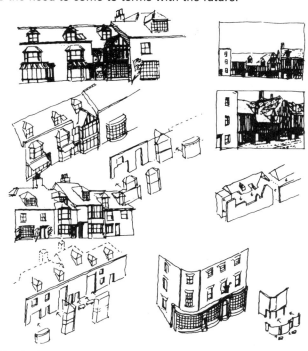

The Argument

Neo-vernacular is obviously wrong in making a jelly mould of the Regionalist tradition. Form as a goal, as Mies van der Rohe pointed out, always ends in Formalism. Such striving is directed not towards an inside, but towards an outside. However, the transformations that have taken place within the medieval frontage type system as represented by a place like Rye are such that the outside of the individual house is now, with its neighbours, the architecture of the street and no longer merely that of the individual house. The facade/s in fact have now become the mediator between the public and private realm. But unlike the additive fabric of the southern European context, which has one homogenous wall for the public realm with accretions mainly in the private, the street facade/wall of a country town in the UK is invariably enriched and extended via time on *both* sides. On closer examination, however, you will see that the accretions in the public realm are primarily architectural in nature, those in the private realm largely concerned with building.

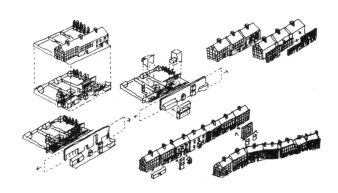

The Natural Relationship

Habraken sees the problem for the architect and planner is that when the *natural relationship* is broken they find themselves pre-occupied with the need to devise forms which formerly came about without him, by means of different forces. The neo-vernacular is a product of such cosmetic ideas. But when we study more carefully the Regionalist tradition we begin to recognise the unique functions of the kind of support structure that existed within the Wealden tradition certainly, as the standard Wealden house type was enriched and extended over a long period of time.

The References

Habraken warns us that we must not allow ourselves to be influenced by forms and constructions which are familiar. *'... I am not suggesting, however, that such forms cannot teach us anything, nor that we shall not need the knowledge and skills implied in these constructions. But today's forms are associated with functions which we want to replace and the danger is that this association, if we are not conscious of it, may prevent us from recognising the unique functions of support structure.'*

The Site

At the foot of East Cliff, by the Landgate, Rye, with views out across Romney Marsh.

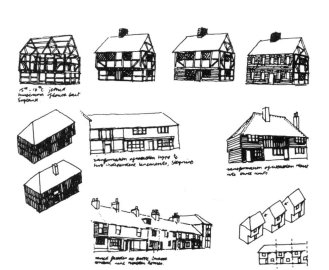

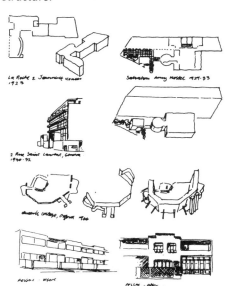

Ahrends Burton & Koralek

FACTORY FOR CUMMINS ENGINE CO. LTD, SHOTTS, LANARKSHIRE

THE REDEVELOPMENT has taken place around and amongst the existing factory buildings in which Cummins have operated for the past 25 years. The production areas have been divided into four distinct elements—Receiving, Machining, Stores and Assembly and Testing and Shipping. These four elements are placed in a progressive sequence, each serving the next.

Above the east/west production flow there is a separate north/south pedestrian circulation system connecting to the car park at a higher level of the site. Three covered bridges provide direct access into the factory at the upper level, clear of materials movement. The two principal bridges will be linked by an upper-level amenity deck which contains the Cafeteria, Medical Centre and Lecture Room. Part of the existing factory space is being converted into a open-plan office.

New production areas of the building are structured on a 15 m sq grid. Pin-jointed, tubular steel columns support welded tubular steel primary trusses. Reinforced concrete stub columns at low level resist possible accidental impact loads from fork lift trucks. Secondary roof structure takes the form of castellated steel joists fixed below the bottom member of the primary trusses. Steel rod hangers connect the primary trusses and castellated beams at one-third intervals across the 15 m span. The roof profile follows this geometric configuration and provides a continuous zone for distribution of primary services. Secondary services distribute within the depth of the secondary structure thus establishing a clear set of differential zones which will maintain a coherent order for distribution routes in the future.

Cladding for roof and walls consists of an inner skin of corrugated structural steel decking (perforated for acoustic absorption) steel spacer purlins and mill finished corrugated aluminium sheeting externally. Cavities are filled with thermal insulation material, vapour barriers and breather paper. Roof and wall glazing utilises green tinted glass and aluminium patent glazing bars.

Interface zones which lie between adjacent production areas are structured by a reinforced concrete frame supporting the first floor walkways and roof level plantrooms.

Energy studies have been undertaken. The buildings are insulated thermally to standards well above the regulation requirements and utilise sophisticated air cleaning and ventilation systems to transfer heat from the high-heat production Machining Areas to adjacent parts of the building. A centralised monitoring system will be installed to control the mechanical, electrical and security systems and to provide centralised maintenance intelligence.

The new factory is built on a sloping site which resulted in a considerable amount of excavation into the hillside to provide a flat area. The surplus earth is formed into a mounded sculpture which serves not only as a windbreaker and a visual screen to the Receiving area but creates a potent landmark on a scale appropriate to the new Cummins factory.

CLIENT: Cummins Engine Company Ltd
STRUCTURAL ENGINEERS: Ove Arup & Partners
QUANTITY SURVEYORS: Monk & Dunstone, Mahon & Scears
BUILDING SERVICES ENGINEERS: Ove Arup & Partners
LANDSCAPE ARCHITECTS: Landesign Group
BUILDING OWNER: Scottish Development Agency
PHOTOGRAPHS: John Donat

Section through perimeter and typical structural bay

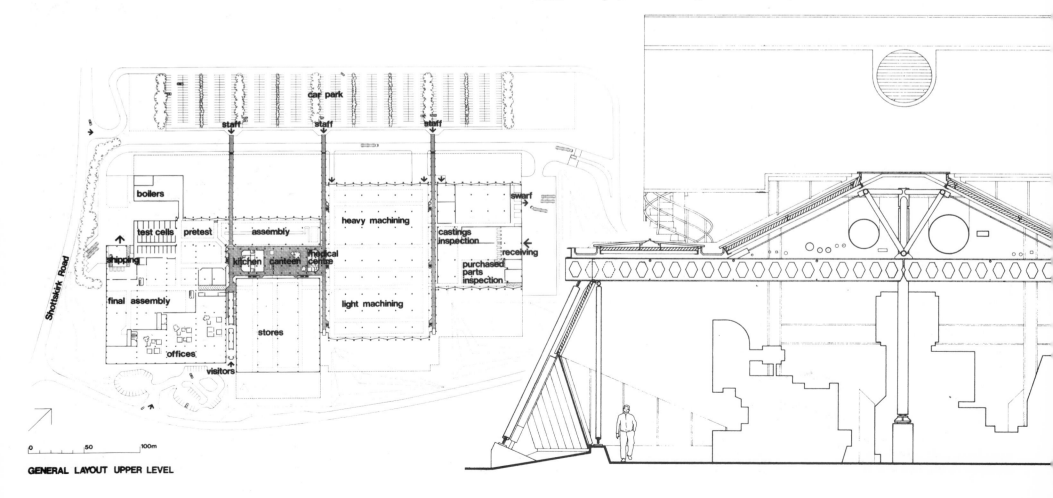

GENERAL LAYOUT UPPER LEVEL

View of end plant room and walkway and exterior of light machining area

View looking west

View of receiving bays to the north-east

Corner junction
Machine shop north perimeter

View of roof showing plant room beyond

Detail of triangulated props

Office conversion of existing north light structure

Detail of NE elevation

View looking east

View of assembly hall

Zaha Hadid
CONVERSION OF 59 EATON PLACE

THE APARTMENT is located in Belgravia in a very sterile, white-washed street with an absence of any nature.

Number 59 was constructed at the turn of the century as a large terraced townhouse and is typical of the style of buildings in the Belgravia area. In common with the properties in the immediate vicinity, the premises proved to be too large for a single occupier and were converted into maisonettes some 14 years ago. The building was constructed as a ground floor and four upper levels, and is divided to form three self-contained maisonettes and a basement.

In early 1980 two acts of urban change took place in Belgravia: an explosion at the Italian Consulate at 38 Eaton Place, which wrecked the entire building; and new urban living injected into 59 Eaton Place.

The clients had modest requirements: they wanted elegance and comfort. They had acquired an apartment which had undergone many changes in the past 20 years and, being stripped of all its ornaments, the house needed a certain newness. The apartment spans three floors and has three vertical conditions:

— the front, which has partly maintained its classical elegance;

— the back, which is an extension added in the mid-1960s, humble and minimal in terms of its materials and overloaded with divisions;

— the middle zone which had confronted the conflicts, had neither the glory of the past nor the comfort of the present but could only look forward to the future.

Our task was to renovate it.

All the ground floor and the old living room were allocated to formal occasions; the only intrusion was the addition of new materials on the floors and a new fire place.

The lobby and dining room underwent the most drastic change to release it from its present state of limbo. A new staircase was installed which extends the public domain to the second floor where a new cloakroom is created.

The top floor houses the clients' private quarters with two master bedrooms—the one coinciding with the formal living room being the most flamboyant, its materials of silk and stone.

The library is abstracted with basic colours, minimum furniture but maximum treatment of the walls to house all the books and mechanical equipment. The gymnasium with jacuzzi at the top of the new extension is the most clinical.

COLLABORATORS: Jonathan Dunn, Kasha Knapkiewicz and Bijan Ganjei
MODELS, COLUMN CONSTRUCTION: Gus Hutcheson
GENERAL HELP: Nan Lee, Wendy Galway, N Ayoubi
ENGINEERS: Ron Wilson and Vincent Grant
QUANTITY SURVEYORS: Alan Thomas & Associates
CONTRACTORS: RL Ruggles & Sons Ltd

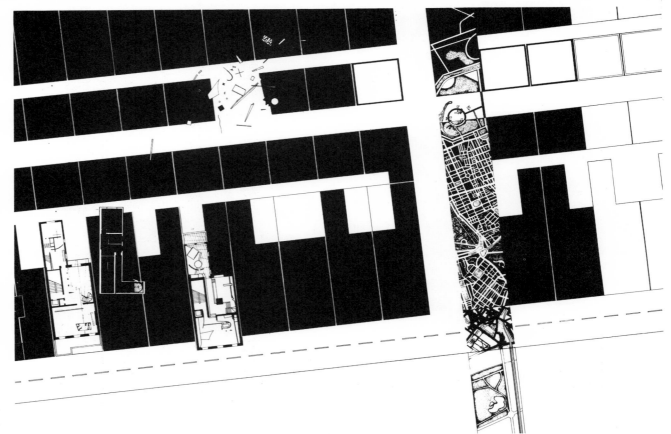

Site and location plan

Overall interior elevations

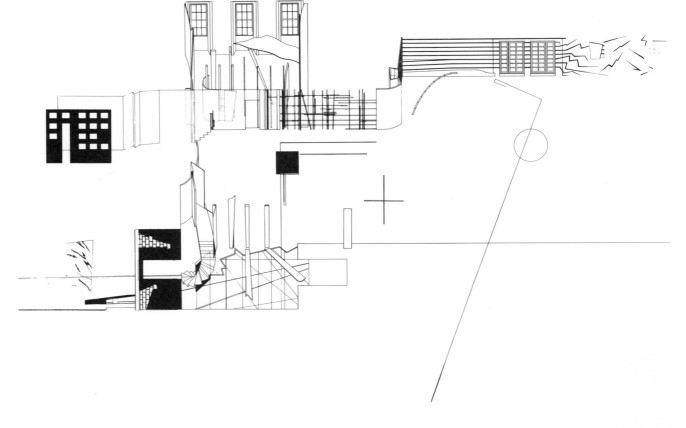

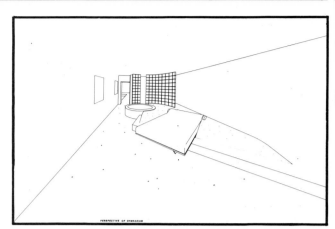

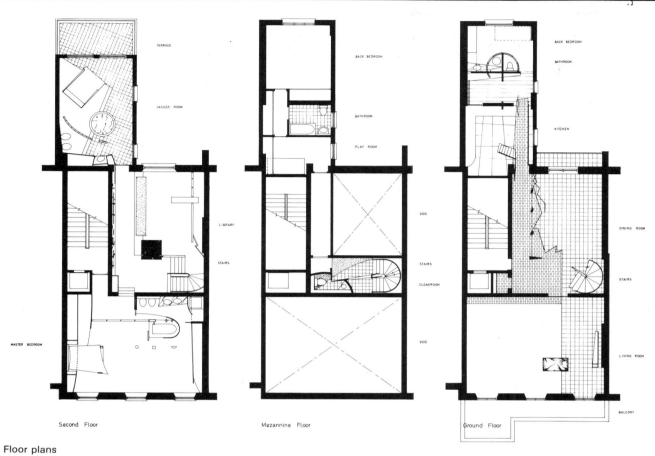

Floor plans

Cross section

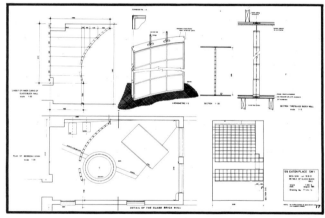

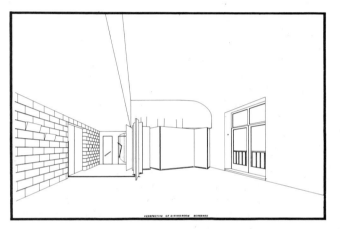

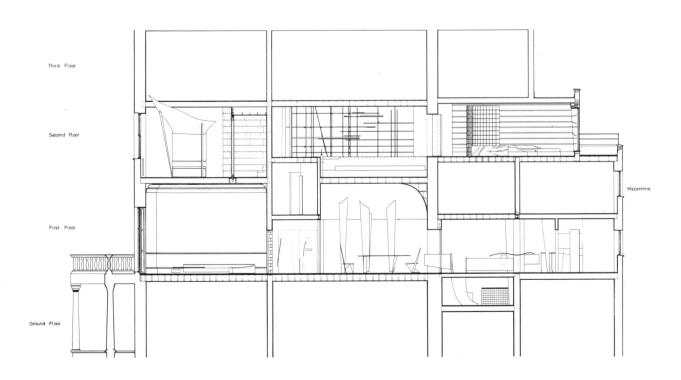

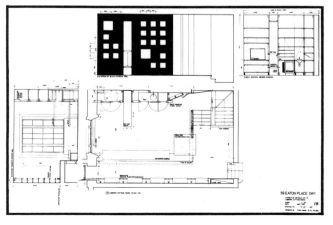

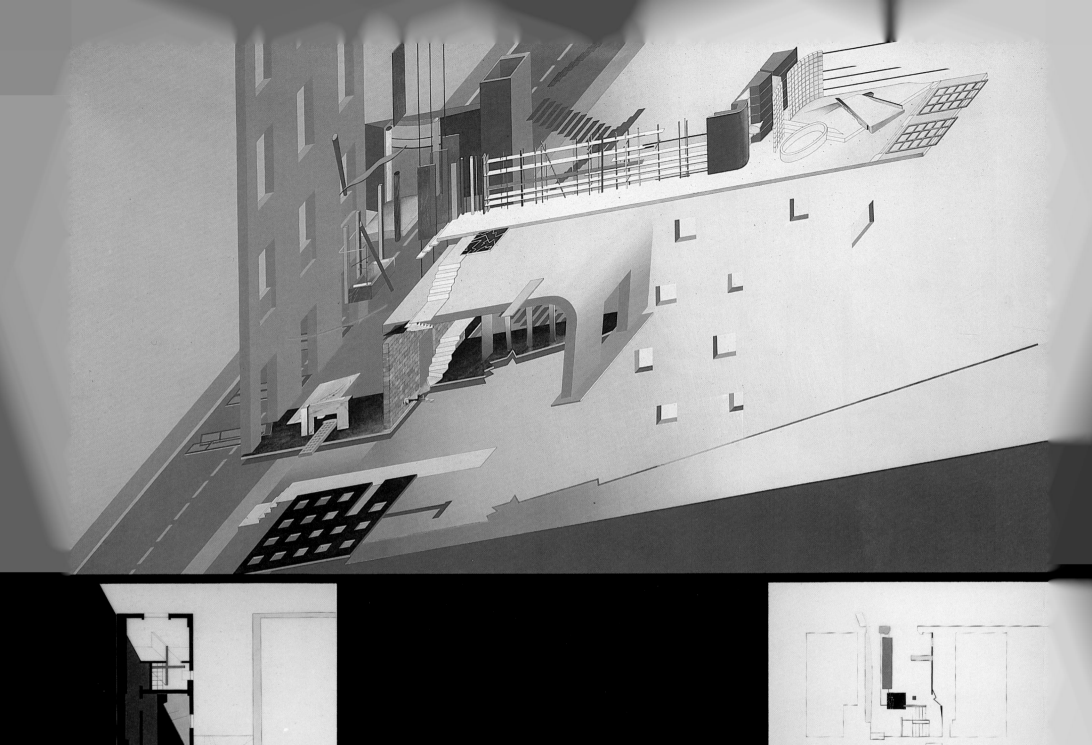

Above, Three towers from the flamboyant, the suprematist to the clinical. From left to right: formal reception room and master bedroom; second tower–dining room and lobby with the new staircases and library; third tower–gymnasium and jacuzzi Left, Ground floor plan. Right, Library plan and early master bedroom plan

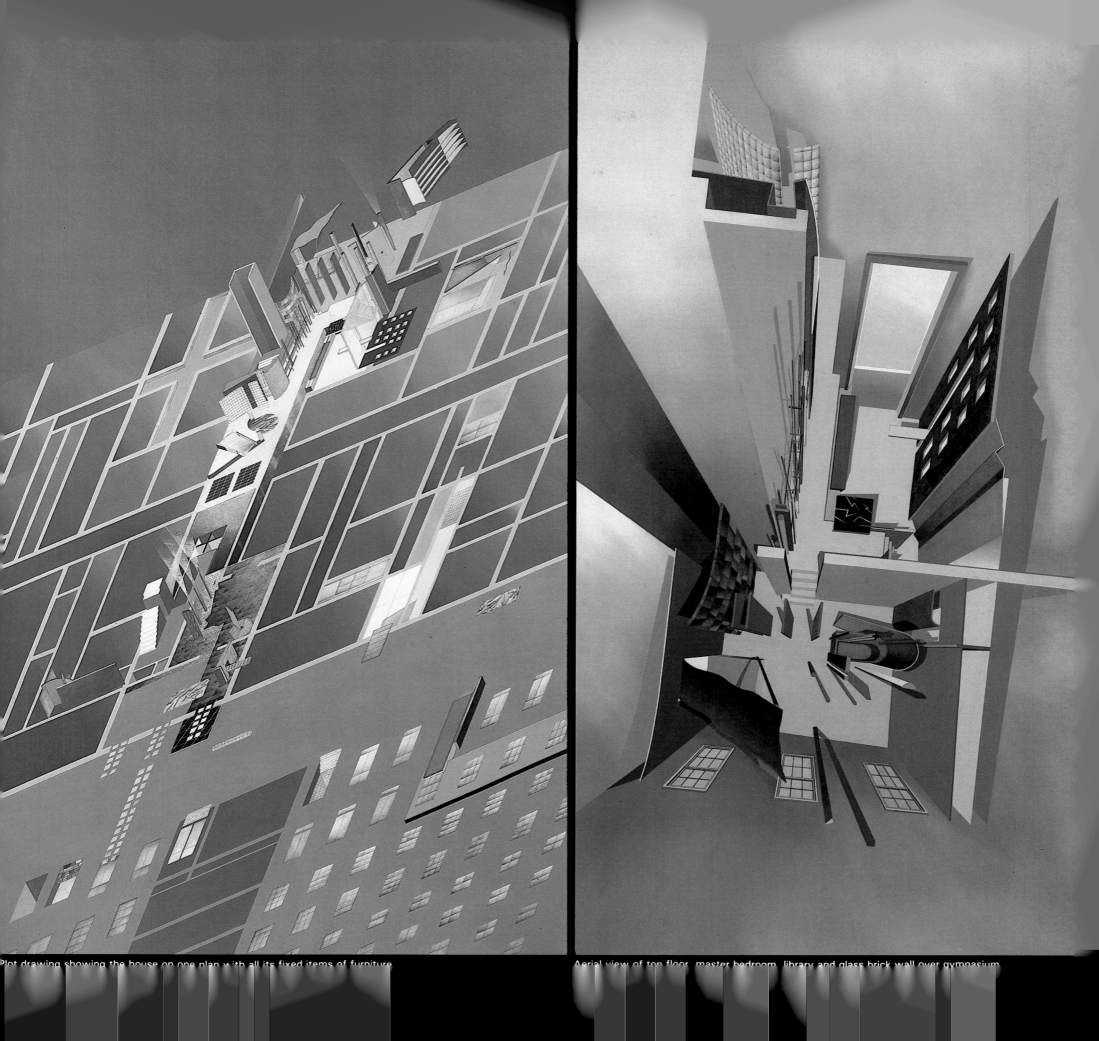

Plot drawing showing the house on one plan with all its fixed items of furniture.

Aerial view of top floor, master bedroom, library and glass brick wall over gymnasium.

Eva Jiricna
DUNLOPILLO HOME

THE COMPETITION asked for a design using Dunlopillo flexible foams, projected as if it were 2,000 AD. The original task, 'Possibilities for the use of foam in the home' soon changed its substance to pose the question 'Is there anything in the home that could not be made of flexible foams?' The submitted design tried to demonstrate this in practice. The proposal was split into three categories:
— products made of flat sheeting material suitable for wall claddings, wall hangings, partitioning, floor coverings, suspended ceilings, softening of hard finishes such as benches, platforms etc;

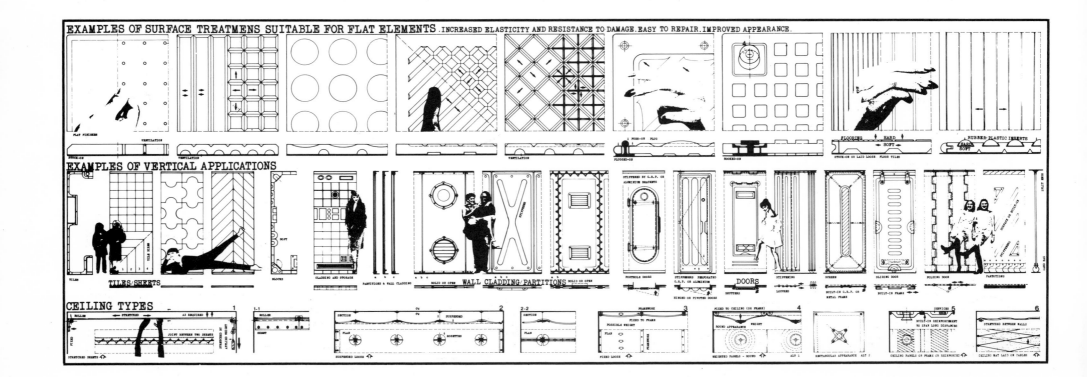

— products made of foam bricks, mainly suitable for furniture of various types;
— products based on a combination of inflated cores and foam rubber cases, foam then gives increased comfort and protection—characteristics which inflatable units used as furniture pieces usually lack.

Dunlopillo agreed to make a prototype which should have demonstrated the possibilities of a partitioning system but due to lack of money and interest the final product failed to prove the point. I still believe in its viability.

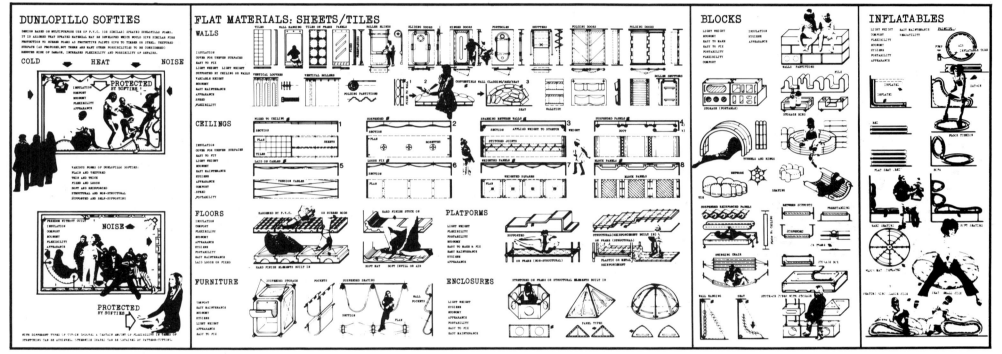

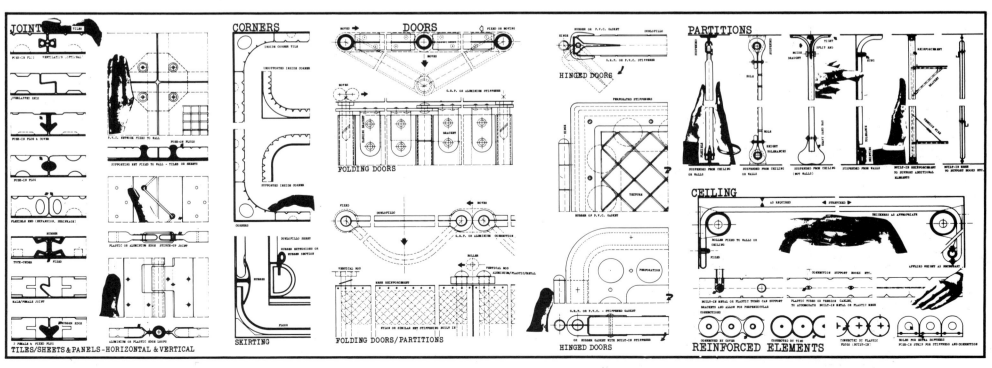

Eva Jiricna
FLAT FOR JOSEPH

ON THE 6TH OF JANUARY, 1981, Joseph to Eva: *'Do me a flat quickly, something rather simple—sort of 1930—I want to move in next month!!'* Two days later a flat was found.

There was only one advantage of a typical central London 1+1 with small, dark rooms, disastrous kitchen and similar bathroom, endless non-functioning walls, doors, screens, non-functioning fireplaces and flowery wallpaper; it had not been converted before by a skilled estate agent and it had no structural walls inside the flat. We freed the maximum amount of space inside the flat and used mirrors and photographs to create the illusion of a larger space.

Joseph moved into the flat in April of the same year the flat having been completed in May.

1 Hall-corridor
2 Bed
3 Shower
4 Kitchen
5 Dining area
6 Living area

Detail of shelf in living area (ph Richard Bryant)

Kitchen (ph Richard Bryant)

View from living area down hallway (ph Richard Bryant)

Chris Dawson
CALIFORNIA INSERTIONS

THESE PROJECTS DEMONSTRATE a strategy towards the remodeling (conversion) of existing buildings and spaces. The 'remodeling' is achieved by the insertion of simple architectonic elements into the existing structure with minimum modification or 'remaking' of that structure. The result is an interplay between new and existing elements setting up tension/harmony, contrast/compatibility relationships.

The insertions here serve the purpose of organizing circulation within the existing building, at the same time rationalizing the configuration of spaces into a coherent hierarchy.

ELIAS RESIDENCE, HOLLYWOOD HILLS

THE CLIENT ASKED for the kitchen to be moved from the upper to the lower level, to create a new interior world whilst leaving the exterior intact, and for additional storage space and the reorganisation of the television and stereo.

The existing house is built in two distinct, adjoining halves on a downhill site. The north half of the house consists of a living space and high-level entry balcony, the staircase going down directly into the living room. The south half of the house is a two storey structure, incorporating bedrooms, kitchen and bathrooms connected to the north half by small openings (one at each level).

A series of parallel 'arcaded' planes are inserted through the plan. These serve to organise circulation and set up a regular rhythm of intervals and openings through the house. The two 'halves' thus become spatially inter-locked both vertically and horizontally.

The staircase is moved from the north to the south half, forcing a physical crossover, further emphasising the interlock of spaces.

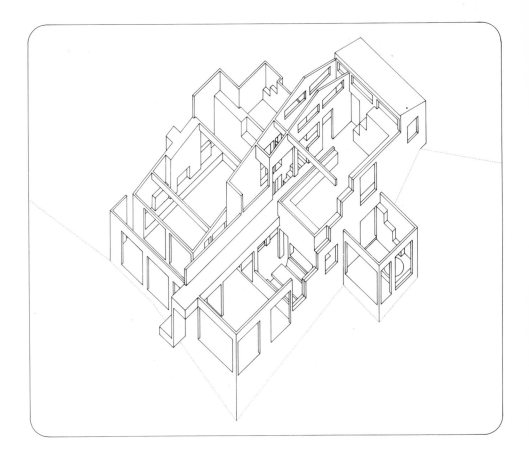

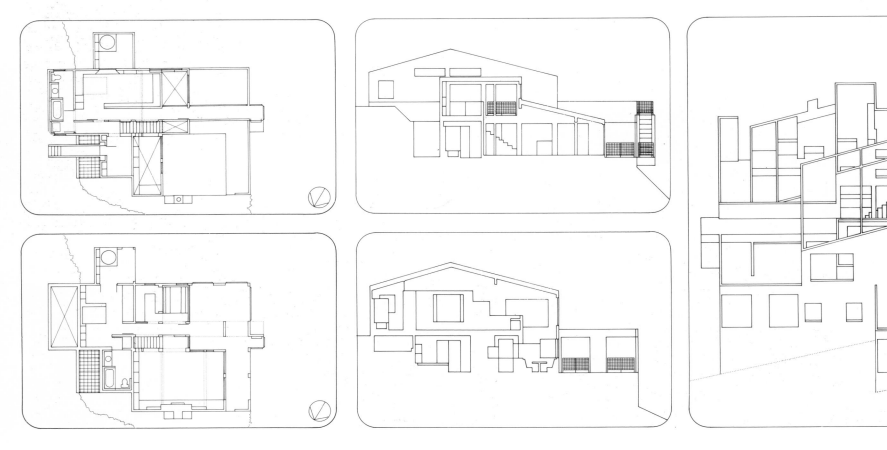

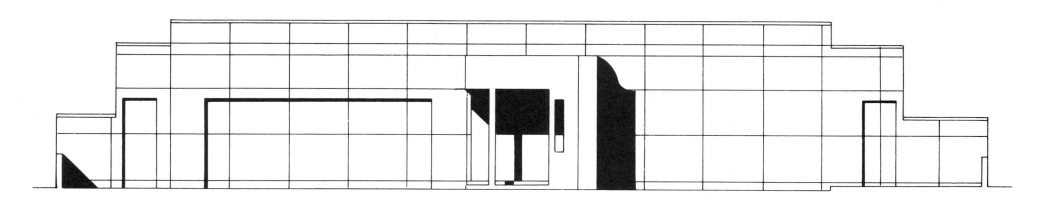

THE CLIENT REQUIRED a new 'street' facade; a new master bathroom; incorporation a jacuzzi and steam room; make the pool area visually private. The existing house is a one-storey structure approx. 5000sq.ft. in area. The site is 180' in length, 80' in breadth with a 40' required setback at the front or street side. The house is a reverse 'L' in plan bounding a swimming pool on the south side. The plan diagram was basically a spine running through the center of the building from front to back along the inside leg of the reverse 'L'. This spine however was interrupted by a small glazed atrium setting up a serious ambiguity in the primary circulation system.

The required new facade is treated as a gridded neutral screen. The plan is organized by the insertion of several parallel 'arcaded' planes. Two of these planes pass through the centre of the plan clarifying the main or 'public' spine. The northernmost of these two planes is irregularly curved and denotes a secondary or 'private' spine running parallel to the 'public' spine.

These primary regulating elements pass through the street facade and form a portico over the front entrance. The arcades set up a dimensional and spatial regularity lacking in the existing plan.

The inserted elements were intended to be coloured – the client however enjoyed the interplay of light on the white surfaces so much that the issue of colour was 'put on the back burner' for a while.

The swimming-pool colonnade

The master bedroom opening on to the pool area   (Martin Residence photos Tim Street-Porter)

View from the street
Circulation spine

Kitchen

Pool
Jacuzzi

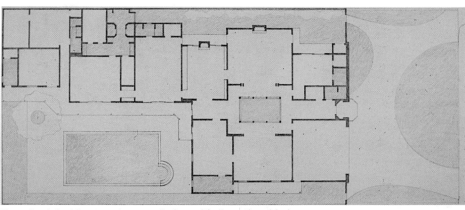

Plan of original house, above and plan with 'insertions' below

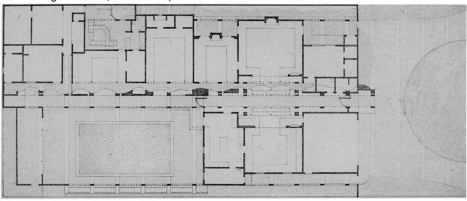

Below, axonometric and, bottom, elevationalised plan

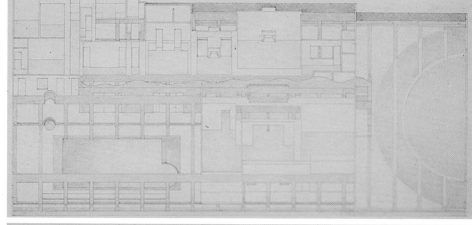

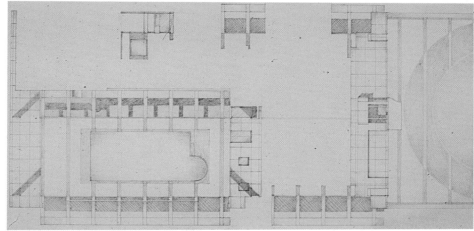

THE CLIENT'S REQUIREMENTS were to add a new family room to an existing 1950s single storey California ranch house. The addition was to be on the garden (south) side of the house. The garden is approximately three quarters of an acre, terraced down and away from the house, incorporates a pool and lawn, is heavily treed and spectacularly lit at night

The strategy here is a little different from the Martin project since an addition rather than a remodel was called for. The garden view from the house is magnificent, and gave rise to the band of glass, uninterrupted by mullions, allowing unimpeded views in all directions.

The addition thrusts out into the landscape and is 'tied back' into the plan by dual means. The new posts exactly mirror in plan the dimensions of the adjoining dining room, implying an overlap of existing and new. A lighting cove runs around the perimeter of this new 'double' space anchoring the addition back through the existing plan.

The new circulation system is defined both by posts and deep-well skylights, which allow sun back into the space.

The curves are generated by the curved terraces which meander round large black acacia trees. The new roof 'floats' over the added space. A new parapet ties the addition into the existing elevations.

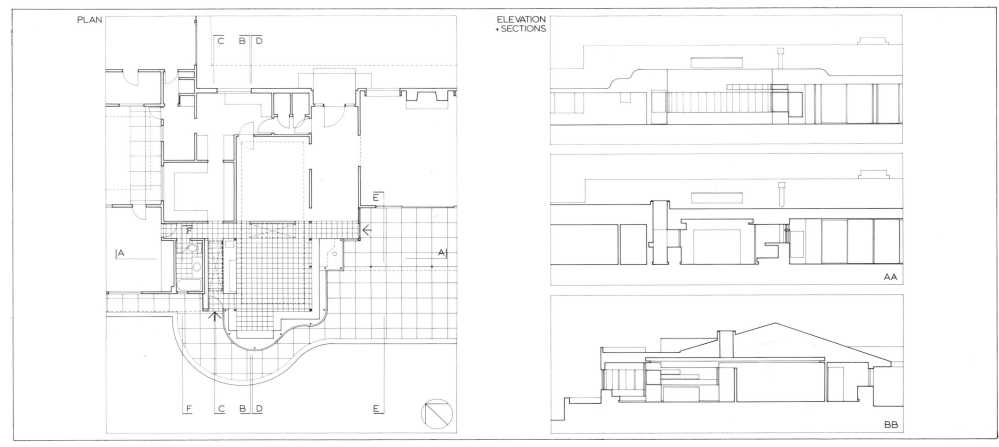

SECTIONS   ORTHOMETRIC

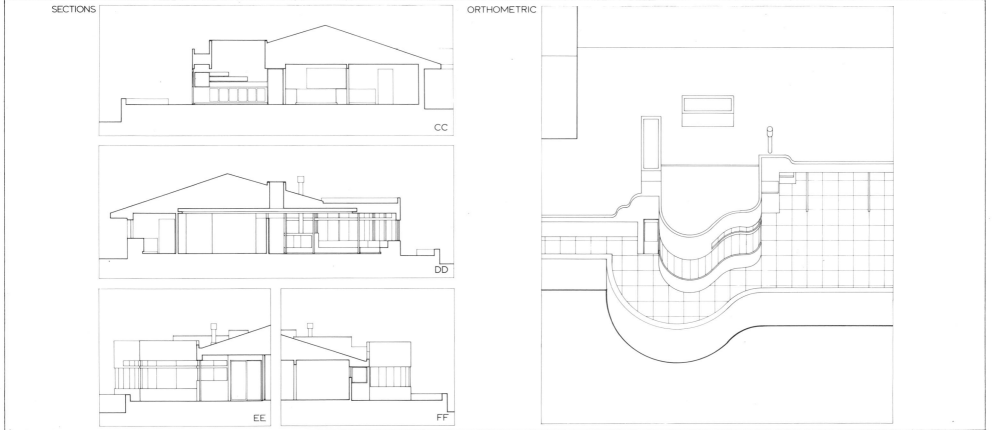

CC

DD

EE   FF

THE EXHIBITION of the life and work of Sir Edwin Lutyens was at the Hayward Gallery from 17th November, 1981 to 31st of January, 1982. It was arranged by a committee under Colin Amery and organised by the Arts Council. We received the commission 18 months after a number of other architects had been tried. Our intention was to design an installation that was in itself a series of delightful spaces alluding to his work, to illustrate what was bound to be an information show. The irony was to 'do' Lutyens in painted chipboard.

The Exhibition is entered through a vestibule which introduces at once an offset axis to the left, bringing one into the first proper space in its centre under the mezzanine. The vestibule should have been covered in hand-marbled paper but it arrived too late to be hung and so it is painted the dark green of the famous post-war volumes of Lutyens' work. At either end are 4' diameter niches with two busts to show immediately the contrasting aspects of his character; the serious establishment architect and the witty inventor of the 'Delhi head'. The niches derive from Hestercombe, the brackets from Reuters entrance doors.
     One enters the next space directly opposite a large photograph of the entrance side of Munstead Wood, to give a taste of Lutyens' work, framed by a long low mock-oak beam and a garden bench standing on a stone plinth. These two elements give an extra emphasis to the low space under the mezzanine in keeping with his 'low' early work. One turns round the plinth, implicitly to the left where a sculpture of a bull leads round the corner into the family and early life section. This has paintings by family and friends and also his school drawings etc. Then, on to Ernest George's office and the work of Lutyens' contemporaries there, before his first works (including Crooksbury) after setting up on his own and meeting Gertrude Jekyll. The Jekyll connection is marked by a re-creation of her fireplace at Munstead Wood; with its over-hanging vaulted chimney and strong circular geometry, as well as her portrait and, more famously, that of her boots. Munstead is shown in some detail through sketch books and an aerial perspective of the original gardens; terminating with a glass cupboard displaying Jekyll above and showing off Lutyens' early use of classical mouldings. The other walls display other early work, including the tentative classicism, culminating in the fabulous Orchards, from which the fire exit doors on the corner were derived. This brings one to the bottom of the ramp, where fire regulations prevented the display of any exhibits. Nepotistically I commissioned my mother to draw a mural for a typical Jekyll pergola planting arrangement in spring and summer. The drawing was printed positive and reversed, then one side coloured and the other side left black and white with the names of the plants annotated.
     At the top of the ramp, two semi-circular openings (Orchards, Tigbourne etc) give a worms-eye view into the marriage bedroom. This room was never realised. Lutyens and his wife always lived in Georgian houses in London in fact and the marriage was

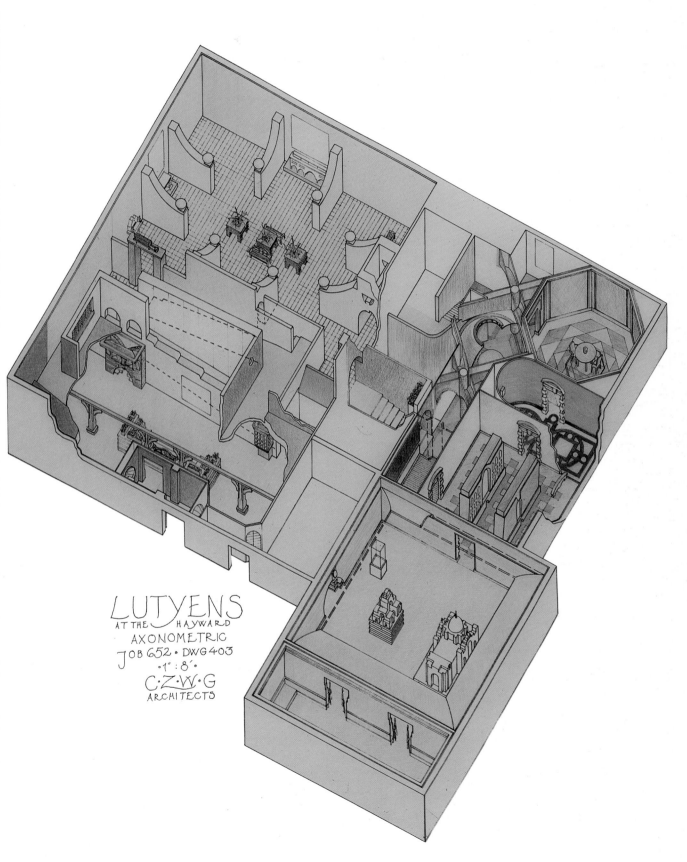

LUTYENS
AT THE HAYWARD
AXONOMETRIC
JOB 652 ● DWG 403
·1°:8'·
C·Z·W·G
ARCHITECTS

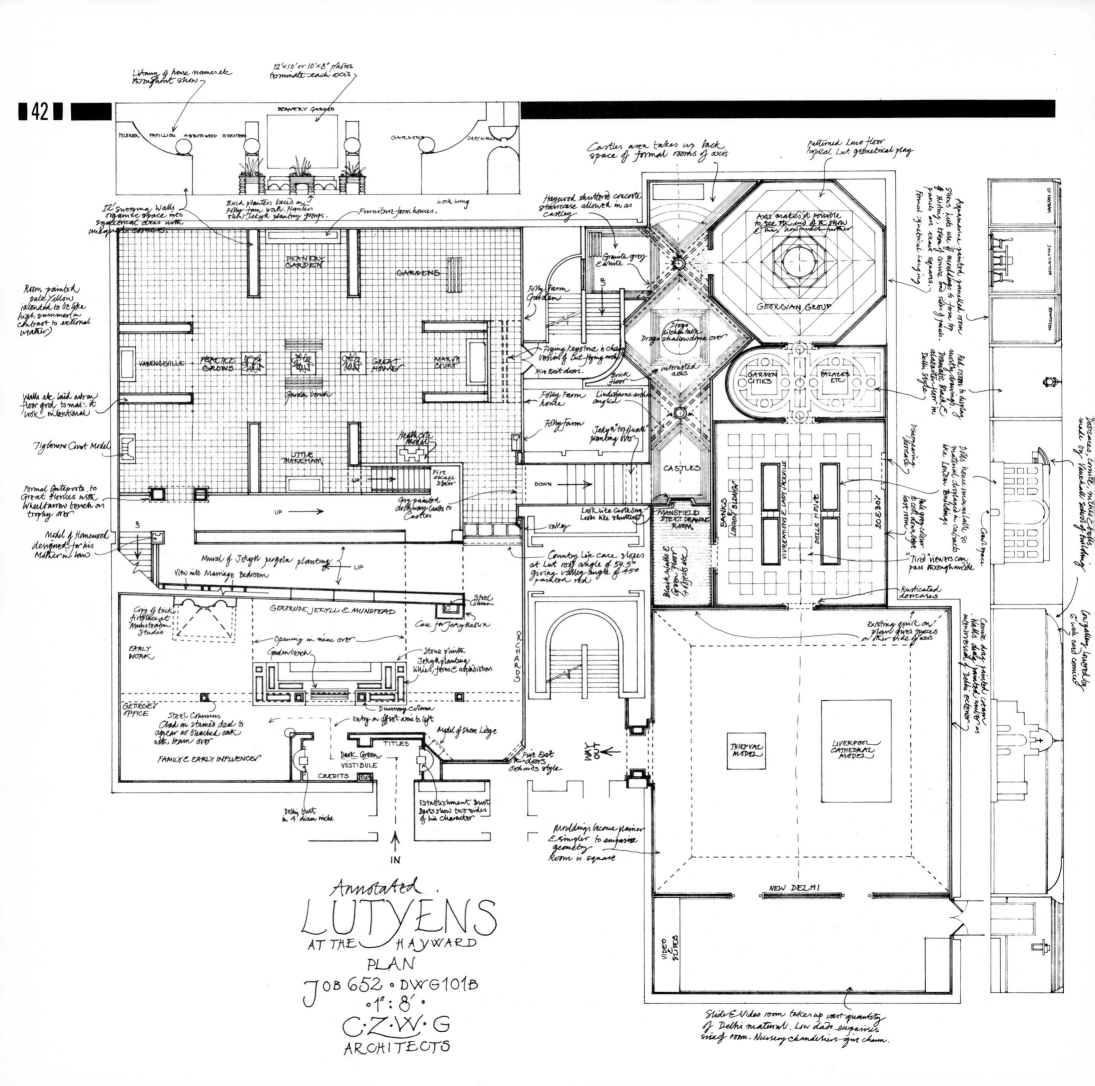

Annotated
LUTYENS
AT THE HAYWARD
PLAN
JOB 652 · DWG 101B
·1":8'·
C·Z·W·G
ARCHITECTS

not successful so the bedroom remained a dream from his courtship letters to her although he had all the furniture made. Thus, the first time it is seen is from below to give it a dream-like quality. The beautiful little casket and its contents which he gave her and other small effects can be seen through a leaded light window from the mezzanine. On the newel post of the stairs on the way up to it is, suitably, a model of Homewood which he designed for his mother-in-law. At that point the visitor can skip the mezzanine and pass through the gate post to the great houses section. What they miss, apart from a second view into the bedroom, is a collection of his furniture designs, including a piano to look like a spinet, a folding library ladder and a section on his office assistants with his desk, measuring cane and favourite reference books, lit by a chandelier and on the walls drawings of unbuilt schemes and office exemplars of lettering. Returning from the mezzanine brings one back, via a glimpse of the next space, to the gate posts whose formality is undermined by the trophy they bear: a wheel barrow garden bench.

The space they introduce is the highest in the Hayward at about 5 m and, although well defined on two sides, leaks away unsatisfactorily at the other corners. To formalise it and provide more hanging space there are eight 600 mm-thick swooping walls with ball finials setting up two symmetrical cross axes but allowing variations in the corners. The four centre bays, so formed, are given four very large photographs intended to be utterly seductive. The four houses allocated to these bays and shown in more detail than the others changed all the time as committee members visited various houses and returned declaring them the best. In the end Le Bois des Moutiers at Varengeville, Little Thakeham, Marsh Court, and, of course, Deanery Garden were chosen. These, and all the main house names, are signwritten onto the walls as a sort of Lutyens' litany. The first image on entering the space is of Tigbourne Court. Seifert's model department made a gorgeous, stone by stone model of the front facade of Tigbourne as well as one of Homewood. The models are all in different styles and scales to try and emphasise the particular qualities of the originals and are hung at suitable heights: Heathcote up high, Folly Farm lower. Varengeville leads onto the free-style houses of Overstrand and the Pleasaunce and here the photographs are hung corner to corner. I could not persuade anyone to have them actually across the corners.

The four big photographs are supported by four suitable pieces of furniture; Varengeville by an art-nouveauish desk, Deanery Garden by a long sideboard and Marsh Court by a rather tall one, and Little Thakeham by a very solid chest which exactly matches the floor colour in the photograph. The centre of the room has rusticated brick planters derived from a Folly Farm balustrade and some benches from its garden as well. The largest corner segment shows the great gardens of Lutyens' collaboration with Gertrude Jekyll; here the material is hung to imitate the multi-material clunch walls of Marsh Court. The whole is dominated by a William

Nicholson painting of a picnic. The Marsh Court back wall is pulled forward away from a fire exit and the passage formed at the back links Folly Farm's appearance in the garden section to its appearance as a great house. The arches are linked by a flying keystone down the length of the passage (this has a very mixed parentage from the beam under Folly Farm's sleeping porch, Homewood's open tympanum and The Mount's strainer arches). Since a special floor could not be sponsored, all the walls, platforms and planters are aligned on the existing 300 mm and 1,200 mm floor grids to make it appear as if the floor was intentional (actually 1' square in 4' squares, the Hayward is in fact Imperial). The whole space is painted a pale yellow to give the effect of a golden, summery Edwardian afternoon.

From this point a stair leads down to Gallery One, a good way to enter a castles section. Lower arches support a high-level planting trough with Jekyll overflowing wall-top plants. Straight opposite is an over-the-roof-top view of Lambay; the floor a patterned brick laid in sand, the wall colour granite grey slightly textured. The space for the castles is a passage interrupted by a diagonally opposed square space, the corners are supported by fat columns which are thus in the centre of the passage. The first arches are half circles à la Lindisfarne central corridor, but angled. The square has the more depressed dome geometry of Drogo with a lantern to make the huge round kitchen table feel at home. Here also the rough-boarded concrete of the Hayward is momentarily allowed to fight back and one of the dome's pendentives is removed to reveal the coffered escape stair ceiling 15 m above. The end of the passage opens out with a wedge shape, echoing the Drogo battlements, formed by what is left over from the next space. The second column marks the change of direction into this space. It is a pale aquamarine octagon denoting the change of style in the Queen Anne/Georgian group including Nashdom and Salutation. This room is the first of the final axial suite, emphasising the new formality and giving the spectator a view in the distance to the end of the show (to help pace it apart from anything else). The octagon is panelled in the Lutyens' manner using the same moulding for the bottom of the cornice, the top of the skirting and the panel stiles. Here the panels are exact squares, the square information panel set centrally and the other material arranged symmetrically. The room has some rather indifferent pale furniture but also a sheet glass light fitting of the wrong date but the right mood.

The floors, in this and the next two rooms are all specially designed and laid in marbled linoleum all with grey in common (in this room in subtle opposition to the pale green) in a pattern formed by placing the corners of squares to touch the centre of the sides of the larger square and so on. The next room runs across the axis with one apsidal end and has a striking floor of squares set in circles in black and alabaster, a black skirting and bright red walls as a good background to, predominantly, drawings of Spanish palaces and garden cities. The apse has the favourite expanding hands clock. This is followed by a choice,

the two freestanding walls in the next space allow the tired visitor to slip through the middle of the room and skip a bit. The between-war years saw a change to large urban buildings, the banks, as well as some more mannerist country houses. So the room has fibrous plaster, heavily rusticated doorcases, one blanked with two 'Lut' doorknobs. It was at this time that he organised Queen Mary's Dolls' House and, since we could not borrow it, the centre walls are themselves in the form of buildings with openings to display the material, but the buildings are more commercial. The floor is a kind of harlequin check in blue and grey as an expression of the wit of the sketches collected here. Around the back one has a display cabinet, lined in mauve velvet, for some gold and brass ecclesiastical plate, and the other has a model of the Poultry bank in a semi-circular arched recess. Only children can experience the cross axis by crawling through the arches in the plinth. Diagonally across the room from the blank door is a real opening into a re-creation of part of his own drawing room at Mansfield Street put together by his daughter Mary with its black gloss wall, apple green floor and witches ball light.

The final principal space displays Delhi, the war graves and Liverpool Cathedral; it is a square of strong horizontal emphasis produced by a 2 m-wide, 800 m-deep coved cornice adapted from the staircase court at the Viceroys' House. The received view is that Gallery One at the Hayward is too low. I decided to make it lower with the cornice, and hot like Delhi with drag-brushed pink walls and a cream cornice. The mouldings fall away to reflect his increasing interest in pure geometry. There are large models of Liverpool, Thiepval and the Cenotaph standing in the space. The axis-ending photograph of the Viceroys' House entrance and dome is flanked by openings to a room for the showing of video and slides, which should have had columns with his Delhi order capitals but economy pushed us into some Union Jacks instead. As well as the shows, the walls are crammed with a mass of Delhi material over a low chair rail, rather as if the Viceroy's wife had done it.

Back out to the sombre final exit of simple half-circle geometrics, there are glass cases for his death mask and hands.

CLIENT: Arts Council of Great Britain
Chairman of Lutyens Committee, Colin Amery
CONTRACTORS: Beck & Pollitzer
FLOORS: Nairn Floors
BRICKWORK: Supervised by the Guild of Bricklayers
FIBROUS PLASTER WORK: Vauxhall College of Building and Further Education
MODELS: R Seifert & Partners and Thurloe Models

First room: garden bench, wall showing early work and... re-creation of Gertrude Jekyll's fireplace at Munstead Wood
Great Houses room: Below, towards Varengeville, long axis and ... right, towards Deanery Gardens, cross axis

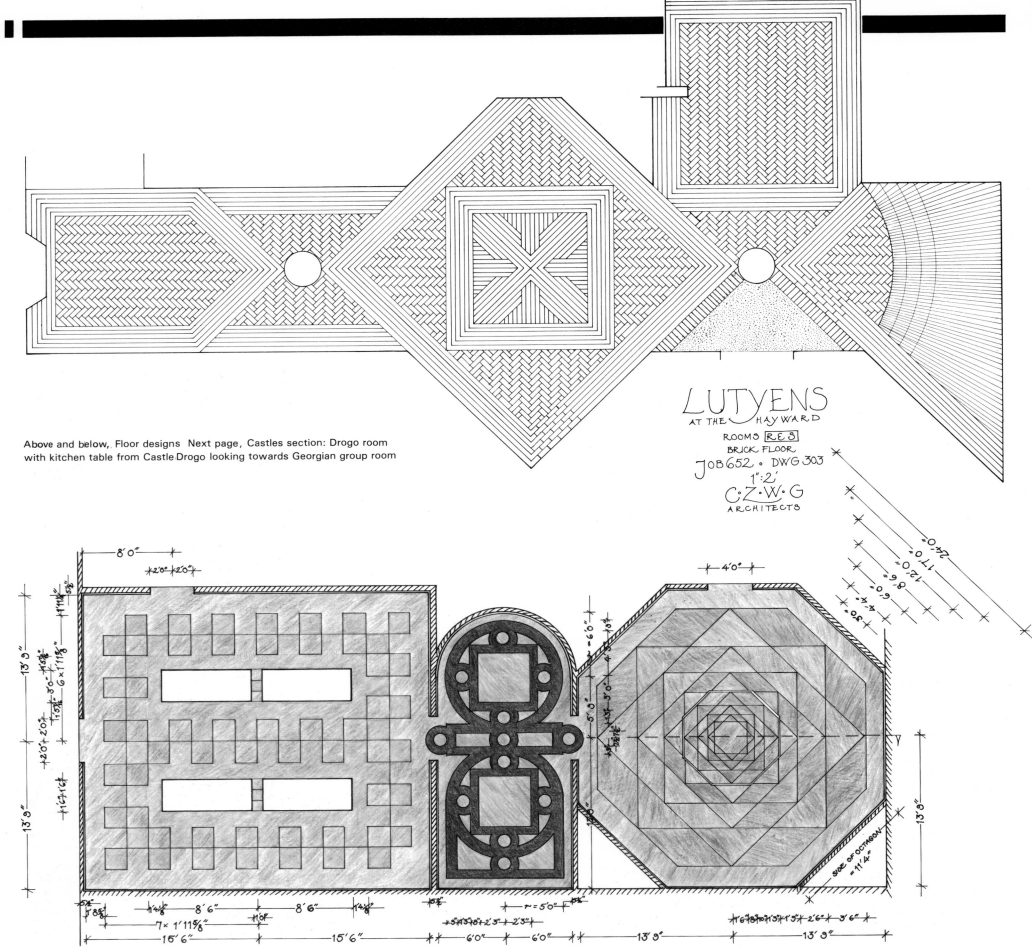

Above and below, Floor designs Next page, Castles section: Drogo room
with kitchen table from Castle Drogo looking towards Georgian group room

LUTYENS
AT THE HAYWARD
ROOMS R E S
BRICK FLOOR
JOB 652 ∘ DWG 303
1":2'
C·Z·W·G
ARCHITECTS

Final room:
Liverpool Cathedral

and Memorial to the Missing , Thiepval

Charles Jencks, in his otherwise generous review in AD News Supplement No 1, 1982 suggests that the exhibition seems closer to straight revivalism than inventive eclecticism. That certainly seemed the issue while I was designing it, but at the time it seemed as if one was being too free. Lutyens being so prolific had an exemplar for almost anything and there seemed no good reason not to reproduce those as the exhibition setting. It was only the vagaries of the Hayward Gallery, the given fact of chipboard and paint construction (and my ignorance) that persuaded me to take any initiative. It seems almost superfluous to be eclectic about an already eclectic designer, straight revivalism would be that automatically. But what one suspects Charlie meant was that it was too nice, too keen to please, it hasn't the fashionable knowing eclecticism of ugly collision. It is true that cornices run all the way around the room, the pediments don't crash into each other or anything else, the mouldings aren't hacked back at 'meaningful' angles, the rustication may be missing but there is no scar. . . . Everyone has got their 'What I learnt from Lut'. What I learnt was that it doesn't have to be ugly to be mannerist.

It is possible to play games, elide styles, swap vocabularies in a way that amuses the visually sophisticated without losing your wider audience. Thus you can carry the good opinion of the profession and the public at once. He must have been almost the last architect not to have a Salon de Refusés attitude to architecture. The suspicion that if ordinary people like it, then it can't be any good really. What is so enviable is the ability to charm the populace while pulling off such architectural gymnastics. Revivalism may be a necessary vocabulary but there is no need to murder it.

Piers Gough

Alsop, Barnett & Lyall

A PICTORIAL DIARY

THIS **PICTORIAL CHRONOLOGY** illustrates a variety of projects carried out by the practice over the last three years. We have always attempted to avoid a 'house style' and trust that the breadth of imagery demonstrates this.

PROJECTS TEAM: William Alsop, Diana Bailey, Mark Cuthbert, Gus Hutcheson, Gareth Jones (artist), John Lyall, David Lyall, Victoria Manser, Amanda Marshall, Peter Newby, Nick Turvey.

Exploration and presentation images for the original Riverside Studios project, Winter 1979

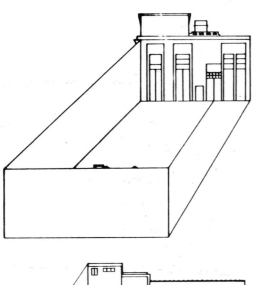

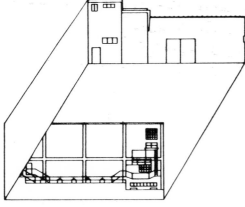

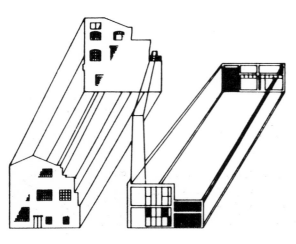

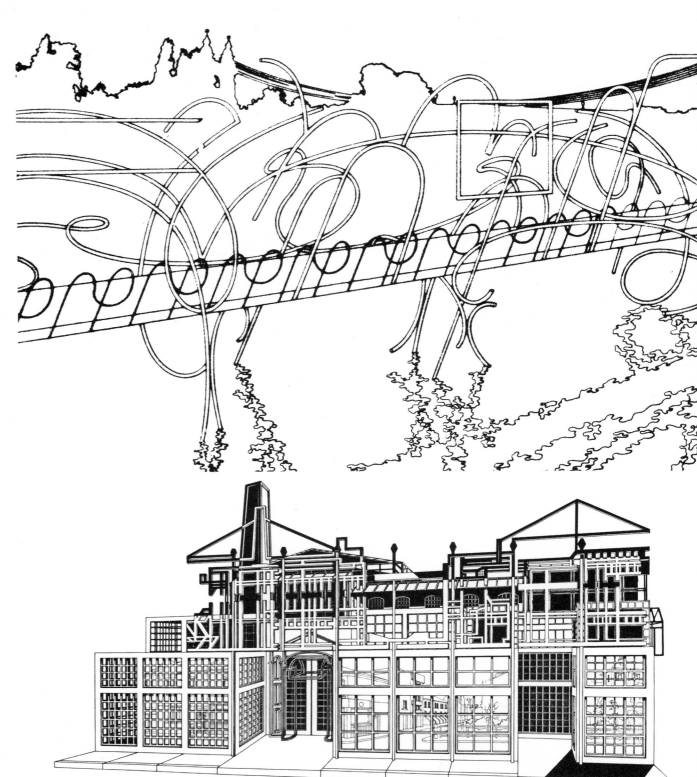

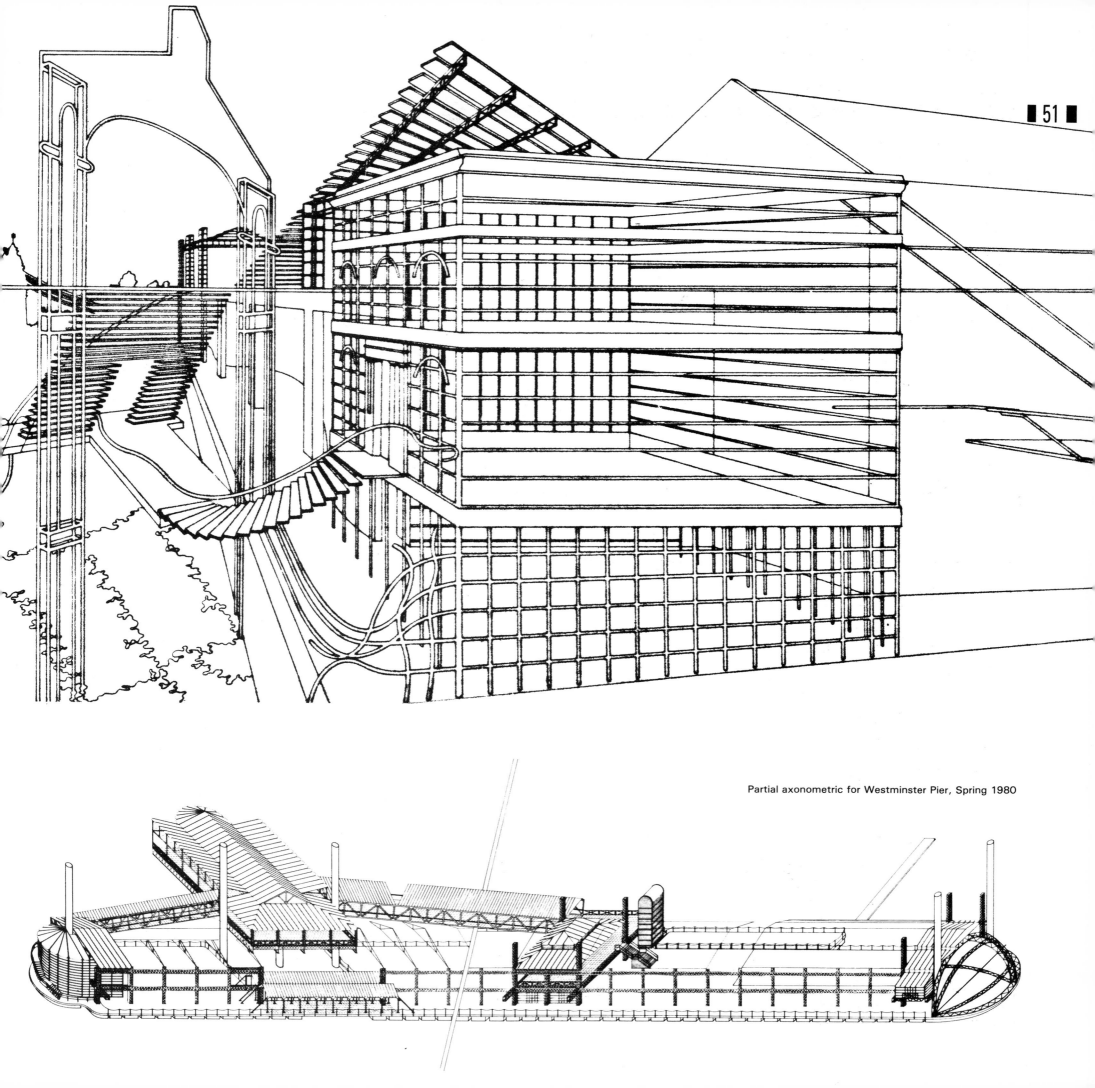

Partial axonometric for Westminster Pier, Spring 1980

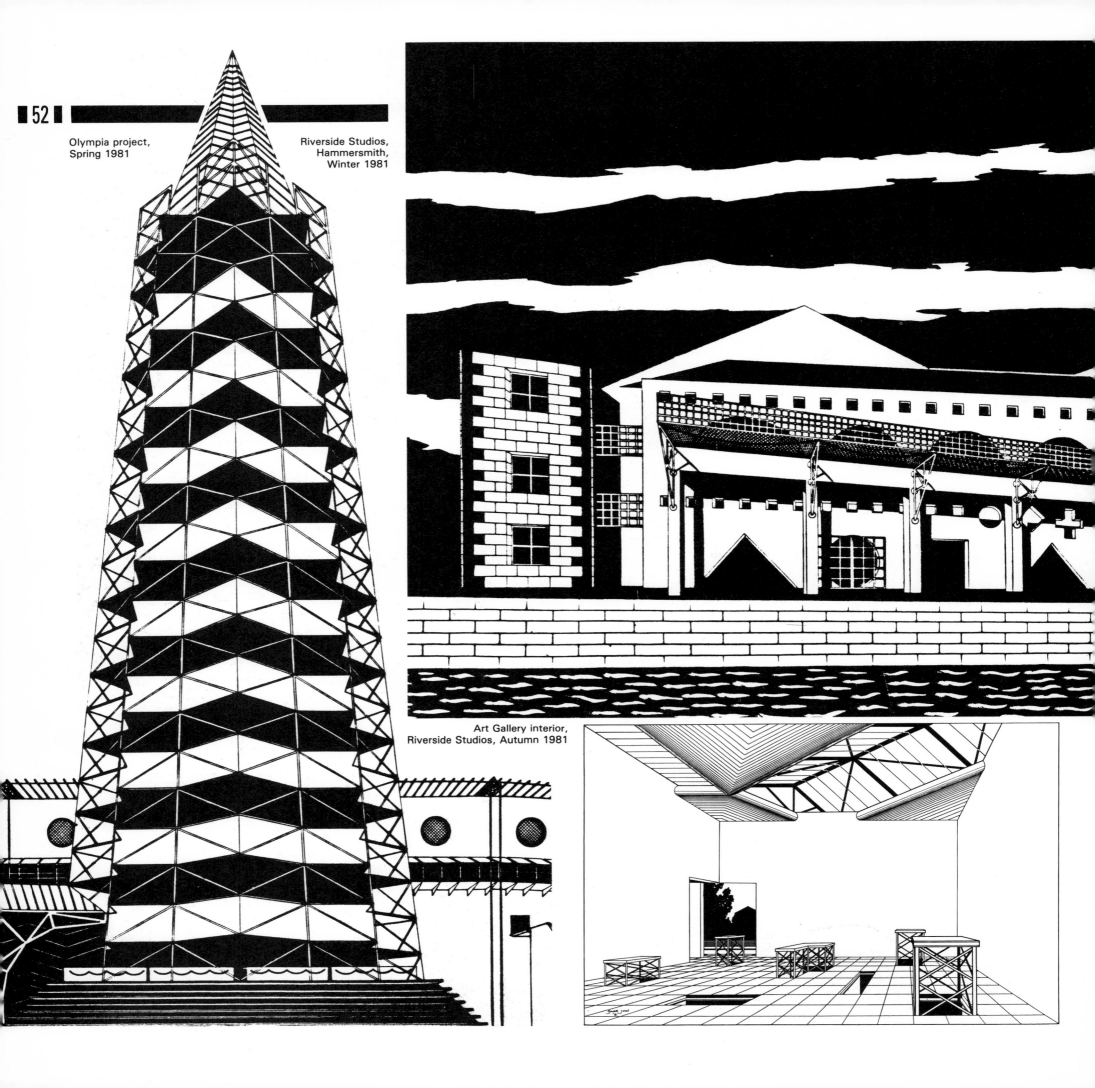

Olympia project,
Spring 1981

Riverside Studios,
Hammersmith,
Winter 1981

Art Gallery interior,
Riverside Studios, Autumn 1981

Entrance detail, Riverside Studios, Winter 1981

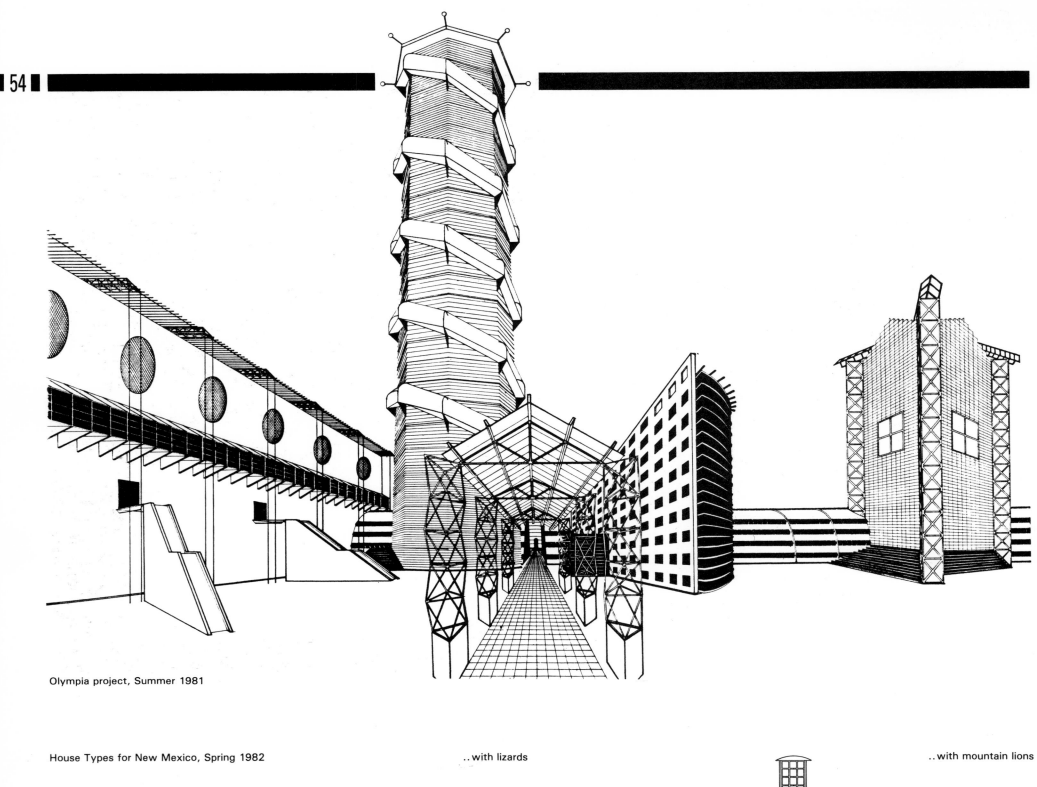

Olympia project, Summer 1981

House Types for New Mexico, Spring 1982   .. with lizards   .. with mountain lions

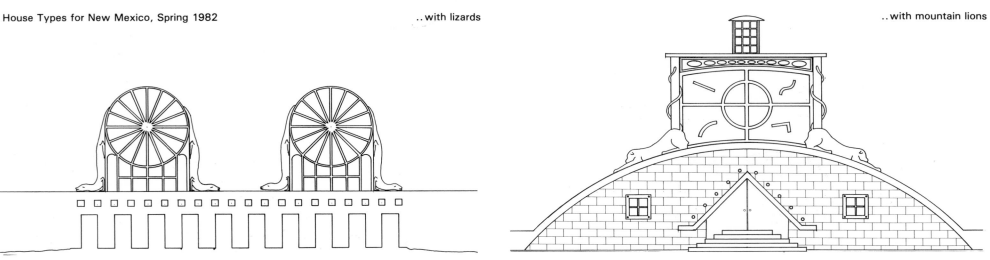

Hampton Competition, Spring 1982

.. with rattlesnake

Arts Centre, Taos, Mexico, Summer 1982

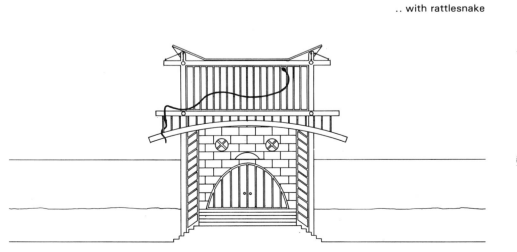

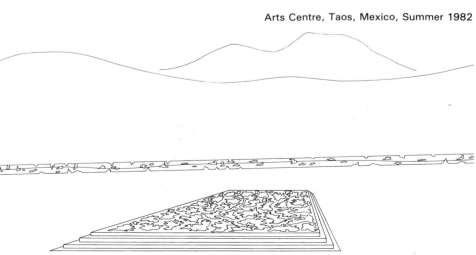

Edward Cullinan Architects
THE UPLANDS CONFERENCE CENTRE, HIGH WYCOMBE, BUCKINGHAMSHIRE

UPLANDS WAS BUILT as a modest country house for a Victorian gentleman on a magnificent site overlooking the Hughenden Valley. The south facing main rooms and facade have been retained for social uses on the ground floor and seminar rooms on the first. The kitchen quarters behind were a warren and these together with other more recent additions have been demolished. Replacing them under a vast new roof is a stair hall leading up to the main divisible meeting room, with a dining room below. Cloisters set off to both sides connecting link blocks and wings of study bedrooms terminated by pavilions. Entrance is through the old house from the south by wicket gate, woodland path from the east, and past (or through) the maze from parking to the west.

The Designers are Edward Cullinan, Anthony Peake, Mark Beedle and Alan Short with Michael Chassay, Sunand Prasad, Robin Nicholson and Elizabeth Shapiro, and building has begun.

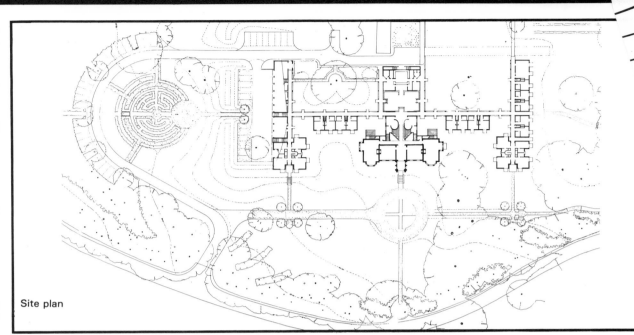

Site plan

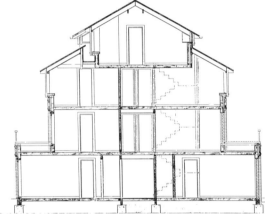

Sections through the study-bedrooms on either side of the old house contain connecting cloister, ground floor rooms opening onto the gardens and first floor through rooms with roof balconies.

The end elevations of these buildings, shown mirrored. . . .

to show that they are the clue to the section of the end buildings which are created from them by placing them back to back, adding floors and opening up the flank to the sun and views.

The elevation of the end buildings.

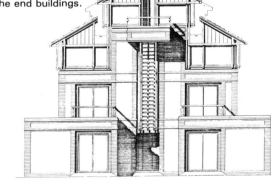

South elevation

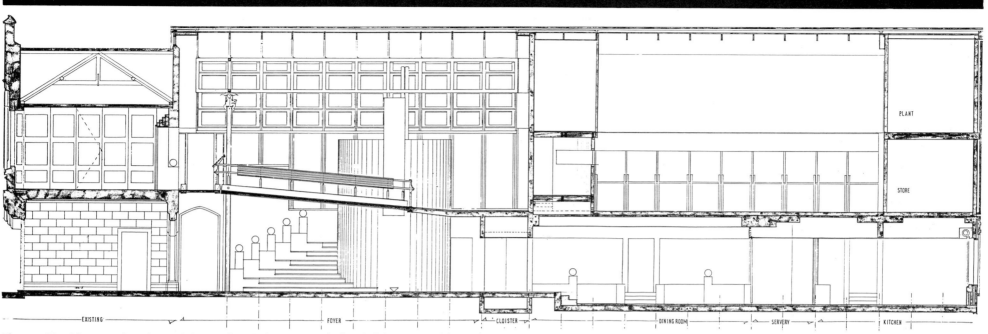

PLANT

STORE

EXISTING · FOYER · CLOISTER · DINING ROOM · SERVERY · KITCHEN

The combined long section shows (left to right) old house, new hall and dining room with meeting room over.

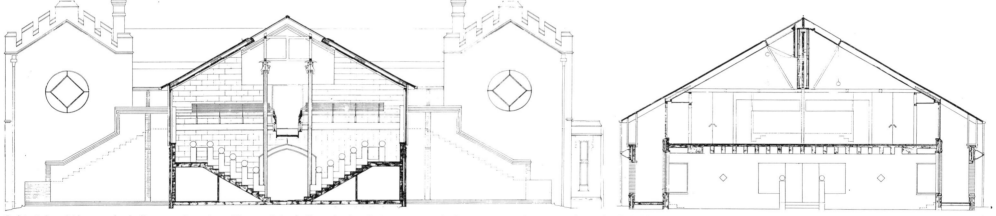

Behind the old house the hall grows from it and beyond the hall... is the dining room with the main meeting room above it, divisible by a descending partition, lit by sliding side windows and by rooflights, blacked out by shutters on counterweights.

Sectional Perspective

North elevation

THE SITE of the proposed rebuilding of the Hurva Synagogue is on the western boundary of the Jewish Quarter in the Old City of Jerusalem — centre of three great religions. It has been the site of a synagogue (twice destroyed) since the 13th Century AD. The Ramban Synagogue, dating from the 10th Century, abutts at a lower level and stands adjacent to the Sidna Omar Mosque to the south. These two buildings generate the geometry of the proposed sunken court which leads east and north terminating at the entrance to the Community Centre. Thus the literal and symbolic foundation of the proposed new Hurva is an historical fragment loaded with cultural memories and embedded in the floor of the City.

The entrance to the Synagogue is from a narrow passage to the west which leads up a few steps to an entrance court. The spatial sequence thereafter comprises the men's entrance Porch; the Assembly, for three hundred men, with the central portion of the Ark wall retained in its original position and bathed in light from the Sanctuary at the east end.

The Community Centre, incorporating a Talmudic Library, Study Hall and classrooms, faces on to the sunken court at a slightly lower level.

Four pairs of towers on each side of the building flank the central space and stand sentinel over it. Their symmetrical disposition makes it clear, on the outside, that the principal space lies between them. Enclosure is completed by four apses, the men's entrance porch, two smaller women's entrance porches to the north and south, and the Sanctuary to the east.

The Women's Gallery, seating one hundred and fifty, is arranged at an upper level on three sides of the Assembly. Stairs incorporated in two of the towers lead to the overhanging roof-strata, from which the surrounding City, the Dome of the Rock, and the Mount of Olives can be viewed — an opportunity to experience landscape, history and people. The dense thermal mass of the roof-strata hovering above the Assembly protects it against glare and heat and stands as a parasol above the events within. The cool night breezes of Jerusalem's microclimate are drawn down the towers by natural convection simultaneously releasing the heat from the building fabric.

The Piazza (formerly part of the site of Louis Kahn's previous proposals) is designed to be integral with the Hurva. It steps gently up from the east over the Community Centre and is envisaged as a marketplace shaded by trees, planting and the canvas canopies of marketstalls.

The design may be thought of as a formally intensified abstraction of the flat roofs, tiny alleys and small squares characteristic of the ancient City. The building is thus part and parcel of its unique context. The central space itself is felt to be a piece of the City set aside for higher purposes.

The building stands on high ground with a gently amplified scale still retaining the grain o... City. From close-to the Hurva is seen to be ris... between and out of other buildings — a... architectural mass, a unity, emerging from the diversity of the City. It is not an isolated monument but an extension of the City itself.

Walls are of stone, incorporating old existing stones. The roof is made of heavy precast concrete sections with external ceramic fascias and the soffit is coffered. Windows are set in deep slots with reversed reveals concealing the frames from the outside.

Light, texture and the acoustical dimension of space combine to stimulate an imaginative response from the worshipper and reflect the inner pulse and rhythms of the design. Emphasis is on smallness and simplicity. The essential idea is that of the assembled community.

The building responds to a set of ideas which seem to have a relevance today, are reasonable in quality and which engage with history. These ideas are about an architecture of urban landscape, which is an extension of the city or the landscape and which seeks to promote and extend human relationships. Buildings are related to other buildings which may be close in space however far off in time, but they do not make stylistic concessions to the past. The buildings in fact are often a metaphor for landscape expressed through the visual organisation of *strata* and towers. These *strata* recall both the streets and squares of the city, the contour lines of hills and they bear witness to the roots of an architectural language inspired amongst other things by natural geological forms.

Aerial view of Old City of Jerusalem

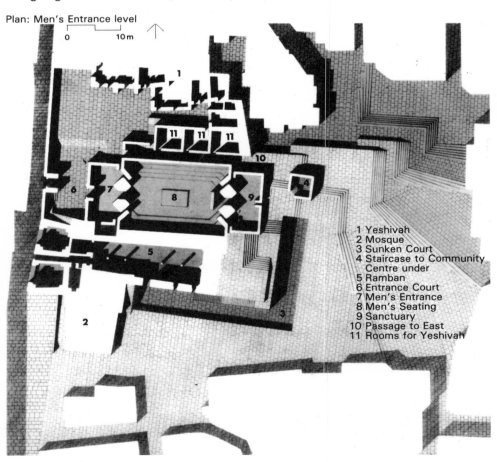

Plan: Men's Entrance level

0   10m

1 Yeshivah
2 Mosque
3 Sunken Court
4 Staircase to Community Centre under
5 Ramban
6 Entrance Court
7 Men's Entrance
8 Men's Seating
9 Sanctuary
10 Passage to East
11 Rooms for Yeshivah

Cross section looking east
Plan: Women's Entrance level

1 Yeshivah
2 Mosque
3 Sunken Court
4 Stair, Ventilation and
  Structural towers
5 Staircase Entrance to
  Community Centre under
6 Women's Gallery

East elevation

Because religious buildings are not unduly constrained by complicated functional demands they have given architects throughout history the opportunity to explore the human significance of space in response to a universal idea. There is no distinct traditional type for the synagogue. The formal vocabulary and the underlying themes of the design of the Hurva have evolved over the years from previous buildings notably the Royal College of Physicians, the National Theatre and the European Investment Bank — all involved with the interpretation of human relationships through the medium of space and the fusion of interior sequences with the grain of urban surroundings. The Hurva continues these themes because they are felt to be appropriate and seem to bear directly on the core issues of religious meaning, just as Palladio's churches not only share features with his villas but were regarded as an embellishment of the city.

To the question *'Does it look like a religious building?'* the answer, today, can only be that it does not look like a religious building.

© Denys Lasdun
8 December 1981

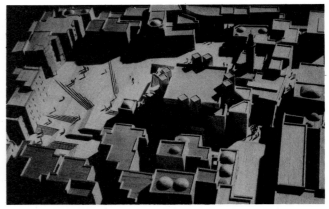

Aerial view of model

ARCHITECT: Denys Lasdun of Denys Lasdun Redhouse & Softley, in collaboration with Josef Schoenberger of Jerusalem.

The work to date has been done in consultation with Ari Avrahami of Jerusalem. The design has been carried out with my associate Stefan Kuszell and assistant, Crispin Wride (of Denys Lasdun Redhouse & Softley). William Curtis and Robert Van Pelt, both architectural historians who studied with Dame Frances Yates, have given helpful guidance during the period of design Drawings: DL invenit, CW delin.

Denys Lasdun Redhouse & Softley
50 Queen Anne Street, London W1M 0DR

Cross section through the Old City showing Dome of the Rock to the east

Derek Walker Associates
A MULTI-USE CENTRE AND FRIDAY MOSQUE, SAUDI ARABIA

A MULTI-USE CENTRE developed for a coastal location in Saudi Arabia comprising speculative offices, corporate offices, hotel and conference centre, shopping, galleries, restaurants, post office, sports centre, exhibition facilities and a small number of high quality apartments attached to the hotel and conference area.

The site levels provide an undercroft for comprehensive servicing areas for all space users. It also integrates parking facilities for some 2,000 cars. An inner two/three-storey arcade links all facilities and the general arrangement of the centre proposes two levels of shaded courtyards. The upper levels can be used for temporary markets, and the lower court is dominated by the Friday Mosque, which is the focal point of the Centre's geometry.

Climatic control was of paramount importance in the design strategies for the Centre. Having run a computer programme on the latitude we divided the solar energy arriving on each face of the building into direct energy from the sun, diffused energy from the atmosphere and reflective energy from the ground for each hour of the year. All known devices were then studied and the four most appropriate and most easily maintained, given the harsh climatic conditions, appear to be over hang, reflective glass, louvres and an American system known as Koolshade. Used in combination these can greatly reduce solar gain whilst at the same time allowing good external awareness.

The Mosque is placed with the mithrab wall facing Mecca at 238 degrees magnetic, forming an interesting geometric inflection within the urban square of the multi-use centre. The hard and soft landscaping and water courses generated in the outercourt areas form a rich setting for the Mosque and its walled courtyard. The Mosque's simple form is developed to the client's specific requirements and the clearly stated religious constraints. The ablutions form the third wall of the Prayer Court and the two blocks are linked by a shaded outer porch which opens on to the Prayer Court. This in turn is enclosed on two sides by 2 m high walls, along whose length run shallow lily ponds. The minarets are placed with bridge links in these water courses.

The Mosque has a continuous run of full-height pivoting doors which transform the Prayer Hall and Prayer Court into one simple indoor/outdoor room. The ancillary rooms of the Mosque are grouped linearly running parallel to the side walls. The side walls also offer entrances to the women's gallery, the Iman's room, the library and the upper plant room. The women's gallery is screened in the classical tradition and the free space generated between these two functional areas provides an uninterrupted hall where the dimensions of the mithrab wall and the main entrance wall are identical.

Ten reinforced concrete columns on a 32.40 m grid cantilever form the ground and support a tubular steel space frame which spans an area of 56×96 m

with a further cantilever of 8 m on each face. External walls are hung from the roof and are made of lightweight cladding in white, translucent double-glazed panels with a framework of stainless steel. The detailed drawing indicates a layering of decoration provided by overlay screens which vary in intensity to the Mosque's internal planning requirements. Light will filter into the internal space through carefully screened translucent wall panels. Artificial light is provided by system lighting contained within the integrated ceiling. The Mosque has air conditioning whose main plant is located within the service and parking area below. Ducting is contained within screen walls and the main ceiling grid. The floors are laid in geometrical patterns corresponding to the grid of the space frame and are in local white marble. The marble forms an upstand to incorporate and isolate the mithrab wall within the structure. This wall is ascending and peaks at the height of the mithrab.

PROJECT TEAM: Derek Walker, David Reddick, R Pummell, N Miller-Chalk, M Wood, Kathy Hines, R Barnes, N Kampmann, R Herron, T Meadows, R Waller.
ISLAMIC ADVISER: Abdul Aziz Samkary
M & E ENGINEERS: Roger Gross, Geoff Morgan
STRUCTURAL ENGINEERS: Felix J Samuely & Partners. Frank Newby, Ian Singleton Green
QUANTITY SURVEYORS: Davis Belfield & Everest Nick Davis, Mike Sharman

Plan of mosque

Axonometric of lightweight mosque

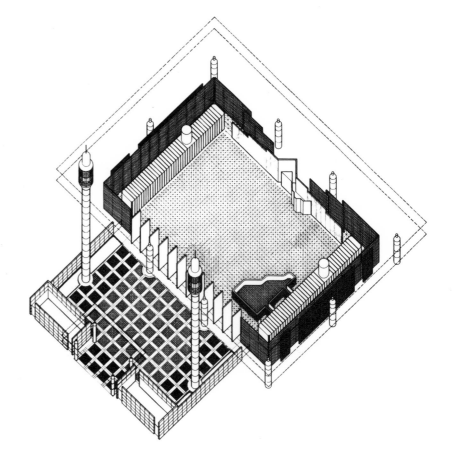

1 Prayer Hall 2 Women's prayer over 3 Courtyard 4 Minaret 5 Entrance 6 Classroom 7 Library 8 Book store 9 Plant 10 Imam 11 Mat store 12 Women's entrance 13 Women's ablutions 14 Men's ablutions

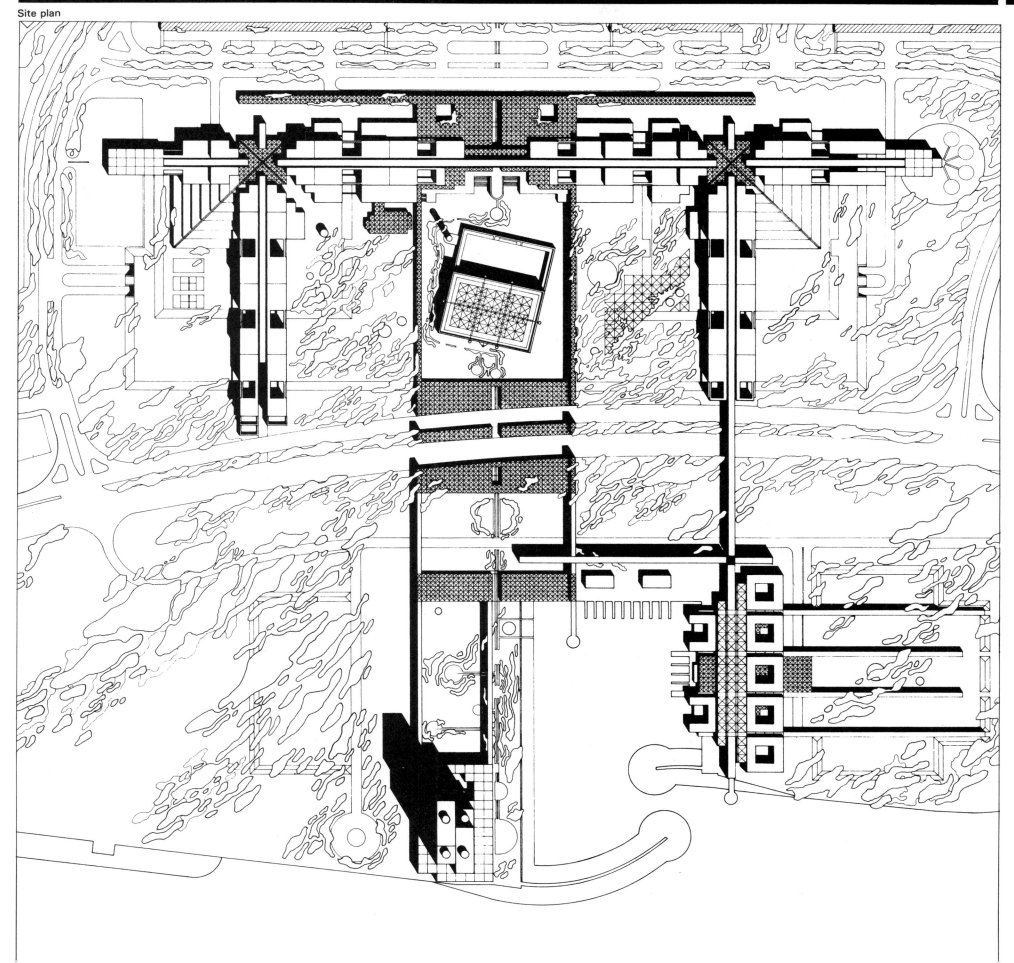

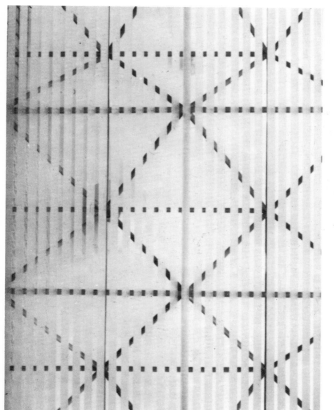

Detail of grid

Detail of roof structure

View of model

Elevation detail

Ron Herron with Walker Wright Partnership
L'OREAL TECHNICAL CENTRE, KENSINGTON

L'OREAL is a multinational group of companies specialising in beauty products. Their British headquarters, of which the technical centre is part, is in a refurbished, recently converted 1930s 'Georgian' building.

The technical centre has four basic functions:
— training of young hairdressers in the specialist techniques of hair colouring and styling, together with a familiarisation programme related to hair products;
— the organisation and running of refresher courses for professional hairdressers in new hair colouring techniques and products;
— the organisation and running of courses for in-house L'Oreal personnel;
— the testing and practical application of new products.

The brief was for a reception area for models and students, three training studios each with a related lecture theatre, a testing studio, staffrooms and a small administrative area.

A simple race track plan was developed, with the circulation 'ribbon' hugging three sides of the existing core. The practical rooms, lecture theatres and offices being located onto the window walls.

It was important to maximise the use of available space so that as much area as possible could be given over to the practical rooms. This is particularly evident in the planning of the practical studios and lecture theatres which are divided by sliding partitions allowing the spaces to be used separately or in combination.

The colour scheme of shades of grey and white provides a cool, clean, salon-like environment and the materials chosen are tough and hardwearing. The white ceramic floor tiles were carefully tested for their resistance to hair colourants! The lighting system takes into account the very specialised requirements of the professional hairdresser, with a mix of colour-corrected fluorescents and tungsten floods.

Special dressing-out units have been designed for the Centre. These are of two types, the first is free standing, incorporating outlets for equipment and holders for hand-dryers or tong holders. These can be moved and plugged into the ceiling power track. The second type of unit is based on a fixed steel column fitted with power outlets, tong and hand dryer holders or brackets for hood dryers, video monitors and audio-visual equipment.

The paraphernalia of the hairdressing business, the dressing-out units, colour mixing stations, crazy long-arm swivel wash basins and 1940s streamlined space flight hair drying 'helmets' on hydraulic arms, placed in a no-nonsense, functional, cool space, makes for a 'salon-set' somewhat different to the High Street or even Mayfair coiffure parlours.

PROJECT TEAM: Ron Herron, Tony Meadows & John Wright
QUANTITY SURVEYORS: Pain & Philips
SERVICES CONSULTANTS: Webber & Lenihan
MAIN CONTRACTOR: Bovis Renovations Ltd
M + E CONTRACTOR: Andrews Weatherfoil Ltd
PARTITIONING: Holzapfel GMBH
HAIRDRESSING EQUIPMENT: Olymp
CEILINGS: Straker Const Ltd

Working drawing of dressing-out units and below, Cut-away isometric

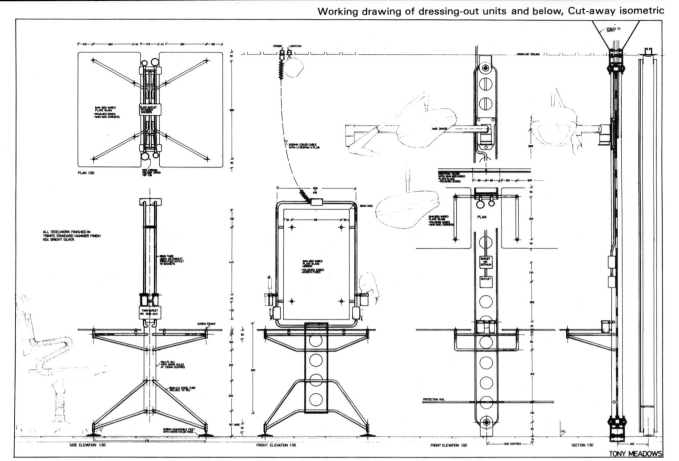

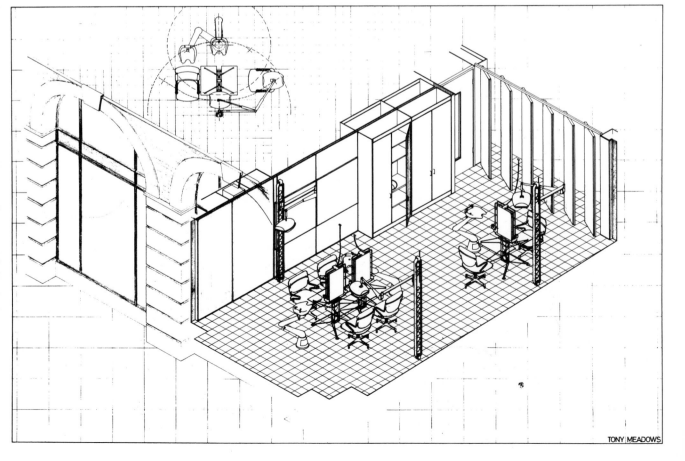

Views of interior of training studio (phs Ken Kirkwood)

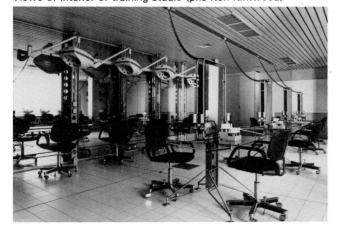

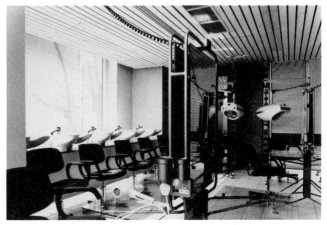

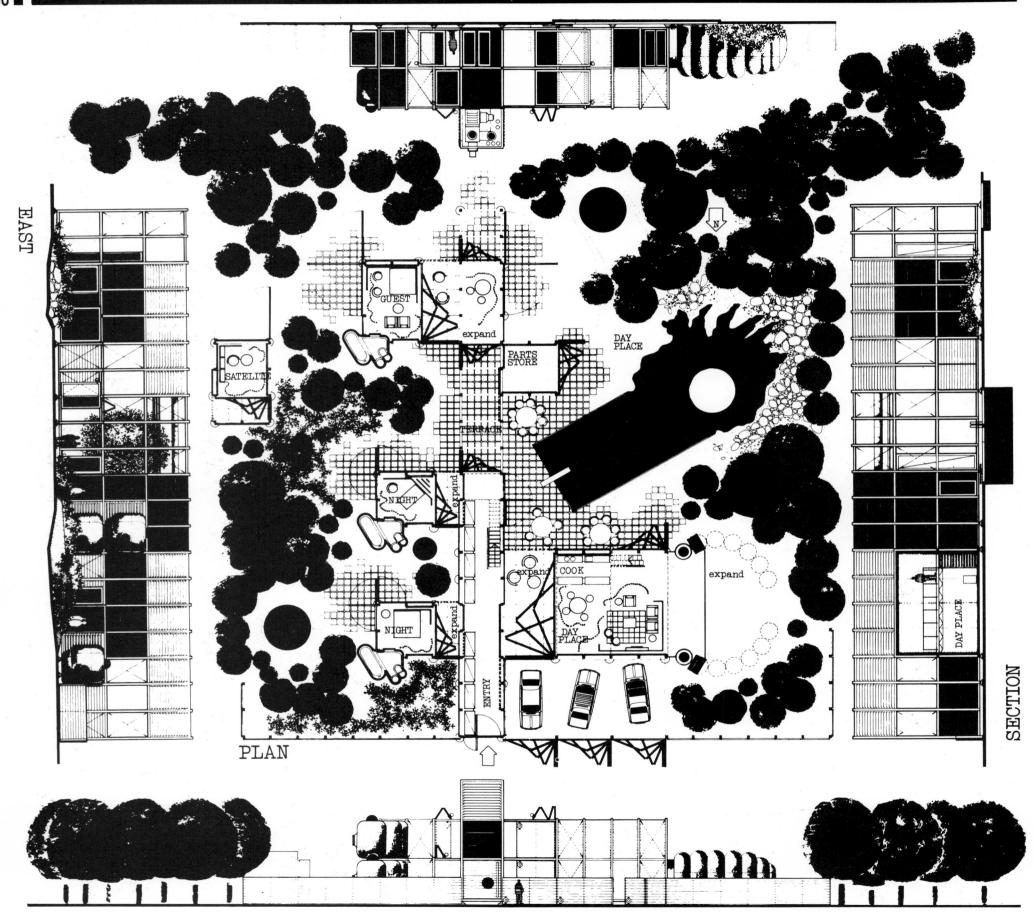

EAST

GUEST

expand

SATELITE

PARTS STORE

DAY PLACE

TERRACE

NIGHT

expand

expand

NIGHT

expand

expand

COOK

DAY PLACE

expand

DAY PLACE

ENTRY

SECTION

PLAN

NORTH

THE URBAN DETACHED HOUSE .... A PIECE OF HISTORY FROM THE IMMEDIATE PAST ..... THE UNBUILT 60s/70s ..... THE RESPONSIVE ENVIRONMENT ..... THE HOUSE FREE OF ITS SITE ..... URBAN MAN AS NOMAD ..... THE ROBOT AS SERVANT ..... THE MOTORISED WALL ..... THE MOVING ROOF ..... PACKAGED PARTS ..... THE POD ..... THE ALL PURPOSE SHED ..... THE OPTIONAL EXTRA ..... OPEN IN USE, CLOSED WHEN UNOCCUPIED ..... THE COMPUTERISED/ELECTRONIC ENVIRONMENT ..... THE INTERIORS AS 'SETS' ..... a RESPONSE TO URBAN MAN'S LOVE AFFAIR WITH STYLE/POST MODERN YESTERDAY, ART DECO BEFORE, NEO FASCISM TODAY ..... THE 'FAD' ..... FROM THE CATALOGUE ..... ELEMENTARIST.

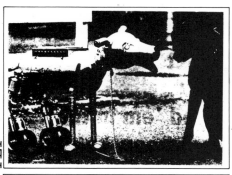

PET

CONTROL

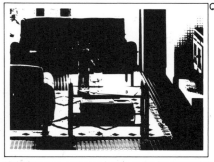

SERVANT

SETS......OPTIONS

MODEL

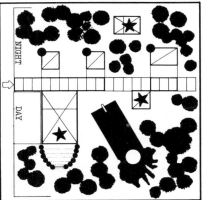

OPEN:DAY

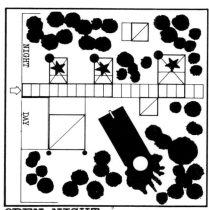

OPEN:NIGHT

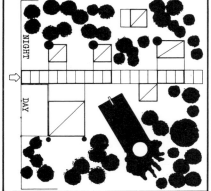

CLOSED

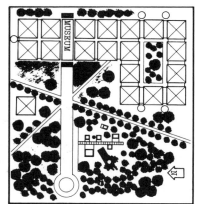

SITE

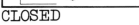

Cedric Price
A GALLERY FOR RENAISSANCE ART, NATIONAL GALLERY, TRAFALGAR SQUARE

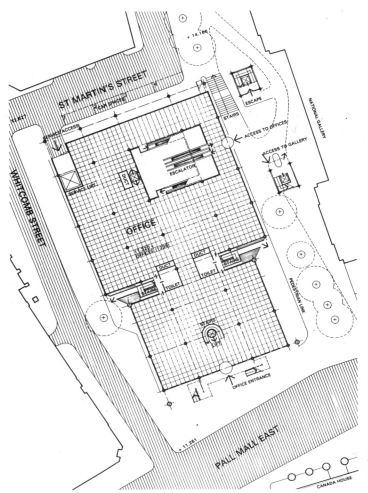

Typical supportive floor, 1980 style

The new neighbour

EXHIBITING PART OF A TIMELESS artistic heritage to the public, 55 million of which own it, does not necessarily require a fixed building in the capital city. Thus, in this project there is an inevitable element of arbitrariness even within the required life span.

Although the present National Gallery — approximately the same age — was a bit of a lash up, re-using as it did the portico columns from old Carlton House, it has enabled a galleried progression for viewing that is worth reinforcing for 125 years but not perpetuating.

The proposal considered the freedom of the voluntary viewer to wander without let or hindrance to be absolutely paramount. However, the opportunities for the displayer to rearrange over this not insubstantial period should be increased.

Thus, whilst the new space feeds trouble-free from the old, a capacity for new spatial delights and operational convenience is the key to its variety. There is theoretically no reason for such a picture casket to have foundations or indeed to always point the same way or to be externally visible at all. It must be safe to people, pictures and insurers and have natural light — that is all.

It is unlikely that the almost sacrosanct nature of the last requirement will last long. Just think of the places where those paintings were first located! However, for financial reasons some more useable space is needed and because of the site available some recognition of the square may be desirable. The supporting structure can, over the projected span, help contain a variety of uses of varied volumes while to hold such a vulnerable point requires the establishment of both tension with adjacent buildings whilst enabling an intriguing visual challenge from both within and without this most punctured of public squares.

This building crowds the street, contrasting its bland, shiny, constantly-cleaned profile with that of the portico of Canada House. Whilst not hiding the central portico of the National Gallery it obscures the feeble pepper pot lanterns though not the Gallery ground level to those approaching from Pall Mall.

It provides uncommitted public shelter within a 'gateway' to the Square. The gallery casket is clad in stainless steel whilst the 'temporary' supportive structures are open to all sorts of finishes. Cream gloss-painted stucco is favoured at present.

The link bridge is of protected steel construction as it, together with the servicing plant it supports, is likely to change considerably over the lifespan of the total development together with the travelling vertical cleaning booms.

The form and finish of the top of the building is most self-conscious as, over the next 125 years, it will be viewed from above by an increasing multitude.

Looking at painting is a quiet, private delight and cannot be accompanied by fireworks as can listening to music. This building is meant to spread delight and wonder through its interior. Externally it is intended to intrigue rather than startle.

CLIENT: Sir Robert McAlpine & Sons Ltd (competition entry)

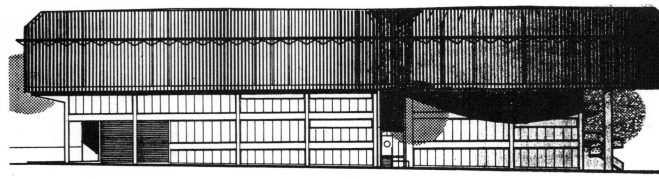

West elevation

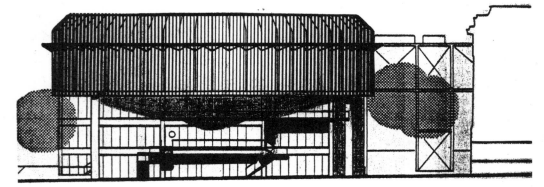

South elevation

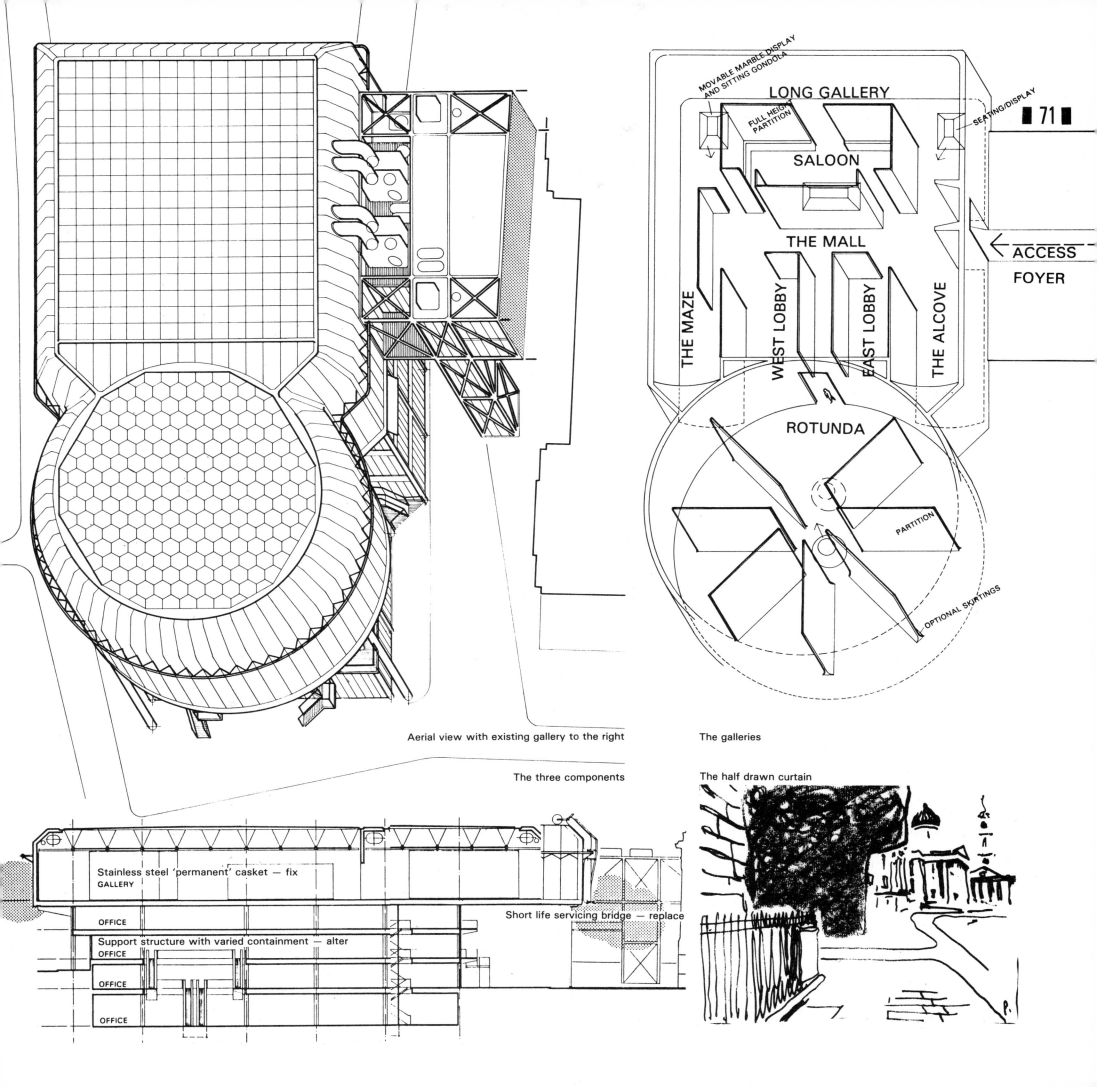

MOVABLE MARBLE DISPLAY
AND SITTING GONDOLA

LONG GALLERY

FULL HEIGHT
PARTITION

SALOON

SEATING/DISPLAY

THE MALL

ACCESS

FOYER

THE MAZE

WEST LOBBY

EAST LOBBY

THE ALCOVE

ROTUNDA

PARTITION

OPTIONAL SKIRTINGS

Aerial view with existing gallery to the right

The galleries

The three components

The half drawn curtain

Stainless steel 'permanent' casket — fix
GALLERY

OFFICE

Short life servicing bridge — replace

Support structure with varied containment — alter
OFFICE

OFFICE

OFFICE

Nicholas Grimshaw & Partners

INDUSTRIAL NURSERY UNIT DEVELOPMENT, PHASE IV, GILLINGHAM INDUSTRIAL PARK, KENT

THE NURSERY UNIT DEVELOPMENT is located at the main entrance to the 120-acre Gillingham Industrial Park in Kent, at present being developed by Grosvenor Developments in partnership with Gillingham Borough Council.

The scheme consists of 15 units of approximately 200 m² planned in two terraces and was directed towards meeting the demand for accommodation of small, perhaps newly-created businesses. Each unit measures 10 × 20 m and has an internal height of 4.6 m. The concrete frame structure (which was designed during the long steel strike in 1980) consists of 200 × 200 mm precast columns and 200 × 400 mm precast beams. The cross-wall construction was completed by inserting 200 mm thick flush blockwork infill panels. Secondary structure between cross walls was avoided by specifying 200 mm-deep galvanised steel roof decking spanning 10 m. The result internally is a clear box, free of the usual steel column and beam projections and associated blockwork pier or board fire protection.

The buildings are clad in maintenance-free silver PVF$_2$-coated steel sheeting fixed horizontally through top-hat sections to horizontal lining trays containing incombustible insulation slabs. Windows and entrance door openings were then cut out on site and GRP window and door frames inserted. Services enter the building through 'hoods' thus retaining maximum usable floor space within the units.

The forecourt areas are surfaced in interlocking concrete blocks which facilitate replacement if disturbed or damaged in the future. A minimum amount of landscaping was disturbed during the construction, and what was disturbed has been supplemented by new tree and dense shrub planting using indigenous species. The development was completed in early summer 1981.

CLIENT: Grosvenor Estate Commercial Developments Ltd
PROJECT TEAM: Nick Grimshaw and Philip McClean
ENGINEER: Peter Brett Associates
QUANTITY SURVEYOR: LC Wakeman & Partners
CONTRACTOR: Willett Ltd
LANDSCAPE ARCHITECT: Brian Clouston and Partners

Construction shots

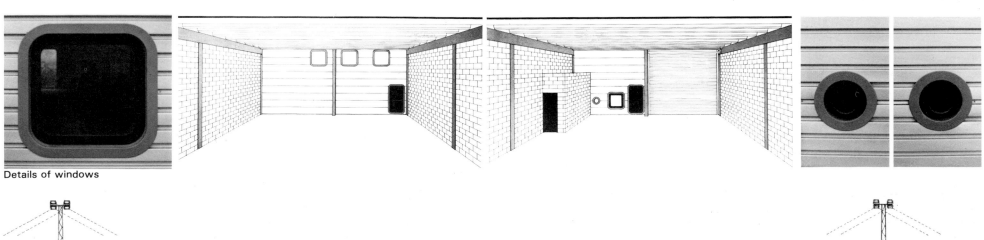

Details of windows

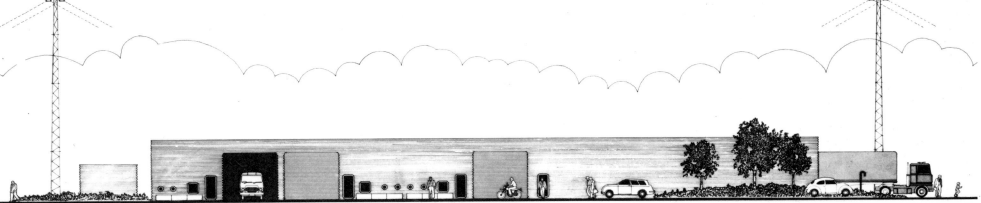

Typical elevation

Nicholas Grimshaw & Partners
SPORTS BUILDING FOR AN INTERNATIONAL CORPORATION

THE CONCEPT OF THE BUILDING is to achieve as much openness as possible. The principal elements required by the brief were:
— a large games hall for volley ball, badminton, indoor soccer and also suitable for social functions
— two glass-backed squash courts;
— a bar, lounge and store;
— a mezzanine level for billiards, snooker and table tennis;
— changing facilities, showers and toilets;
— a managers' office.
Unnecessary partitioning has been avoided but netting or glazed walls are used where separation is required. Continuing the open theme, pre-made elements

View of model and detail showing netting walls and cross bracing of structure

SPORTS HALL FOR IBM (UK) LTD, HURSLEY PARK, WINCHESTER

THE NEW SPORTS HALL is located in the grounds of the IBM Laboratories at Hursley Park, just outside Winchester. The brief was to provide a multi-purpose sports hall to the existing IBM social club, suitable principally for badminton and other indoor sports but to be used also for occasional social functions.

After researching existing sports buildings it was felt that the usual solution of a brick box was neither desirable nor appropriate, especially in such a sensitive setting.

The principal and most striking element of the design is the external structural framework consisting of five trussed portal frames made of tubular sections which span 18 m and 5.25 m centres. Inside, a very clear, flush-walled internal space is achieved. The structural framework serves to break down the bulk of the building both by the articulation of the frames themselves and also by the patterns their shadows cast on the silver cladding. The framework relates to the trunks, boughs and branches of the trees surrounding the site.

The cladding panels are self-finished, foam-cored, steel-skinned and bolted

Views of building (ph Jo Reid & John Peck)

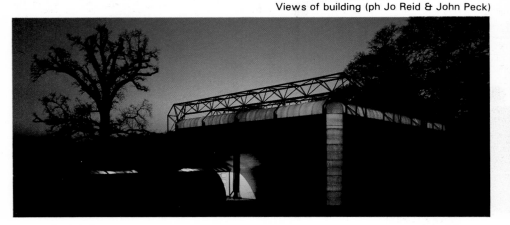

South-west elevation

Long section

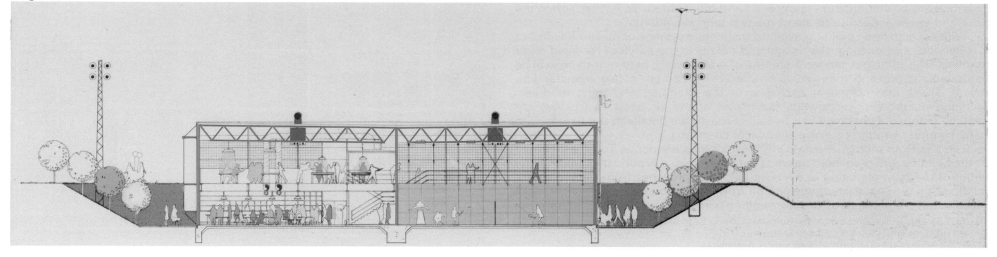

SPORTS BUILDING FOR AN INTERNATIONAL CORPORATION

such as prefabricated squash courts and modular toilet units are to be used and slotted into the overall building framework.

The main structure is a 1.40 m deep flat truss at 4 m centres spanning 16 m to 180×180 RHS columns. This means that there is a central line of columns and this spine is used to separate the large games hall from the collection of smaller elements which composes the rest of the building.

The cladding is of silver PVF_2-finished, steel-skinned, foam-cored sandwich panels. The panels are bolted to cleats on the main structure and also to 160×160 UB lightened mullions. To break down the mass of the building, bands and blocks of glazings coupled with bands of strong colour are employed. The cross bracing of the structure is exposed and highlighted. To further soften the mass, the eaves are radiused along the two long elevations.

With such an open building, with no suspended ceilings or plaster finishes to hide services and ducting, the design and details of the services received close attention. The principal service elements of water tanks, heat pumps, electrical distribution board and main service runs are contained in two free-standing towers. These are located at each end of the changing and toilet modules. Radiating out from these towers, the routes of the air ducts and cables are carefully planned. Great care had been taken with the details of the fixings with many coming from the catalogues of yacht chandlers.

The site is an industrial estate with few striking elements. To give a setting for the building, grass covered mounds are to be created around the building, the height of the mounds being at eyelevel as one approaches from the main DEC building. A patio is provided, opening off from the bar on the southern corner of the building, the gradient of the surrounding banks forming a sheltered suntrap.

PROJECT TEAM: Nick Grimshaw, Mark Goldstein, Simon Bean and Don Gray
STRUCTURAL ENGINEERS: FJ Samuely & Partners
QUANTITY SURVEYORS: Michael F Edwards & Associates
SERVICES ENGINEERS: Ronald Hurst Associates

Model of structure

SPORTS HALL FOR IBM (UK) LTD, HURSLEY PARK, WINCHESTER

to cleats welded to the main frame and to the gable mullions. To enable extension of the building along the east-west axis the mullions have been detailed to allow the entire gable wall to be unbolted and taken down. The enlarged building would then include prefabricated squash courts and give more play floor space.

The eaves and corner panels are formed from curved, double-skinned transluscent blue panels. This gives a neutral internal light without glare.

The roof is suspended at the node points of the trusses with special turn-buckle connectors to a lightweight metal deck with insulation board. It is covered using a single-membrane, welded PVC roof. The use of PVC components allowed the complicated upstands at the connectors to be easily formed and sealed. The interior of the building is open and flush-walled. This gives maximum clear space for sport. The floor is of sprung beech. The hall is lit with high level uplighters reflecting off the underside of the roof deck to give an even light level across the hall. The temperature and ventilation are maintained by two external heat pumps, slung in cradles from the main frame, with the air chanelled through exposed ductwork. The power cables are all taken in one high-level face-fixed duct.

Detail of structure (ph Jo Reid & John Peck)

CLIENT: IBM (UK) Ltd
PROJECT TEAM: Nick Grimshaw, Mark Goldstein and Simon Bean
STRUCTURAL ENGINEERS: FJ Samuely & Partners
QUANTITY SURVEYORS: Michael Edwards & Associates
SERVICES ENGINEERS: Ronald Hurst Associates
MAIN CONTRACTOR: Wiltshier Ltd

Nicholas Grimshaw & Partners
AZTEC WEST, BRISTOL

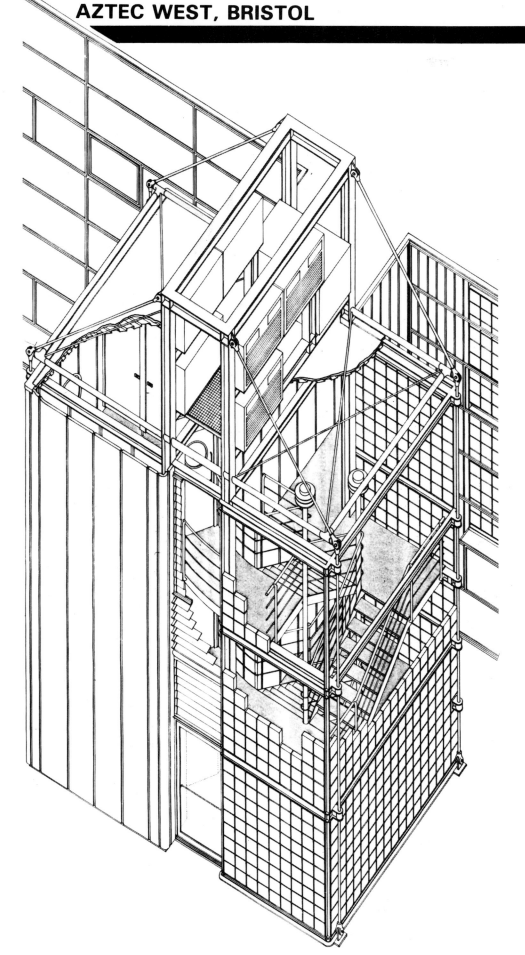

HI-TECH OFFICE SPACE on two floors for use by Digital Equipment Co. This forms Phase One of a two-phase development which will eventually double the accommodation and extend the building to form a complete square with a central courtyard.

The design incorporates several unique features aimed at accommodating the rapidly changing requirements of the hi-tech office user:

— The general arrangement of served and servant spaces with the latter outside the main volume reduces costs, gives a much better nett to gross ratio of 92%, gives natural ventilation to toilets and escape stairs, allows construction to suit function without compromise and, without the need for protected corridors, leaves the main served area completely free and unobstructed.

— The structure is based on a 14.4 m^2 module with columns on a 7.2 m grid and pairs of primary beams at first floor and roof level. This allows the structure to be extended in either direction without affecting the existing building and also reduces the structural depth of these elements, and hence the height of the service zones.

— The main envelope is clad entirely in mirrored DG units with relocatable opening lights. 50% of the skin has opaque insulation panels zipped to the inside of the cladding grid which allow instant relocation of 'windows and walls' without affecting weather-tightness.

— The power and telecommunication distribution is via fully accessible floor trunking on a 2.4 m grid.

— Heating and air circulation is based on a ceiling void/plenum system with secondary fans mounted in interchangeable ceiling tiles to pull warm air down where necessary.

— High efficiency floor-standing uplighters with complete mobility give variable lighting conditions when and where required without affecting the ceiling layout.

CLIENT: Richard Ellis on behalf of Electricity Supply Nominees Ltd
PROJECT TEAM: Brian Taggart, David J Richmond and Alan Robshaw
STRUCTURAL ENGINEERS: Peter Brett Associates
QUANTITY SURVEYORS: Gardiner and Theobald
SERVICES ENGINEERS: YRM Engineers
MAIN CONTRACTOR: Wimpey Construction UK Ltd

Left, Axonometric of stair tower

Perspective of building on site

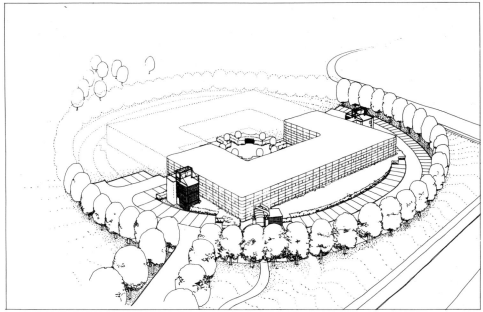

THE CLORE GALLERY FOR THE TURNER COLLECTION will be the first element in the development of the Queen Alexandra Hospital Site for use by the Tate Gallery, and it was essential to position the new building in a way that would not inhibit further development. Certain visually important buildings of the Hospital complex are to be retained and integrated with the new building. The Lodge on Bulinga Street/Millbank will be retained. At the moment it is used by the Ministry of Defence and, when available to the Tate, will be ideal for garden functions and tea rooms, with offices and VIP accommodation above. We will also retain the Hospital entrance building on Bulinga Street which may overlook a future sculpture garden and be used as a library/bookshop and for archives. Other remaining Hospital buildings are to be used for offices and storage. The retention of the Lodge with its counterbalancing relationship to the Royal Army Medical College to the south-west preserves the contextual setting of the Tate and maintains the symmetrical balance of the Gallery about its entrance portico. Nevertheless, the Clore Gallery will have its own separate identity and be clearly seen from Millbank across the gardens of the Tate. The existing plane trees will be maintained and new lawns laid across Bulinga Street to the Lodge.

ARCHITECTS: James Stirling Michael Wilford & Assocs with PSA Museums and Galleries Group
PROJECT TEAM: Russell Bevington, Peter Ray, John Cairns, John Cannon, Robert Dye, Lester Haven, Walter Naegeli, Sheila O'Donnell, Philip Smithies, Stephen Wright
CONSULTANT STRUCTURAL ENGINEERS: Felix J Samuely & Partners
CONSULTANT M + E ENGINEERS: Steensen Varming Mulcahy & Partners
CONSULTANT QUANTITY SURVEYORS: Davis Belfield & Everest
CONSULTANT PUBLIC HEALTH ENGINEERS: John Taylor & Sons
CONSULTANT LANDSCAPE ARCHITECT: Janet Jack

1 Up view of entrance to Clore Gallery 2 Up view of rear elevation facing towards Vickers Tower
3 Section perspective of upper level gallery 4 Perspective of lecture theatre
Opposite page: View of the entrance to the Clore Gallery from the Tate pavilion across the sunken terrace (ph Dennis Crompton)

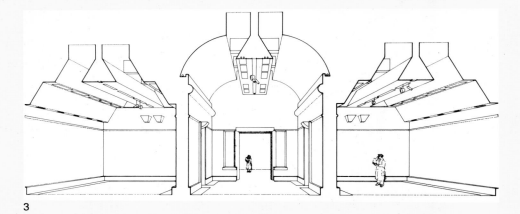

3

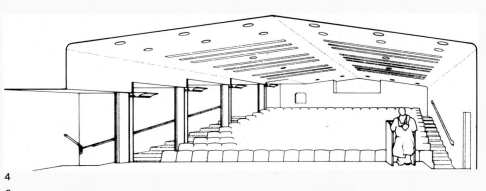

4

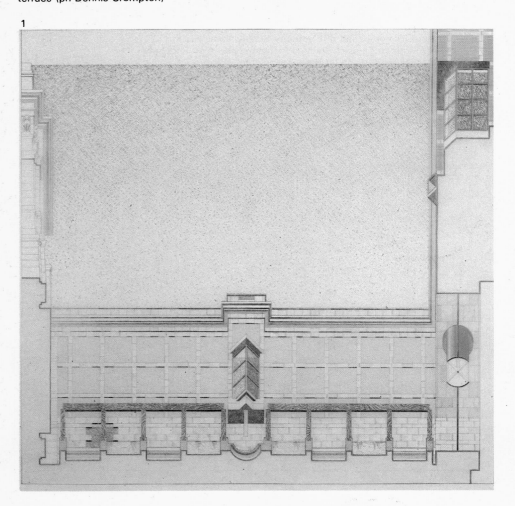

1

2

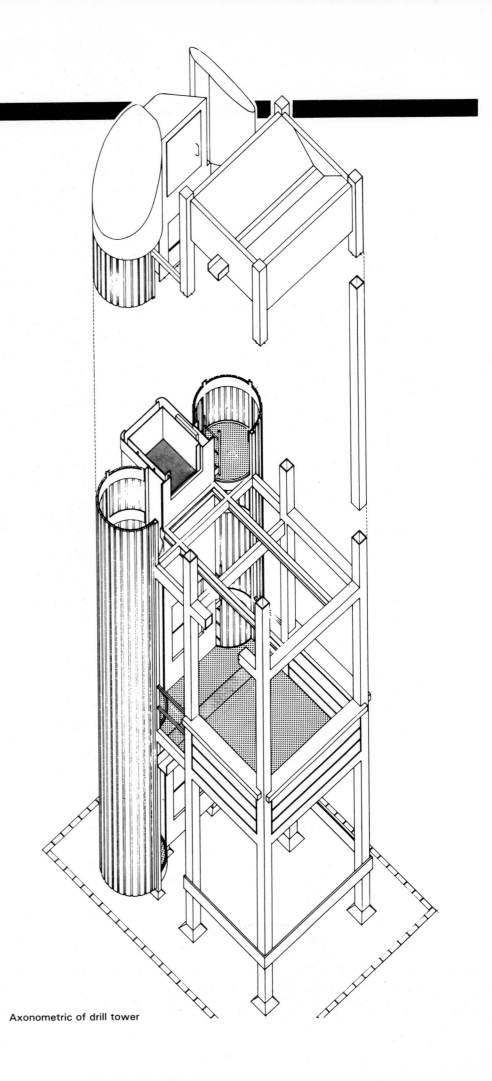

Interior of tubular ladder shaft

Small goods hoist

Axonometric of drill tower

DRILL TOWERS FOR
THE LONDON FIRE BRIGADE

THE LONDON FIRE BRIGADE have over 110 stations in the Greater London area and most of these stations have a drill tower on which firemen practise their rescue and fire fighting routines. The tower is therefore essential to the Brigade in maintaining a state of readiness and competence. Many of the existing towers are unsafe or do not comply with the latest Home Office standards which were drawn up in 1980. The GLC's department of Architecture and Civic Design was asked to survey these towers and it was found that it would be too expensive to adapt many of them and therefore a programme was initiated to produce a series of prototype towers which complied with the 1980 Home Office standards.

There are three main elements in the design of the new towers: the four drill platforms, the two ladder tubes and the lift shaft between the tubes.

The ladders to each level are contained inside two tubular shafts; they run for one storey only at a time and are staggered to prevent a fall of more than 10 feet by anyone using them. The tubes are clad in lightweight 'Planja' steel sheeting.

The lift shaft contains a small goods hoist and this allows practice equipment to be hoisted to each level to be used in drills.

PROJECT TEAM: Peter Jones, Jake Brown, David Cook and Vincent Pilato
STRUCTURAL ENGINEERS: Eric Voller (GLC)
ELECTRICAL ENGINEERS: Trevor Mason (GLC)
QUANTITY SURVEYOR: Michael Adams (GLC)
SITE CONTRACTOR: Mabey Construction Ltd
STEEL FABRICATOR: Fairfield Mabey Ltd

Views of exterior of ladder and lift shafts

Foster Associates

DESIGN FOR A CORPORATE HEADQUARTERS FOR HUMANA INC, LOUISVILLE, KENTUCKY

AT THE BEGINNING OF 1982, Foster Associates were invited to take part in a limited competition to design a new corporate headquarters for Humana Inc, in Louisville, Kentucky. Our response was a cluster of towers, the main offices with a triangulated perimeter structure enclosing internal vertical columns carrying the floor loads and service towers propped against the rigid perimeter structure.

HUMANA PROJECT TEAM: Wendy Foster, Norman Foster, Birkin Haward, Loren Butt, Roy Fleetwood, Richard Horden, Jan Kaplicky, Annette le Cuyer, Winston Shu, David Chipperfield, Vakis Hadjikyriacou
STRUCTURAL ENGINEERS: Jack Zunz, Bob Emmerson, Ian Gardner
QUANTITY SURVEYORS: Bob Ridgewell, Danny Flynn, Ray Liechti
MODEL MAKERS: Neil Holt and Nick Morgan
PHOTOGRAPHER: Richard Davies

Left . INFLUENCES   Right , Model in context

Aerial view with montage of building on site

Base of model

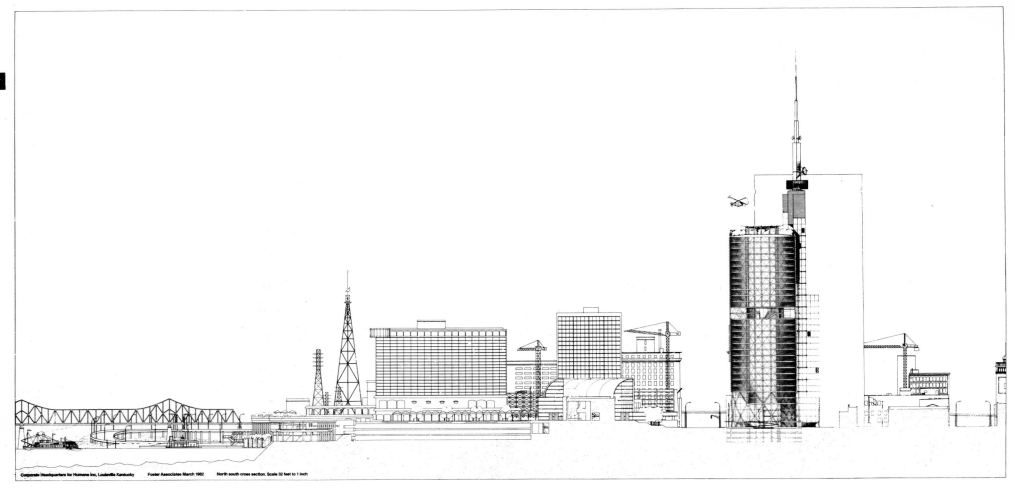

Corporate Headquarters for Humana Inc, Louisville Kentucky   Foster Associates March 1982   North south cross section. Scale 32 feet to 1 inch

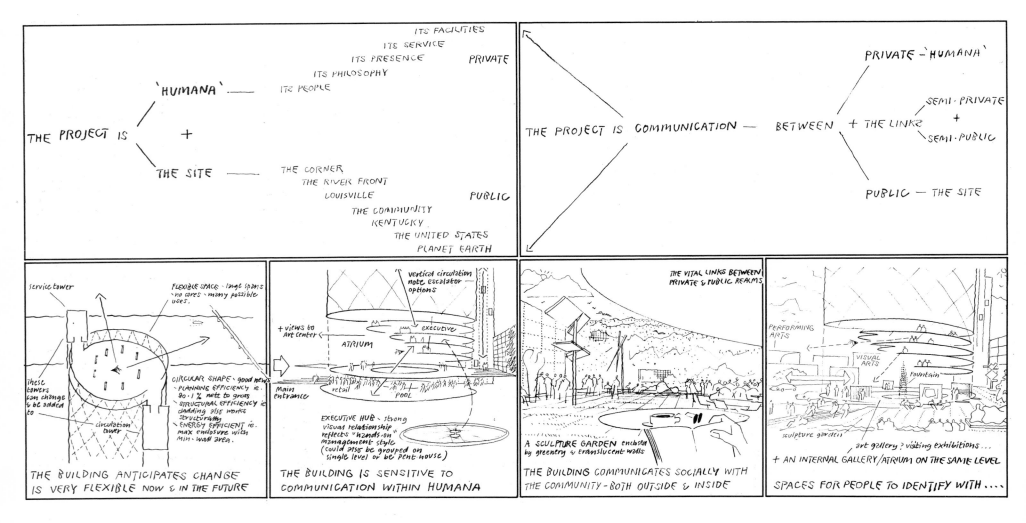

ITS FACILITIES
ITS SERVICE
ITS PRESENCE   PRIVATE
ITS PHILOSOPHY
'HUMANA' — ITS PEOPLE

THE PROJECT IS   +

THE SITE — THE CORNER
THE RIVER FRONT
LOUISVILLE
THE COMMUNITY   PUBLIC
KENTUCKY
THE UNITED STATES
PLANET EARTH

PRIVATE - 'HUMANA'

THE PROJECT IS COMMUNICATION — BETWEEN + THE LINKS

SEMI-PRIVATE
+
SEMI-PUBLIC

PUBLIC — THE SITE

---

service tower
FLEXIBLE SPACE - large spans - no cores - many possible uses.
these towers can change & be added to
circulation tower
CIRCULAR SHAPE · good news:
- PLANNING EFFICIENCY ie. 90·1% nett to gross
- STRUCTURAL EFFICIENCY ie cladding also works structurally
- ENERGY EFFICIENT ie. max enclosure with min. wall area.

THE BUILDING ANTICIPATES CHANGE IS VERY FLEXIBLE NOW & IN THE FUTURE

---

vertical circulation note escalator options
+ views to Art Center
executive
ATRIUM
Main entrance
retail
POOL
EXECUTIVE HUB · strong visual relationship reflects "hands-on" management style (could also be grouped on single level or be pent-house)

THE BUILDING IS SENSITIVE TO COMMUNICATION WITHIN HUMANA

THE VITAL LINKS BETWEEN PRIVATE & PUBLIC REALMS
A SCULPTURE GARDEN enclosed by greenery & translucent walls

THE BUILDING COMMUNICATES SOCIALLY WITH THE COMMUNITY - BOTH OUTSIDE & INSIDE

PERFORMING ARTS
VISUAL ARTS
Fountain
sculpture garden
art gallery? visiting exhibitions...
+ AN INTERNAL GALLERY/ATRIUM ON THE SAME LEVEL

SPACES FOR PEOPLE TO IDENTIFY WITH ....

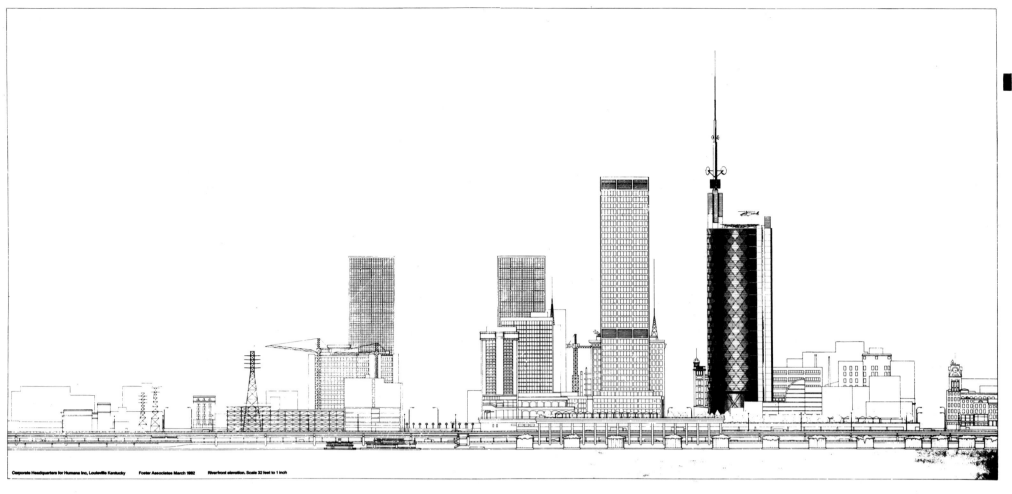

Corporate Headquarters for Humana Inc, Louisville Kentucky   Foster Associates March 1982   Riverfront elevation. Scale 32 feet to 1 inch

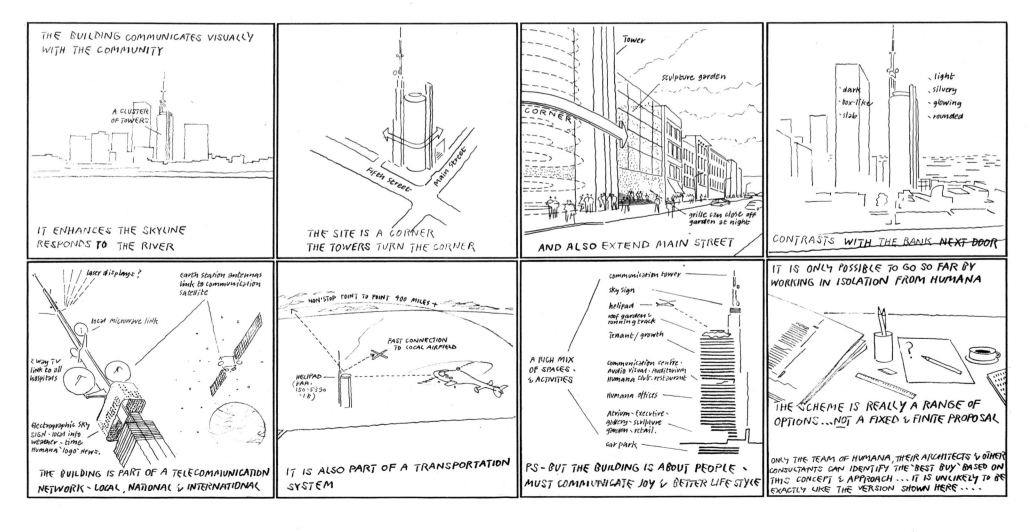

THE BUILDING COMMUNICATES VISUALLY WITH THE COMMUNITY

A CLUSTER OF TOWERS

IT ENHANCES THE SKYLINE RESPONDS TO THE RIVER

Fifth Street
Main Street

THE SITE IS A CORNER THE TOWERS TURN THE CORNER

Tower

sculpture garden

CORNER

grille can close off garden at night

AND ALSO EXTEND MAIN STREET

---

light
silvery
glowing
rounded

dark
box-like
slab

CONTRASTS WITH THE BANK NEXT DOOR

---

laser displays?

earth station antennas link to communication satellite

local microwave link

2 way TV link to all hospitals

Electrographic sky sign - local info weather - time Humana 'logo' news.

THE BUILDING IS PART OF A TELECOMMUNICATION NETWORK - LOCAL, NATIONAL & INTERNATIONAL

NON-STOP POINT TO POINT 400 MILES +

FAST CONNECTION TO LOCAL AIRFIELD

HELIPAD (FAA - 150-5390 -1B)

IT IS ALSO PART OF A TRANSPORTATION SYSTEM

---

communication tower

sky sign

helipad

roof garden & running track

tenant/growth

A RICH MIX OF SPACES & ACTIVITIES

communication centre - audio visual - auditorium Humana club - restaurant

Humana offices

atrium - executive - gallery - sculpture garden - retail.

car park

PS - BUT THE BUILDING IS ABOUT PEOPLE - MUST COMMUNICATE JOY & BETTER LIFE STYLE

IT IS ONLY POSSIBLE TO GO SO FAR BY WORKING IN ISOLATION FROM HUMANA

?

THE SCHEME IS REALLY A RANGE OF OPTIONS... NOT A FIXED & FINITE PROPOSAL

ONLY THE TEAM OF HUMANA, THEIR ARCHITECTS & OTHER CONSULTANTS CAN IDENTIFY THE 'BEST BUY' BASED ON THIS CONCEPT & APPROACH ... IT IS UNLIKELY TO BE EXACTLY LIKE THE VERSION SHOWN HERE ....

Corporate Headquarters for Humana Inc, Louisville Kentucky   Foster Associates March 1982   North south cross section. Scale 16 feet to 1 inch

Corporate Headquarters for Humana Inc, Louisville Kentucky   Foster Associates March 1982   North elevation. Scale 16 feet to 1 inch

DESIGN FOR A NATIONAL GERMAN INDOOR ATHLETICS STADIUM, FRANKFURT

Exterior and interior of model

IN ITS ULTIMATE FORM athletics is a fusion of the body and mind—the mechanical and the spiritual. Our approach to architecture and the design of this building is the same—an attempt to integrate humanistic ideals; sun, light, views both in and out, ambience, gentle forms, with advanced 20th-century engineering—maximum spans with minimum materials—sparse, elegant and very economical. The arch form creates the maximum internal span—functional but enjoyably symbolic—with the minimum external bulk. Each part of the building is clearly expressed with materials appropriate to their location and function. On the outside the base of the building is landscaped with greenery, internally the base is sculptured concrete, with inside walls and floors of cast glass and stainless steel trim, both hard wearing and maintenance-free. All spaces receive natural light—either direct or diffused. The engineering of light and energy are important ingredients in the scheme. The main arena level is slightly depressed into the ground to ease access to the public level and create the most sympathetic relationship on the site with the existing landscaping and adjoining buildings. The glazed end walls are recessed to give shadow and create covered outside viewing areas which offer protection to bystanders; they also create a sense of occasion and entrance.

STRUCTURAL ENGINEERS:Ove Arup & Ptnrs with Boll & Ptnr
QUANTITY SURVEYOR: Davis Belfield and Everest
BUILDING SERVICES ENGINEER: MDA Dunstone GmbH
                                        Schmidt Reuter
LIGHTING: Bartenbach and Wagner
ARCHITECTURAL RENDERING: Helmut Jacoby

Below, cross sections and longitudinal section. Opposite, site plan and details of cross section and longitudinal section.

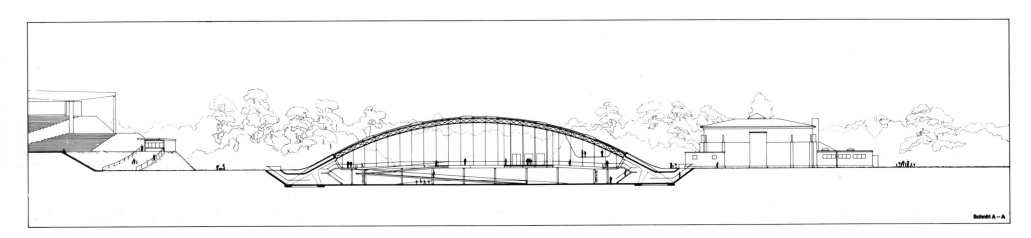

Schnitt A – A

Schnitt B – B

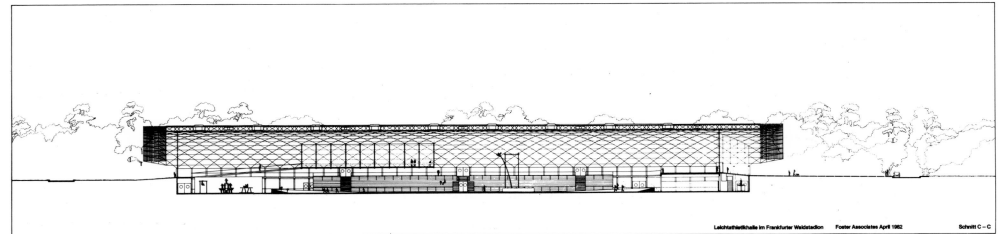

Leichtathletikhalle im Frankfurter Waldstadion   Foster Associates April 1982   Schnitt C – C

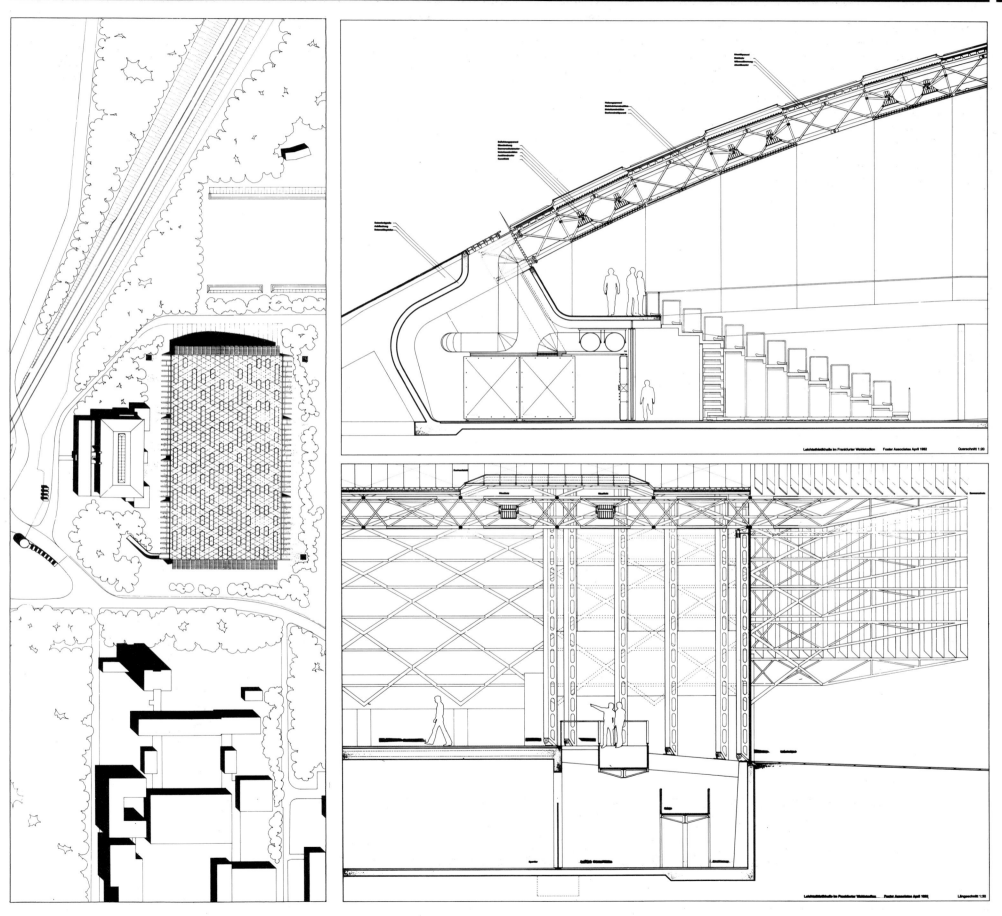

IN ACCORDANCE with their expansionist policy, Renault UK Ltd have purchased 16 acres of land at Westlea Down for development as a Parts Distribution Centre, improved regional offices and Training School. In the first phase of construction is intended to build 20,000 m² of warehouses and a further 4,000 m² of offices or the management of the Distribution Centre, the Regional Office, a showroom or cars and vans, restaurant facilities and an After Sales Training School.

All the activities of the building will be contained within one overall structure which is made up of a set of 24 × 24 m modules. The column grid of 24 m relates rst to the various types of racking used in the warehouse, providing a high egree of flexibility in its layout and also serves as an overall planning grid llowing the building to make maximum use of the irregular shape of the site.

CONSULTING ENGINEERS: Ove Arup and Partners
STRUCTURAL ENGINEERS: Ove Arup and Partners
QUANTITY SURVEYORS: Davis, Belfield and Everest
MANAGEMENT CONTRACTOR: Bovis
ACOUSTICAL ENGINEER: Tim Smith
OFFICE PLANNING: Quickborner Team

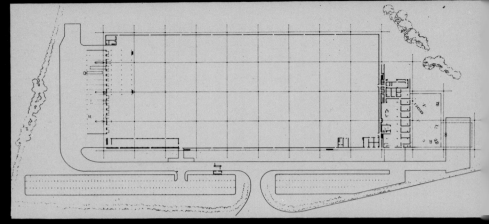

Site plan

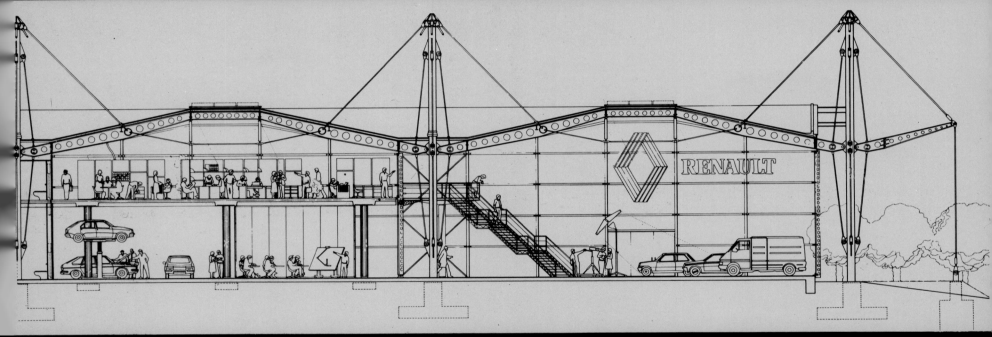

Detail of long section showing offices, After School Training and showroom

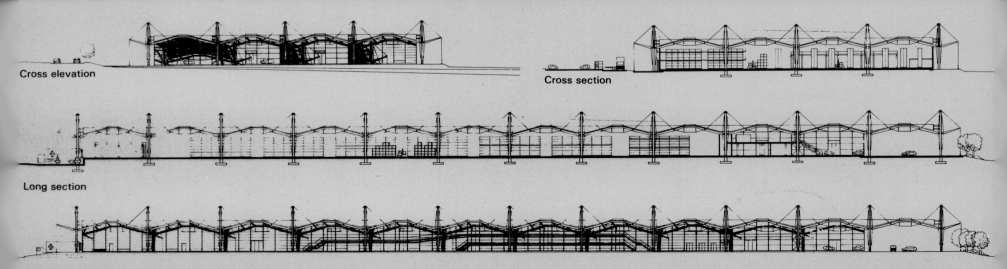

Cross elevation

Cross section

Long section

Long elevation

Corner elevation in context

Detail of roof/wall juncture

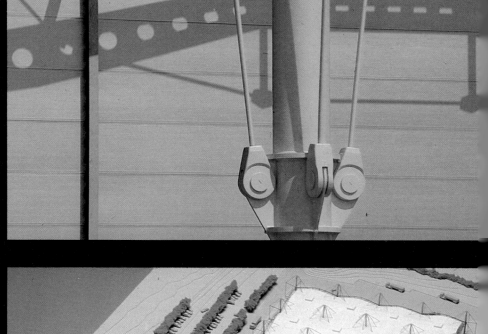

Details of structure
Aerial views: building on site and model (ph of building: Sealand Aerial Photography, Chichester)

Alan Stanton
THE TATE GALLERY PAVILIONS

THE TATE GALLERY commissioned us to design two summer pavilions to house a working studio (for Winsor and Newton) and a cafe on the lawn facing the river. The pavilions were originally planned to be placed on either side of the Tate's portico but work on the adjacent Clore Gallery necessitated their re-location to one side of the entrance.

The working studio provides paint, brushes and canvas for the public and allows them to discuss techniques and materials with painters and technical advisers. The cafe serves as a summer time coffee shop for visitors to the Gallery.

Notes on the Design—Formality and Informality

The gallery suggests theatre to us—a stone backdrop set on the river, the gardens a stage. We find ourselves making tents that are both decorative sets and characters with bold, flat faces, backs and fronts—scaled up, shaped and dressed to animate the Thames.

Setting temporary, flapping canvas against the Gallery's stone classicism reminds us of popular feast and ritual. Tents become banners, may-poles, totems, jousting marquees. Common public festivities are set against the more private and sober functions of the Gallery's interior (market stalls beneath the loggia, the fair at the castle gates).

A Clothes Horse

We have invented a kind of clothes horse. A simple flat angular frame that can be dressed according to occasion and season. A trestle, a gibbet. Wind vanes added on a post at the top to move and clatter in the wind. Birds on a flagpole, a head for the body.

Clothes

A soft, curved bell shape is formed in fabric between a suspended ring and three points along the frame above. A taught, vaulted space within and a suggestive shape without that decently requires to be dressed.

This dressing—the tabard with its flat, cut-out shapes and flapping layers is made to contrast with the inner form. Metal spars and straps stitch through and stretch to hold its shape. The design is not definitive. Future functions may prompt an extension of the wardrobe.

We have chosen cotton canvas fabric—a traditional tent material with its own character that takes on a patina of use, grimed by rain, bleached by sun it casts a diffuse creamy light inside. It can be coloured and painted.

Inside

A tower-figure inhabits each of the spaces, greets you as you enter, offers paints, brushes, food and light.

PROJECT TEAM: Alan Stanton, Peter Rice, Andrew Morris, Bill Logan, Amarjit Kalsi, Kathy Kerr
COLOURS & VANES: Wendy Robin
CONTRACTOR: Clyde Canvas Ltd
LIGHTING: Concord with Wotan Lamps
W + N INTERIOR: Beck & Pollitzer

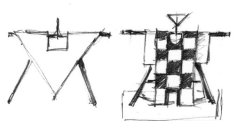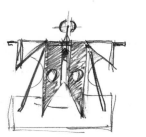

Alternative 'clothing' sketches

Preliminary sketch of pavilions on initial site

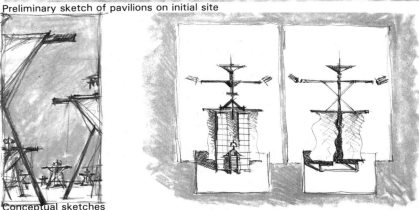

Conceptual sketches

Views of pavilion (phs Martin Charles)

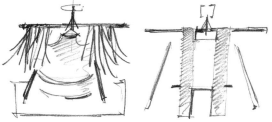

Right , View of pavilions from entrance to Tate Gallery

View of interior of working studio (ph Martin Charles)
Front elevation of model

Mark Fisher
DESIGN FOR ENTERTAINMENT

China

The Wall

The Pyramid

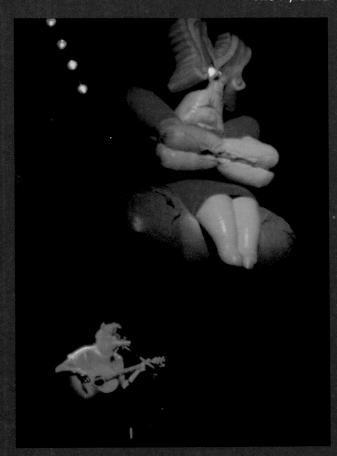

Mark Fisher
THE BRITANNIA ROW GANTRY

THE GANTRY BEGAN LIFE as a study for rebuilding a 32 m high pyramid shaped roof to cover an outdoor concert stage. At the climax of the concert the top half of the pyramid was to break loose and fly away. On a tour of America in 1975 an attempt was made to achieve this effect using a structure of American design. The attempt failed when the flying half of the structure crashed during a concert in Pittsburgh, wrecking several cars.

The new design was based around a lightweight steel gantry 18 m square, the top of which formed a dock for the helium filled flying half of the pyramid. The steelwork was designed so that it could also be erected as a stage cover capable of carrying loads of lighting and PA equipment up to 20 tonnes. In this configuration a tension membrane roof covered the pyramid dock, carried on 18 m long bow girders of 75 mm diameter steel tubes.

Prototype junctions for the helium filled inflatable tube frame of the aerostat were completed in July 1978, and the steelwork was fabricated in the same year. The project was abandoned before the aerostat was built. However, the canvas roof was completed and the gantry has been in use as a stage cover since 1979 in both the UK and Europe.

The design of the gantry was markedly different from other designs for portable stage roofs. Because of the exceptionally large wind loads it was expected to carry when used as a base for the pyramid, and the large free spans which were required, the steelwork was bound to weigh about nine tonnes. This meant that the most expedient way of getting it into the air was to use cranes. Once the presence of cranes on site was accepted, there was little advantage in making the structure from a large number of separate components individually liftable by men. By making the structure from a smaller number of large sub-assemblies the number of joints was reduced, resulting in considerable savings in weight. But, it also made the structure unusually bulky, requiring two 40 ft flatbeds to transport it.

The girder frame was assembled on the ground by an erection crew of ten men aided by two 15 tonne hydraulic cranes. The connections between sections of truss were made by bolted flange plates. After the outer frame was complete the bow girders were sprung and pinned into place. The synthetic canvas roof was lifted on in one piece using the two cranes simultaneously, and tied down by the erection crew. Working lights, rigging points and fixings for side sheets were installed when the structure was still on the ground.

The two cranes lifted the completed roof high enough for the completely assembled legs to be pinned into place at hinge joints. They then lifted it higher, the legs swinging then rolling into position on pneumatic tyred wheels fixed to their bottom ends. Once the legs were perpendicular their free corners were bolted into place and the whole structure was dropped onto prepared bases like a giant coffee table.

After the cranes were cast off, bracing stays were run to convenient positions around the structure or to various forms of mass anchorage, skips of rubble or dead men buried in the ground. Erection usually took ten to twelve hours.

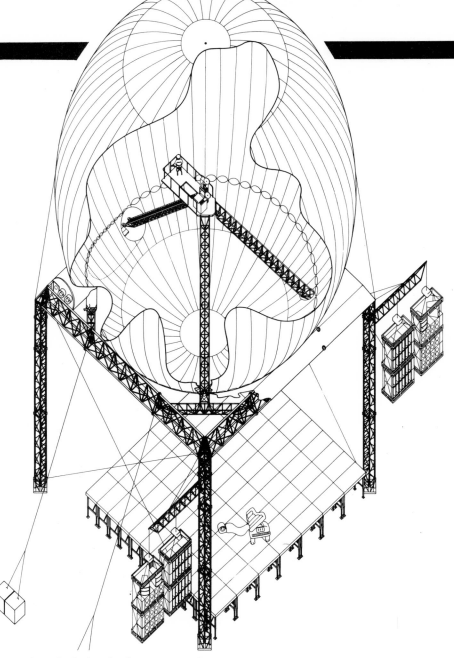

Proposal for spherical projection screen roof.
Axonometric view showing projection position.
The PA is flown in baskets from outriggers at each side of the stage.

ERECTION OF THE GANTRY:
The canvas roof is lifted into position by cranes

The completed roof at ground level before lifting

During lifting; the hinged legs are running on wheels.

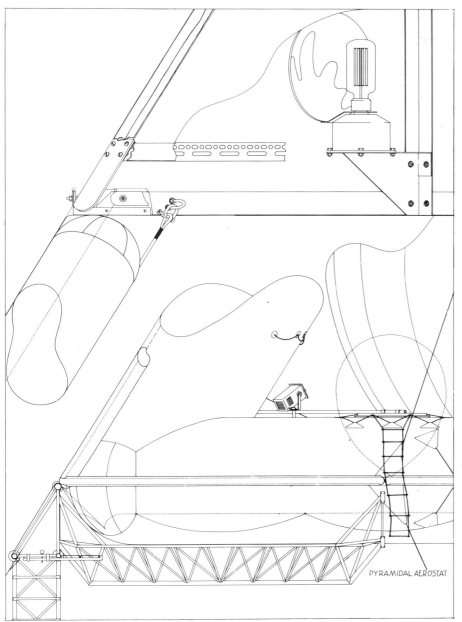

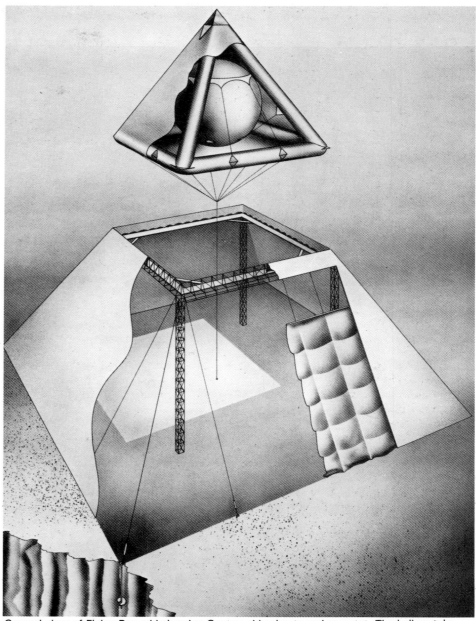

Details of the Flying Pyramid. Above; lamp house at apex. Below; corner of inflatable tube frame and gantry dock. Two sizes of inflatable tube were used to form sharper arrises.

PYRAMIDAL AEROSTAT

General view of Flying Pyramid showing Gantry, side sheets and aerostat. The helium tube frame of the aerostat was only neutrally bouyant. The spherical ballon was required to lift the cladding and provide positive bouyancy.

THE GANTRY IN USE, NURENBURG 1979:

The cranes are cast off after the legs have been set on prepared bases.

The lighting installation is flown from the main girders on chain hoists.

The Gantry is flanked by three storey PA wings dressed with shrims.

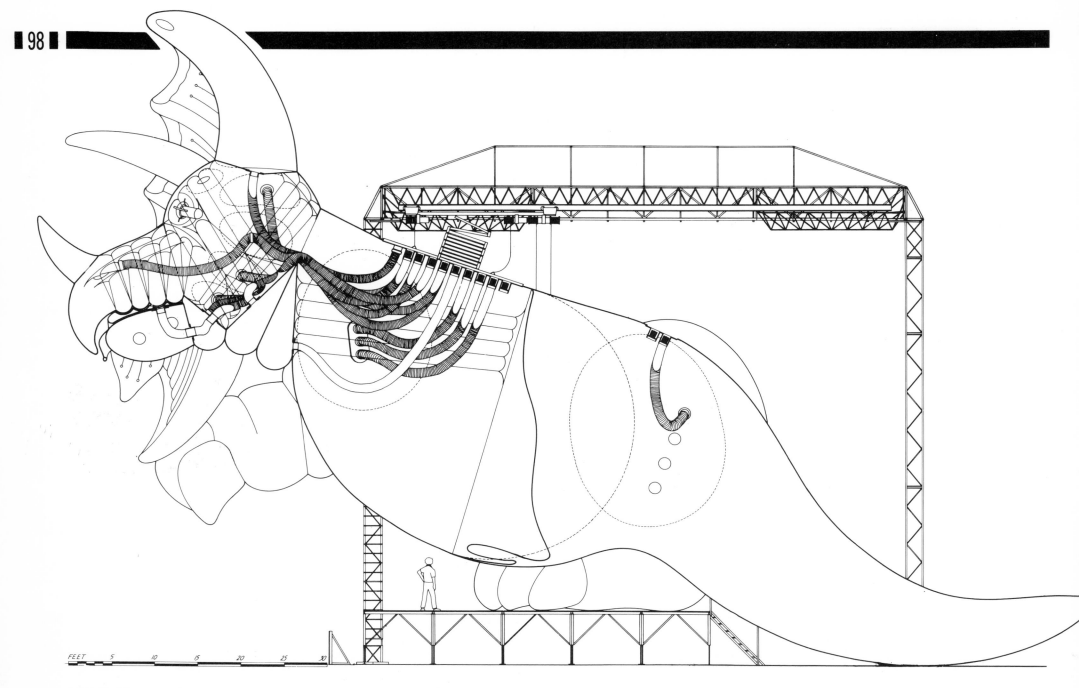

FEET 5 10 15 20 25 30

Inflatable Dinosaur project.
Section through Gantry and beast.

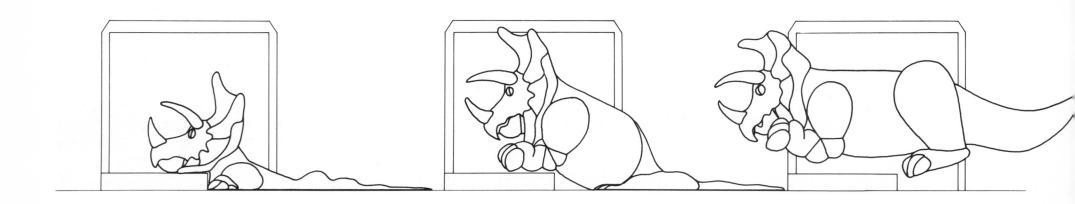

A series of projects executed in 1978 incorporated the gantry and exploited its capacity to carry heavy and unusual loads. The dinosaur explored the construction and rigging of a large inflatable puppet with limited articulation of the arms, neck and jaw. The process of simultaneously lifting and inflating the puppet was used later in puppets built for The Wall.

The Oasis Truck Stop presented popular American iconography at a scale appropriate to the arenas encountered on that continent. The drawings were done against the background of the Olympic Stadium in Montreal. The pop-out worms and waitresses on the inflatable trucks were an extension of ideas first tested in inflatables built for Pink Floyd's 'Animals' tour in 1977. The spherical screen was proposed as a display system for laser and wide-angle 70 mm projection.

CLIENT: Graeme Fleming, Brittania Row Lighting Ltd
STRUCTURAL ENGINEER: Jonathan Park

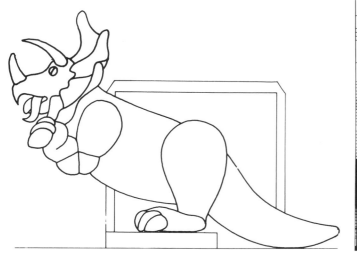

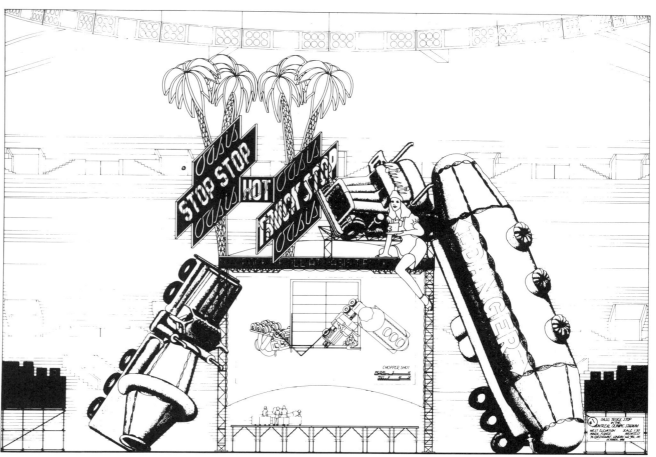

Oasis Truck Stop project.
Front elevations showing inflatable trucks, waitresses and worms

Mark Fisher
THE WALL FOR PINK FLOYD

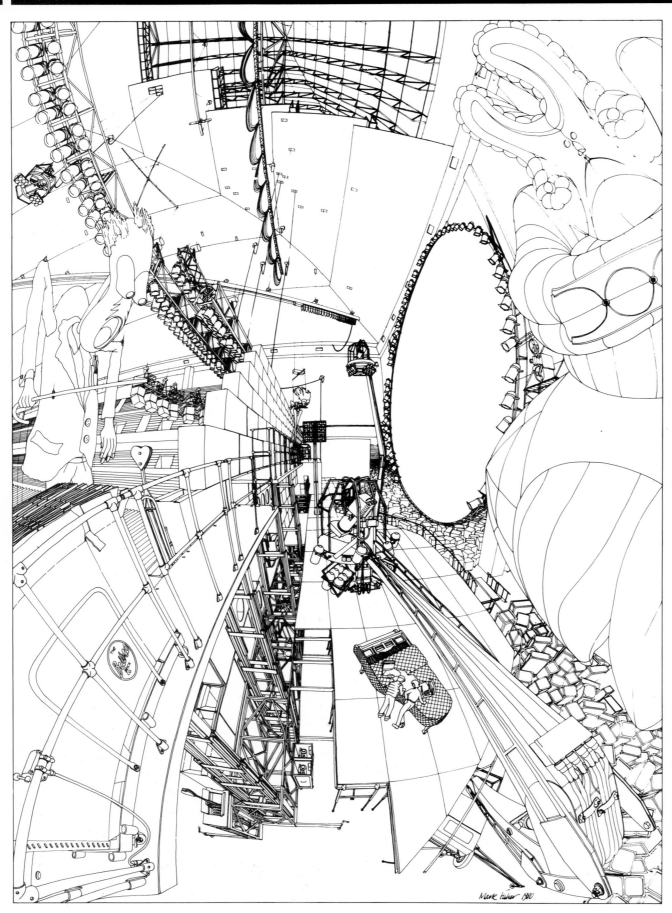

ROGER WATERS' PLAN FOR THE WALL as a live concert was well developed when work began on the design. It was first performed in Los Angeles in February 1980.

The audience entered the arena to find vestiges of a white crumbling wall emerging from the seats at each side of the stage, as if it had intruded into the arena. During the first half of the concert the 60 m wide gap between the two crumbling ramparts was filled with bricks, leaving openings at the bottom so that the band could be seen behind it. Simultaneously, 10 m high inflatable puppets appeared, sculpted from cartoon figures invented by Gerald Scarfe. The last of the 1.5×0.75 m bricks was placed on the final chord of the first half of the concert, and the return to houselights revealed a 12 m high wall stretching 70 m across the arena.

The second half of the concert began with the band concealed behind The Wall. As it progressed, Roger Waters was presented to the audience in the armchair of a *trompe l'oeil* hotel room which folded out from The Wall and Dave Gilmour appeared on top of The Wall to sing and play. Later the whole band appeared on a stage in front of The Wall. In the closing stages three synchronised projectors presented animated film on The Wall behind the band and as they left the stage The Wall toppled and fell, cued to a sound effects tape.

The concerts were designed for presentation in American style indoor arenas. Built either for ice-hockey, basketball, or sometimes both and with a five-a-side football surface for good measure, well equipped arenas of this kind can be found almost everywhere in the world except the UK. They normally run a broad mix of events on a tight schedule, putting financial pressure on rock productions to get in and out quickly. Dress rehearsal for The Wall was 30 hours after commencing load-in. The arenas offer no theatrical facilities except ample supplies of seats, electric power and crowd control!

The Wall was constructed from large interlocking bricks. Each brick was a rectangular sleeve of fire-proof dual-wall cardboard. The sleeve was open top

SKETCHES EXECUTED DURING THE DESIGN OF THE CONCERT:
Concert opening. The cardboard wall emerges from the seats at each side of the arena.

and bottom, with the top edges returned inside to form stiffening beams. Tabs at the bottom of the sleeve mated with the open top of the sleeve below, or with slots in the stage floor. The bricks packed flat for transport and were moved around the stage on trolleys.

Telescoping support columns were located beneath the stage at 3 m centres. As the bricks were placed in position the columns extended under remote control, rising up inside the sleeves to make contact with the stiffening beams and thus stabilise The Wall. Behind the support columns were five 6 m long platforms mounted on pairs of telescoping columns. These platforms lifted The Wall building crew and their bricks into the air as The Wall grew in height.

At the top of each support column was a lever. The lever was centered when The Wall was being built, and thus passed without interference through the voids in the bricks. To demolish The Wall the lever was pitched either forwards or backwards as the column was retracted. Each brick the lever passed was destabilised sufficiently for it to topple to the ground. The descent of the ten columns was syn chronised to make The Wall collapse course by

THE WALL IN LONDON
(Above) Section and rear elevation. The division of the wall into scaffolding flanks with a mechanical centre section is shown.

(Below) Plan. The wall divides the stage into a forestage and backstge. Each had a complete set of instruments and microphones. The drumkit on the forestage was set on a hydraulic lift.

Proposed construction methods. Left, from a rolling platform. Right, from hydraulic manlifts.

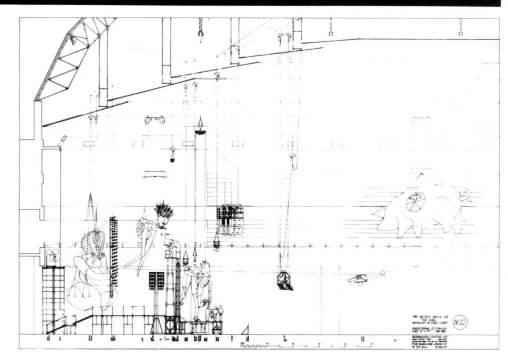

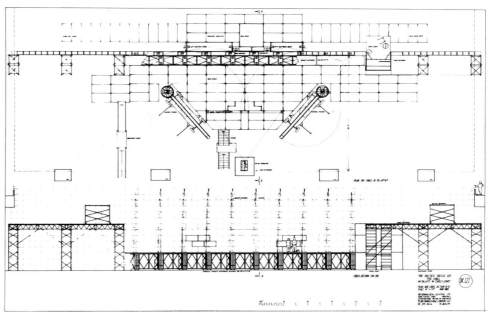

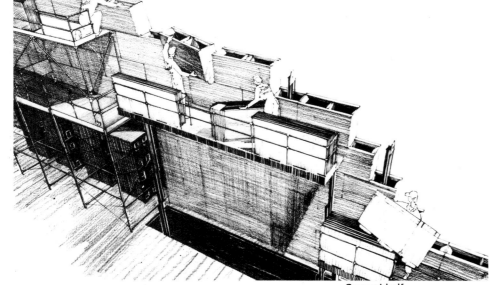

The band play on the forestage.

Second half.
Projection on the wall; inflatable hammers under the roof.

After the collapse; one of several proposed endings to the show.

Manlift sub-assembly at full extension

Manlift and support column sub-assembly.
The demolition lever on the support column is centred.

Demolition lever in knockdown position

Telescopic machinery being set on arena floor.

Demonstration collapse

Inflatable pig on 40m traveller track

Twin hydraulic columns assembled into manlift.

Twin hydraulic column crate

Demolition lever detail

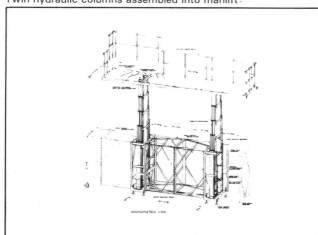

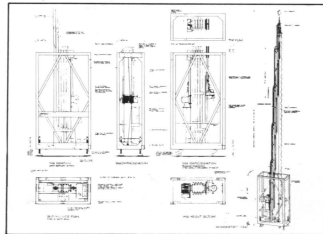

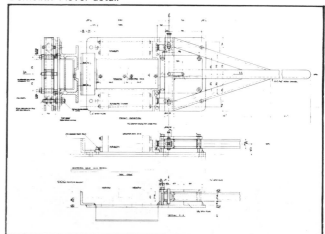

course. This made the bricks land close to the base of The Wall.

The show was transported from arena to arena in standard 40 ft air ride trailers. The mechanical parts of the telescopic columns were therefore built into crates designed to an appropriate packing module. To allow rapid transfer from the trucks to the arena each crate was mounted on heavy duty castors and fitted with pulling and lifting bars at convenient heights.

On the arena floor the crates were spaced apart by modular frames. The frames were stiffened with internal bracing arranged in a way which allowed the stage crew to step through them easily. The frames turned the telescopic machinery into a single box truss 30 m long which formed the foundation of The Wall. Lightweight decks on the upper surface formed the manlift platforms and column trapdoors. A proprietary staging system butted up to the truss leaving clear access beneath for electrical and hydraulic distribution and maintainance.

Loading in and assembling the centre wall foundation took six to eight hours. To the left and right of the centre section The Wall was constructed from bricks tied back to scaffolding. In each venue the bricks and scaffolding were tailored to fit flush to the arena seating. During the show the outer ramparts were built up by men working from platforms rolling on top of the scaffolding. When The Wall was demolished the bricks thus placed collapsed in sympathy with the centre section.

In the air above the stage, rigging to the arena roof supported lighting trusses and pods, drapes, screens, traveller tracks for the inflatables, and several tons of PA equipment. To facilitate installation and maintenance each item was supported by one or more precisely located chain hoists. More than 60 hoists were attached to the roof structure of each arena by elaborate bridles of steel cables.

The show was transported in 13 trailers, including one trailer entirely filled with 2,000 bricks weighing 11 kg each.

DIRECTOR AND SCRIPTWRITER: Roger Waters
ART DIRECTION: Gerald Scarfe
ARCHITECTURE AND INFLATABLES: Mark Fisher
STRUCTURAL ENGINEER: Jonathan Park
LIGHTING DESIGN: Marc Brickman

Support column crate

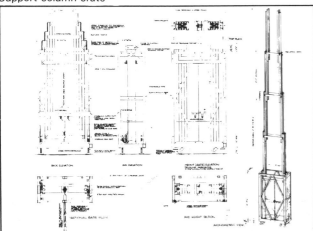

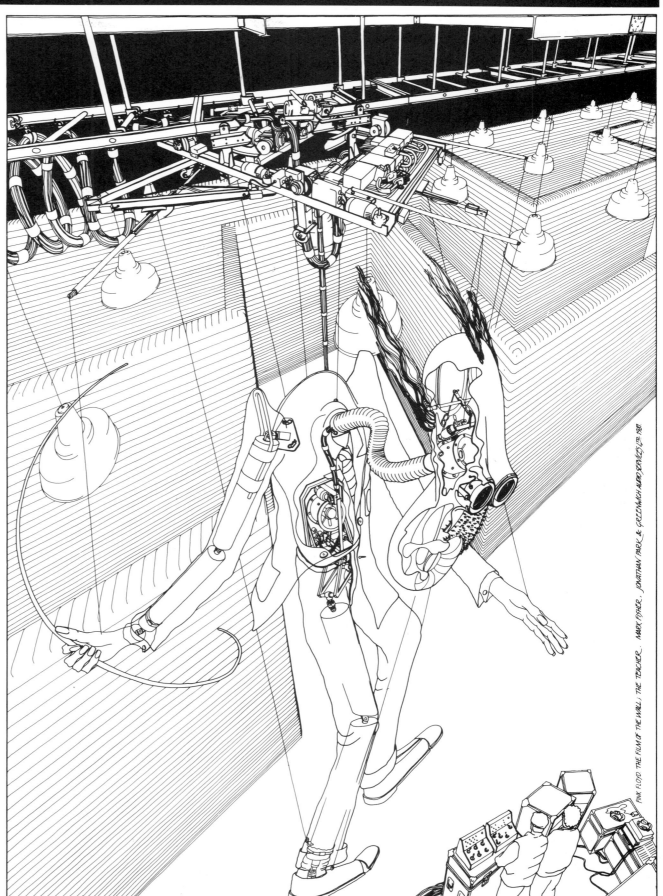

PINK FLOYD: THE FILM OF THE WALL; THE TEACHER. MARK FISHER, JONATHAN PARK & GREENBACH AUDIO SERVICES LTD 1981

Mark Fisher

Sketch of proposed outdoor concert in Shanghai Football Stadium. The design incorported a billboard upon which custom-designed posters were to be constantly changed during the concert.

JEAN-MICHEL JARRE is a composer and producer who creates music using only computers and electronic synthesizers. He performs his music on a range of equipment. Some of it is commercially available, and some of it is specially built.

Since the general thawing of attitudes towards the West in the 1970s, Chinese radio has broadcast a limited amount of contemporary Western music, including most of Jarre's repertoire. A small amount of Western popular music is also available on disc and tape, although it is so expensive that few Chinese people can afford to buy it.

In 1980 Jarre visited China to lecture and to demonstrate electronic music at the Conservatoires of Peking and Shanghai. The interest this aroused led to an invitation from the Chinese Bureau of Culture for him to return to China and present more formal concerts of his music. The concerts were to be the first live performances of Western popular music ever presented in the People's Republic of China. Jarre's previous concert experience included a huge free concert given at the Place de la Concorde in Paris in 1977, during which several million people crowded into the streets to hear his music. He wanted the concerts in China to take place in urban spaces of similar size in both Peking and Shanghai, to make his music accessible to as many people as possible.

The staff at the Chinese Bureau of Culture responded with interest to the

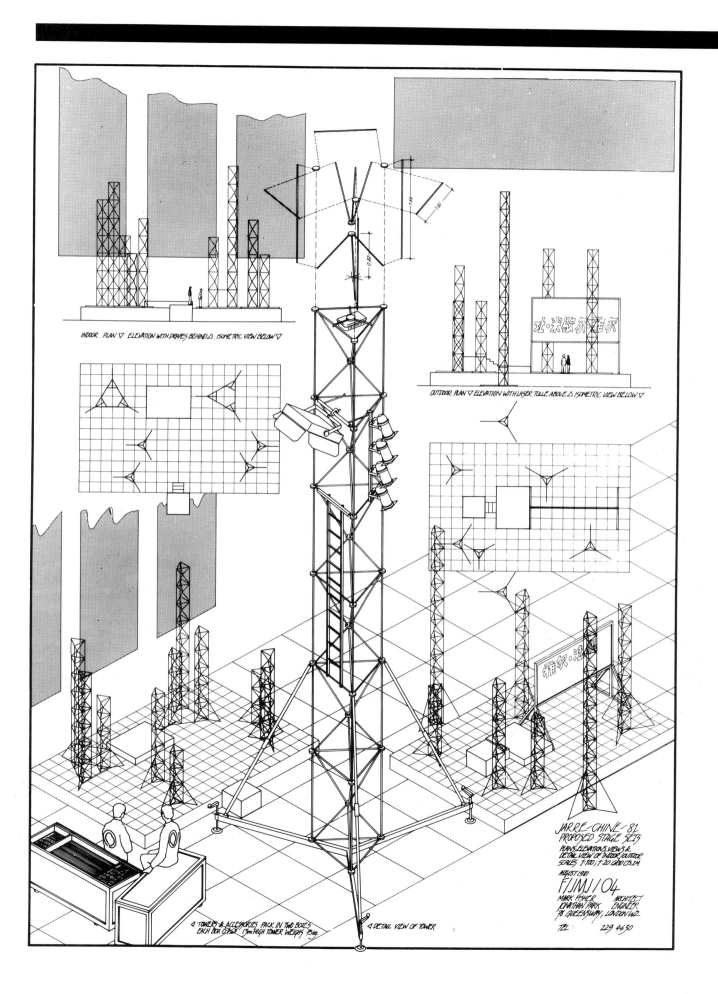

INDOOR. PLAN ▽ ELEVATION WITH DRAPES BEHIND △ ISOMETRIC VIEW BELOW ▽

OUTDOOR. PLAN ▽ ELEVATION WITH LASER TULLE ABOVE △ ISOMETRIC VIEW BELOW ▽

北・米歐尔雅沢

雅沢・・

JARRE - CHINE - 81
PROPOSED STAGE SETS

PLANS, ELEVATIONS, VIEWS &
DETAIL VIEW OF INDOOR /OUTDOOR
SCALES 1:100, 1:20 GRID IS 1M

AUGUST 1981

F/JMJ/04

MARK FISHER   ARCHITECT
JONATHAN PARK   ENGINEER
78 QUEENSWAY, LONDON W2

TEL: 229 4630

◁ TOWERS & ACCESSORIES PACK IN TWO BOXES
EACH BOX 0.75 x 2. 15m HIGH TOWER WEIGHS 75kg.

◁ DETAIL VIEW OF TOWER

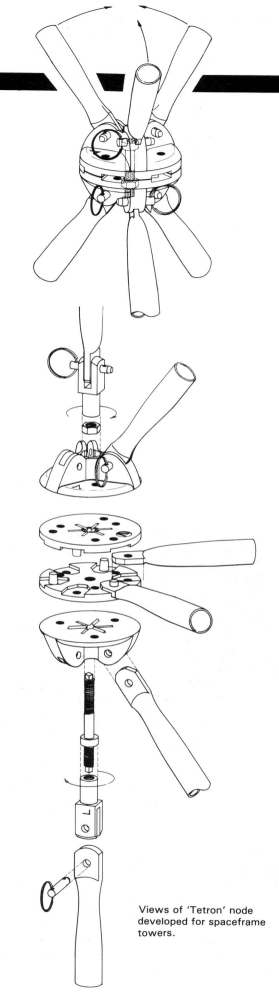

Views of 'Tetron' node
developed for spaceframe
towers.

Sketch of proposed outdoor concert, Shanghai Football Stadium. The stage was placed in the middle of the field. A black gauze for projected laser effects was suspended between two lighting towers.

Sketch of proposed indoor concert, Shanghai Municipal Gymnasium.

Chinese workers assembling spaceframe towers.

technological paraphernalia which customarily accompanies rock concerts of that size. But at the same time, faced with such a novel situation, they were determined to maintain strict control of the audience. They knew that this would be achieved most easily by restricting the concerts to small sports arenas. After a year of difficult negotiations Jarre agreed to perform the concerts in two indoor arenas, one seating 18,000, the other 12,000, and one football stadium seating about 60,000. The football stadium concert was cancelled after the production team arrived in China.

In spite of their strict control of the presentation of the concerts, the Chinese Bureau of Culture did not plan to bear much of the production cost. It was met instead by the sale of film rights in the West. Although the Chinese wanted to see the full splendour of a Western rock concert, such a production, even when filmed in China, would be of little interest to Western TV viewers. A comprehensive graphic design programme was undertaken to establish an image comprehensible to both the Chinese and Western audiences. To the Chinese it described the arrival of foreigners with magical synthesized music in the literal style of their contemporary graphic art: to Western viewers it presented a strong, unfamiliar and slightly exotic image.

The technical specification for the concerts created logistical problems. Most Western rock bands travelling in the Far East carry only their musical instruments with them. Sound and lighting equipment is rented locally and the concerts are often visually less ambitious than productions in Europe or America. For Jarre's concerts, all the equipment was transported from Europe except a few loudspeakers which were rented in Hong Kong. After creating a minimal lighting design and selecting the most compact and lightweight equipment, a point was reached where the mass of freight could only be reduced by leaving stuff out. The equipment making up the inflexible core of the show weighed 15½ tonnes. Any opportunity for savings in freight costs lay in the design of the stage set into which the equipment would be incorporated.

The set was formed by a group of tall free-standing aluminium towers. The synthesizers stood at the bases of the towers whilst heavy loads of lights, cables, and occasional engineers hung from the top. The towers had to be as light and compact as possible when travelling. This was achieved by designing them as space frames in which the longest bars were 1.6 m long. No existing system could be found which combined sufficiently light weight with known structural performance, rapid assembly and even faster disassembly. Jonathan Park invented a system using custom cast aluminium nodes connected to mass produced aluminium tubes with fastpins. The tension rods clipped into right and left hand threaded clevises which screwed onto the studs which held the mating parts of the node together. The tension was set using torque wrenches with custom heads which engaged directly on the clevises. Working under supervision a crew of eight Chinese assistants assembled the towers in five hours.

The tallest towers stood 13 m high and weighed 75 kg. The whole stage set, which included additional rigging and effects for the outdoor concerts, and a set of 3 m high aluminium and canvas screens, packed into two boxes weighing 200 kg each and accounted for only 5% of the gross shipping weight of the production.

DIRECTOR: Jean-Michel Jarre   STRUCTURAL ENGINEER: Jonathan Park
PRODUCER: Francis Dreyfus   GRAPHIC DESIGN: Kate Hepburn
LIGHTING DESIGN: Gerald Lafosse

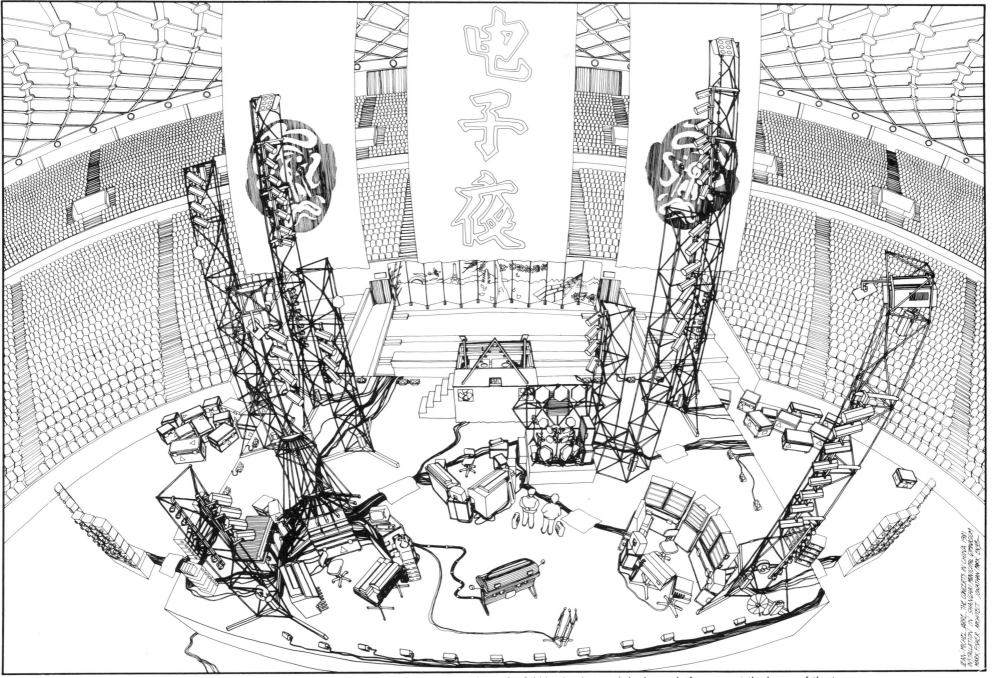

View of stage set, Shanghai Municipal Gymnasium. The positions of the four synthesizer musicians, the fold-back mixer and the laser platform are at the bases of the towers

Renton Howard Wood Levin Partnership
OFFICE BLOCK, 250 EUSTON ROAD, LONDON

THE OFFICE BUILDING, completed in August, 1981 after a twenty-two month construction programme, has a gross area of approximately 209,000 square feet, made up of general office space, leisure facilities, a cafe and a public house.

It consists of two separate blocks. The higher, street perimeter block is mirror-glass clad and provides a barrier against traffic noise for the square and housing. The three-storey low block is brick clad to relate to the housing in scale and materials and completes the fourth side of the square with housing on the other three sides. The two blocks are linked by a glass barrel-vault roofed arcade.

The high block has three wings served by two circulation cores designed so that the east wing may be let off separately from the rest of the building. The west, Hampstead Road wing has office accommodation in the basement in addition to that on the other levels. The central, Euston Road wing has parking for 36 cars in the basement and office accommodation on the ground and six upper levels with plant rooms at seventh floor level. The east, North Gower Street wing has parking for 34 cars in the basement and office accommodation on the ground and five upper levels.

The low block incorporates the leisure centre on the two basement levels and the cafe and public house at ground floor level. Office accommodation is provided on the ground and two upper levels. Entrance to the leisure centre is on the ground floor level with access down its own staircase to the gymnasium, three squash courts and their related viewing gallery and changing rooms. As the centre is to be used by office workers during working hours, there is a separate entrance from the office area. In the evenings and at week-ends, the centre will be open to members of the public.

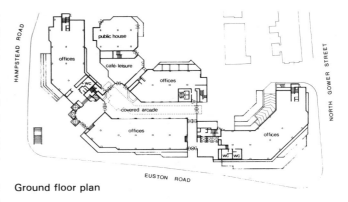

Ground floor plan

PROJECT TEAM: G Levin, G Mann, J Tebbutt and L Broer
STRUCTURAL ENGINEERS: Ove Arup and Partners
QUANTITY SURVEYORS: Gardiner & Theobald
M & E ENGINEERS: Matthew Hall Mechanical Services Limited
M & E CONSULTANTS. Rybka, Smith & Ginsler
M & E QUANTITY SURVEYOR: Mott, Green & Wall

View of office block from Euston Road

John S Bonnington Partnership
SALMIYA ISLAND AQUARIUM AND DOLPHINARIUM, KUWAIT

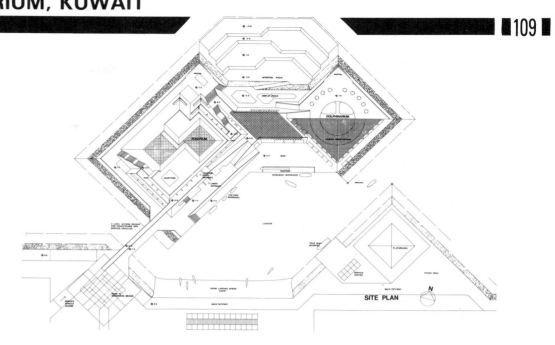

DIRECTLY OFFSHORE from the Salmiya district of Kuwait is a narrow underwater shelf suitable for building an island. It is therefore proposed to construct the aquarium on a purpose-built island approximately 20,000 m² and 50 metres from the coastline.

The aquarium will be an educational as well as leisure facility and includes a 200-seat auditorium and a library/study centre. The superstructure is an *in situ* reinforced concrete frame on the 6-metre planning grid.

The internal public areas of the aquarium are designed to give the illusion of descending into the sea. The visitor first enters one of the pyramid spaces which contains the shoreline exhibit. In the centre of the second pyramid shape is the main spectacle of the aquarium; the reef tank. This is the largest tank in the building (8 m diameter × 11 m deep). It will have a central simulated reef and will contain large and gregarious fish species. The visitor will descend by a helical ramp around the reef tank as if he were descending into the sea.

The public display of the dolphinarium consists of a kidney-shaped show pool and two circular holding pools. A glazed wall to the front of the show pool permits underwater viewing.

CLIENT: Municipality of the Government of Kuwait
STRUCTURAL ENGINEERS: Harris and Sutherland
BUILDING SERVICES & INTERIOR DESIGN: John S Bonnington Partnership

SITE PLAN

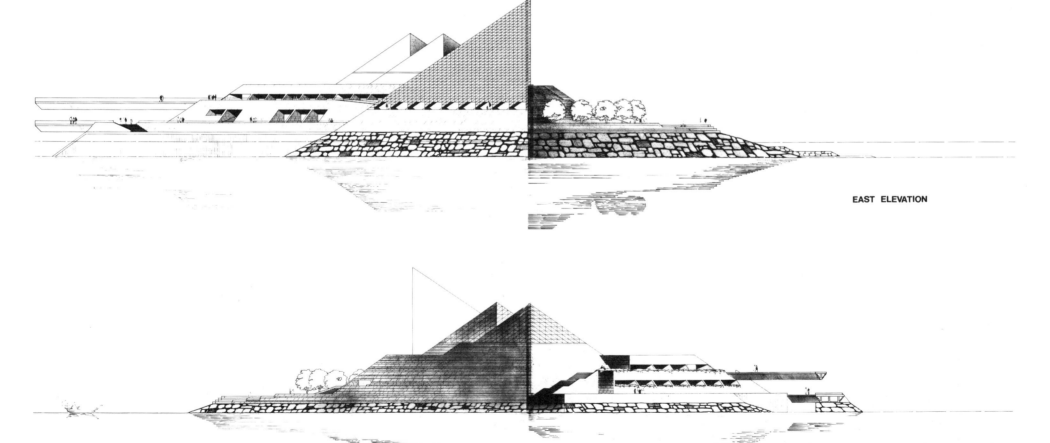

EAST ELEVATION

WEST ELEVATION

Powell Moya & Partners
INTERNATIONAL CONFERENCE CENTRE, WESTMINSTER

THE INTERNATIONAL CONFERENCE CENTRE is being built on the north half of Broad Sanctuary—a site vacant for nearly 50 years. The brief includes three independent conference areas:
— an auditorium for 700, press/public gallery, full SI and projection facilities, with separate secretariat and foyer/lounge space;
— a main conference suite, with rooms for 450, 225, 60 and 60, full SI facilities, related offices, lounges for delegates and interpreters and a VIP dining room;
— a separate high-level conference room for 200 with full SI and projection facilities, offices and lounge.

CLIENT: Property Services Agency
ARCHITECT: Powell Moya & Partners with PSA (DCA)
MANAGEMENT CONTRACTOR: Bovis Construction Ltd.

East elevation   Photomontage of proposed building on site

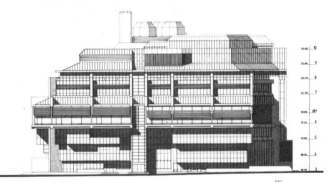

The Law & Dunbar-Nasmith Partnership
PITLOCHRY FESTIVAL THEATRE, SCOTLAND

ATHEATRE with a raked auditorium on a steeply sloping site has to be designed in section as much as in plan. The public entrance leads into the foyer, which in turn leads into the 540 seat auditorium at the crossover aisle to emerge once more at ground level. The views from the site to the north are spectacular by any standards, and the positioning of the theatre and the design of the foyer have been carefully considered to take full advantage of these.

STRUCTURAL ENGINEERS: Ove Arup & Partners
QUANTITY SURVEYORS: James D Gibson & Simpson
SERVICES ENGINEERS: John C R Pearce
CONTRACTOR: J Fraser Construction Ltd
THEATRE CONSULTANTS: John Wyckham Associates

Level 1 and 2 plans   View of theatre from the Tummel River

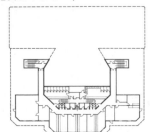 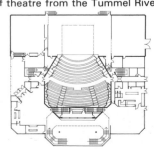

Jeremy & Caroline Gould
MILLFIELD LIBARY AND RESOURCES CENTRE, SOMERSET

North elevation (ph John Donat)

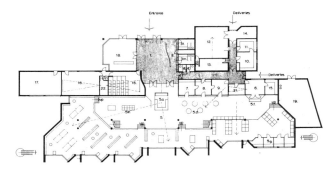

Ground and lower floor plan

Aerial view of model

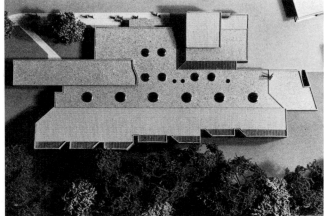

THE BUILDING WAS 'ON SITE' in November 1978 and was completed in March, 1980. The brief divides into four main areas:
— the Library Hall for 35,000 books, 42 carrels and 200 table spaces with librarian's offices and a Programme Preparation Room;
— Audio-Visual Centre with a TV Studio and Recording and Distribution Room;
— two Viewing Rooms, one with a raked floor, with projection box and a spare classroom defined in the brief as 'spare space' to become an extension to the library if required;
— Entrance Hall, WCs and Bookshop.

It was clear to us that the new building had to make a definite statement so that it could become 'the new centre of school activities' that the brief demanded. Thus we put the building parallel to the Butleigh Road and the form of the building 'stacks' up in horizontal layers towards the north against the trees. From the north, the building steps forward and upward forming a massive wall leading to the school entrance. On the south, horizontal forms are exaggerated emphasising the length of the site. On the north, the verticals are emphasised and the scale is larger, designed to be seen through the trees.

CLIENT: Millfield School
STRUCTURAL ENGINEERS: Clarke Nicholls & Marcel
QUANTITY SURVEYORS: Jeffreys & Vaughan
SERVICES ENGINEERS: Ewbank Design Partnership
MAIN CONTRACTOR: Melhuish & Saunders Ltd

View of main entrance (ph John Donat)
Interior of entrance hall looking west (ph John Donat)

Arup Associates
BAB AL SHEIKH DEVELOPMENT, BAGHDAD

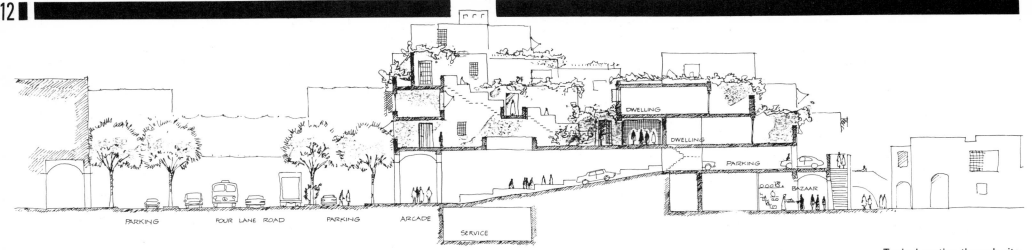

PARKING   FOUR LANE ROAD   PARKING   ARCADE   SERVICE

Typical section through site

IN MARCH 1981 Arup Associates won a design competition for a commercial and housing development in Baghdad, Iraq. They were appointed together with the runners-up Carlfried Mutschler & Partner of Mannheim, Germany, to proceed with the detailed design in order to commence construction in January 1982.

The site adjoins a new road that will bisect the conservation area of Bab Al Sheikh and the historic Al Gaylani mosque which is located close to the centre of Baghdad.

The proposal is to create an urban boulevard that would provide the opportunity for commercial activities to develop on both sides of the new road and to integrate housing into the scheme at upper levels. At a central point along the road, a pedestrian bridge incorporating shopping will link the site to the mosque in order to re-establish some continuity to the conservation area. The street facade is to be a double wall that will form a continuous arcade at ground floor level and provide additional rooms and terraces to the housing above. It will be the organising element that will give a cohesion and special identity to the new street.

The Arup scheme has incorporated an eight storey building that relates to the existing building around Al Kilhany Square at the southern end of the site. This building has a large central vaulted space around which the office accommodation is placed. Shops, a cinema and some sporting facilities occupy the lower levels and the rear of the site. The bulk of the development consists of shops and offices on two lower levels and stepped courtyard housing varying in height from six to two stories across the depth of the site. The 175 housing units are planned on a structural module of 5 metre bays with service zones every 25 metres. The central bridge link will incorporate a public square and relate to a large shopping facility on the site designed by Carlfreid Mutschler. Additional shopping and housing will be planned into the Mutschler scheme behind the double street facade wall.

CLIENT: Amanat al Asima
ENGINEERS: Arup Associates
QUANTITY SURVEYORS: Arup Associates

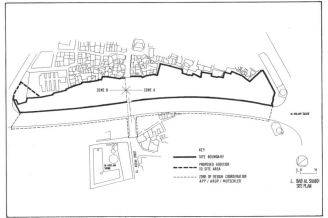

Site plan — conceptual principles

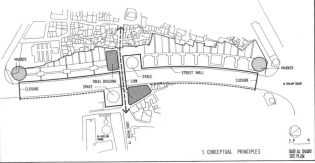

Site plan showing boundary of new scheme
Climate control diagram

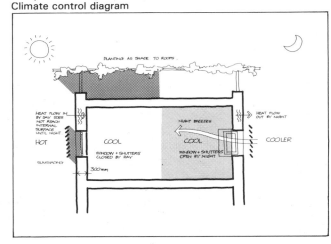

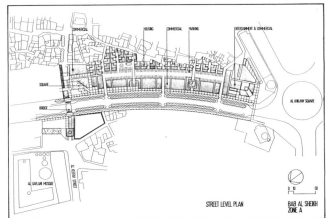

Co-ordinating section

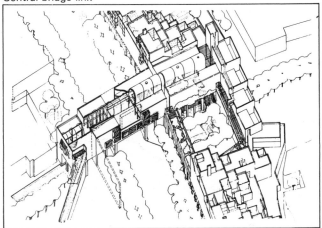

Street level plan
Central bridge link

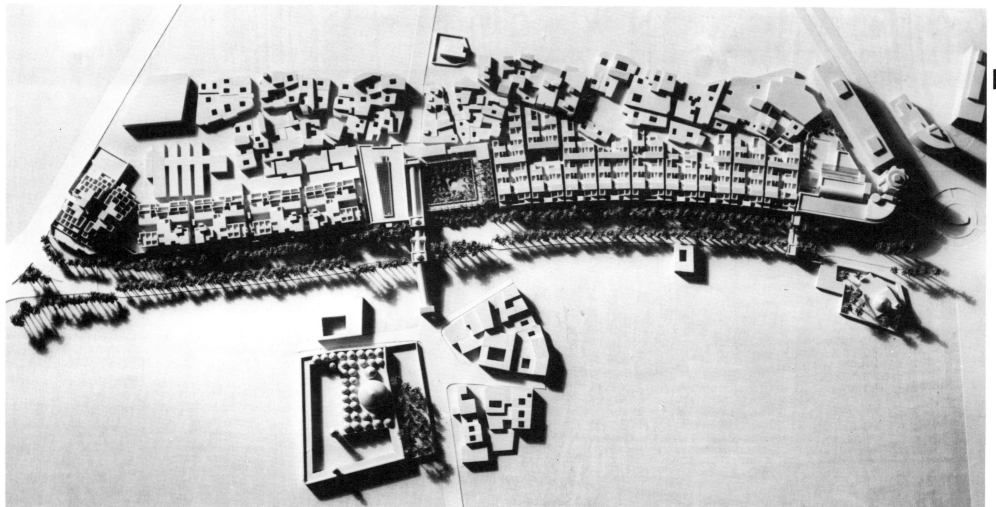

Development model

BEDFORD SCHOOL RENOVATION

ON THE NIGHT of 3/4 March 1979 the Bedford School Main Building was largely destroyed by fire. During the same month Arup Associates were appointed as architects for the restoration or rebuilding of the Main Building, including the Great Hall, approximately 31 classrooms, three staff rooms and five offices.

The original building designed by EC Robins was completed in 1892, and is a listed Grade II historic building. Apart from the staircases and their associated rooms and lobbies at the east and west ends of the building, the fire damage was extensive and the only reusable elements of the building were the external brick walls and a few of the internal walls. Two important considerations weighed heavily against reconstruction. Firstly consent would be required for demolition, and secondly a large part of Bedford School's history and tradition has been associated with this significant building and should be maintained. It was therefore agreed that work should proceed on the renovation of the main building.

The only major change on the exterior is on the south elevation where a porch (incorporating a reading room at first floor level) is added to form the new entrance from the School quadrangle. It is constructed in brick and stone with a large arched opening to match the north-east and west gables, and provide architectural emphasis and interest to the south facade. All the detailing matches the original so that it appears as a contiguous part of the Main Building. The renovations were completed and the School ready for occupation by September 1981.

CLIENT: Harpur Trust
ENGINEERS: Arup Associates
QUANTITY SURVEYORS: Arup Associates
CONTRACTOR: Laing Management Contractors Ltd

Burnt out interior

South elevation (ph Crispin Boyle)

Assembly hall after renovation (Crispin Boyle)

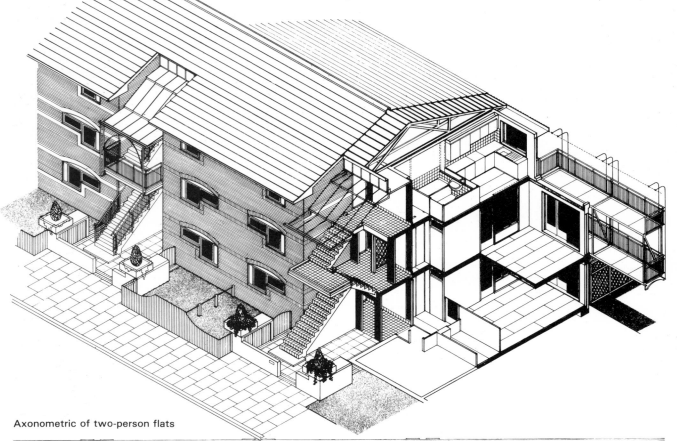

Axonometric of two-person flats

THE **PLANNING BRIEF**, based on the newly amended mandates of the Greater London Development Plan, required housing to be built to a density of 100 habitable rooms per acre, resulting in the following mix of dwelling types; 72 two-person, one-bedroomed flats; 9 three-person, two-bedroomed flats; 14 four-person, two-bedroomed houses; 12 five-person, three-bedroomed houses. This gives a total number of 107 dwellings. In addition:

— Emphasis on two-person dwelling to redress the under provision in the overall Highgate New Town redevelopment area, with a minimum of 50% being for elderly people.

— Balmore and Doynton Streets to be closed at their junctions with Dartmouth Park Hill.

— All family dwellings to be located at ground level (in compliance with D of E recommendations) with back to back garden layouts where possible.

— Dwellings to be designed with brick external walls and pitched roofs.

The three-storey block containing the flats runs from north to south along Dartmouth Park Hill and was conceived as a building presenting two faces. The public entrance side which describes the curved linear nature of the street is modulated to suggest a series of repeating villas, an illusion of individual houses. The private side is orientated into the site with large windows and balconies which clip onto the flat facade.

CLIENT: London Borough of Camden
PROJECT TEAM: Sidney Meades, Bill Forrest and Oscar Palacio
STRUCTURAL ENGINEER: Ove Arup & Partners
QUANTITY SURVEYOR: Oswald E Parratt & Partners
SERVICES ENGINEER: Pell Frischmann & Partners
MAIN CONTRACTOR: J Murphy & Sons Ltd
CONSULTANT ARCHITECTS: Colin St John Wilson & Partners
STRUCTURAL ENGINEERS: Ove Arup & Partners
QUANTITY SURVEYORS: Davis Belfield & Everest
MECHANICAL ENGINEERS: Steensen Varming Mulcahy
                & Partners

West elevation of A2 block
Site plan

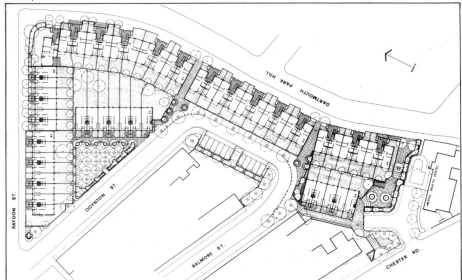

Floor plans for two, three, four and five person houses and flats

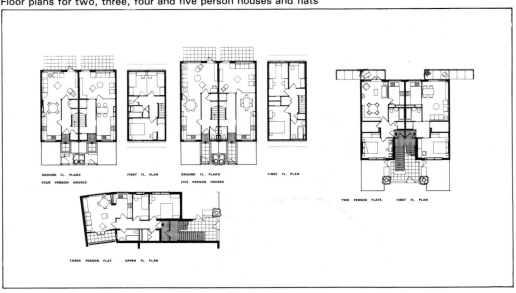

East elevation of two-person flats from Dartmouth Park Hill
(ph Martin Charles, courtesy *Architects' Journal*)

Left: Footpath between A^2 and A^1 block from Doynton Street
(ph Martin Charles, courtesy *AJ*)

West elevation of two-person flats
(ph Martin Charles, courtesy *AJ*)

A$_3$ block, two-person flats from Dartmouth Park Hill

Doynton Street from Raydon Street
(ph Martin Charles, courtesy *AJ*)

De Blacam & Meagher
NATIONAL PEAT MUSEUM, DUBLIN

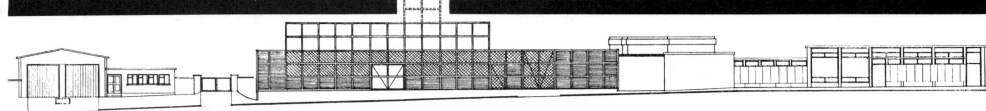

Street elevation

THE BRIEF WAS TO PROVIDE an industrial and archaeological museum to show and explain the history, development and future proposals for the peat bogs in Ireland. The museum consists of four sections: Natural History; Archaeology; Industrial History and Conservation together with office accommodation for district staff, with a total floor area of approximately 1,000 m².

The concept of the display is the contrast of the natural objects and plant material set in daylight against glass and perforated metal. Thus, the exterior walls consist of steel framed clear glazing, glass block and brickwork while the internal walls are designed in such a way as to be an integral part of the exhibition itself. They consist of painted, perforated steel pivoting wall panels and 'glass cases' ('occupiable double glazing').

STRUCTURAL ENGINEERS: Ove Arup & Partners
QUANTITY SURVEYORS: Seamus Monahan & Partners
MECHANICAL ENGINEERS: Varming Mulcahy Reilly Associates

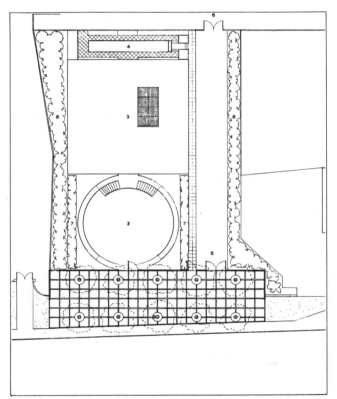

Site plan

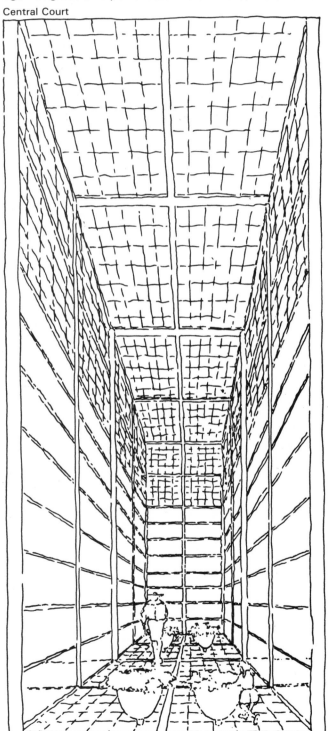

Central Court

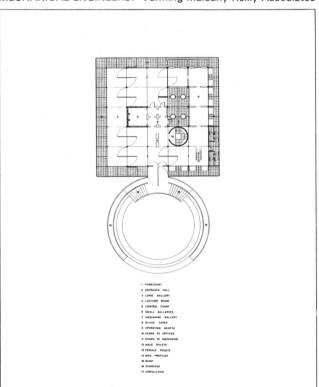

Plan

1 FORECOURT
2 ENTRANCE HALL
3 LONG GALLERY
4 LECTURE ROOM
5 CENTRAL COURT
6 SMALL GALLERIES
7 MEZZANINE GALLERY
8 GLASS CASES
9 OPERATING HEARTH
10 STAIRS TO OFFICES
11 STAIRS TO MEZZANINE
12 MALE TOILETS
13 FEMALE TOILETS
14 BOG PROFILES
15 RAMP
16 STAIRCASE
17 CIRCULATION

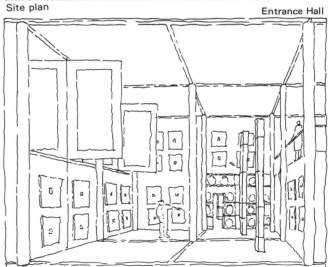

Entrance Hall

Glass Cases

Edward Jones & Margot Griffin
ARCHIVES BUILDING FOR KARL FRIEDRICH SCHINKEL, BERLIN

ADJACENT TO THE CHARLOTTENBURG PALACE and its gardens, the site is conspicuous in its relationship to a series of historic axes, thereby prompting the perennial distinction between monument and city fabric and ideas concerning gateway or the rhetorical entrance to the 19th-century city.

The building is programmatically small (2,000 m²) in comparison with the metropolitan improvements associated with its ambitious context. It is to contain architectural archives, a gallery, a theatre and an 'architectural' garden. This is to serve as a memorial to Schinkel and his School and also to act as a live museum for the city of Berlin.

Five obvious and interrelated architectural typologies are proposed along the axis—a columned portico (entrance to the theatre and palace grounds)—a circular theatre (lectures for 120 people and for larger audiences)—a square pavilion (museum)—a winter garden (cafe and expanded exhibitions)—a linear and cellular building (archives). The building programme and the 'architectural' garden have been combined as: 1 water garden (as a space between the Schinkel Pavilion and the archives), 2 winter garden (forming the referential space between the museum and the archives), 3 roof garden approached by a grand public staircase. The belvedere within the roof garden finally gives visual connections to the local district.

Sectional isometric

Site axonometric

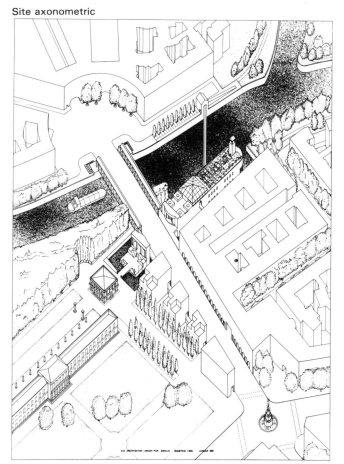

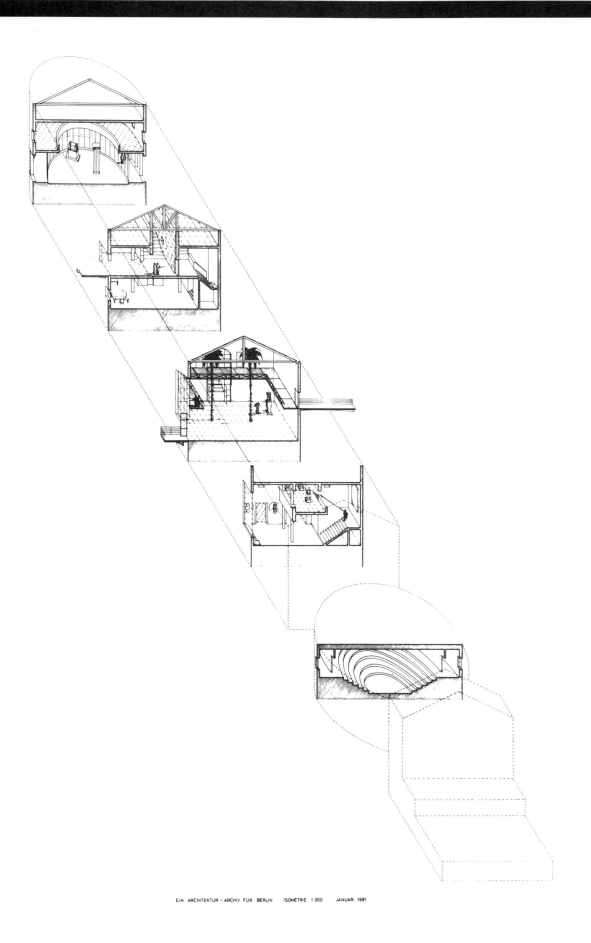

EIN ARCHITEKTUR - ARCHIV FÜR BERLIN   ISOMETRIE 1:200   JANUAR 1981

Colin St John Wilson & Partners

ADMINISTRATIVE BUILDING FOR ABBEY NATIONAL BUILDING SOCIETY, MILTON KEYNES

Views of Model

THIS PROPOSAL WAS SUBMITTED in a limited competition for a building to house part of the Central Administrative functions of the Abbey National Building Society on a 6.2 acre site in central Milton Keynes.

The accommodation was to provide for 500 staff initially in an office area of approximately 7,000 m², a computer function of 3,250 m² and a staff restaurant and plant area of an additional 1,850 m². Expansion space was planned for 6,500 m² of training facilities, deeds storage, and printing works.

The building is prominently sited on raised ground, fronting to the east onto the main axis of the town centre (Midsummer Boulevard) and, to the south, Grafton Gate which is clearly visible from the railway station.

Four intentions determined the building form. Firstly it is inflected in order to address itself to approach from the two main fronts (east and south). Secondly, the undulating facade would introduce a curve into Milton Keynes for a change. Thirdly, this sculptural form is reinforced by the use of brick wall-mass to contrast with the faceless 'packing-case' architecture surrounding it. Fourthly, the building advertises its identity by means of the pyramidal roof, (recalling the familiar Abbey National symbol) which sits on the Staff Common Room.

The need for energy conservation and the desire to open up the building to its country setting led to a building form which mixes natural with mechanical ventilation, natural light with 'topping-up' from artificial sources, and only the Computer Suite is fully sealed and air-conditioned. The result was predicted to effect a 50% reduction in energy consumption when compared with the conventional deep plan fully air-conditioned office building.

STRUCTURAL/MECHANICAL ENGINEERS: Ove Arup & Partners
QUANTITY SURVEYORS: Monk & Dunstone

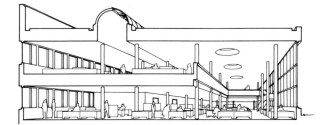

Sectional perspective

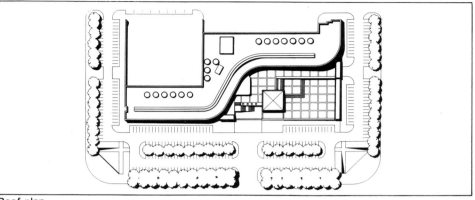

Roof plan

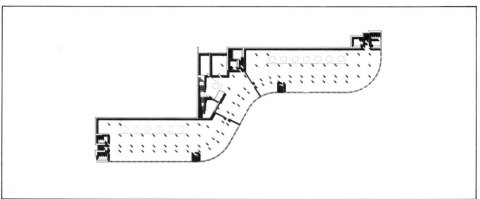

First floor plan

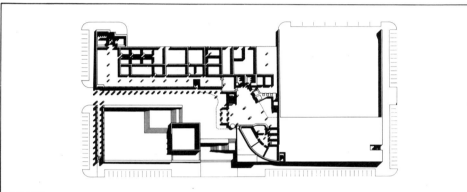

Ground floor plan

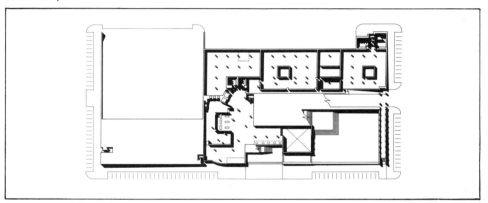

Lower ground floor plan

South elevation to Grafton Gate
East elevation to Midsummer Boulevard

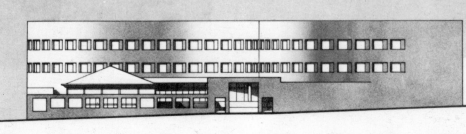

Colin St John Wilson & Ptnrs

THE BRITISH LIBRARY, EUSTON ROAD, LONDON

IN VIEW OF ITS SIZE (200,000 m²) the building is designed to be constructed in (up to seven) stages, each one technically self-sufficient and balanced as a library function: thus two ranges of building (closed-access reading rooms on the west, open-access reading rooms and library offices on the east) are connected by a common entrance hall, catalogue-room and other central shared facilities with main book-storage distribution in deep basements.

The building form is developed from these basic terms in the contextual relationship of St Pancras on

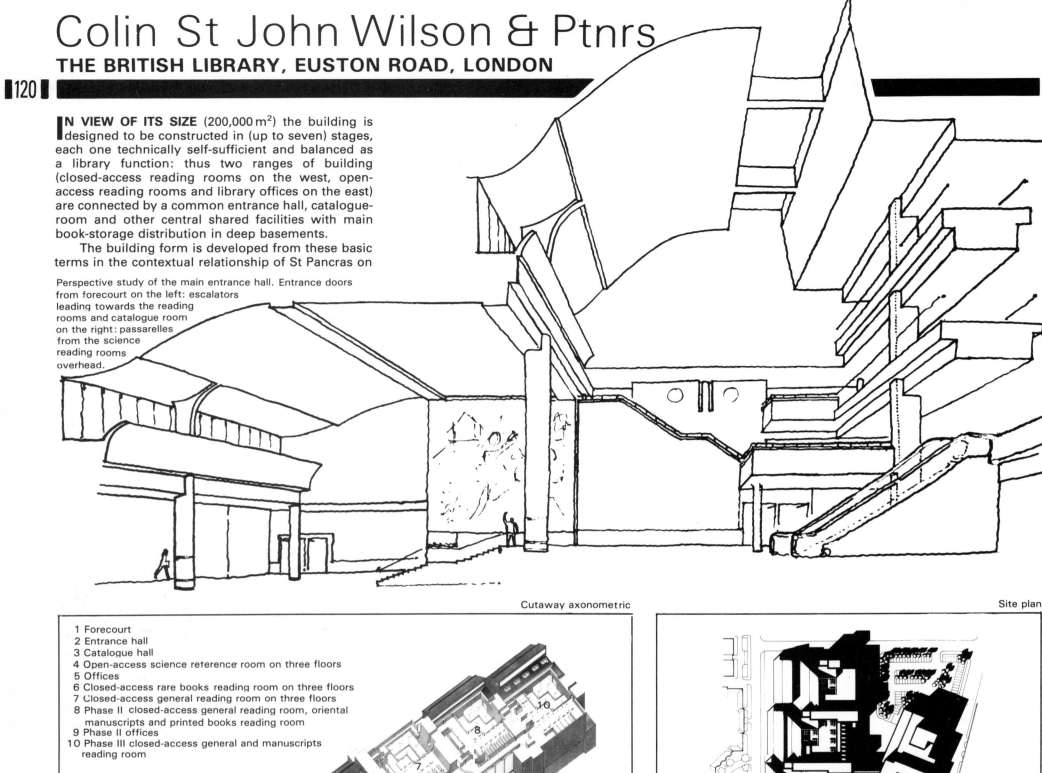

Perspective study of the main entrance hall. Entrance doors from forecourt on the left: escalators leading towards the reading rooms and catalogue room on the right: passarelles from the science reading rooms overhead.

Cutaway axonometric

1 Forecourt
2 Entrance hall
3 Catalogue hall
4 Open-access science reference room on three floors
5 Offices
6 Closed-access rare books reading room on three floors
7 Closed-access general reading room on three floors
8 Phase II closed-access general reading room, oriental manuscripts and printed books reading room
9 Phase II offices
10 Phase III closed-access general and manuscripts reading room

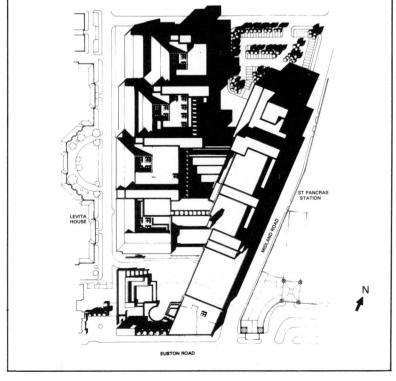

Site plan

the east and Levita House (the LCC's version of Vienna's Karl Marx Hof!) on the west with attendant planning restrictions upon building height, set-back off main entrance facade etc.

While the interior design evolves directly from the different patterns of use in readership and library services, the exterior form is necessarily less direct since it must make sense out of the dilemma of discontinuity to which any phased building is subject. (Symmetry with missing parts is a one-winged duck.)

The construction started in April of this year.

CONSULTANT ARCHITECTS: Colin St John Wilson & Partners
STRUCTURAL ENGINEERS: Ove Arup & Partners
QUANTITY SURVEYORS: Davis Belfield & Everest
MECHANICAL ENGINEERS: Steensen Varming Mulcahy & Partners

Interior of entrance hall

Pinchin & Kellow
STUDIO FLATS, ST AUBYN'S ROAD, LONDON

THIS **PROJECT** for thirty two studio flats is currently under construction in Crystal Palace, London, SE19. Completion date is February 1983.

CLIENT: Croyden Churches Housing Association
ENGINEER: Austin Trueman Associates
SERVICES: Zisman, Bowyer & Partners
CONTRACTORS: Glenlion Construction

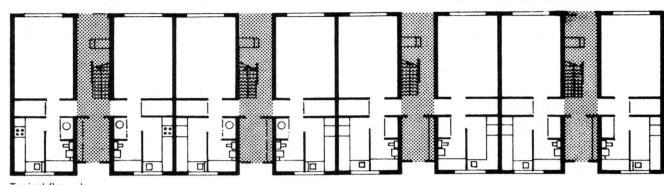

Typical floor plan

From the parts to the whole...

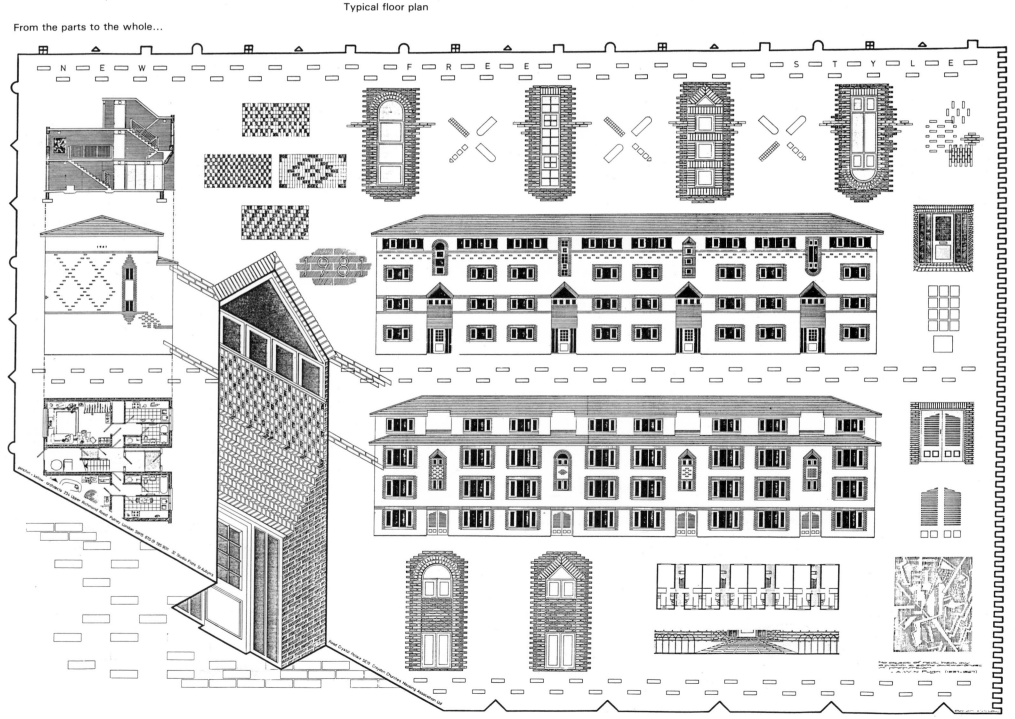

Bob Allies & Graham Morrison
READING ENTERPRISE MALTHOUSE PROJECT

THE BRIEF WAS TO PROVIDE the following features:
— a small flexible theatre space seating up to 330 people and capable of accommodating a wide variety of performances. It should also double as a television studio;
— a restaurant which could be managed separately;
— a bar with its own stage which would also serve the theatre;
— meeting rooms and rehearsal spaces;
— dressing rooms, stage and administrative spaces.

The public spaces are to be capable of operating independently from other activities in the building and as occasions demand (such as a jazz festival or children's TV programmes) flow freely from one to another so that restrictions on movement are minimised.

The Malthouse currently has an incomplete gable, resulting from an earlier adjacent demolition and it was decided to complete the fourth face of the building with a pedimented roof over the new theatre/studio space. The stairs and entrances appear externally as new elements, glazed to reveal the changed nature of the older solid structure. The spiral stair facing the canal and main road stands as a marker with its neon-banded structure and neon 'Malthouse' weather-vane.

The television monitors hung from the glazed control room over the foyer and the views from the stair and glazed lift into the major spaces enable the activities of the Malthouse to be both apparent and accessible to the casual visitor to the bar and restaurant. The controlled flexible technology of the television studio is used throughout the building and confirms the new and exciting use which the old, well-known structure has been given.

CLIENT: Reading Enterprise
PROJECT TEAM: Bob Allies, Graham Morrison,
Jim Clay and Peter Higgens

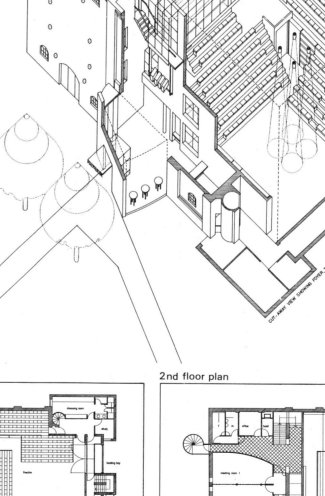

Axonometrics

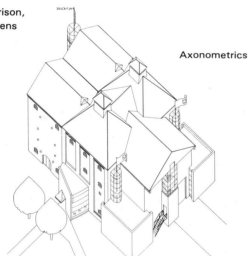

The building in context

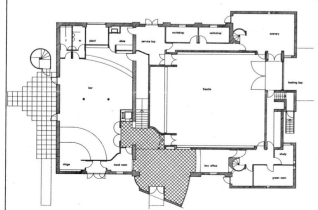

Ground floor plan

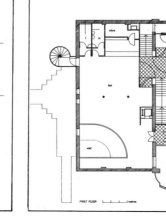

1st floor plan

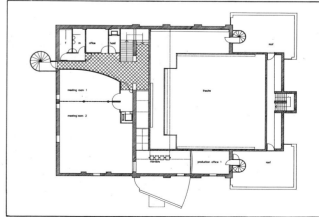

2nd floor plan

Peter Cook & Christine Hawley
LAYER CITY

The Outriders of Layer City

THIS PROJECT IS A DIRECT DEVELOPMENT of the earlier projects that involve 'meshed' and 'layered' approaches to territoriality, in particular the 'Shadow House'.

It is also to be read as directly in the line of occasional earlier 'city' projects such as 'Plug-In City' (1964–66), 'Instant City' (1968–70) and 'Arcadia' (1976–80) whereby a series of architectural inventions are deliberately set against an urban idea which is semi-realistic, semi-abstract.

The urban development suggested is pitched at around 25,000 persons per km². The intention is to set up a series of differing but overlapping 'atmospheres', each with its own character and structure. These, instead of being clearly zoned or demarcated (as in most 20th-century planning) are deliberately overlapped or 'layered'. The same attitude is taken towards the relationship of basic road structuring and linear open-space structuring. The provision of roads is relatively close-packed and evenly distributed: as a network rather than a hierarchy ... elaborate crossing systems and artificial 'interchange' points replaced by a continuous series of overlaps by the built layers.

HOUSE OF TWO STUDIOS

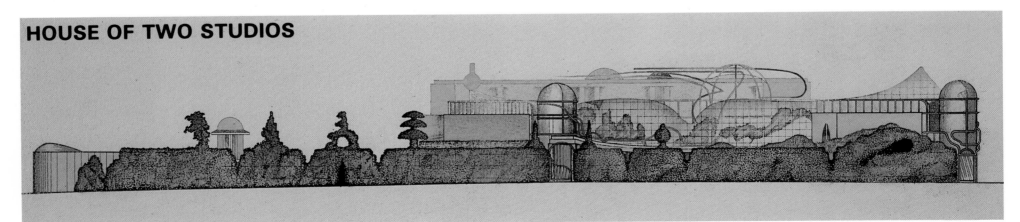

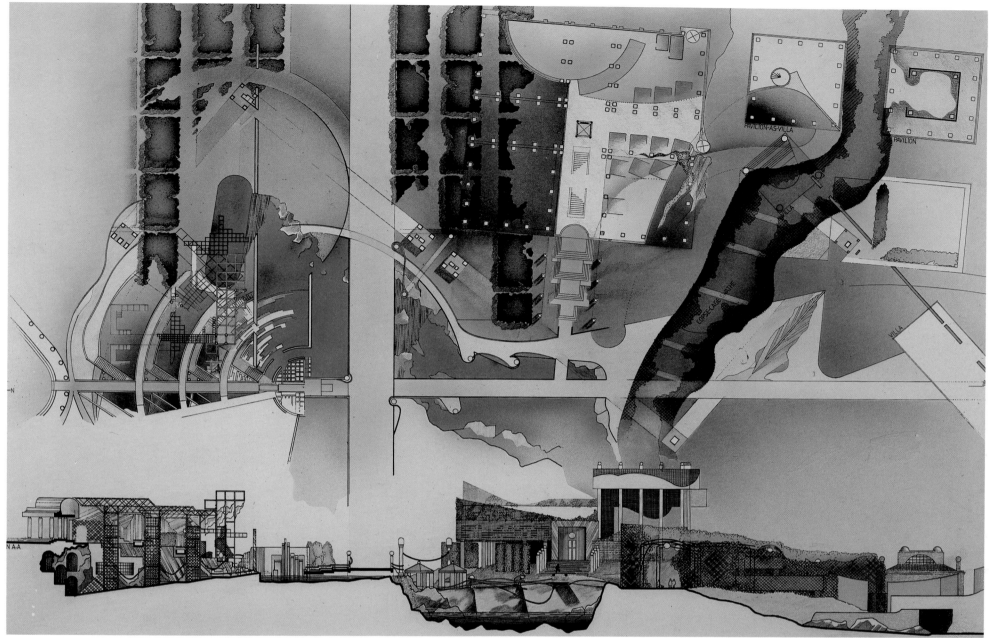

Plan of Layer City, south-east from the Shadow House

IN HISTORY the Romans regarded baths as places where acts of immersion and exercise were combined to promote bodily well-being, whereas the more contemplative bagnios of the 17th and 18th centuries used a course of chambers and steam rooms to cleanse both physically and cerebrally.

The overpowering blanket of morality that produced municipal baths in England in the 19th century and 'functionalism' that produced parallel institutions in Scandinavia and Germany are not the models here. Rather a place in which to extend the atmosphere of 'hotel', 'ocean liner' or the beauty parlour along with an internal garden.

The new Porchester Baths would be redeveloped as an all year round resort, with the reintroduction of gracious refreshment and a degree of indulgence in the act of bathing.

The developed section drawing shows all the pools and the restaurant. The Turkish and Roman baths and some of the private pools are to the right of the drawing. The main pool lies in the centre, with the access gallery to the library above.

PORCHESTER BATHS

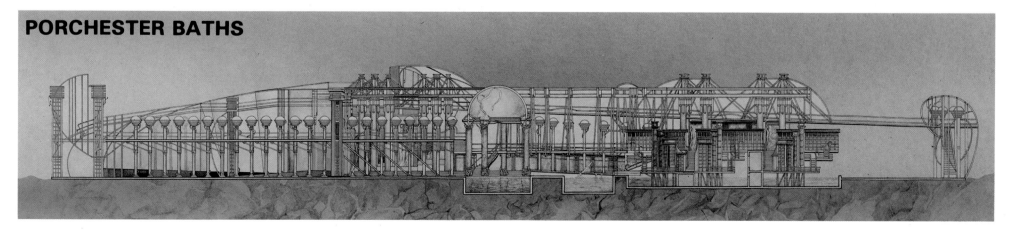

Darbourne & Darke

SEMI-RURAL BOLZANO

THE SCHEME WAS A PREMIATED DESIGN in an invited international competition. The competition, was for a larger area than there is at present, and invited alterations or suggestions on the development of the whole Semirurali Area. However, one design aspect was obligatory: a pedestrian deck developed in the first phase (planned by Professor Carlo Aymonino) was to be continued in the second. This site was originally developed during the early 1930s with the resettlement of Italians from the Veneto area into the now predominantly German speaking Sud-Tirol town of Bolzano. This development was of low-density two-storey flats set in small gardens. The pressure of German speaking people from the countryside around Bolzano, wishing to settle in town, has promoted a planning policy of increasing low-density housing without expanding the perimeter of the town, where the surrounding mountains allowed, into good agricultural land. The Semirurali Area became a site for residential redevelopment to a higher density. The project consists of 360 subsidised housing units each with parking for one car, a primary school for 350, an infant school for 200, kindergarten for 75, and a crèche for 45.

The primary early design consideration led away from high structures towards closely clustered low buildings, resulting in a courtyard form of housing which evolved from an observation of this form in the older, denser sections of Bolzano. The height of these courtyard dwellings means no lifts or excessive public stairs. The courtyard access is linked by the planted pedestrian decks which are not overall, but cover parking only.

The assembly of dwelling provides a series of spaces leading to the courtyard, which functions as a semi-private space, cool in summer, warm in winter. Causeways provide raised surfaces linking the main pedestrian routes. From these routes, the space alternates between public access and private space for small gardens, play areas or generally communal gardens.

CLIENT: Institute for the Promotion of Social Housing of the Province of Bolzano

Site plan

Site section

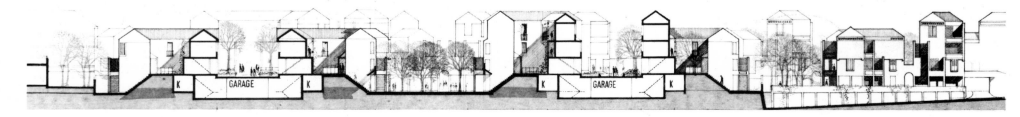

Doug Clelland & Eric Parry Partnership

NEW HEADQUARTERS FOR SSL LTD, OXFORDSHIRE   AD PROJECT AWARD • COMMENDATION

Projection of the central space at each level

SOLID STATE LOGIC LTD design and manufacture electronic computer aided console desks for sound studios in the recording, radio and television industries. Both they and their customers share a hermetic and internalised world: the conceptual world of electronics. Our main intention was to reconcile this technological world and the wider horizons of human experience in order to create a fertile and stimulating workplace. We chose to base our thinking on the nature of two constant human phenomena, work and dwelling. The theme of work encompasses a hierarchy which ranges from the mundane and prosaic to the realms of morality and imagination, whilst that of dwelling implies a sensibility for the poetics of place and the profundity of nature.

This range of meanings coincided with our clients' desire to inhabit a place of work which offered a rich environment for thinking, action and the gestation of ideas. They had decided that although a location on an industrial estate would be economically advantageous in the short term, it would only provide the lowest common denominator with respect to fulfilling their conditions for work. The site in Stonesfield was given, as was the schedule of spatial requirements. As the building developed so did the client company resulting in an expansion of the design brief to include both the interior design and the landscaping of the site. This did not require new proposals, and was merely a logical extension of the point already reached in the building process. This situation was possible because the client had already chosen their builder and paid directly for labour and materials.   The building process was geared to cash flow, had a particular flexibility, and was coordinated by a management group made up of the client, builder and architect.

The building is organised around a coherent centre which affords a clarity to the layers of solid and transparent walls which frame the spaces and the light. On the ground floor, the production suite of rooms is designed to flow around a dark and calm space which implies the base of the building. The four walls which enclose this space are designed to suggest the world of nature beyond. The first floor also gathers around the centre, but the space is light and open with layers of semi-transparent enclosures which accommodate the multiplicity of activities that comprise research, development and administration. The tower, a room for solitude and thought, marks the vertical hierarchy and offers a retreat. By an appropriate use of solid and moveable walls, all the rooms and spaces have been designed to satisfy the dual needs of privacy and communication among colleagues, whilst local servicing is provided on each floor. In this building we were trying to discover a shared culture which could underpin architectural practice, and address the continuity of human values.

The building developed, both externally and internally, as an artistic and literal 'construction' in the sense that each part could be composed and modified

Site plan: The building is one of a series of elements which, by means of entrance, avenue, grove, portico, lawn and landscape establish the structure of the long site.

East to west section

Working sketch of ground floor soffit

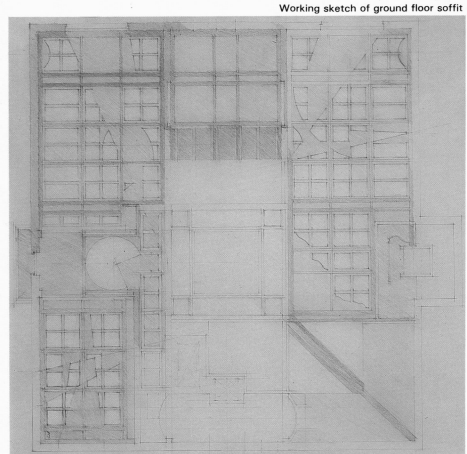

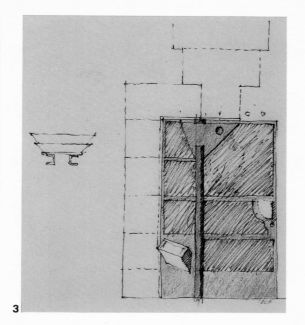

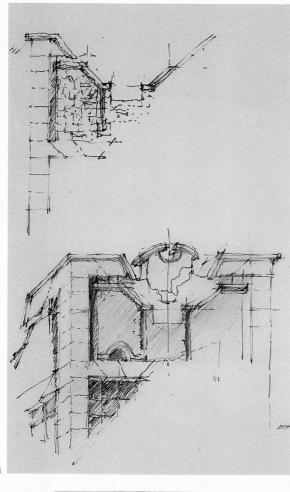

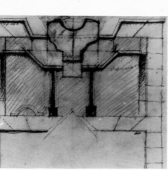

1 Tower   4 Bay window
2 Tower   5 Mural
3 Door   6 Fountain

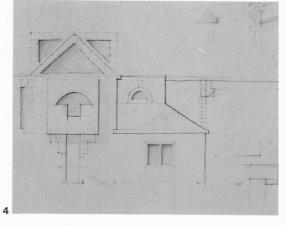

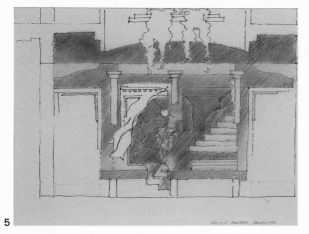

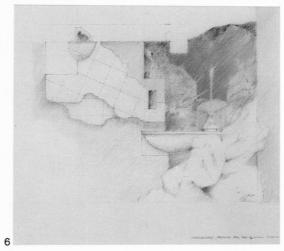

Working model for waterpiece

from the scheme which, at 1:100 received planning approval, and at 1:50 received building regulations approval.

The innovations accepted by the client for site organisation meant that instead of a weekly inspection of the site the reverse happened; a weekly visit to the city and the larger world. The challenge was accepted to reconcile the potential of a building with the constant pressures that stultify design. The days were occupied by dialogue with the client and the craftsman, and the nights by thinking and drawing.

The typical drawing board practice during construction, (when constructional details become enlarged images of 1:50 drawings) was replaced by a process which continuously recomposed the building within the 'dotted lines' of the scheme drawings used for statutory approvals. Each piece was thought through as a poetic theme; definitive images as sketches were invented; constructional details were drawn up; and the piece built. This process of site based composition, while still requiring a multitude of working drawings, is rooted in the potency of the sketch and the day to day world of the building site. It fundamentally challenges the neutrality and autonomy of the drawing board, just as our architectural intentions challenge the neutrality and autonomy of a building as an 'object'. Instead, the process reflects the conditions of concrete reality inasmuch as it places the power of imagination through the sketch, and actual day to day construction through time spent on site at the top of the list of architectural priorities. Some examples may suffice to suggest how the process gleaned poetry from the day to day reality of the site.

The external wall—The requirements of the District Council stimulated a search for the architectonic potential of stone faced blockwork and precast stone; the integration of pieces of excellent craftsmanship from demolished buildings; the roofs not just as cover, but as pointers to the centre of the building; the composition of facades informed by the passage of the days and the seasons; the facades as link to, and penetration from, the village and the countryside.

The potential of a window—Each facade, as the illustrations show, is a response to its orientation; the space and character of each room are unique, this is confirmed by the asymmetry of window placement; the building and its reconciliation with the day and the night by using a wall rather than the parasitic reflection of the landscape; the interplay between energy saving fabric and theatricality; the balance of transparency with solidity.

A soffit as a composition—By negotiating the bottom 50 mm from the structural slab, by plundering the roof timbers from a demolished chapel in Surrey, by solving the integration of horizontal cable runs and the need for acoustic absorption, by placement of the composed elements on top of the steel shuttering in order to accentuate the role of the windows and the location of the centre, a ceiling has been left which may be readable in many ways over the years during the moments between work.

High technology—The decision to limit expense on 'active' environmental technology appeared only worthwhile for poetic intention if the 'passive' could be pushed to its limits. 'Multi-Beton' low-temperature underfloor water grids and an air-to-water heat pump, when used in conjunction with the insulated cavity walls, provided the neutralisation of high and low peak external temperatures—not expressed, but embedded.

The Hall of Counterpoint—The central space of the ground floor is designed as a reference point for the building, its theme being the cave. The darkness and calm allude to more primary aspects of human existence. Some of the elements which articulate the theme are at present incomplete, but even so, it is here that dwelling in a work place takes on its most poetic and imaginative garb.

The elements of the Hall—The floor of marble pieces set in epoxy alludes to the cave yet, it is soft underfoot, implying the interpretation of nature through artifice. The four walls which enclose the Hall are designed to suggest elements of nature beyond the building. The east wall, its theme being the threshold between route and centre, is a colonnade, composed of a piece from a demolished chapel and two columns. The south wall contains a hollow, thematically considered as a place for memory to settle. It is composed within a frame of doors and a mirrored entablature. The north and west walls are as yet incomplete. The theme of the ceiling is a canopy to the cave. Above the centre of the floor, a conical oculus reveals the stair to the tower room high above. Four

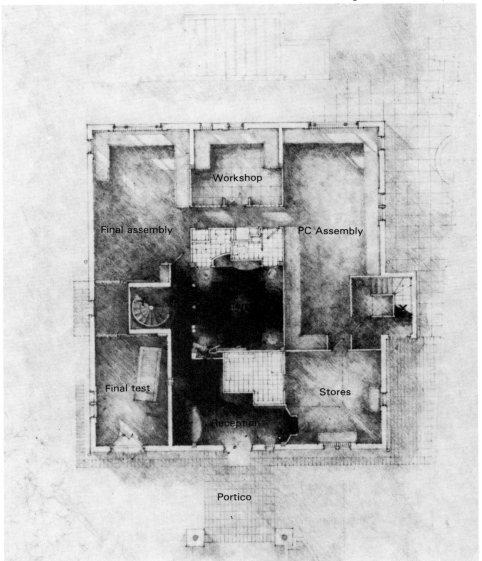

Ground floor plan

square floor lights in the corners of the space allow diffuse light from elsewhere above to penetrate the darkness. The geometry, with its use of the circle and the square, is precise and the inverse of the geometry of the floor.

Unfinished elements of the Hall—The west wall will be painted with a mural which is an evocation of ascension and distance. The north wall, also at present incomplete will hold a construction which, with its four water sources and rugged three dimensional quality, will allude to the grotto. These six surfaces of the Hall by their differing characters but consistent relationship to the whole will

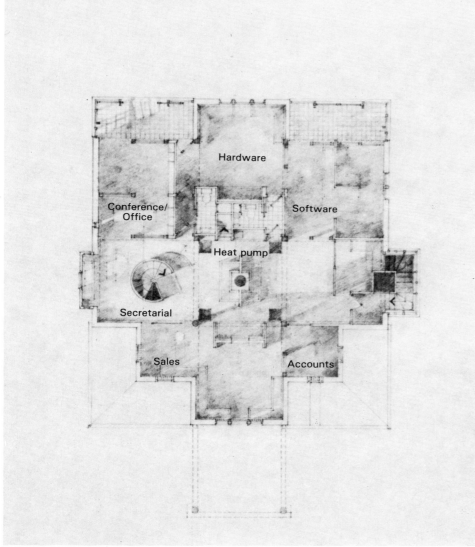

First floor plan, morning

- Hardware
- Conference/ Office
- Software
- Heat pump
- Secretarial
- Sales
- Accounts

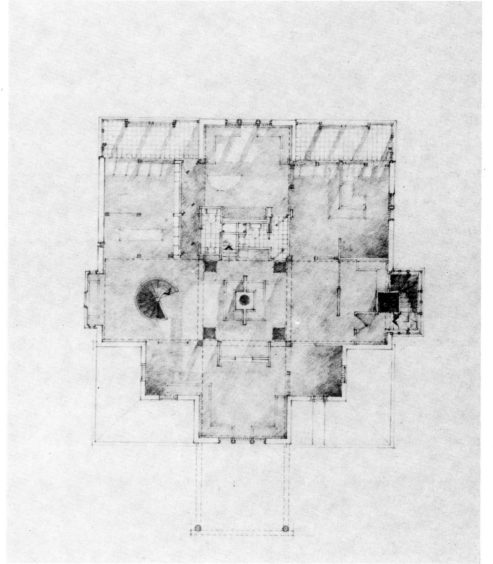

First floor plan, afternoon

complete the unity of the space.

    The Tower—Originally conceived as a plant room of one type, it has become a plant room of quite another, a retreat for the people of the company. By way of a stair, metaphorically 'Jacob's Ladder', the centre of the building at its height becomes a place to be alone; the north parapet framing the sun as it passes over the valley beyond, while to the south the openness refers to the valley, the countryside, nature, dreams and the beyond.

STRUCTURAL ENGINEER: Michael J Pereira (London
BUILDING CONTRACTOR: Drew Warren (Oxon)
HEATING: H Page & Son Ltd (London)
PLUMBING: Ivan G Langford (Oxon)
ELECTRICAL: Paul Glennister (Oxon)
WATERPIECE: ADBC Workshop (London)
PHOTOGRAPHS: Richard Davis, Peter Wilson, Pauline Cord and the authors

We should like to thank many friends and colleagues for their contributions and in particular Dalibor Veseley

Berman and Guedes

TOWCO HOUSE, DRAWING OFFICE EXTENSION

Towco House facade

Axonometric of Abbey Crescent

ABBEY CRESCENT, OXFORD

THREE BUILDINGS ON THE THAMES—All these buildings are luxury flat developments.

22 Narrow Street: The original 1950s engineering works' building consisted of two arms around a courtyard; a floor and a half was added and the central courtyard was glazed to cover a steel access stair and glass lift.

26 Narrow Street: Working from an empty site the new building has a powerful glass cylinder making bay windows; the base reads like the stern of a ship and the whole is crowned with a projecting glazed tympanum.

28 Narrow Street: The facade of this derelict Victorian warehouse was demolished and a new facade developed from the model of a Venetian Palazzo with powerful corbelled windows flanking a Serlian window group, topped with a heavy cornice and too small a pediment (the drawings were lost by the bricklayers, so the pediment was built from memory). The new fourth floor was built into a galleried structure re-using the original framework of the roof and cast iron columns.

CLIENT: Mr & Mrs Hoffenberg
ENGINEERS: Nos 28 & 26, Campbell Reith and Partners Nos 22, C Whitham & Partners

In colour on previous page

TOWCO HOUSE DRAWING OFFICE EXTENSION—This is a small building hitched onto the back of another with two tough blank side walls decorated with striped brickwork and chunky stepped gables. The long south wall is more elaborate and precise: a mahogany grid filled with different materials, iron gates, opaque brown armour-clad glass, bronze sunscreen and mirrors.

CLIENT: Town and Country Mechanical Services
ENGINEER: C Withan & Partners
QUANTITY SURVEYORS: Buckley & Surtees
MECHANICAL AND ELECTRICAL ENGINEERS: Towco Ltd

ABBEY CRESCENT, OXFORD—This neglected triangular site facing south over the Thames was chosen by the client as the site for 74 bedsitter flats, 10 one-bedroomed flats and two houses. The plan consists of a large crescent of three-storey blocks arranged as 'villas' linked with low-roofed staircases. There are strong horizontal bands of coloured brickwork which, together with the fenestration, unify the scheme and define the base, centre and galleried attic. Construction is due to begin in July, 1982.

CLIENT: The Cherwell Housing Trust
ENGINEER: Ian Howdrill Associates
QUANTITY SURVEYOR: Ridge & Partners

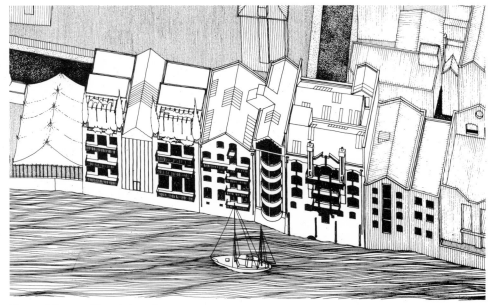

View of Narrow Street riversite

No 22 Narrow Street   No 26 Narrow Street with adjacent site, No 28 (ph John Donat)

Conversion of 22 Narrow Street

New building at 26 Narrow Street

No 28 Narrow Street

28 NARROW ST E14

Keppie Henderson & Partners

RESTORATION OF THE WILLOW TEA ROOMS, GLASGOW

AD PROJECT AWARD ● BRONZE

WHEN DALY'S DEPARTMENT STORE moved to the Sauchiehall Centre from the building of which the Willow Tea Rooms formed a part, The Arrowcroft Group bought the building with the object of refurbishing it into a number of smaller shops with storage and offices on the upper floors.

At that time the only parts of the Willow remaining in more or less original condition were some of the plaster panels; the main stair and balustrade, part of the balcony at the rear of the ground floor, two fireplaces heavily overpainted, some panelling and a fireplace on the upper floors and, of course, the Room de Lux stained glass and doors.

When planning permission was granted the Planning Department imposed 20 conditions to ensure that the building would be put back (within reason) into its 1904 condition. In May 1979, Keppie Henderson & Partners were asked by Arrowcroft to act as consultants with regard to the Willow Construction.

A considerable number of alterations and much pseudo-Mackintosh work has taken place over the years, all the non-Mackintosh additions were taken out of the building, together with the old electrical and heating systems. Part of the Mackintosh work was removed for safekeeping and that which had to remain was protected by plywood. The original panelling and cover strips were 5/8" thick solid timber but in many parts plywood and blockboard pieces were found, materials not used in 1904. Wherever possible solid timber was used but some of the timber of the required width and quality is simply unavailable nowadays.

The shop front itself was not as much of a problem as it appeared at first sight, because the original fixings still remained the front could be positioned reasonably accurately. The ironwork of the staircase remained substantially intact but that forming the screen on the restored balcony front had disappeared long ago. The decoration scheme was perhaps the most complicated to track down. We only found one piece of original wall fabric covering. This was the same material as that used in the Ingram Tea Room where much of the original stencilled decoration remained behind the wall linings of the Cloister Room. The material with which the walls of the Willow is lined, is as close a match in modern materials as we could get.

What remained of the original ironwork, the Room de Lux doors and the Margaret MacDonald gesso panel have been brought out of store and reinstalled, fireplaces and grates remade, replacement window handles and special tiles cast, to complete the reconstruction of the fabric. It now depends on the tenant as to how he will use the building and how he will furnish it to complete the reconstruction.

CLIENT: Arrowcroft Management Ltd
PROJECT TEAM: GG Wimpenny, Keppie Henderson and Partners
ARCHITECT (BUILDING ALTERATIONS): Carl Fisher Sibbald & Ptns
STRUCTURAL ENGINEERS: HL Waterman & Partners
QUANTITY SURVEYOR: Cobb Blyth & Associates
MECHANICAL & ELECTRICAL ENGINEERS: Ramsay & Primrose
CONTRACTOR: Gilbert Ash (Scotland) Ltd

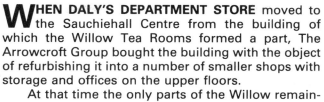

Restored facade

Restored interior (phs Gillanders & Mack)

Richard Rogers & Partners
INMOS MICROELECTRONICS FACTORY, NEWPORT, SOUTH WALES

Microchip

THE FAST TRACKING NATURE OF THE PROJECT required the design to be responsive to any site and capable of being built in a range of sizes. During the design process, a number of sites were considered. The final decision was to locate the factory at Newport, Gwent, close to major transport routes and with a good range of skilled and unskilled labour.

A building was required that provided office and ancillary space, as well as facilities for microchip wafer production. Speed of design and construction were critical factors. A further constraint on the design of the building was the phenomenally high quality environmental control required by microchip projection facilities. Air in the production area had to be absolutely clean to cut down on the failure rate of

Car parking zone

Main access road
External tanks and service zone

Production zone

Main circulation spine

Office and laboratory zone

Courtyards and lawn

General amenity green space

Existing woodland

Phase 2   Phase 1

Site plan

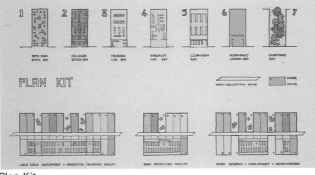

Plan Kit

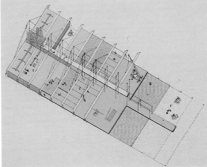

Building process

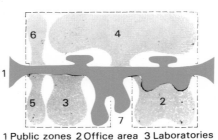

1 Public zones 2 Office area 3 Laboratories
4 Clean room 5 Plant room 6 Shipping and
receiving 7 Courtyard

Zoning diagram

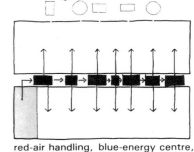

red-air handling, blue-energy centre, yellow-special services

Services diagram   Early sketch

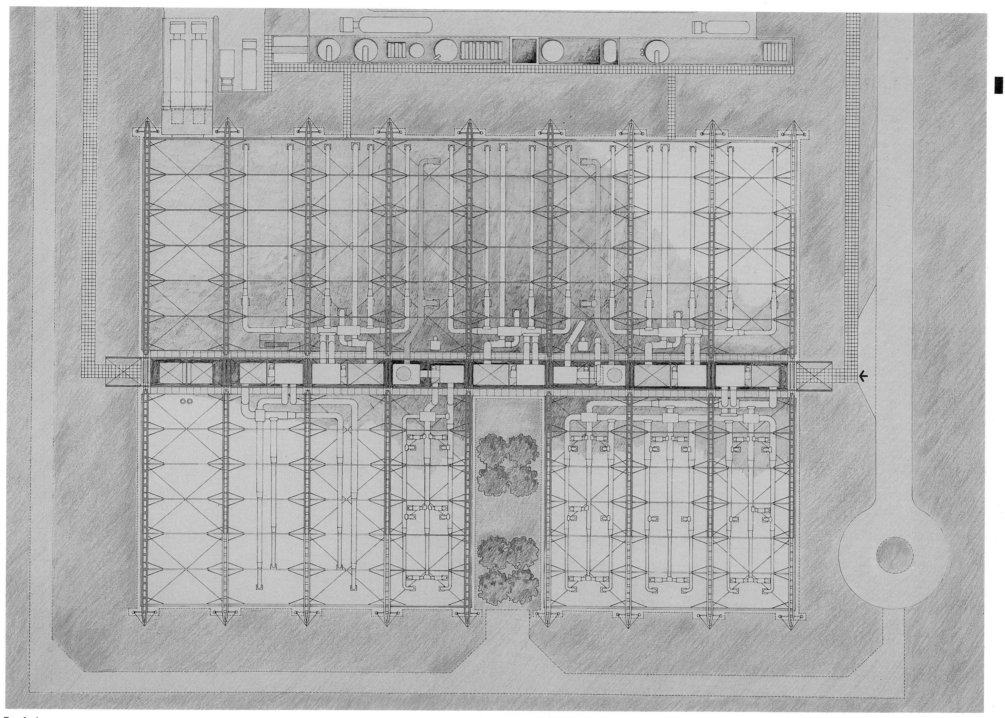

Roof plan

Model of structure

wafer production, a process highly sensitive to dust. The architects added to this brief a series of guidelines from which the building evolved:

— the design should be able to respond successfully to changes in the brief as the programme evolved during construction;
— the building should act as both a high performance, precision, production machine and as a friendly and stimulating environment for employees;
— the design should allow for maximum flexibility and potential growth and change in order to be able to meet the needs of a new and fast evolving industry;
— the design and construction of the building should suit the client's fast building programme.

The building design evolved as a single-storey steel structure conceived as a kit of rapidly erectable parts with maximum off-site prefabrication. The basic concept of the building is a central linear circulation and service spine with lateral wings of specialised activities. The spine, 7.2 m wide and 106 m long, acts as an internal street, generous enough in size to contain vending machines, public telephones, seating, meeting places, planted areas, library and information displays, and waiting areas for the offices. It provides easy visual security control and is intended to link up with future phases of building on the site, so that all the facilities in all the buildings are readily available to all staff. Offices and restaurants are on the south side of the spine, and the clean production room to the north. The main air supply equipment is grouped in localised modules allowing minimum duct runs above the spine; ducts being taken across the roof to the point of use. Production wastes are collected in linear floor trenches and production supply services are distributed on walls within the production zone. The layout of the building is infinitely extendable along the spine, with the addition of more of the 13 × 36 m bays possible on the Newport site.

An 8-bay scheme was proposed as the first phase of a 20-bay final development, set at the east end of the site so that extension could take place in a westerly direction in the future. The very large clean room facility and the shipping and receiving bay occupy the complete north side of the spine. The south side has one bay kept as an open landscaped courtyard, offering daylight and sheltered open space

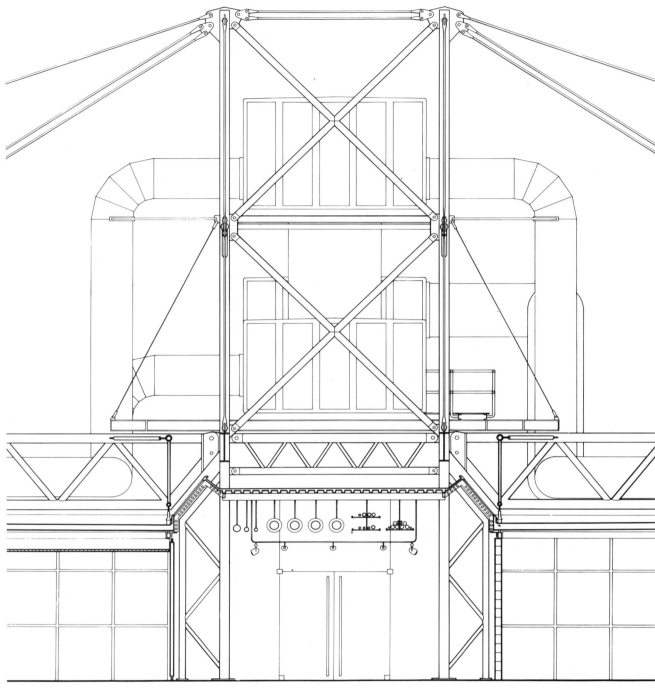

Detail of elevation

Section

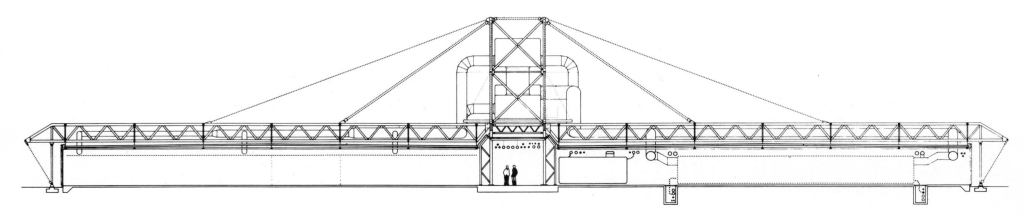

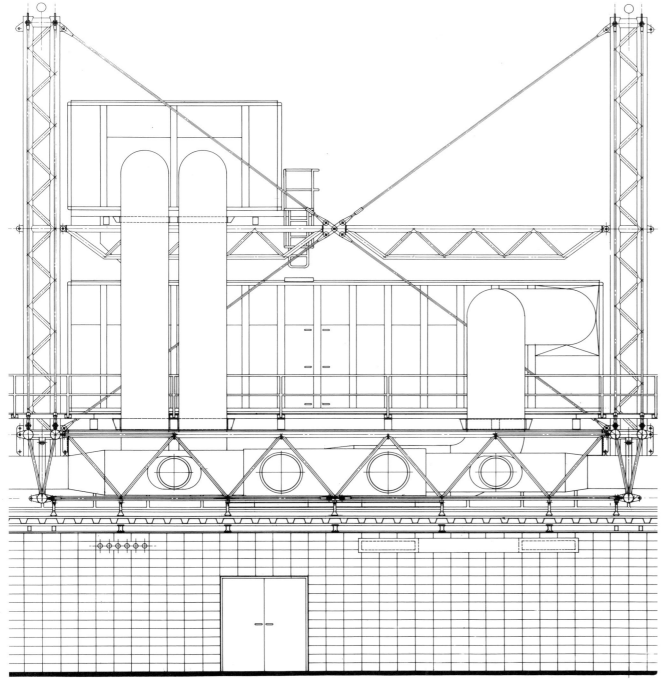

next to the main block of offices and the restaurant. Assembly labs and the main pipes service plant room occupy the western three bays of the south side.

The production zones on the north side of the building include the clean room which is separated from the spine by locker rooms in which personnel must change into special clothing. The locker rooms also act as an air lock/anti-dust barrier between the spine and the clean room. The clean room itself has smooth, non-dusting white finished walls, floors and ceilings, and specialised very high volume air scrubbing and cleaning equipment to maintain the purest possible atmosphere and a steady temperature and hygrometric conditions. Services from the plant room—hot and cold water, chilled water, compressed air—run at high level in the main spine, servicing the modular HVAC units.

The structure is a tubular steel assisted span tension structure, supported by tension tie rods from the spine towers. The structural system provides uninterrupted column-free spaces for maximum internal flexibility. The roof is fabricated from 6 m span steel decking with thermal insulation and a 5-layer roof membrane. The external walls are based on a system of standardised mullions which will accept any type of infill: single glazing, double glazing, transluscent or opaque panels. This allows the client to alter walls and finishes as he wishes. The initial design proposed double glazing on the office areas and solid insulated sandwich panels for the production areas.

North elevation spine

CLIENT: Inmos Ltd
PROJECT TEAM: Julia Barfield, David Bartlett, Pierre Botschi, Mike Davies, Sally Eaton, Michael Elkan, Marco Goldschmied, Kunimi Hayashi, Tim Inskip, Peter McMunn, David Nixon, Richard Rogers, John Young
STRUCTURAL ENGINEERS: Anthony Hunt Associates
QUANTITY SURVEYORS: Hanscomb Partnership
SERVICES ENGINEERS: YRM Engineers
CONTRACTORS: Laing Management Contracting Ltd
MODEL: Mark Bullimore

North elevation

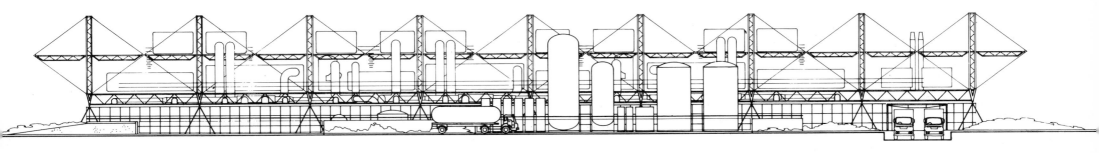

CONSTRUCTION SEQUENCE

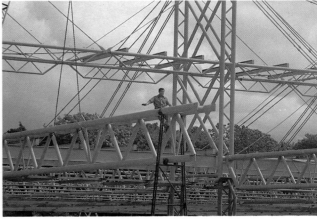

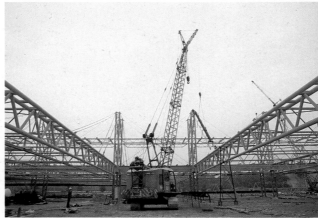

Detail of grid

A day out of the office at INMOS (ph Nicholas Sargeant)

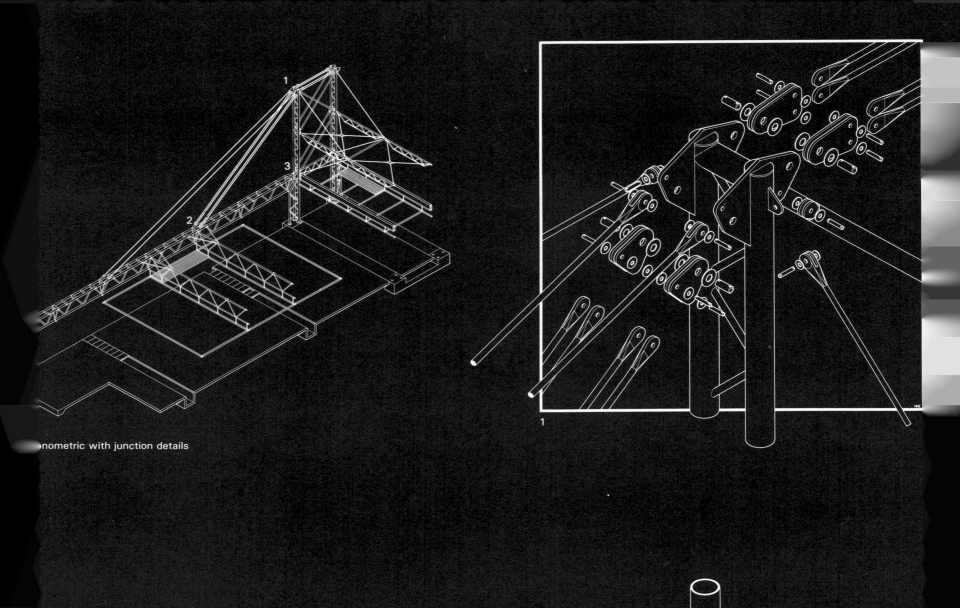

nometric with junction details

1

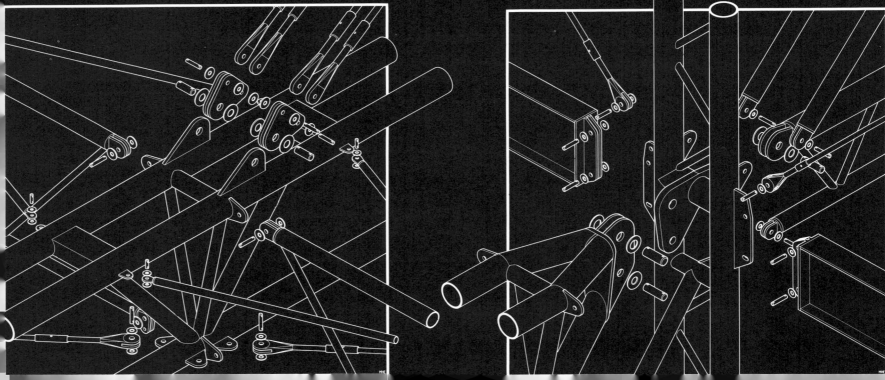

Construction shot (ph Pat Hunt)

View of external tanks (ph Pat Hunt

Richard Rogers & Partners
PATSCENTER, PRINCETON, NEW JERSEY

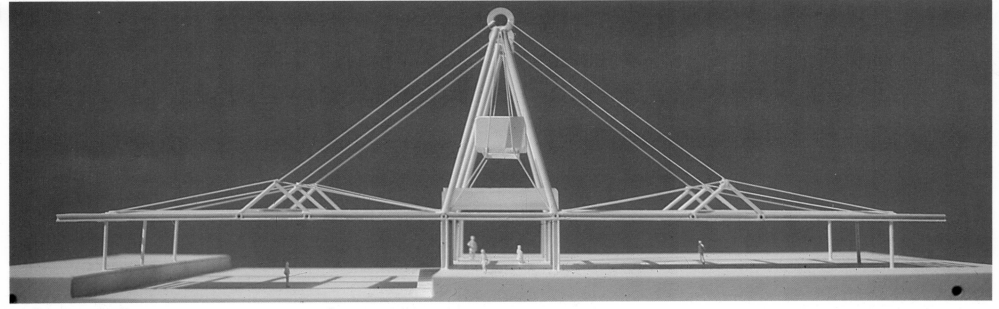

Model of structure

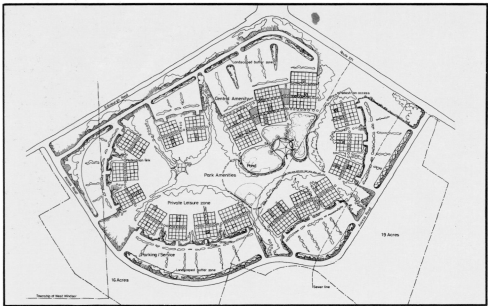

Site plan

Kit of parts

THE FIRST PHASE of a research and development facility is the 'gateway' building of an industrial park to be developed on a 100-acre rural site six miles east of Princeton, New Jersey. It has a level 10-acre site with an option on a further 16 acres for future development. The site is located only 50 miles from both New York City and Philadelphia and is approximately one hour's travel from three major airports. Scattered developments in the surrounding countryside house a number of prodigious research and development facilities including RCA, J&J, Squibb, Exxon and Siemens.

Patscenter was established in North America in early 1980, housed in 11,000 square feet of speculative office accommodation 2 miles east of Princeton town centre, some five miles from the new site. In March 1982, with a rapidly increasing staff of around 30, Richard Rogers and Partners were appointed to design a new facility.

The principal objectives were:

— to provide for the expansion of Patscenter with a custom-designed building offering maximum flexibility;
— to permit further growth of Patscenter in North America;
— to enable PA Management Consultants to integrate on the site at a later date if required.

Other requirements included a very high level of freedom of circulation and staff contact, flexibility in the arrangement of offices, labs and services, and the provision of a wide structural grid or totally free space. The north elevation, looking onto Route 571, the main access to the site, should have a strong visual impact, expressing Patscenter's simple but high quality image.

The design strategy resulted in a single-storey suspended steel structure, rapidly erectable as a kit of parts of standard components prefabricated off site. The basic building concept is a central linear spine. This glazed arcade houses services, circulation and related activities. Open laboratory and office zones, as well as meeting rooms and administration facilities are located within clear-span spaces to either side of the 8 m-wide by 80 m-long arcade. The services are centrally located in a bay by bay system. The first phase is for 40,000 square feet and the completion date is summer 1984.

CLIENT: Patscentre International
PROJECT TEAM: Pierre Botschi, Marco Goldschmied, John McAslan, Gennaro Picardi, Richard Rogers, John Young
STRUCTURAL ENGINEERS: Ove Arup & Partners/Robert Silman Associates (USA)
QUANTITY SURVEYORS: Hanscomb Associates Inc (USA)
SERVICES ENGINEERS: Ove Arup & Partners/Syska and Henessy Inc (USA)

Rogers Patscentre

KNOLL INTERNATIONAL, THE THIRD GENERATION OFFICE SYSTEM

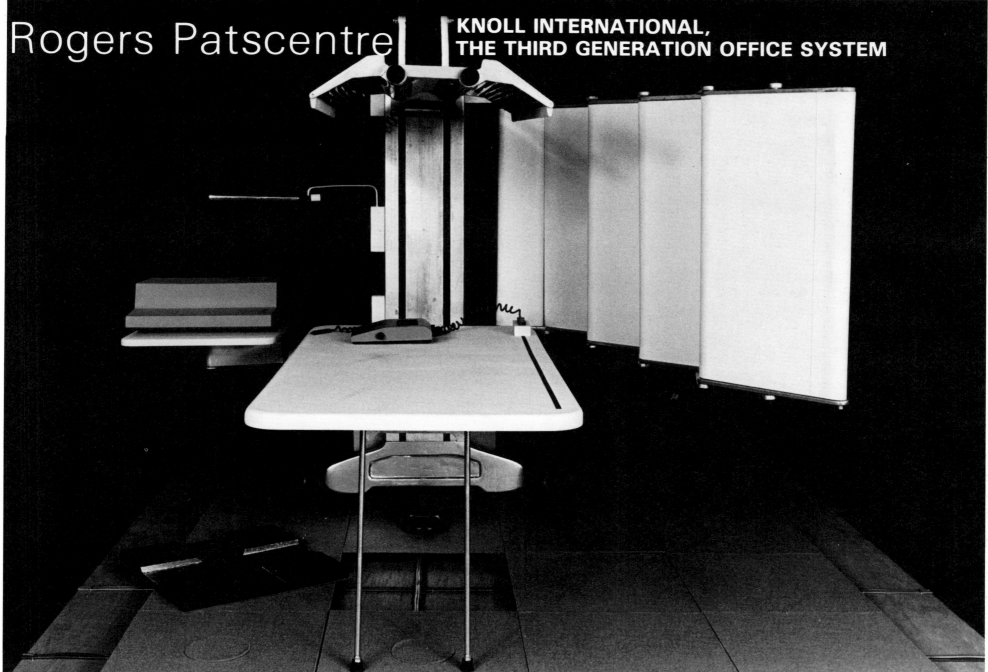

View of model

THE OFFICE HAS EXISTED for just over 100 years. Born out of the industrial revolution, it was made possible by the telegraph, telephone and transportation that allowed administrative functions to be consolidated in one specialised place.

First generation offices soon adopted ideas of efficiency from factory mass-production lines and became larger paper processing plants in the first open plan spaces. Some 20 years ago the office underwent a major transformation—responding to needs of adaptability in a fast-changing society. Closed and open office spaces combined to form an open, flexible space—the landscaped office. Although office furniture designed for those needs—second generation systems—has evolved in an attempt to respond to the changing context, there has not been a major reappraisal of the office and office systems since that time.

This project thus examines the needs of tomorrow's office in the light of recent research and, in combination with the potential offered by newly developed technologies, proposes the creation of the Third Generation Office.

In all current debates about the existing office environment, three areas of concern become apparent.

GENERALISATION—The majority of today's offices are equipped with generalised lighting, generalised air conditioning, standardised equipment and planning layouts. In this environment individuals have little or no control and choice, and there is thus dissatisfaction with standards of visual and acoustic privacy, thermal control, space and equipment. Flexibility is limited by office management and there is thus a need for a 'responsive' office.

COMPLEXITY—Many office systems are complex and heavy with a large number of elements, special joints and fixings that are difficult to stock, order, assemble and change. Changing the 'flexible' office is often a job for the specialist. There is thus a need for rationalisation.

THE PROBLEM OF SERVICES—The multiplicity of power and communications cables and air ducts found in all offices poses major problems of organisation and connection. Services often inhibit change as well as being visually chaotic. The growth of the use of electronic data equipment in the office can only aggravate this situation. The accommodation of services will be a prime factor in the design of a future office system.

It is commonly accepted that two major events—the second communications revolution and the end of cheap energy—will both have a major impact upon the office of the future. Specifically:
— there will be a growth in cheap artificial intelligence (the silicon chip revolution);
— there will be major developments in communications technology (optical fibre transmission, commercial broadcast satellites);
— there will be a need for major energy savings (as

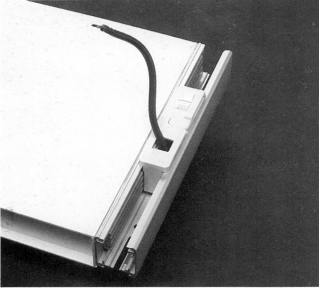

The desk track

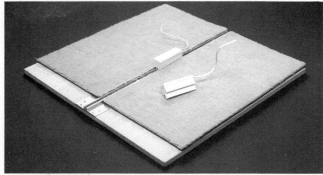

Floor services

Acoustic testing of louvre screen system

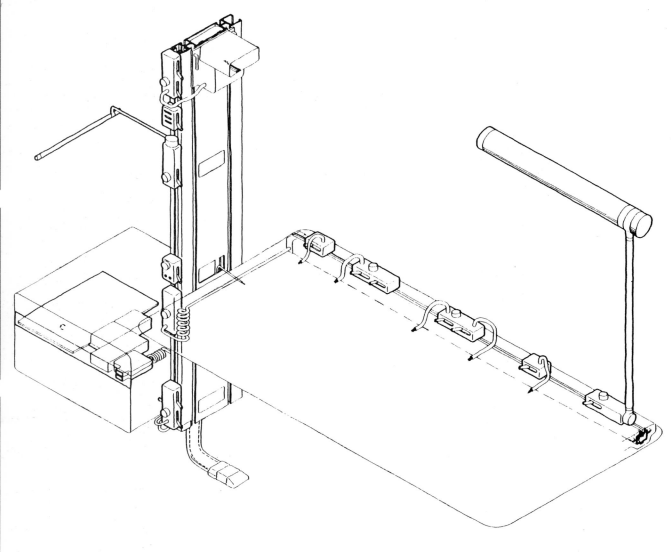

Power and data track system

costs increase as new electronic data processing equipment makes demands for energy).

Although the long term effects are very much open to speculation it is possible that:

— automation in the factory will move people from the factory shop floor into the office;

— automation of clerical jobs will move staff into administrative and executive roles (thus creating a demand for an improved, varied office environment);

— improved communications will allow greater staff mobility within and outside the office (the 'satellite' home office and scattered small office units become reality. Within the office an individual may use several work places rather than occupy one place permanently).

As a response to this the office will be tailored to the needs of the individual. He will be able to tune his own acoustic and visual privacy, regulate personal lighting and thermal conditions and arrange the configuration of his work-place and equipment. In open office space this will create a more varied environment.

MOBILITY—The office will allow people to move from task to task and place to place. It will function in a variety of different environments. In the open office, units will move with staff quickly and easily, in response to increasing needs for fast change. Units will be compactly stored when not in use and will be able to operate in traditional enclosed offices, or at home.

RATIONALISATION—The office will be made from a minimum number of standard components that meet all the functional needs of the office of the future. Standard components, assembled in the factory to form complete units, will allow the product to be tuned to changing markets. In the office the user will modify his unit at the turn of a knob. What was, in previous systems, 'assembled' or 'set up', will 'fold out' or 'open up' and both components and complete units will be easily stored. Materials will be selected for maximum performance and minimum weight.

Mass-produced components with integrated and simplified details will be manufactured.

ENERGY INTEGRATION—Units will have integrated power and data distribution systems using both present and future transmission systems. The office unit will be 'intelligent'. Control systems coupled to data processing and communication systems will allow the user to communicate with or through his unit in a wide variety of ways. The office will also be energy economic. Power consuming equipment will be chosen for energy efficiency. 'Intelligent' responsive control of energy systems will allow power to be contoured more closely to actual needs, with consequent savings in energy. The office system will include an overall services distribution system. Cables, pipes, etc will be 'consolidated' into service components and run in a 'service floor'.

During design development, the many aspects of office design and technology were considered and investigated in close collaboration with engineers and

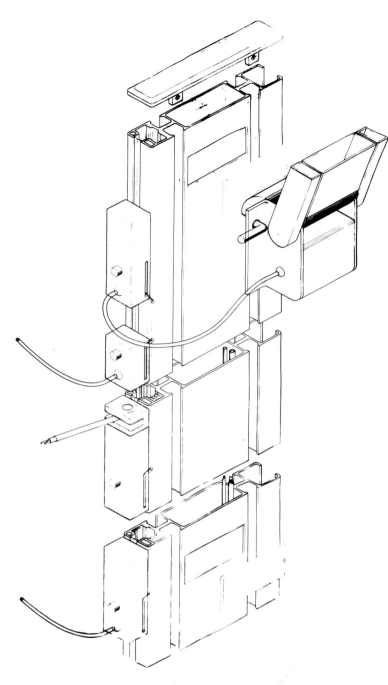

Detail of power and data track system

Environmental canopy – lighting reflector mock-up

technicians at Patscentre:

Power, Communications and Control—Overview of future requirements, available technology, system configuration.

Air-Conditioning—Individual comfort criteria, review of system options, development.

Service Floor—Review of alternative systems, materials, development.

Lighting—Lighting levels and types, available technology.

Acoustics—Review of open-office acoustics, new technology, materials.

Storage Systems—Review of range of storage needs, dimensional standards, rationalisation, waste paper compaction.

Dimensional Co-ordination—Anthropometric, ergonomic needs related to other dimensions.

Materials—A general survey of available materials and new developments.

Design Co-ordination—During the development of the specific areas of research, a series of design studies and tests were carried out integrating research and ideas.

THE DESK TRACK—The potential future requirement for power at a single work station has been estimated at 1–2 kw. In order to give a flexible distribution and a variable capacity system, power and data are delivered around the unit by a track system. This contains three power circuits (air, lighting and peripherals and a data track).

FLOOR SERVICES—In order to overcome the problems commonly associated with floor service distribution systems, a number of ideas and alternatives were investigated. They were based upon:
— service 'plug' points at close centres;
— single connectors;
— consolidation of service lines and connectors;
— plenum service floors.

ACOUSTICAL RESPONSE—The ability of the individual to control (open and shut) his acoustic environment gives potential psychological as well as physical benefits and allows him to 'signal' his need for privacy or open communication. Acoustic elements are therefore operable and responsive.

LOCAL ENCLOSURE—An acoustic enclosure is most effective when it is as close as possible to the noise source or shielded volume (eg an acoustic helmet, or phone booth). The degree of openness/enclosure necessary has been studied. Acoustic elements are therefore relatively small (when compared to traditional walls) and wrap around the sound zone. The unit has a retractable canopy and screen system.

ABSORPTION—Acoustic surfaces are highly absorbent to stop noise at source and absorb sounds coming into the enclosure.

ENVIRONMENTAL CANOPY LIGHTING—A variable fluorescent task light 'canopy' element gives even, non reflecting light at desk level and together with ambient up-lighting units provides a more efficient varied and contrasting illuminated environment. It consists of an operating range of orientable collimating reflector wings and semi-focusing fresnel sleeves.

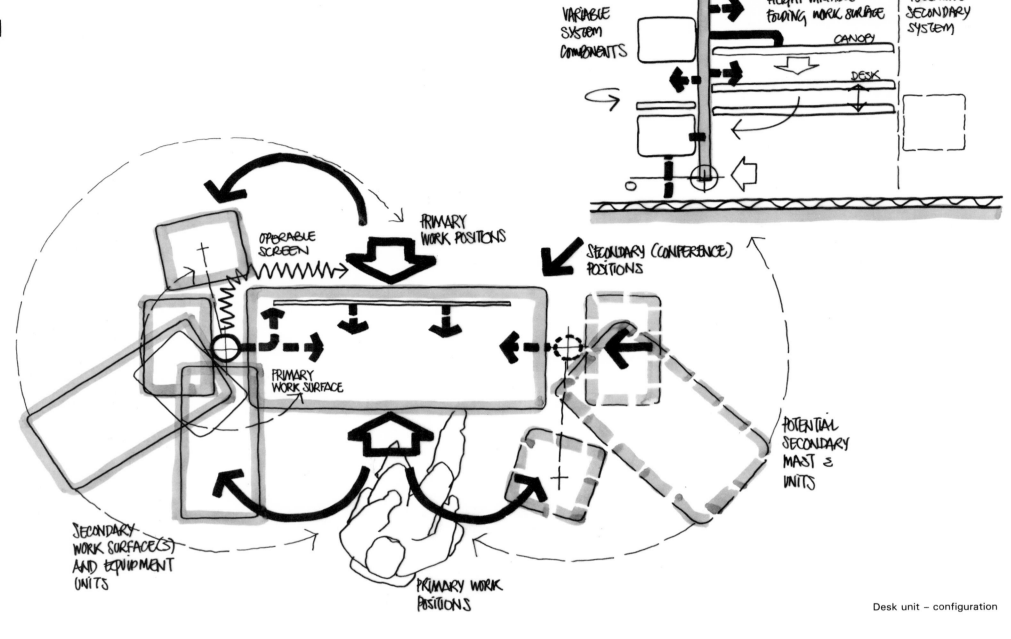

TROLLEY | **FOLDING UNITS** | **POTENTIAL SECONDARY SYSTEM**

VARIABLE SYSTEM COMPONENTS — HEIGHT VARIABLE FOLDING WORK SURFACE — CANOPY — DESK

OPERABLE SCREEN — PRIMARY WORK POSITIONS — SECONDARY (CONFERENCE) POSITIONS — PRIMARY WORK SURFACE — POTENTIAL SECONDARY MAST & UNITS — SECONDARY WORK SURFACE(S) AND EQUIPMENT UNITS — PRIMARY WORK POSITIONS

Desk unit – configuration

The Basic Module

The system is based upon an integrated, mobile, personal work module. Although sold and delivered to the office as a ready-to-use unit, it is in fact made from an assembly of standard components that, in other combinations, form a complete office environment. The assembly of the majority of these components is restricted to the factory and flexibility in the office is achieved by foolproof user-operable elements. The module rests and moves over a thin service tile floor system, and plugs into a socket for power, data and water lines. The module is made of an assembly of the following components:

Mast/Chassis Unit—A vertical structural mast that carries air, power and data is mounted on a wheeled chassis.

Service Module/Controller—A service module package connects to the mast and contains air-handling, electrical and electronic process and computing equipment. Different mechanical/electronic components may be plugged into the module. The service module is controlled from the desktop controller—an interface keyboard and display screen. The user controls the module's 'intelligent' functions through this unit. A mast track plug and adaptor system allow equipment, lighting, etc to be connected to the track.

The Environmental Canopy—The canopy, attached at the head of the mast, acts as an 'umbrella' over the desk surface. It provides acoustic shielding and absorption, light (in the form of a unique non-veiling reflector/lamp unit), masking sound, and air diffusion. The user can control height and position, as well as the light, air and sound functions.

The Desktop Unit—The desk work surface folds up alongside the mast when not in use—or when the module is being moved. Another adjustment allows the height of the surface to be varied from machine height to standing work height. Two control knobs under the surface release the counterbalancing mechanisms for both these functions. The desk is equipped with an integral power/data track.

The Machine Table—A swing-out machine support table allows a typewriter, word processor or VDU to be used in conjunction with the main desk surface. A swing-out fluorescent light is attached to the mast track above the table.

Acoustic Louvre Screen—A folding, light-weight acoustic screen allows the desk to be used on all sides (for conference) and (when closed) as a private enclosed work station. The louvres offer different choices of visual and acoustic privacy as the screen is opened out.

The basic component range is extended by other components to form a complete office system.

PROJECT TEAM: Alan Collins, Simon Conolly, Simon Davey, Mike Davies, Jude Douglass, Gordon Edge, Roger Huntley, Tim Inskip, Amarjit Kalsi, John Lipton, PE Mitchell, R Pettigrew, DR Plummer, Richard Rogers, Alan Stanton, John Young
MODELS: Julia Barfield, John Holmes, David Mark
CONSULTANTS AIR CONDITIONING & LIGHTING:
Sound Research Laboratories, Ove Arup & Partners
PHOTOGRAPHS: Jocelyn Van den Bossche

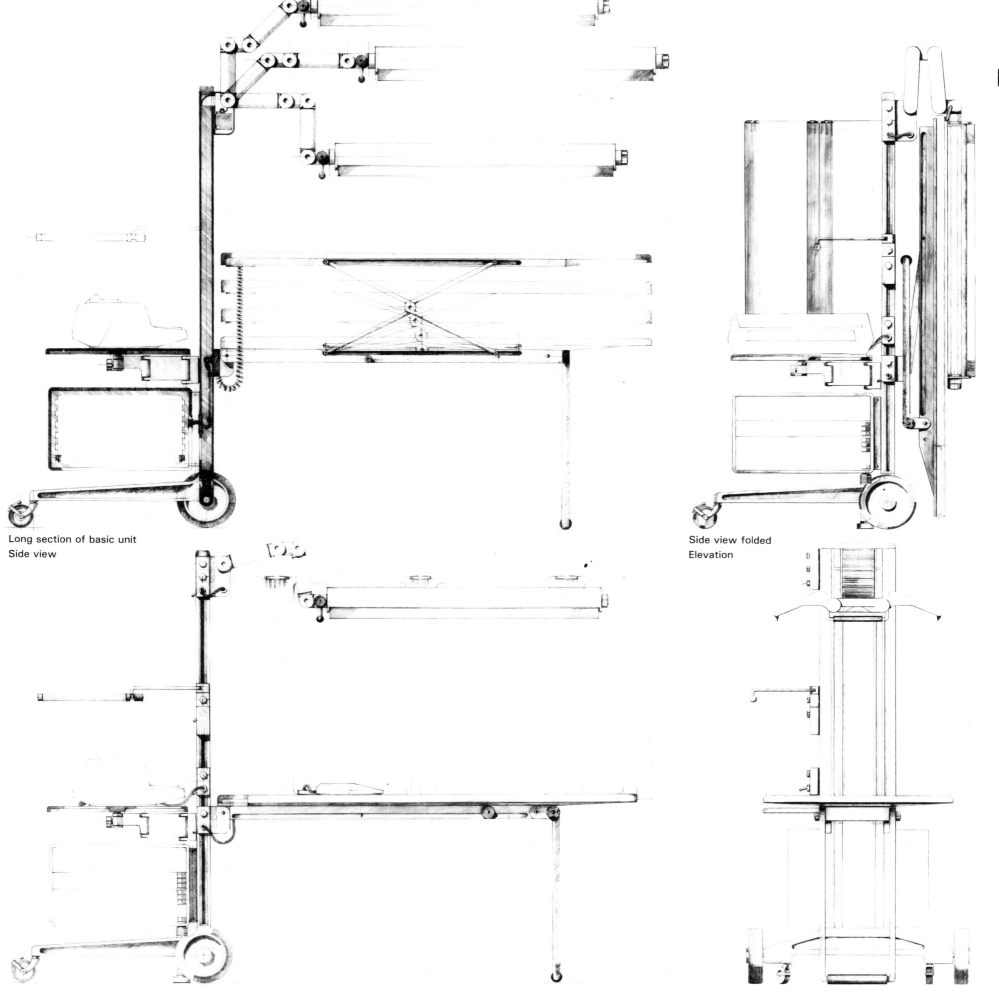

Long section of basic unit
Side view

Side view folded
Elevation

The basic component range is extended by other components to form a complete office system...

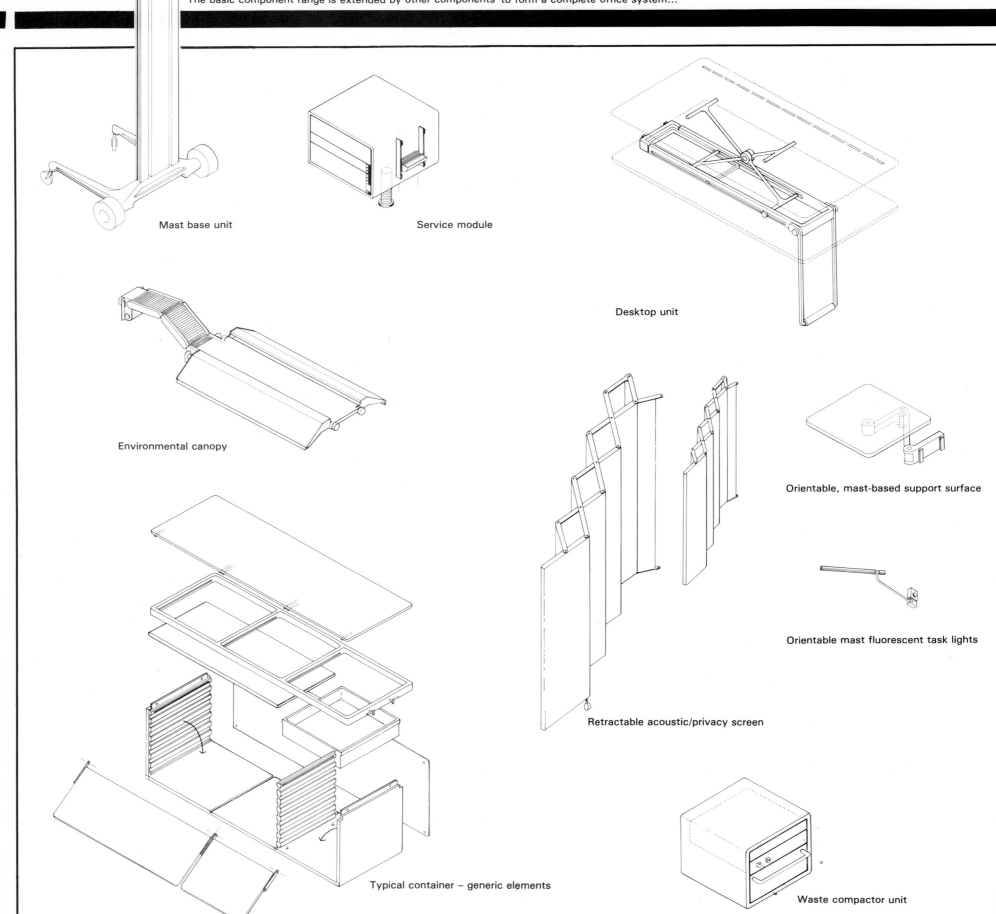

Mast base unit

Service module

Desktop unit

Environmental canopy

Orientable, mast-based support surface

Orientable mast fluorescent task lights

Retractable acoustic/privacy screen

Typical container – generic elements

Waste compactor unit

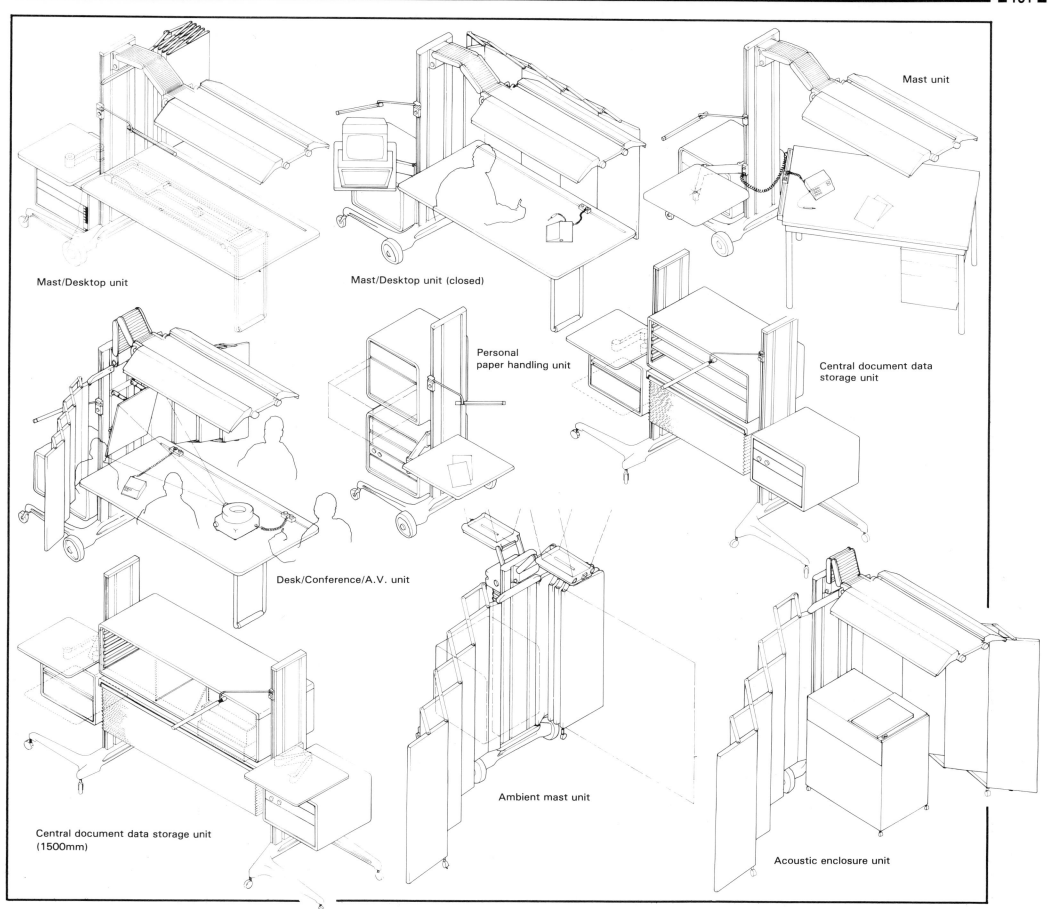

Mast/Desktop unit

Mast/Desktop unit (closed)

Mast unit

Personal
paper handling unit

Central document data
storage unit

Desk/Conference/A.V. unit

Central document data storage unit
(1500mm)

Ambient mast unit

Acoustic enclosure unit

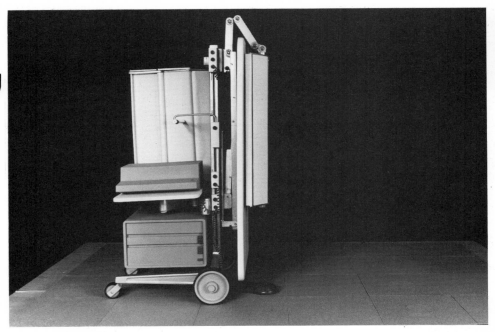

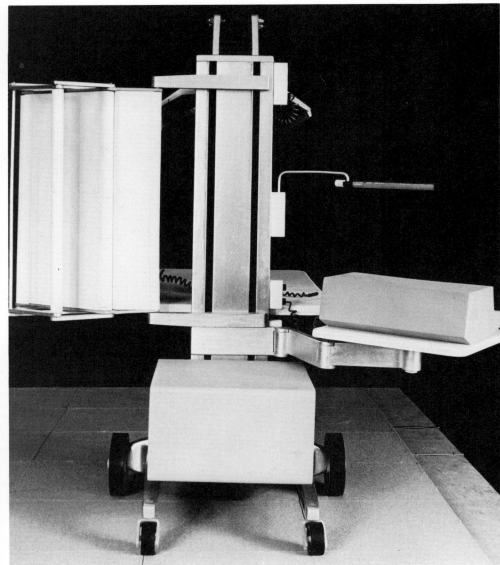

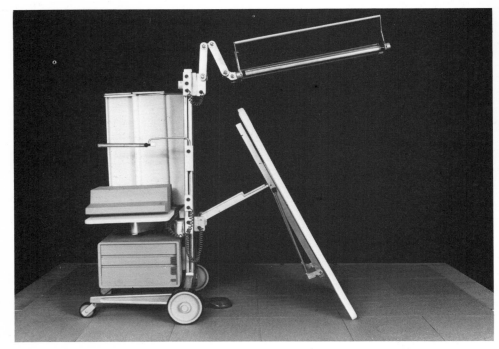

Photographs showing different positions and applications of the basic unit

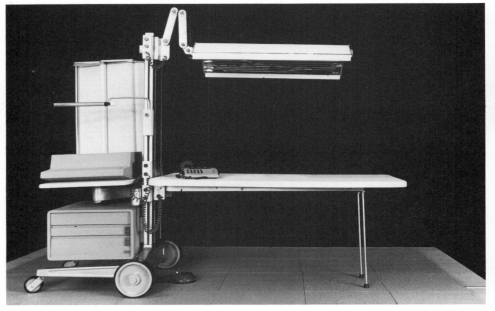

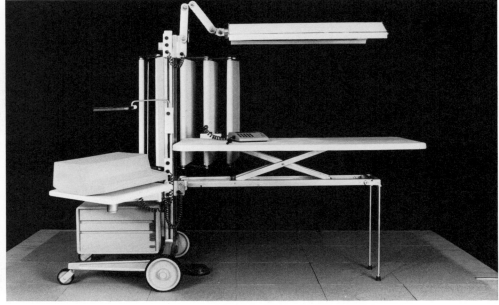

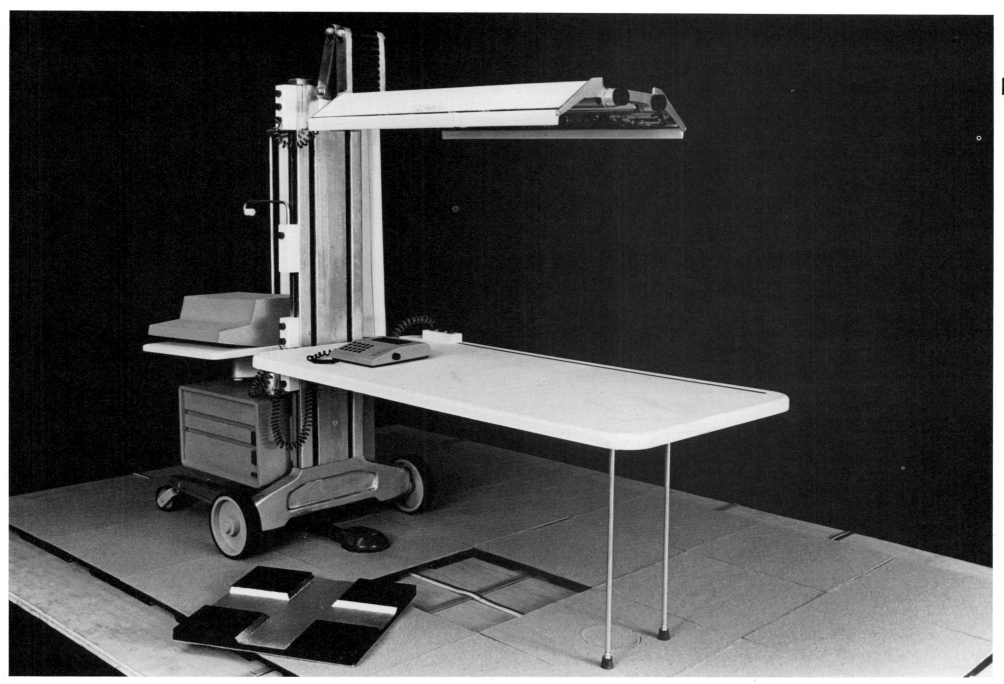

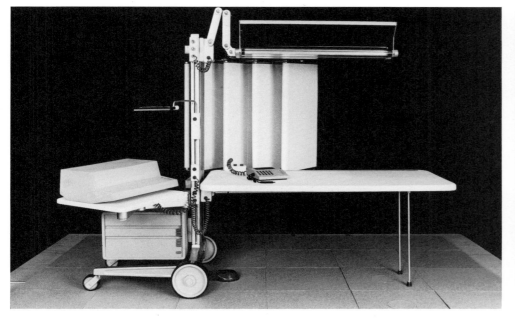

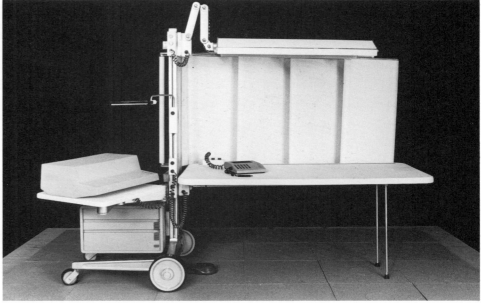

Building Design Partnership
EALING CENTRAL AREA DEVELOPMENT

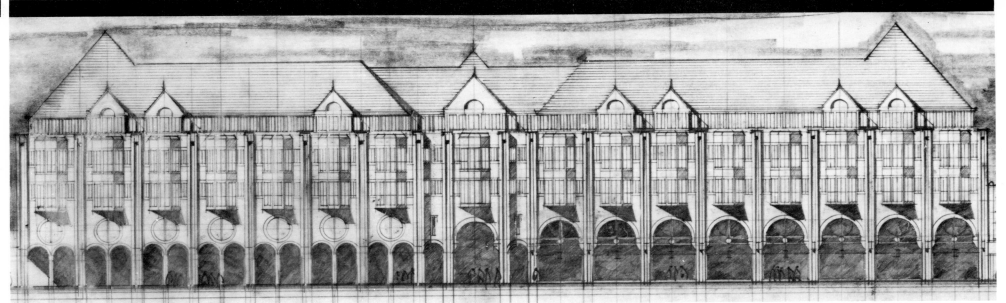
High Street elevation

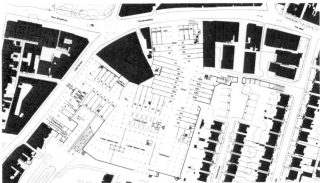
Site plan

Perspective of central court
East elevation

FROM AN ARCHITECTURAL STANDPOINT this scheme is one of the most controversial in the firm. At the competition stage the brief made it quite clear that the winner would have to fit in with the character of Ealing and, since being appointed, there has been great insistence on our keeping and developing the spirit of the scheme as submitted.

Escalators rise from the High Street level into the lower part of the atrium which is walled and floored in Travertine marble and which has a gallery from which the courts on either side can be viewed and entered. These courts are luxuriously landscaped and built over the first floor car park. They are separated by a 3-storey high glazed atrium of triple-arched section. Two glass lifts rise from the main level of the atrium to give access to three floors of offices.

A dominant feature of the shopping plan is the large court which functions as a town square at the heart of the development. It is here that the three main shopping malls converge. It will be formally planted with four rows of trees which focus on the balconied twin towers rising from a still, reflecting pool at the east end.

The twin towers give access to the seven levels of car parking and the library on the east side.

CLIENT: JL Development Services Ltd
ARCHITECTS, CIVIL, STRUCTURAL & MECHANICAL ENGINEERS:
Building Design Partnership
QUANTITY SURVEYORS: Guthrie & Partners

View of model with twin towers and part of car park

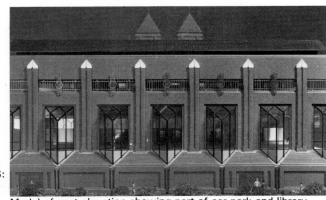
Model of east elevation showing part of car park and library

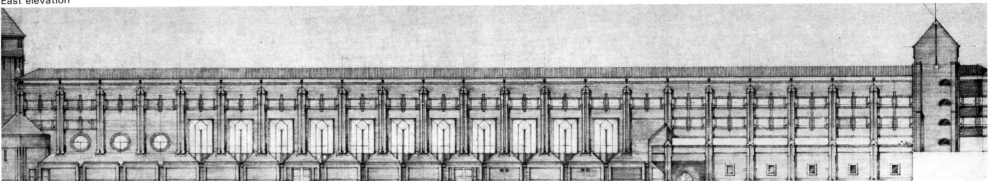

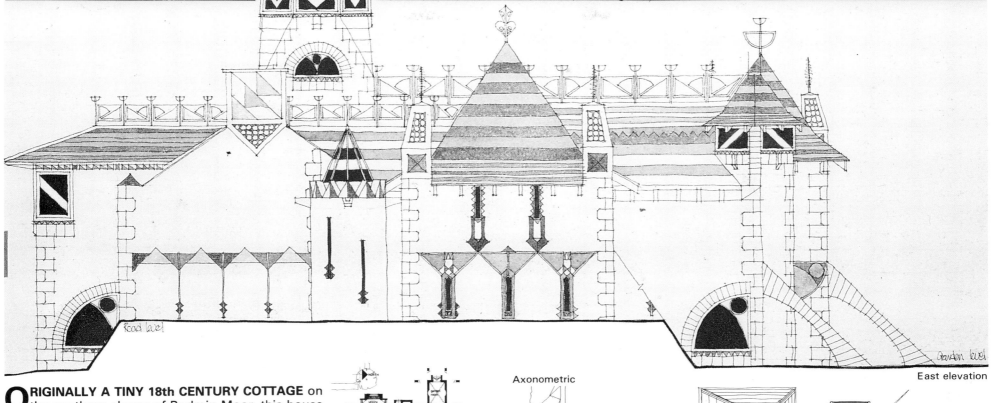

East elevation

ORIGINALLY A TINY 18th CENTURY COTTAGE on the southern slopes of Bodmin Moor, this house belongs to the painter, photographer and author Graham Ovenden. He wanted to enlarge the cottage to provide space sufficient for the needs of a family and guests, studio accommodation for painting and photography and spaces large enough and stylistically suitable to house a significant collection of 19th century furniture.

This building was conceived prior to the formation of the 'Ruralist Brotherhood', of which Ovenden is a member, and whilst it is not an 'official' Ruralist building, it shares much of the philosophy of the Ruralist group of painters; with their admiration for some of the great artistic personalities of the past.

Ground and first floor plans

Axonometric

View from the south-west

Demetri Porphyrios
HOUSE IN GREECE

THIS IS A HOUSE in the northern outskirts of Athens. The sloping terrain of the site together with the restricted frontage to the street and the direction of the view establish an east-west axis. The house, therefore, is doubly frontal: to the west it faces the street; to the east it looks towards the city of Athens.

The brief for the house was conventional except for two points the client insisted upon: first, that there was to be an interior swimming pool with adjoining exercise rooms; second, that upon entering the house one should clearly perceive its organisation.

It was this latter aspect which, together with the site conditions, generated the design *parti*. The entry hall, measuring 6×6×9 metres, has a split level staircase that leads to the swimming pool below and to the reception areas above. The corridor that serves the first floor bedrooms pierces the entry hall and becomes a high level gallery. The private and public areas of the house are brought together, therefore, in the entry hall itself. And yet, the skylit timber roof, the Doric columns *in antis* supporting the gallery above, the balcony in the centre and the base in marble give the impression of a covered court.

The reception rooms are arranged in sequence and open onto a pergola that faces the garden. Below is the arcaded porch of the swimming pool. Facing the street, another pergola highlights the staircase that connects the parking area with the house. Finally, the circular staircase serving all three levels of the house terminates in a belvedere that affords a memorable view of the city of Athens and of the sea beyond.

In this way, the house is composed of a number of distinct syntactic types: the pergola, the *treppenhaus*, the tower and the rectangular house proper. These types are composed in an additive manner and never lose their identity except for a certain qualification of their edges at the points of interface. Similarly, the overall figurative character of the house derives from the confluence of several iconographic types: the rusticated base, the entry porch, the pedimented entry, the belvedere tower and the familiar double-pitched roof of the house proper.

Internally, the reception rooms are 4 metres high and their individual as well as composite dimensions are always multiples of the series 2–4–6. The swimming pool, delimited by engaged pilasters and pilasters *in antis*, acquires the importance of a public room.

The construction is in reinforced concrete with stone facing externally and Pentelic marble facing for skirtings, floor surrounds, staircases, balusters, fire surrounds and window sills. The roofs are in timber, close-boarded and tiled. The roof to the entry hall as well as the joinery in the house are in stained and varnished oak. The two Doric columns of the entry hall are unfluted and in solid Pentelic marble; they have been saved from a Neoclassical house recently demolished. All ironmongery is in brass. Floors are in tongued-and-grooved oak boards except for the floors to the corridors and bathrooms which are in chequerboard dark green and white marble. The floors to the exercise rooms adjacent to the pool and those of the pergolas and porches outside are in Pelion stone slabs. The walls and ceilings throughout the house are plastered and painted off-white and white respectively. Externally, the house is rendered and painted in brushed yellow ochre.

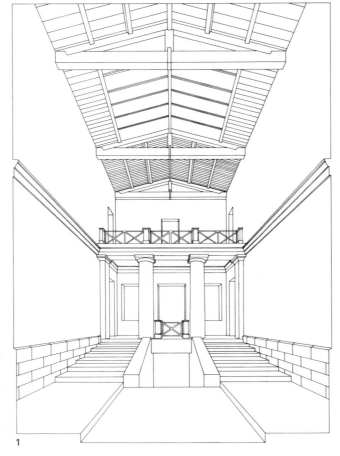

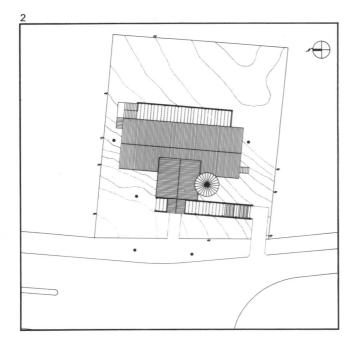

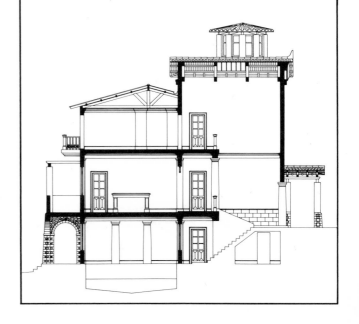

1

Entry Hall

1 Interior perspective of entry hall

2 Site plan

3 Transverse section

4 Front elevation facing the street

5 Side elevation facing the garden

6 Street level plan, ± 0 and+1m

7 Garden level plan, -2.40m

8 First floor plan, +5m

PRESENTATION DRAWINGS: A Zannas

4

5

6

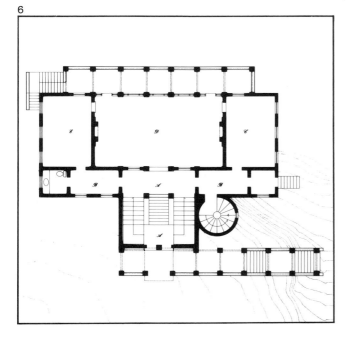

7

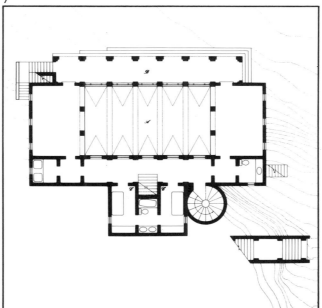

8

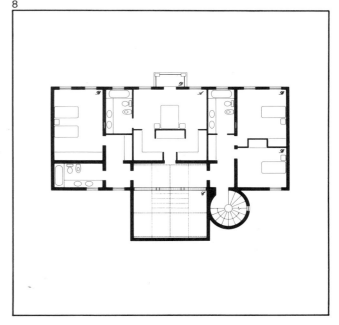

Rick Mather Architects
REBUILDING AND REFURBISHMENT OF 4 ETON VILLAS, LONDON

THIS HOUSE WAS REMODELLED to suit the needs of a psychiatrist and psychologist who both work and live in the house. The bottom floor was converted to a suite for their professional work and the top three floors for the private quarters. New terraces were excavated and french windows made to give a direct connection from the two ground floor consulting rooms to the garden. The first floor (where much of the original detailing was still intact) was little changed. The top two floors were opened into a large living space by removing and rebuilding virtually everything from the second floor upwards. The third floor was lowered, opened out with a new dormer, french windows, and roof garden, and omitted at the front to extend second floor living room up to the roof and through three new electrically operated roof lights. New bathrooms, cloakroom and new passenger lift (for the clients' old age) were added to the side bay.

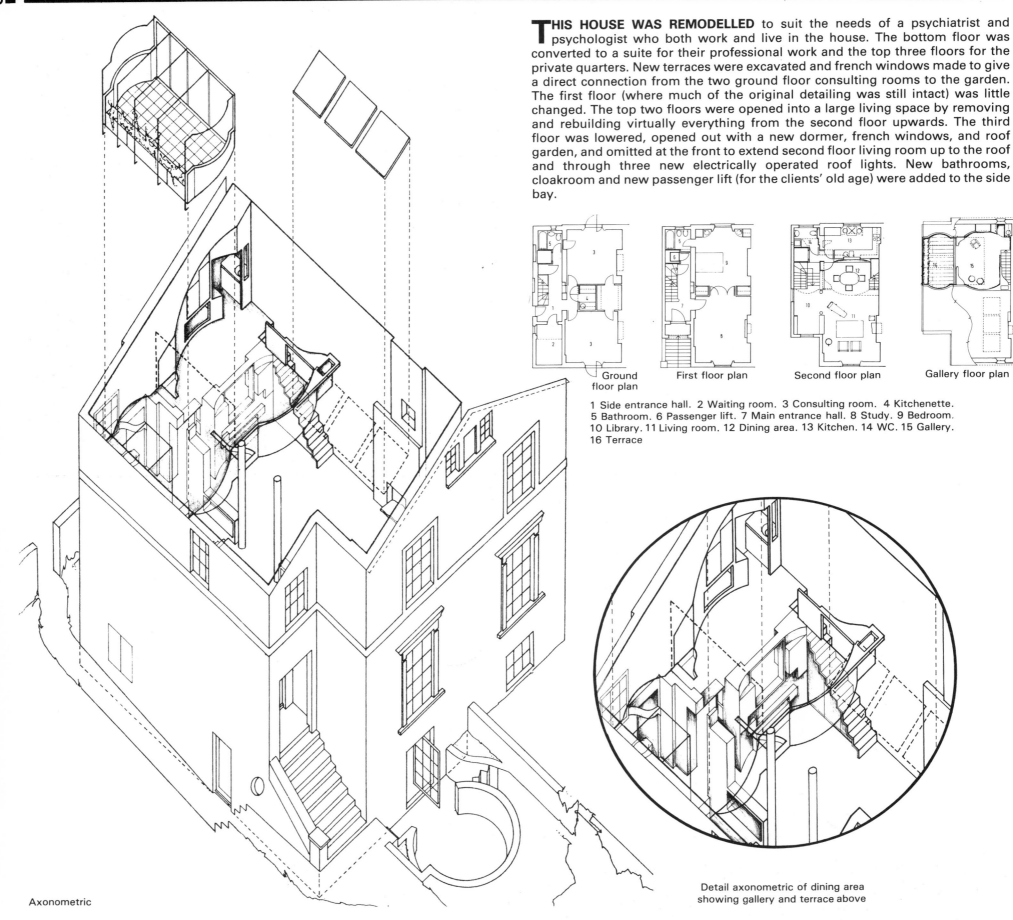

Ground floor plan

First floor plan

Second floor plan

Gallery floor plan

1 Side entrance hall. 2 Waiting room. 3 Consulting room. 4 Kitchenette. 5 Bathroom. 6 Passenger lift. 7 Main entrance hall. 8 Study. 9 Bedroom. 10 Library. 11 Living room. 12 Dining area. 13 Kitchen. 14 WC. 15 Gallery. 16 Terrace

Axonometric

Detail axonometric of dining area showing gallery and terrace above

The clients use the lower part of the house during the day when they can enjoy the view to the garden or a quick cup of coffee in the sunshine between patients. In the evening they use the top which catches the best daylight and weather permitting, enjoy a cocktail on the roof terrace in the late evening sun.

The house is part of a row of semi-detached early Victorian villas approached through a long garden. Care was taken to retain and reinforce the existing look by using the same detailing for the new french windows on the bottom floor, recessing the roof terrace into the roof making it almost invisible from the street, restoring any of the old detailing that had been lost, and rerendering the outside to match the original colour and marking. The project was completed in September 1980.

DESIGN TEAM: Rick Mather and Bill Greensmith

Roof lights over living area

Interior and exterior (Photographs Ken Tam)

NEW HOUSE, GIRSBY MANOR, LINCOLNSHIRE

THE CLIENT'S BRIEF was for a much smaller building than the original country house, preferably all on one floor and with immediate access to a conservatory and protected terrace that could be used in all seasons. To increase the apparent scale of this building to fit the big site three devices are used:
— the south elevation is maximised by arranging the main rooms in a line toward the major views;
— the east and west elevations are increased by adding an entrance court which also incorporates the existing gate, game larder and tower into the new design;
— the height of the new house is exaggerated by using an inverted roof and building a new tower. The tower also terminates the drive and balances the old tower diagonally opposite.

DESIGN TEAM: Rick Mather and Bill Greensmith

Perspective of house in context

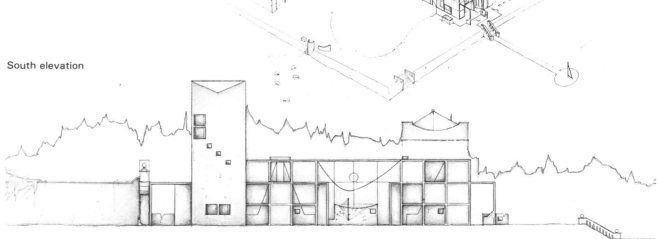

Plan

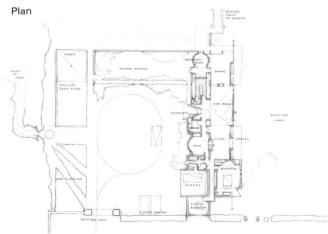

South elevation

John Outram
FACTORIES AT KENSAL ROAD, NORTH LONDON

KENSAL RD plays with the traditional language of the facade to say that the gods of the city to which this facade is dedicated are personifications of the three Mythologies of Modernism — the gods of Rationality, of Matter and of Vitality.

ARCHITECTS: John Outram and Tony McIntyre
CLIENT: McKay Securities Group Ltd
STRUCTURAL ENGINEERS: Peter Brett Associates;
                Rom River Co Ltd; Reconsteel Ltd
QUANTITY SURVEYORS: Close Morton & Partners
MAIN CONTRACTOR: Haymills (Contractors) Ltd

Oblique view of Kensal Road elevation

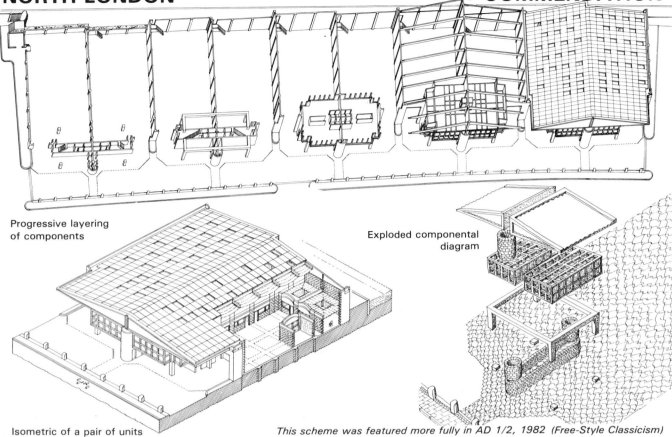

Progressive layering of components

Exploded componental diagram

Isometric of a pair of units

This scheme was featured more fully in AD 1/2, 1982 (Free-Style Classicism)

Cambridge Design
DAVIES' SCHOOL OF ENGLISH, CAMBRIDGE

THE EXISTING SCHOOL OF ENGLISH BUILDING, together with two similar Victorian villas on either side will be incorporated within the new scheme. The new complex will extend onto the adjoining sites and will provide a school of 15 classrooms with ancillary accommodation for teachers and study areas using computer links, a 250 seat multi-purpose lecture hall, 75 seat library resource centre, language laboratory, administrative offices and an 80 seat cafeteria.

    The building has at its centre the multi-purpose hall which extends up through three storeys of the building and through glazed screens provides a display of the functions of each floor. The construction is due for completion in April 1984.

CLIENT: Enrocentres-Zurich, Switzerland
STRUCTURAL ENGINEERS: FJ Samuely & Partners
QUANTITY SURVEYORS: Davis Belfield & Everest
SERVICES ENGINEERS: YRM Engineers   Section through model

View of model from south-east showing the cafeteria at the back which looks onto the Botanical Gardens

Levitt Bernstein Associates
HOUSING AT FERRY STREET, LONDON

Axonometric of scheme

A RANGE of one, two and three bedroomed houses, with a 20–25% provision for the elderly was the brief. All the dwellings were to have living rooms positioned so as to take advantage of the spectacular views to the South, across the Thames and towards Greenwich. In addition, all the family houses were to have gardens to the front and rear.

The problem was one of distributing the buildings around the site so that they would relate to the adjacent buildings, the street frontage, and to the riverside. The solution was to distort two basic terraces of narrow-frontage houses.

A planning requirement for a public riverside walk, with access from Ferry Street led to the positioning of a central pathway on the axis of the Cutty Sark opposite, and funnelling out at the riverside to the full width of the site.

CLIENT: Circle 33 Housing Trust Ltd
STRUCTURAL ENGINEERS: Ove Arup & Partners
QUANTITY SURVEYORS: Rider Hunt & Partners
SERVICES CONSULTANTS: Dale & Goldfinger

Riverside elevation

Brown & Parnaby
COMMERCIAL BUILDING, BRITISH COLUMBIA

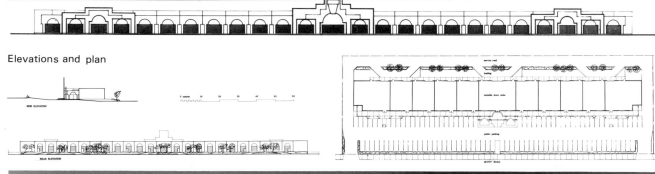

Elevations and plan

T HIS IS A BRASH COMMERCIAL BUILDING in a brash commercial context which provides a simple economical enclosure for standard rentable units for use as shops, offices or service premises. The site is on a secondary highway—a commercial strip—on the fringe of Greater Vancouver. The developer's success will depend upon attracting customers and tenants to his site in competition with dozens of other similar commercial developments.

The simple form arises directly from the shape of the site and its relationship to the highway. To maximise floor space and frontage the building is long (156 m) and shallow (17 m). Architectural expression is applied in a series of layers on the public face of the building.

Colour is the final and critical element in the composition. The basic colour is green ranging from the palest pastel shade to strong deep tones. Each panel is a different colour with a gradation from the centre to the ends to suggest a curved facade— breaking, and at the same time confirming the monotony of the colonnade. Construction is intended to start in early 1982.

DESIGN CONSULTANTS: Brown & Parnaby Architects
PROJECT INITIATION AND MANAGEMENT: Stene Associates, Canada

Left : Perspective of street elevation (perspective: Barry Lundahl, photo: Commercial Illustrators Ltd, Vancouver)

Graham Smith
TUC BUILDING, WHITEHALL

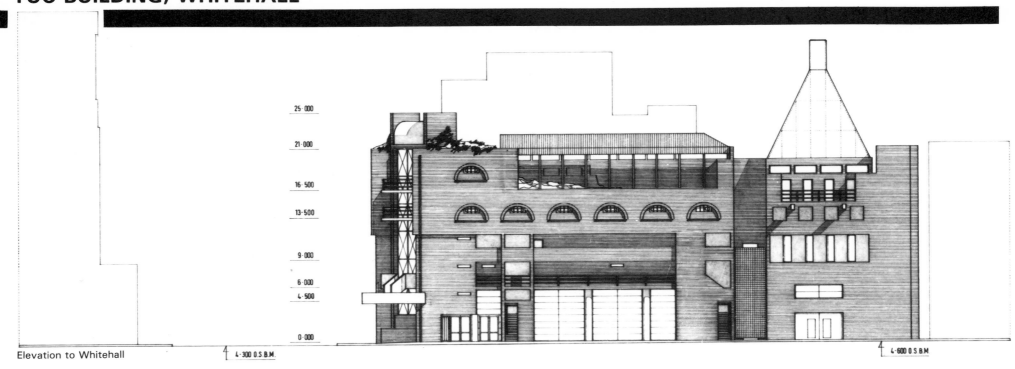

Elevation to Whitehall   4·300 O.S.B.M.   4·600 O.S.B.M.

THE PURPOSE OF THIS PROJECT was to insert a building into Whitehall which would expose the role of a building as a monument, and its capacity to represent attitude and value. The TUC brief evolved from the thematically determining context with which the proposed building was to establish a dialectic. The historical significance of Whitehall as a synonym for government, as prime civic space for public gestures of acclamation and dissent was to be appropriated and inflected by another institution.

The Private Building situated along the secondary route of Richmond Terrace includes a training college, specialist departments and a printing hall; it internalises its most important spaces which extend into the Assembly Chamber. Surrounding this Chamber which takes the form of a large debating chamber and presidium; and fronting predominantly onto Whitehall are the official and public areas including exhibition space, a museum, public and press galleries and Secretariat building. This area, surmounted

by a shed 'baldachino' is the animating core of the whole building and provides a setting for the fundamental act of protection through assembly.

The Council Chamber at the apex of the Secretariat building accommodates the body elected to represent and negotiate, and has an external building balcony both overlooking the Cenotaph and undermining the Royal balcony opposite.

AIR SERVICES CONSULTANT: Keith Hanson (Max Fordham & Ptnrs)

Section A   Section C   Richmond Terrace elevation

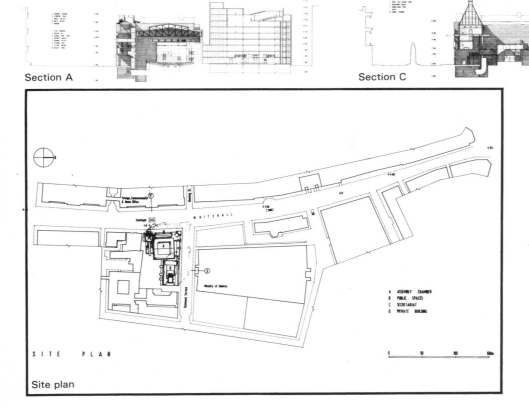

Site plan

A   ASSEMBLY CHAMBER
B   PUBLIC SPACES
C   SECRETARIAT
D   PRIVATE BUILDING

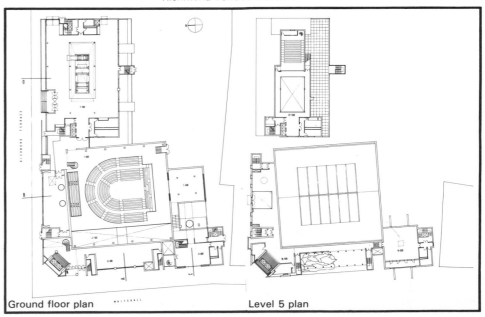

Ground floor plan   Level 5 plan

Michael Gold
LIBRARY FOR THE ROYAL MILITARY COLLEGE OF SCIENCE, SHRIVENHAM, WILTSHIRE

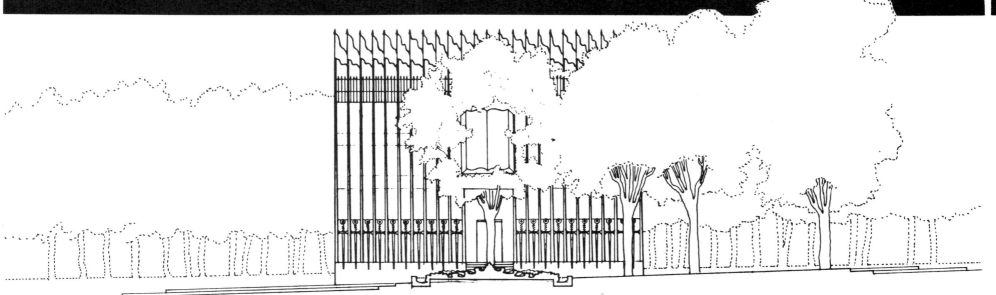

Entrance elevation

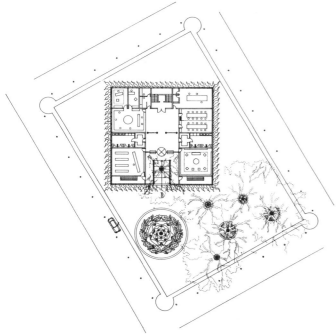

Ground floor plan

THE **EXTERIOR OF THE LIBRARY** is of bronzed glass, with the building set on a black asphalt surface edged by stone pavings. The asphalt is inlaid with gold ceramic tiles around the building and various coloured tiles around the five tree pits. Inset in the surface, in front of the entrance, is a round pond (placed over an existing reservoir) in which is placed a stainless steel 'rose' garden.

In the courtyard (8 × 8 m) is an oak tree, which is trained through the south facade screen to yield an impression that is 'captured' by the building. There is a progression from the entrance gates, up the steps in the courtyard lined with twisted metal handrails, through the bronzed revolving door above which is an 'open book' shaped window, into the lobby, past the gilded rope barriers, on to the lift and up, to turn back to the main library floor above. This progression consists of a series of axial compositions collecting a somewhat heraldic imagery corresponding to various associations drawn from the nature and use of the particular building.

Heraldic symbols are employed as metal flags on the top frieze of the exterior of the building, they are enamelled with the colours and emblems of the various regiments, services and other bodies of the military.

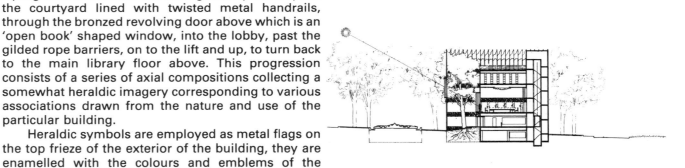

Cross section

Section through entrance

Basement

First floor

Gallery

Top floor

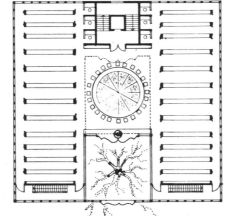

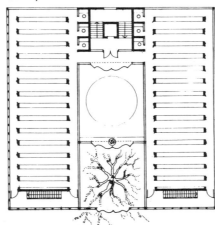

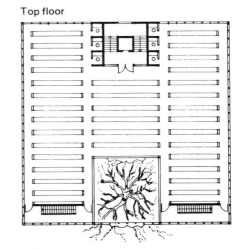

Sansom Cross Architects

LIBRARY FOR THE ROYAL MILITARY COLLEGE OF SCIENCE, SHRIVENHAM, WILTSHIRE

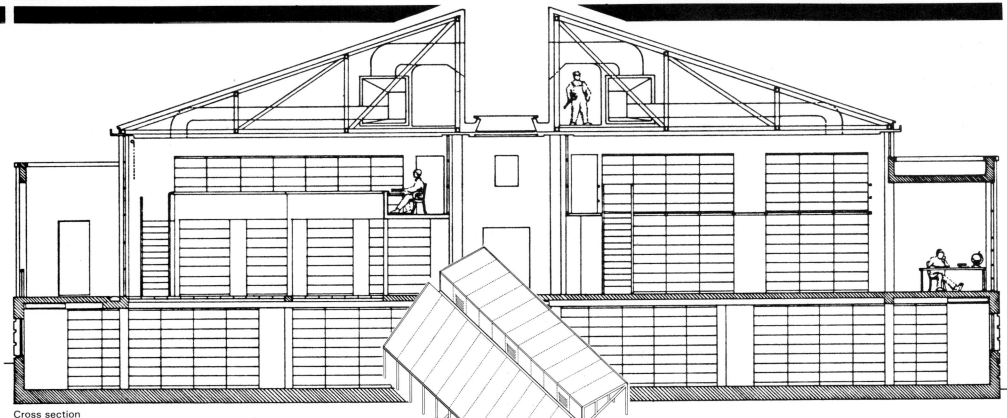

Cross section

REJECTING THE CASUALNESS of many recent libraries, this project was inspired by the simple clarity of older buildings and the tradition of military structures. Sited in an exposed position, it was intended to complement the Sandhurst Building south of it and to establish a new order on the north side of a proposed pedestrian precinct. The main rooms are double height in the centre of the ground floor with specialist spaces at the corners. Textbooks and reserve stacks are at basement level. On a reinforced concrete podium a steel structure stands to span the main rooms. A silver-grey metal roof would glisten above in contrast to the brick around the ground floor and rusticated stone below. This was a competition submission of 1981.

Sandhurst building

Model

Exploded axonometric

Perspective of building in context

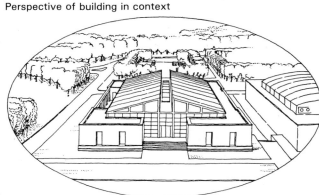

Model

Pentagram
RECONSTRUCTION OF THE GLOBE THEATRE

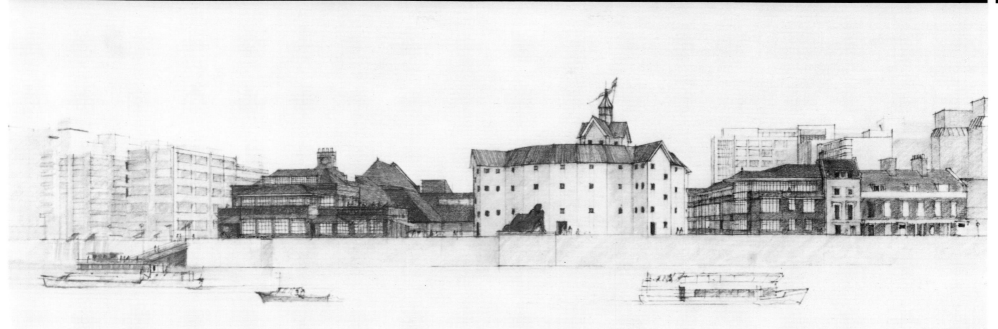

Riverside elevation

THE GLOBE THEATRE COMPLEX is seen partly as an educational tool, a centre for Shakespeare studies and also as a performance space where the Elizabethan Theatre can be recreated. The Globe itself will be as authentic as possible and as uncomfortable, no doubt as the original.

The small covered theatre in the complex is a reconstruction of Inigo Jones' 'Cockpit' Theatre, based on the drawings discovered not long ago in Worcester College, Oxford. In the Elizabethan tradition there is no elaborate staging, plays in the Globe will take place in the afternoons in summer, by daylight. The Cockpit is a winter theatre and there will be a natural ventilation and lighting system. The problem of relating the Globe and the Cockpit to the matrix of modern buildings with complex usages is inevitably arguable. The theory that has been followed is to accept that the theatres are craft buildings and that the others should be too. They are also very much reduced in scale and the museum is really a connecting shed between the larger monuments. The flats are broken into verticals to contrast with the simple white Globe, and the red brick of the adjoining Provost's House on Bankside will run through all the new buildings. The Cockpit will be in a similar colour but if possible in the 2″ bricks of the period.

Conjectural reconstruction of original Globe Theatre

Section through the new Globe

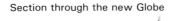

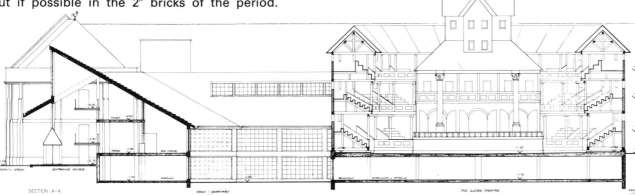

SECTION A-A

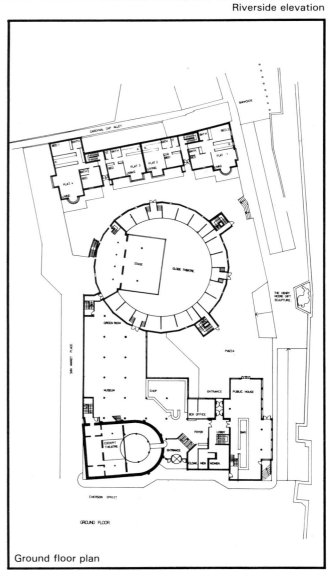

Ground floor plan

Peter Bell & Partners
TWO HOUSES IN CAMDEN TOWN

THE PURPOSE OF THIS PROJECT is to design two houses which exploit the corner location and the difference between their middle and end of terrace positions. The echelon plan provides corner views and west light for both houses on the street side, and the shared statutory off-street parking behind the gardens. The houses are of exposed brick cross-wall and timber construction, and aim for a richness of detail which is both elegant and self-explanatory. To this end all timber is dowel jointed, for economy (of bolts) and in pursuit of a rigorous structural purity.

PROJECT TEAM: Peter Bell and Stephen Greenberg

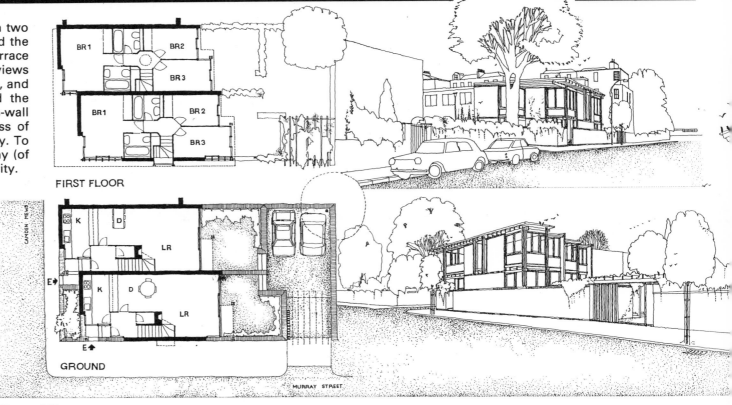

FIRST FLOOR

GROUND

John Melvin & Partners
HOUSING FOR CHILDLESS COUPLES, ISLINGTON

IF WE ARE TO TRANSCEND THE BRIEF from one of mere housing to that of place and home-making, which we see as the architect's prime responsibility, then a notion of home has to be sought. A clue can be found in the very language we use. A dwelling place in old English is 'eard' and a dwelling is 'eardian', thus steward, guardian and warden are all connected by the same root and common thread of meaning, being of protection and of looking after. Therefore, the notion of dwelling should not stray too far from this essential quality and function.

CLIENT: The London Borough of Islington
PROJECT TEAM: John Melvin and Angus McLeish
STRUCTURAL ENGINEERS: Jaffet, Gubbay & Partners
QUANTITY SURVEYORS: Burrell, Hayward & Budd
SERVICES ENGINEERS: J Lewin & Associates
MAIN CONTRACTOR: Whyatt Builders Ltd
View of front elevation to Blackstock Road (ph Martin Charles)

Greenhill & Jenner Partnership
WANDSWORTH SHIFTWORKERS' NURSERY, LONDON

THIS NURSERY FOR 50 CHILDREN up to five years old is designed to operate 14 hours a day for the benefit of local working parents. The backland site, about a third of an acre within the perimeter of St Georges Hospital, London SW19, is contained by a 2 m high brick boundary wall and the blank faces of existing buildings. The nursery consists of a central nave, bounded on the road side by service rooms and to the rear by quiet rooms and ancillary spaces linked to the main play space by sliding folding doors.

CLIENT: Wandsworth Child Care Campaign
STRUCTURAL ENGINEERS: S Richardson
QUANTITY SURVEYORS: BWL Smith & Associates

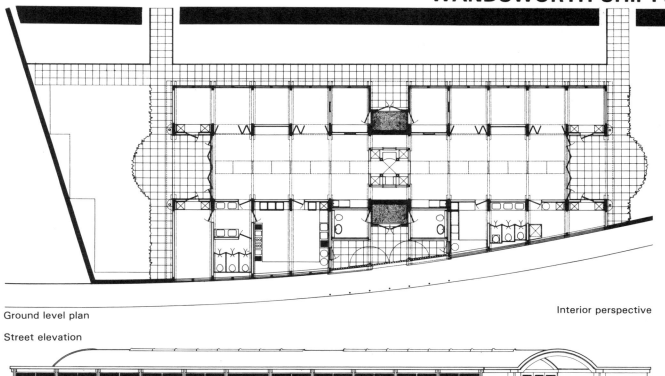

Ground level plan

Street elevation

Interior perspective

Rock Townsend
CONVERSION OF A MEWS WAREHOUSE, SOUTH-EAST LONDON

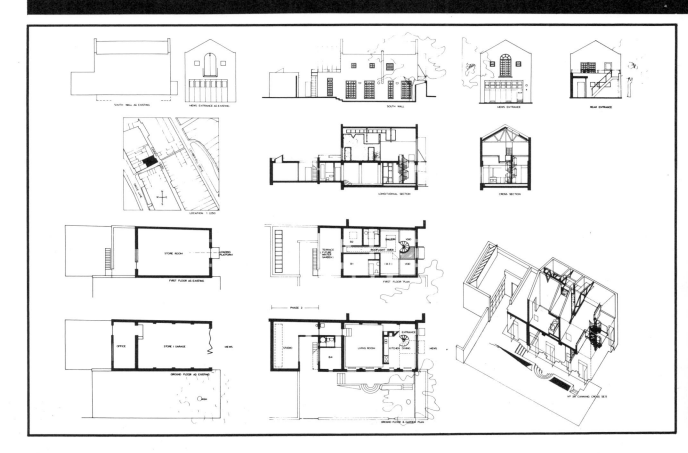

THIS HOUSE WAS CONVERTED from a small warehouse and garage in a mews. The concept of the house revolves around the kitchen/dining space which is double height, exposing the full form of the building. The two levels are linked with a staircase which leads to the gallery, this area is roof-lit and is used as a workspace. The rooflight extends along the length of the house, lighting the short corridor and the bedrooms via the triangular openings at the apex between the walls and the roof. The landing is linked to the former first floor front landing opening by a metal bridge. From here fine views are available up and down the mews and into the entrance and dining space below.

CLIENT: Paul and Carol Vinycomb
PROJECT ARCHITECT: John Eger
CONTRACTOR: Chouter and Son Ltd

View of interior

Site section

THE PRIMARY INTENTION of the layout is to create compact streets of terraced houses of a scale appropriate to the location in Milton Keynes. 152 dwellings were required, the majority of which are houses, a mixture of seven, six, five, three and two person dwellings.

Courtyard blocks terminate the axes of the streets and also act as gateways for the pedestrian access to the main shopping area which lies beyond a formally landscaped zone. This landscaping responds to both the main distributor road to the north-west and the cycle path crossing the site.

In order to form a distinct edge to the open space to the south-east, the ends of the terraces are marked by the returning of the pitched roofs as hipped gables, with large oriel windows set in the flank walls facing onto the open space. The perimeter is further defined by short terraces, placed orthogonally to the streets which are indented, behind pergolas, to screen parking from the distributor roads and the open space.

A clear distinction between public and private realms is maintained: entrances and integral garages are positioned directly off the street, while 'squares' contained behind the blocks provide play spaces immediately accessible from private rear gardens.

CLIENT: Milton Keynes Development Corporation
STRUCTURAL ENGINEERS: FJ Samuely & Partners
QUANTITY SURVEYORS: Davis, Belfield & Everest
SERVICES ENGINEERS: Dale & Goldfinger

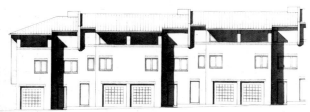

Elevation of three-storey street

Site plan

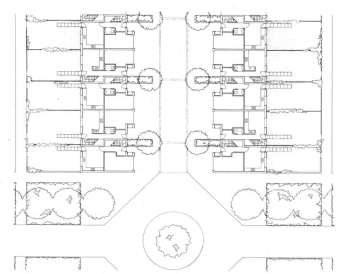

Ground floor plan with combinations of four, six and seven- person houses

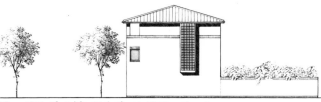

Elevation of gable end, three-storey street

Axonometric of three-storey street

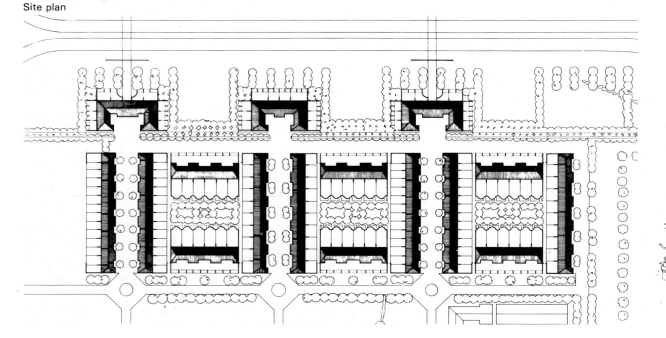

SINGLE PERSON HOUSING, HARINGEY, LONDON

View of facade (ph Martin Charles)

THE SITE FOR THIS PROJECT is a narrow strip of land with views over London to both the north and south. The site is flanked on either side with 11 and eight storey residential blocks.

The brief required accommodation for 34 two-person and two one-person units. A four-person caretakers unit was also required together with a laundry, common room and kitchen, porter's office and ancillary plant rooms. There are loadbearing brick cross-walls and piers, with reinforced concrete floors and roof slabs. The external finishes are facing brick piers and faced flank walls with brick soldier courses at floor slab levels. The windows are high-performance stained timber opening casements with spandrel panels of glass blocks.

CLIENT: London Borough of Haringey
STRUCTURAL ENGINEERS:
FJ Samuely & Partners
QUANTITY SURVEYORS:
Monk & Dunstone,
Mahon & Scears
SERVICES ENGINEERS:
London Borough of
Haringey
GENERAL
CONTRACTOR:
H Fairweather
Ltd

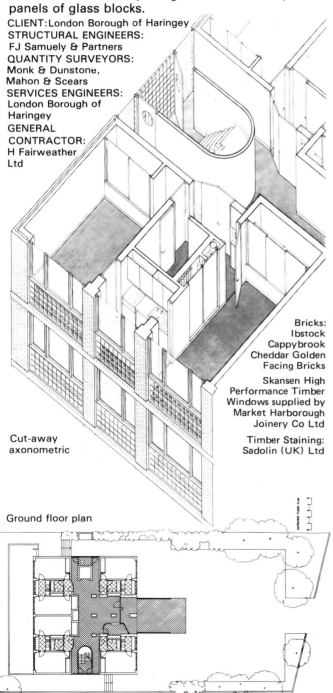

Bricks:
Ibstock
Cappybrook
Cheddar Golden
Facing Bricks

Skansen High
Performance Timber
Windows supplied by
Market Harborough
Joinery Co Ltd

Timber Staining:
Sadolin (UK) Ltd

Cut-away
axonometric

Ground floor plan

Julyan M Wickham Architects
HOSPITAL FOR THE DOUBLY HANDICAPPED, BOEKEL, HOLLAND

THIS PROJECT PROPOSES a place for the treatment of people who are both mentally and physically handicapped. It forms part of a hospital complex which specialises in the treatment of psychiatric conditions. The hospital, which was established in the late 19th century, is today a major centre in Europe, housing some 500 patients and over 600 doctors, nurses and other staff. The scale of the hospital and its gradual development over the last 100 years has produced a complex of pavilions each concentrating on a specific condition or activity and forming as a whole a village of a kind.

The pavilion for the doubly handicapped is designed to house 30 patients and will have facilities for various treatments both psychiatric and physical. The patients fall into three broadly defined groups; the new admissions, those who can be resocialised, and the chronic.

The brief called for three separate wings or houses for the patients' living accommodation, a central area for the psychiatric treatments and leading off this area a complex containing the hydro, physio and ergo therapy areas, the programme required many small spaces on one floor.

Thus the combination of the context: with its avenue to the south and closely surrounding buildings on all other sides; the requirements of the brief; a series of interrelated wings needing much perimeter wall surface to light and ventilate many small spaces; and our wish to provide a series of intervening garden courts of varied openness, quality and use suggested to us the use of a chequer board plan arrangement as a starting point.

Each living wing is approached from the central area leading into the day spaces—which consist of the dining hall off which are the living room and kitchen, all relatively open to each other and their adjacent garden courts. Each of the day spaces relates to at least two outside spaces, sometimes very enclosed, sometimes very open, sometimes very public and hard, sometimes more or less private and soft and sometimes shared, always in different combinations. By contrast to the day spaces the night spaces are more closed and private since they are areas where the inhabitants can retreat into their own private world. The rooms, which look for the most part outwards onto the larger world of the hospital complex, are wrapped around their service rooms— the bathrooms, lavatories and shower rooms, with the intervening corridor forming a route occasionally looking out over the complex or top lit, and widening into a small hall at the entrance to each room. The wing for new admissions (house 1) to the south west is the farthest from the main entrance court and has the most protected external spaces. However, it enjoys close contact with the central area and shares a garden court with the wing which contains those patients who are to be resocialised (house 2). This is the middle or south east wing which in itself overlooks the main entrance court and the pavilion containing the shops, barber, tobacconist and newsagent which is to be placed in the oval square at the junction of the avenue and the entrance road. House 3, the

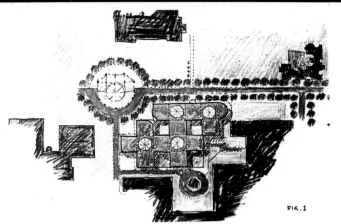

Chequerboard arrangement

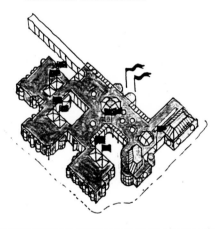

Schematic axonometrics

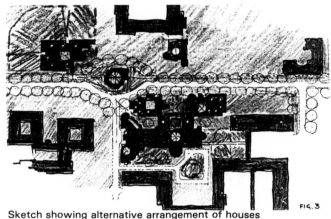

Sketch showing alternative arrangement of houses

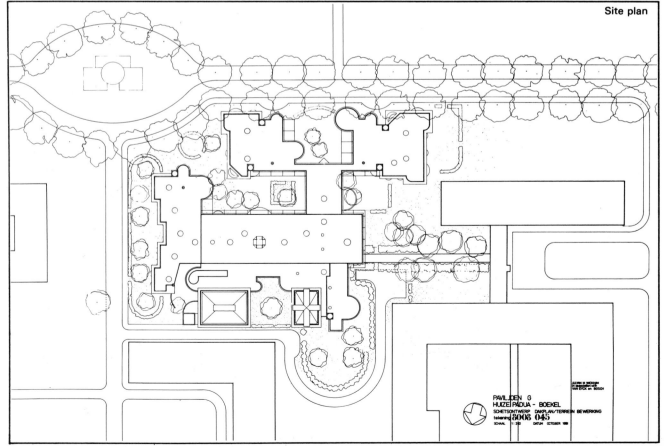

Site plan

PAVILJOEN G
HUIZE PADUA - BOEKEL

wing for the chronic, to the east is separate from the other two. Its day spaces are again overlooking the main entrance court to allow maximum external stimulus, but here the night (more private) spaces are given their own garden on the outside and a more street-like internal corridor which provides access to the rooms from the day spaces and this time has a separate hall leading from it to the service areas.

CLIENT: Huize Padua-Boekel
PROJECT TEAM: Julyan M Wickham with Desmond Lavery, Tess Wickham, Jamie Campbell, Chaiuw Lim and Douglas Streeter

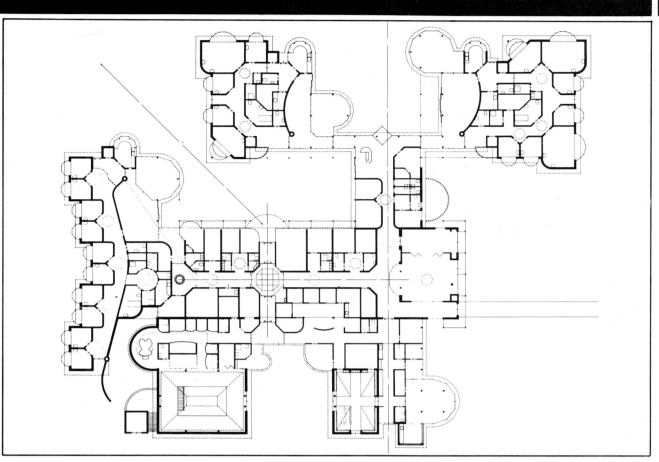

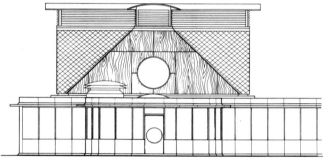

Detail of west elevation

Floor plan: we had to avoid long straight corridors which could seem even longer to those patients with a limited action radius and symmetrical arrangements which may have a disorientating effect. However the preferable asymmetry must not lead to a sense of chaos but a high degree of recognition.

North elevation

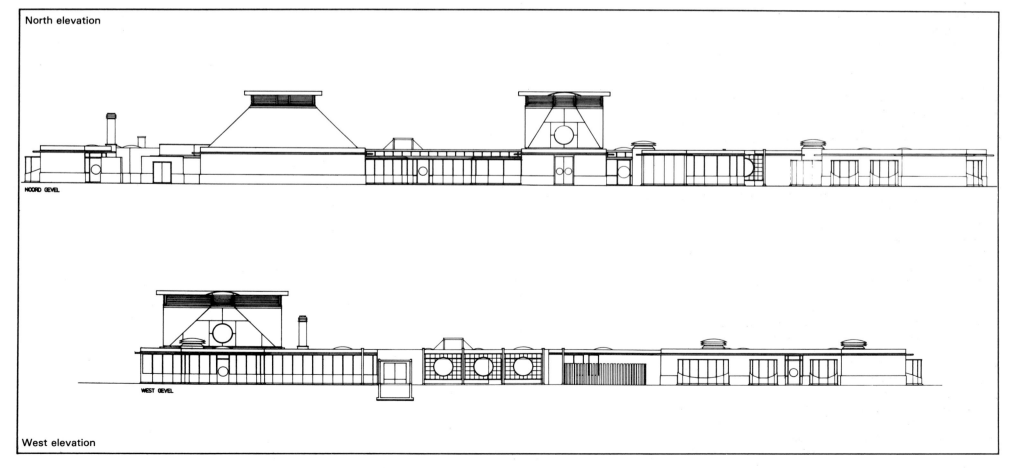

West elevation

James Gowan
HOUSE PROJECTS, HAMPSTEAD

THE PREOCCUPATIONS OF THE 1956–63 HOUSE SKETCHES[1] were all concerned with how a family might develop from a modest beginning; a small domestic core containing kitchen, bathroom and stairway. Future additions were shunted onto this with much energy and dramatic effect and there was a relaxed attitude towards the use of a mish-mash of materials. Aalto and Van Doesburg furnished some of the credentials and brutalism still had its pungency, even if it lacked an audience. This is also true for the rear facade of our Kensington studio house[2] in Southwell Gardens; with two-tone brickwork, fair face concrete rainwater head and arched lintel, inaccessible splendours which would never be gazed upon.

If intention is the guide, the current house projects eschew most of the old war-horses; general considerations and long-term strategies such as prototypes,

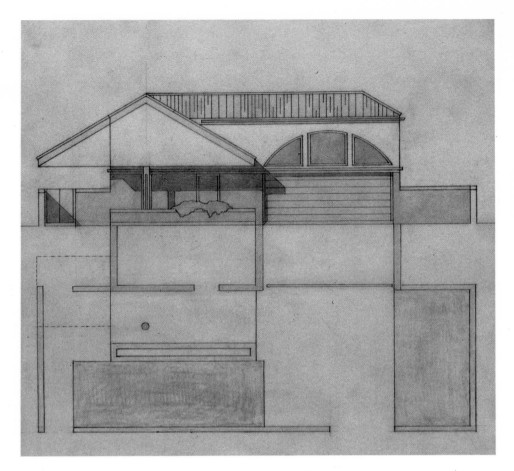

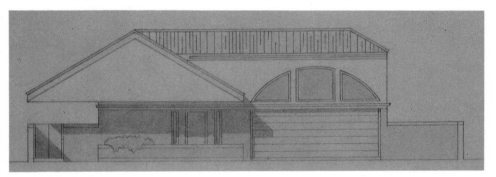

James Gowan & Anthony McIntyre
DIY SUPERMARKET FOR SAINSBURY'S HOMEBASE, BROMLEY, KENT

IN DECEMBER 1981 we were invited by Sainsbury's Homebase, a DIY supermarket chain, to submit a design in limited competition for a store in Bromley, a part of South London. Our submission was completed by mid-February and its overriding intention, to domesticate an industrial shed, did not engage the imagination of the jury who, it was reported, were looking for a strong idea.

The brief calls for a shop and facilities of about 2,500 m² plus a garden centre and parking for 125 cars. Apart from a section being open at weekends for the sale of plants, the requirements are very much those of a standard supermarket. The site, at a mainroad intersection, has fallen into disuse. It is littered with

caravans and much else and its childrens' boating pool is now abandoned.

There was no perfect answer to the brief requirements, but it was felt that the usual expedient of landscaping the building into oblivion would be inadequate to the problem, considering that we were dealing with an object at least 16 m high and some 70 m long. The materials are brick and tile facings. Variants were tried using the Sainsbury house-colours, green roof, orange and white banded brickwork, but after much deliberation it was felt best to reserve these rich Kipling resonances for some future commission in a warmer, more expansive clime.

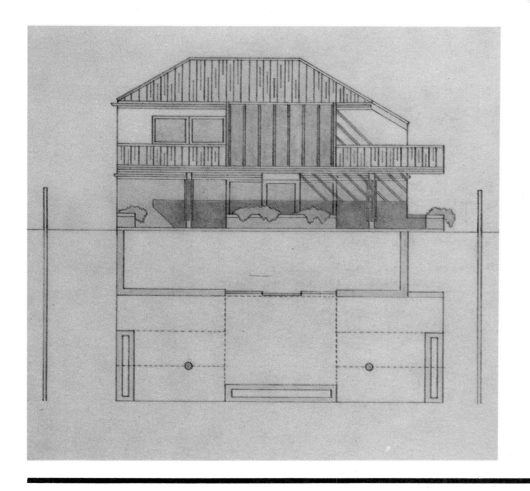
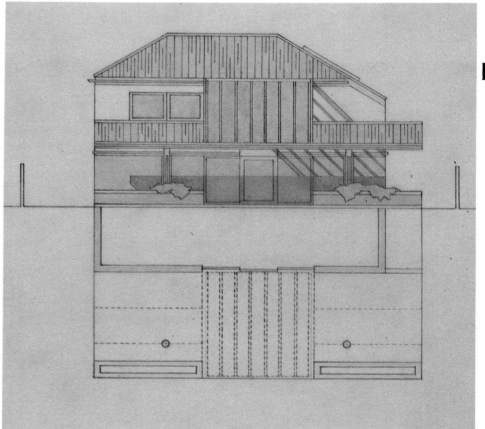

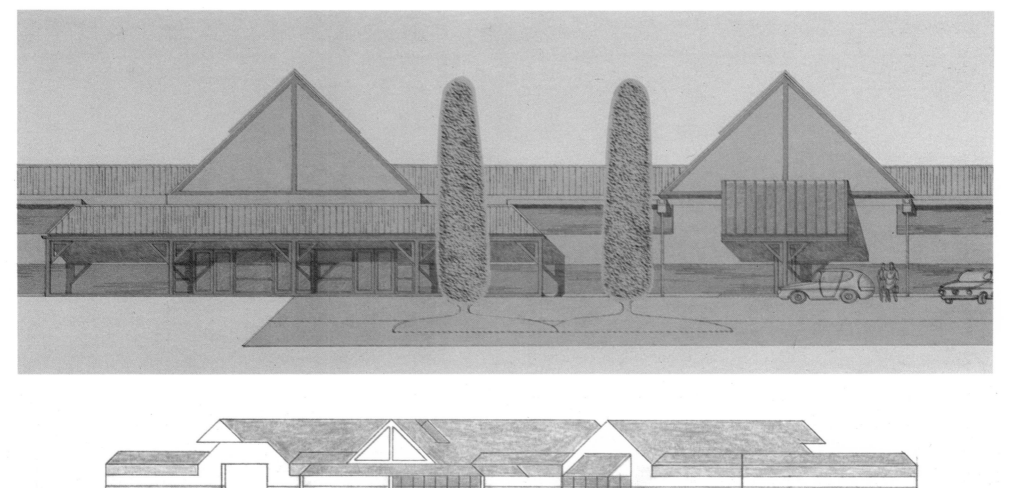

HOUSE PROJECTS, HAMPSTEAD

the establishment of a correct style and so forth. These dwellings are arranged to slip into a gap in the solid structure of the status quo: a 60 foot frontage of secluded land in timeless, leafy Hampstead. To the north is a near neighbour blocking views of West Heath and to the south, the garden of a Consulate.

The aesthetics engage convention and the rule-book. In one design the classical temple front and the Diocletian baths are invoked for a most modest purpose: the porch and garage. In another, an unused affection finds a place in the scheme of things at last: the propped structure of the railway bunker. Norman Shaw seemed a useful source for oriels that were linked with a sense of movement and Alexander Thomson, rather than Halicarnassos, came to mind with the classical pile-up: the Vincent Street church, possibly. One recalls from the scribbled notes on his drawings that Jefferson was quite open about his sources. They tended to be classicist models which he considered to be ideal whereas the house sketch references that have been suggested are less overt and reverential; but that is a fine distinction if one is reflecting upon the shift in taste that has taken place in the last twenty years, from experimentation to orthodoxy.

1 Architectural Monographs 3, p 55 Academy Editions   2 idem p 21

Axonometric

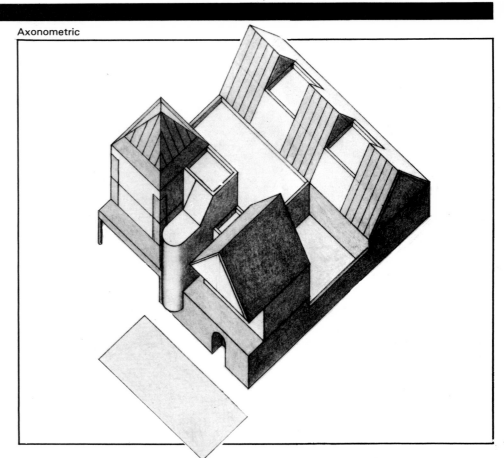

Elevation

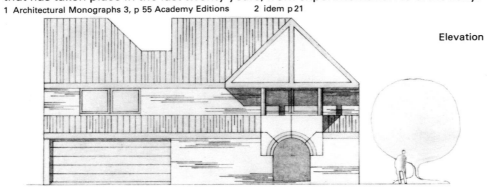

DIY SUPERMARKET FOR SAINSBURY'S HOMEBASE, BROMLEY, KENT

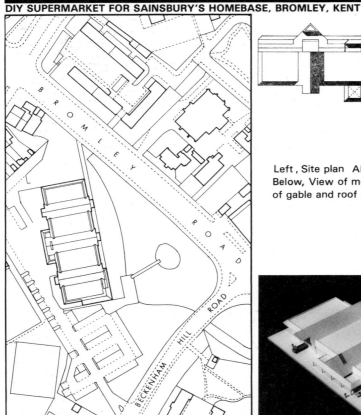

Left, Site plan Above, Preliminary study
Below, View of model   Right, Elevation
of gable and roof plan

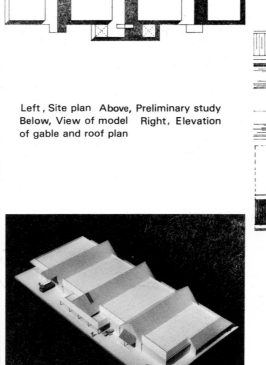

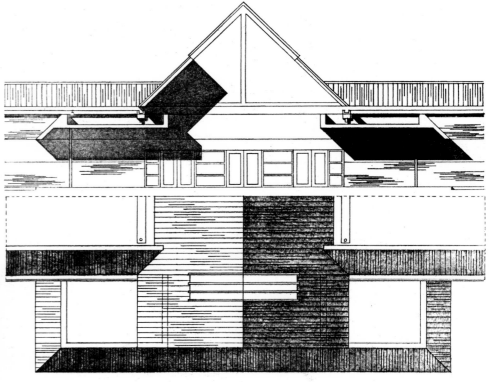

0   10   15   20 M

Elevation studies ..

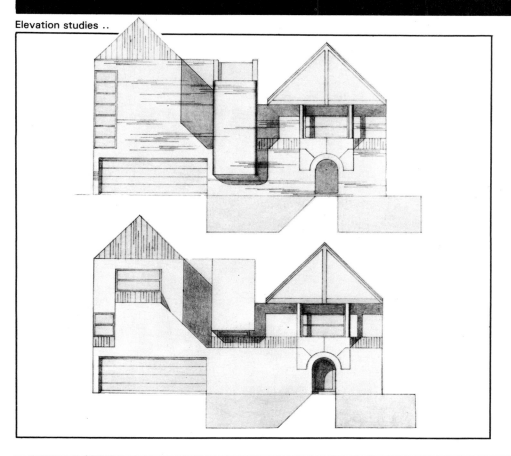

.. and sketch floor plans

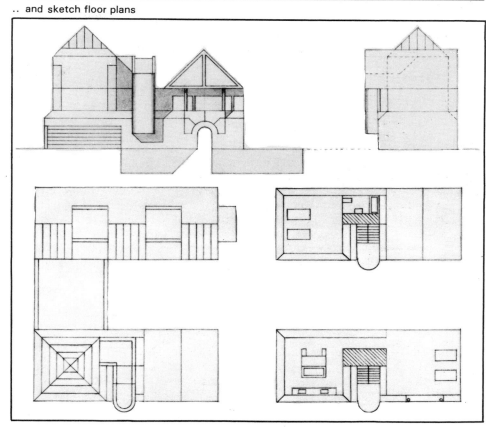

Entrance facade: view from south

Peter Wilson and Julia Bolles-Wilson

FOUR STUDIES FOR A LONDON SEMI-DETACHED TERRACE FACADE

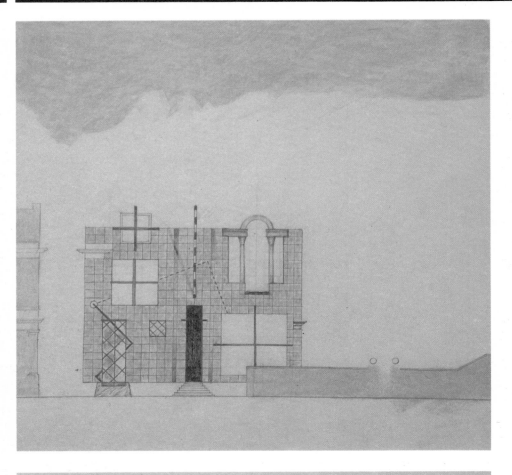

Terry Farrell Partnership

Vauxhall Cross competition entry, 1982, views of model
(ph Satish Patel, model C&B Models)

Terry Farrell Partnership

TERRY FARRELL PARTNERSHIP OFFICES, 8 PADDINGTON STREET, LONDON

PHOTOGRAPHS: J Mortime

WHEN, IN 1980, TERRY FARRELL started practising from the same offices that had for ten years previously housed the Farrell Grimshaw Partnership, a series of carefully intentioned changes were carried out that dramatically altered the internal environment.

Inside, the major axis of the office is now defined by a colonnade of 6 columns that in their different ways provide incidents and define spaces and axes. The columns are not merely decorative. In a small office even columns have to earn their keep and these occupy no floor space as they sit on essential space-consuming objects. The first two of the columns are hollow and linked to the heating system which previously, at ceiling level, was performing below requirement. Central filing cabinets are located below the next pair, together with power, light and telephone distribution for all adjoining work spaces. Filing cabinets are sited below the 5th and 6th columns and in the one hollow rectangular column are the telephone, professional and other directories.

The partners' office leads directly to a small courtyard lightheartedly decked out to resemble a beach. The scene is complete, with canvas windbreak, lifebelt, sand, waves, seascape and outdoor furniture. Here, in the centre of London, the office can, without sand in its sandwiches, enjoy an hour on the beach in its lunch hour.

PROJECT TEAM: Simon Sturgis, Josef Foges, Simon Hudspith, Doug Streeter
Terry Farrell and John Chatwin work on all projects

View through to sea-scaped courtyard

Staircase to first floor

View down office from entrance, columns three and four with filing cabinets

Axial axonometric

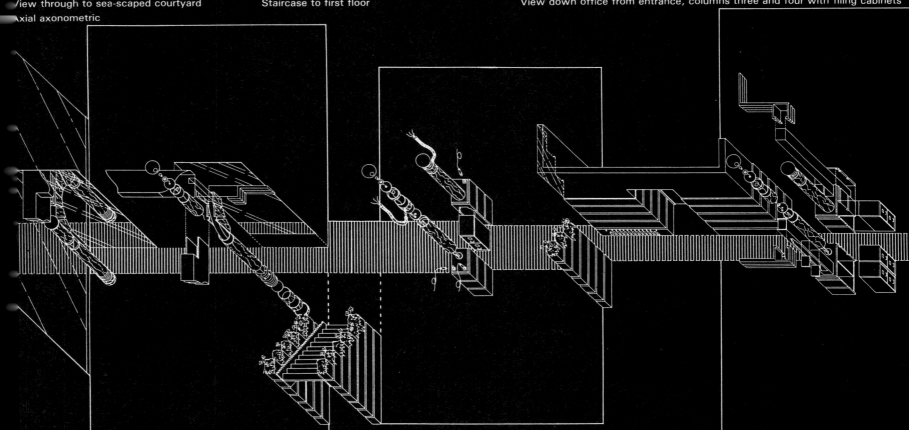

THE SITE IN COVENT GARDEN is owned by the Royal Opera House who plan to extend their premises by building a second auditorium. The building itself developed from two different influences. First, the current work of the office which includes both Alexandra Pavilion and the previous Clifton Nurseries in Paddington and second, the building's architectural context. The problem of creating a facade and a building of appropriate scale and appearance for this historical context was resolved by adopting a classical portico, based on the precedent of Inigo Jones' nearby St Paul's Church, and extending it in a 'temple' form to become the underlying image of the design.

The roof of the building is fabricated from Teflon-coated glass fibre, the first instance of the use of this material in Britain. Teflon was chosen because it combines a 20% daylight transmission with an appearance from the outside of relative solidity in keeping with the 'temple' concept.

The portico facade facing King Street is an everchanging feature of the building containing planting and light displays that change with the seasons. Resting on 6 columns, the pediment is a steel framework and here, as elsewhere; the architectural detail deliberately alludes to classical details whilst playfully distorting them. Four of the facade columns are made of plywood but appear solid and are painted 'stone' colour. The capitals appear solid but are of post-formed perspex and incorporate light sources. The 'Doric' columns are topped by an entablature that has no architrave and no cornice. Instead the frieze has triglyphs that are hollow, illuminated letters with discontinuous upside-down dentils on the top.

PROJECT TEAM: Craig Downie, Alan Morris, Richard Solomon

ENGINEERS: Arup Lightweight Structures
CONTRACTOR: Wiltshier London Ltd

Clifton Nurseries, Paddington (ph Jo Reid)
Facade to the piazza (ph Jo Reid & John Peck)

Column head, Covent Garden (ph G Challifour)

Interior with detail of roof structure
(ph Jo Reid & John Peck)

Terry Farrell Partnership
CRAFTS COUNCIL GALLERY, 11-12 WATERLOO PLACE, LONDON

A YEAR AGO, the Terry Farrell Partnership was appointed by the Crafts Council to prepare plans for the enlargement and complete revitalisation of their premises on the western side of Waterloo Place.

The Craft Council's requirement was to provide approximately 2,000 sq ft of gallery space capable of sub-division into three separate areas; slide index and information area; reception and sales areas; storage and conservation area for their collection of crafts objects and the facility for their public display; a substantial conference/meeting room; office space for about 12 exhibition and information staff; workshop and storage space.

The newly-acquired building—No 11 Waterloo Place—has a ground floor 2 ft above the existing gallery (although the two mezzanine areas are on the same level). By changing the main entrance from No 12 to No 11, lowering the entrance door and an 8 ft wide strip of floor, it has been possible to form a new ramped entrance area which provides easy wheelchair access around the entire ground floor, and to introduce a lift so that disabled people can also visit the mezzanine slide index and information centre, and the conference/committee room in the basement. This ramped entrance area has generated the main architectural strategy of the building; the creation of the main axis from entrance to stair, and a cranked cross axis through the two main gallery spaces.

PROJECT TEAM: John Langley, Clive Wilkinson, Alan Morris
ENGINEERS: Cyril Blumfield & Partners
QUANTITY SURVEYORS: Michael Edwards & Associates

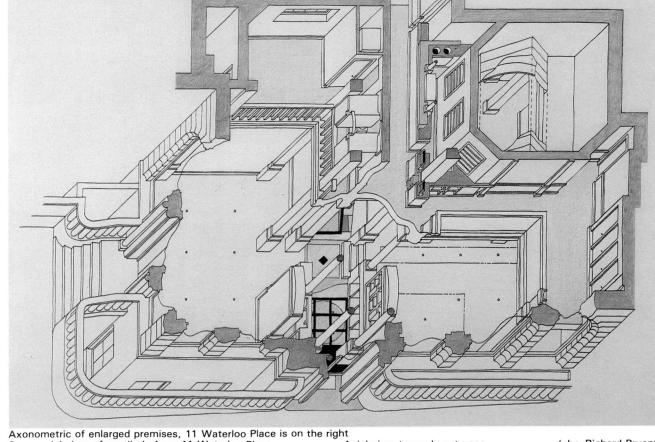

Axonometric of enlarged premises, 11 Waterloo Place is on the right

Stairway to mezzanine

Cross-axial view of vestibule from 11 Waterloo Place

Axial view towards entrance   (phs Richard Bryant)

WOOD GREEN NORTHERN INDUSTRIAL DEVELOPMENT, HARINGEY, LONDON

THESE SIX BUILDINGS on five inner city infill sites represent a unique partnership between Haringey as landowner/planning authority and funding and architectural expertise co-ordinated by a developer to produce a systematic approach to the rejuvenation of decayed industrial/residential areas to the east of Wood Green Central Area. The objective was to retain existing substantial industrial property and to redevelop those sites which were vacant or where buildings had outlived their useful life, to provide increased employment and a unifying architectural element to the whole industrial area. The concept was generated by:

— the manoeuvering geometry of large articulated vehicles and site parking requirements;
— the desire to achieve maximum site coverage (over 60%) and building subdivisibility;
— the contextual relationship of each site on the main street frontages and constraints posed by surrounding buildings and negotiations with 21 separate adjoining owners.

PROJECT TEAM: John Petrarca, Geoff Warn, Peter Tigg, Simon Hudspith (Middlesex Polytechnic)
PHOTOGRAPHS: Jo Reid & John Peck

Kingfisher Place,
(escape doors and glazing for future mezzanine)

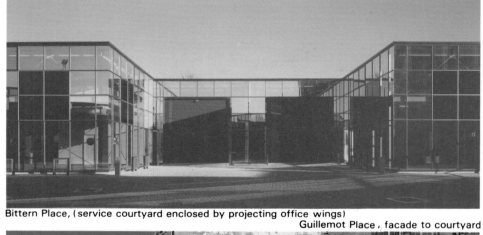

Bittern Place, (service courtyard enclosed by projecting office wings)

Ironic column

View down spiral stair

Guillemot Place , facade to courtyard

View of core

Detail of door, Mallard Place

Aerial perspective indicating relative position of five sites

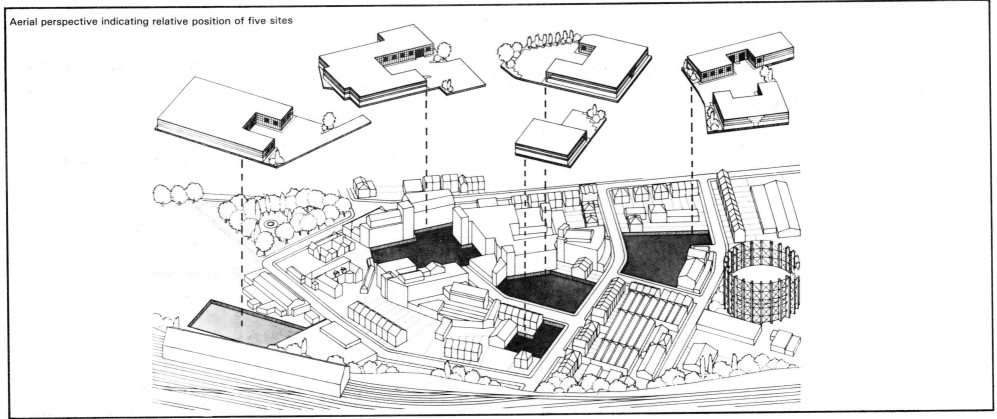

Erosion of urban block

A wall with window

Preferred condition – internal court

Establishing an order

Extending the urban fabric

Access to courtyard

Plan of Bittern Place site

Axonometric

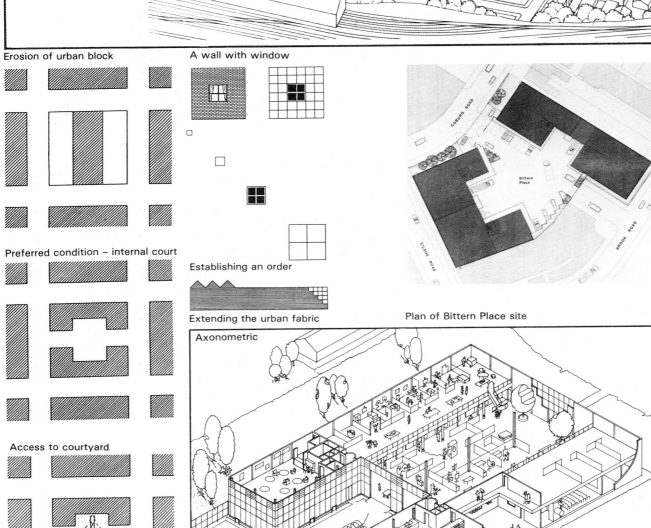

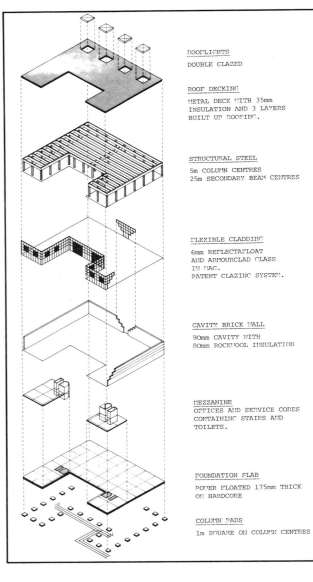

ROOFLIGHTS
DOUBLE GLAZED

ROOF DECKING
METAL DECK WITH 35mm
INSULATION AND 3 LAYERS
BUILT UP ROOFING.

STRUCTURAL STEEL
5m COLUMN CENTRES
25m SECONDARY BEAM CENTRES

FLEXIBLE CLADDING
6mm REFLECTAFLOAT
AND ARMOURCLAD CLASS
IN MAG.
PATENT CLAZINC SYSTEM.

CAVITY BRICK WALL
90mm CAVITY WITH
80mm ROCKWOOL INSULATION

MEZZANINE
OFFICES AND SERVICE CORES
CONTAINING STAIRS AND
TOILETS.

FOUNDATION SLAB
POWER FLOATED 175mm THICK
ON HARDCORE

COLUMN PADS
1m SQUARE ON COLUMN CENTRES

HOUSE ON THE PWLLHELI PENINSULA, NORTH WALES

Ground floor plan

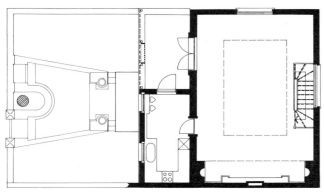

1 Bedroom one
2 Bathroom
3 Garage
4 Bedroom two
5 Shower room
6 Guest bedroom
7 Conservatory
8 Entrance hall

Elemental axonometric

View from south (ph Oliver Richards)

THE HOUSE is nearing completion in Pwllheli in North Wales. It faces south overlooking dunes towards the sea.

Timber frame panel construction was chosen on economic grounds and the house is structurally divided into two halves which are split open by a conservatory. This full-height space is crossed by a bridge and tapers from its narrowest point, the entrance lobby, towards the sun and view. The conservatory is covered by a conical barrel vault which concludes in a giant oculus window and it forms the principal spatial element in the design.

Oliver Richards, Paul James, Terry Farrell in partnership.
Peter Southgate (site architect)
QUANTITY SURVEYORS: Michael Edwards & Associates

Front elevation

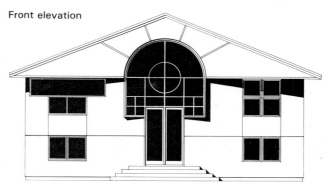

PRIVATE HOUSE, ST JOHNS' WOOD, LONDON

First floor plan

View of entrance
(ph Richard Solomon)

Ground floor plan

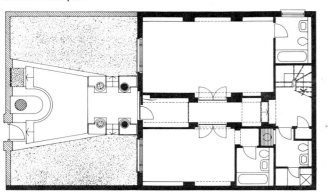

THE HOUSE WAS BUILT when this area of London was surrounded by ponds and fields and was known as The Vinery. The ground floor contained stables with a well-lit studio above. The brief was to convert this into a family dwelling.

The entrance layout set out to give scale to the garden and is ordered around the front 'double' door, framed by the porch and its columns. The strong axis set up is shifted when one penetrates the building. Play on symmetry to achieve an appropriate scale within restricted spaces was a theme throughout. In the front elevation a false window in the trellis completes the facade while ensuring an openness to the balcony.

Detail of cornice moulding (ph Satish Patel)

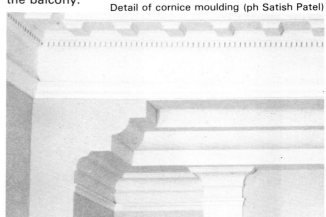

ALEXANDRA PAVILION, ALEXANDRA PALACE, HARINGEY, LONDON

WHEN THE VICTORIAN ALEXANDRA PALACE was gutted by fire it was determined to replace it with a temporary building. Shelter Span Ltd were the successful tenderers for a design and building package based on a simple brief for the superstructure and an outline plan.

The standard Shelter Span system comprises an enclosing membrane of PVC-coated fabric panels which are supported on a rigid structure of aluminium portal frames. The technique of fixing the fabric derives from sail technology and consists of a luff groove set on the structural member into which is slotted a bolt rope attached to the edge of the fabric panel. The bolt rope is slotted in from one end of the luff groove and is held in position by a continuous lip. In their fabrication the panels are tailored to double curved patterns using welded seams and the luff groove allows them to be simply but effectively tensioned in position. The stable double curved form of the panels prevents their wear and tear through flapping in the wind while at the same time creating the attractive scalloped appearance. In the Shelter Span system the luff groove is combined with an inexpensively extruded aluminium section which can be bent at the elbows to form portal frames.

ARCHITECTS: Terry Farrell Ptnrs (Oliver Richards/Michael Glass) in conjunction with Dr Peter Smith, architect/planner to Alexandra Palace Development Team
ENGINEER: Peter Rice with Ian Ritchie
PHOTOGRAPHS: Jo Reid & John Peck
M & E ENGINEERS: Ronald Hurst Associates

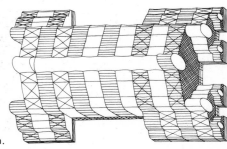

Liverpool Garden Festival Building, competition entry, 1982.

This structure was designed using a similar system to that of Alexandra Pavilion.

View of interior of Alexandra Pavilion

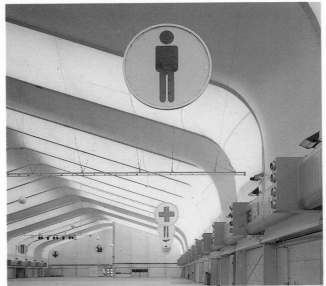

AD PROJECT AWARD ● COMMENDATION

Terry Farrell Partnership
LOW-COST HOUSING

**MAUNSEL HOUSING SOCIETY,
SELECTED SITES IN AND AROUND LONDON**

IN THE MID 1970s we undertook ten suburban housing schemes on small infill sites on the outskirts of London; they ranged from eight to 36 houses. The sites had been acquired by two Housing Associations from developers and builders following the '73 property crash; generally they all had planning consent for blocks of flats from four to eight storeys high.

We developed a very simple, narrow frontage plan form, based on the Georgian terrace house — especially in its capacity to have a raised front door, and allow the incorporation of a separate basement flat. A standard timber-framed construction was developed for all schemes, but each site used different cladding materials or elevations.

Although a local firm of contractors was used for each site, the main super-structure was undertaken by one subcontractor, who had been selected in a serial tendering procedure which had grudgingly been agreed to by the DOE — despite the fact that it showed savings of up to 30% of yardstick on some schemes. This contractual technique allowed the advantages of factory production and common construction details to be applied to each site, without the loss of individuality introduced by the local builder undertaking all ground and finishing work.

PROJECT TEAM (Both Projects): Dave Clarke, Josef Foges
PHOTOGRAPHS: Graham Challifour

Oblique view of Crawley green Road

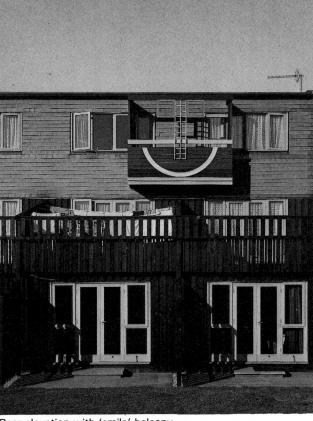

Rear elevation with 'smile' balcony

OAKWOOD 13-18, WARRINGTON NEW TOWN

WHILST THE MAUNSEL SCHEMES were under construction we were appointed by Warrington New Town to design two larger residential schemes either side of a local park in Oakwood. These commissions allowed us to develop the timber frame techniques explored in the Maunsel schemes to include ideas of adaptation by occupiers.

The site, on the southern edge of a large Second World War Ordnance Depot, was divided by an old drainage ditch, with extensive old foundations and obstructions to the north, and large areas of peat mounding and new woodland growth to the south. An early decision was the concentration of new development in the northern portion to make best use of expensive substructure work and to retain as much young woodland as possible. The scheme was arranged as a series of separate, easily identifiable cul-de-sac 'lanes' having direct access from the local distributor road, and each terminating in a woodland path. The lanes themselves have been detailed to allow shared access by car and pedestrian, and detail design places a high emphasis on front hedge, front gate and house plot. Besides the lane and footpath system, the remainder of the site has been developed as large back gardens, eliminating as far as possible public open space — what belongs to everybody belongs to nobody, here at least.

Isometric with landscaped surfaces

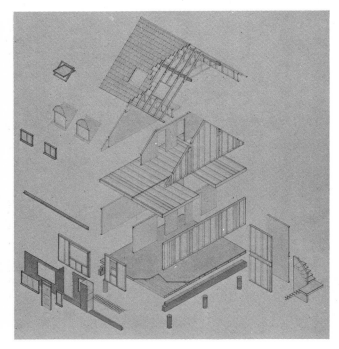

Exploded axonometric

NEW HEADQUARTERS FOR BREAKFAST TELEVISION (TV-AM) CAMDEN TOWN, LONDON

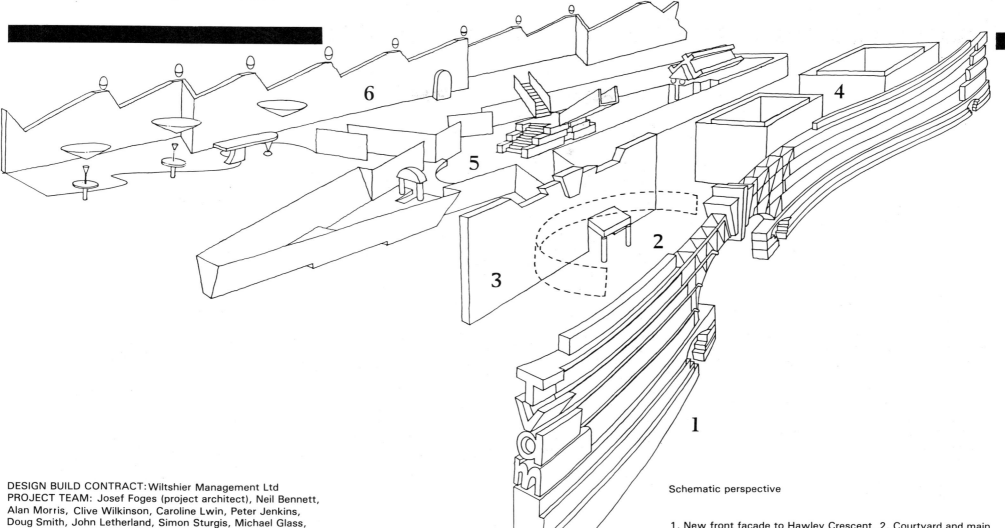

Schematic perspective

1. New front facade to Hawley Crescent 2. Courtyard and main entrance 3. Re-modelled existing facade 4. Two new television studios added 5. Modified existing double height atrium space 6. Re-modelled north wall to Regents Canal

DESIGN BUILD CONTRACT: Wiltshier Management Ltd
PROJECT TEAM: Josef Foges (project architect), Neil Bennett, Alan Morris, Clive Wilkinson, Caroline Lwin, Peter Jenkins, Doug Smith, John Letherland, Simon Sturgis, Michael Glass, Craig Downie and Satish Patel
ENGINEERS: Peter Brett Associates
M & E ACOUSTICAL CONSULTANTS: Sandy Brown Associates

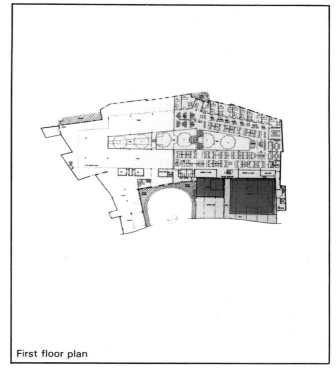

A COMMISSION to convert a disused two storey garage in the heart of North London's Camden Town into a new headquarters for TV-AM (Britain's national breakfast TV channel) has produced one of the most challenging projects executed by our office so far.

Having a long, curving frontage to a one-way street, sandwiched between the remnants of 'rag-trade backstreet' and the run-down Regents Canal, the site became an exercise in layering between these two extremes.

On the street entrance side the layer is a new billboard facade behind which are the blank walls of the studios and the only penetration through the facade is an archway leading to an elliptical entrance courtyard.

The rear layer of the canal side facade is a romantic and colourful adaptation of the existing saw-toothed wall with new additions of balconies and a new house which cantilevers over the towpath.

Inside the building, midway between these two facades and running parallel with them, is an existing linear atrium surviving from the old building which rises through two storeys. This central garden space focuses the wide range of activities contained within the complex.

Ground floor plan

First floor plan

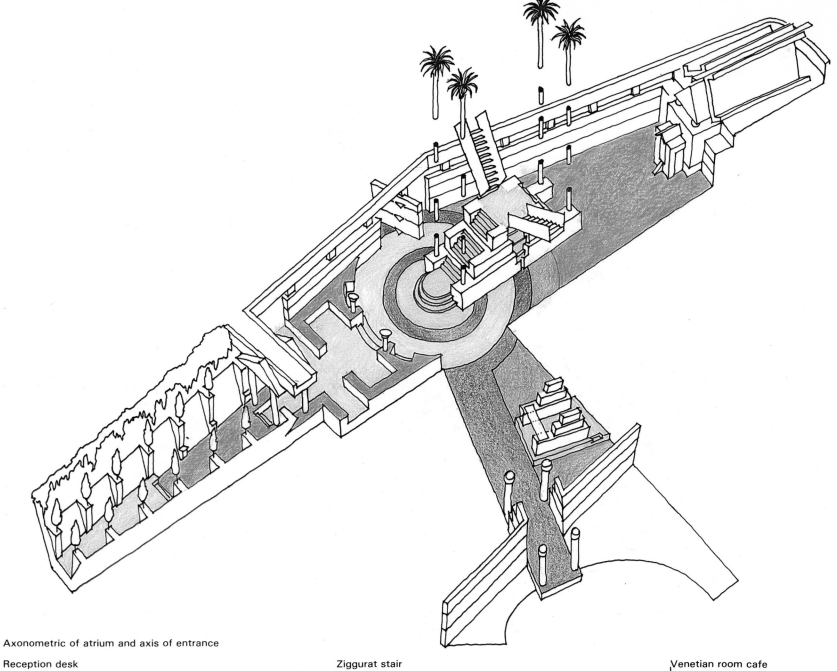

Axonometric of atrium and axis of entrance

Reception desk

Ziggurat stair

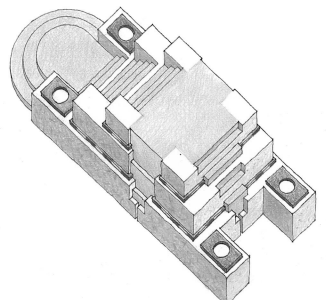

Venetian room cafe

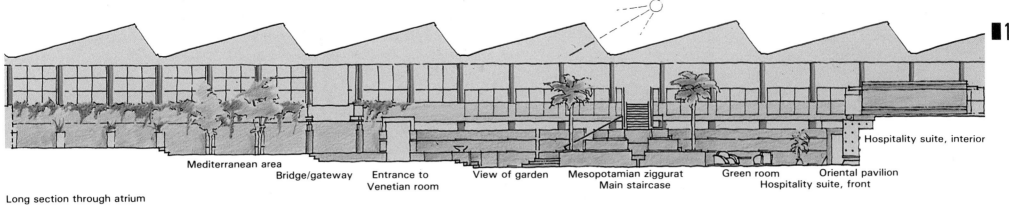

Hospitality suite, interior

Mediterranean area
Bridge/gateway
Entrance to
Venetian room
View of garden
Mesopotamian ziggurat
Main staircase
Green room
Oriental pavilion
Hospitality suite, front

Long section through atrium

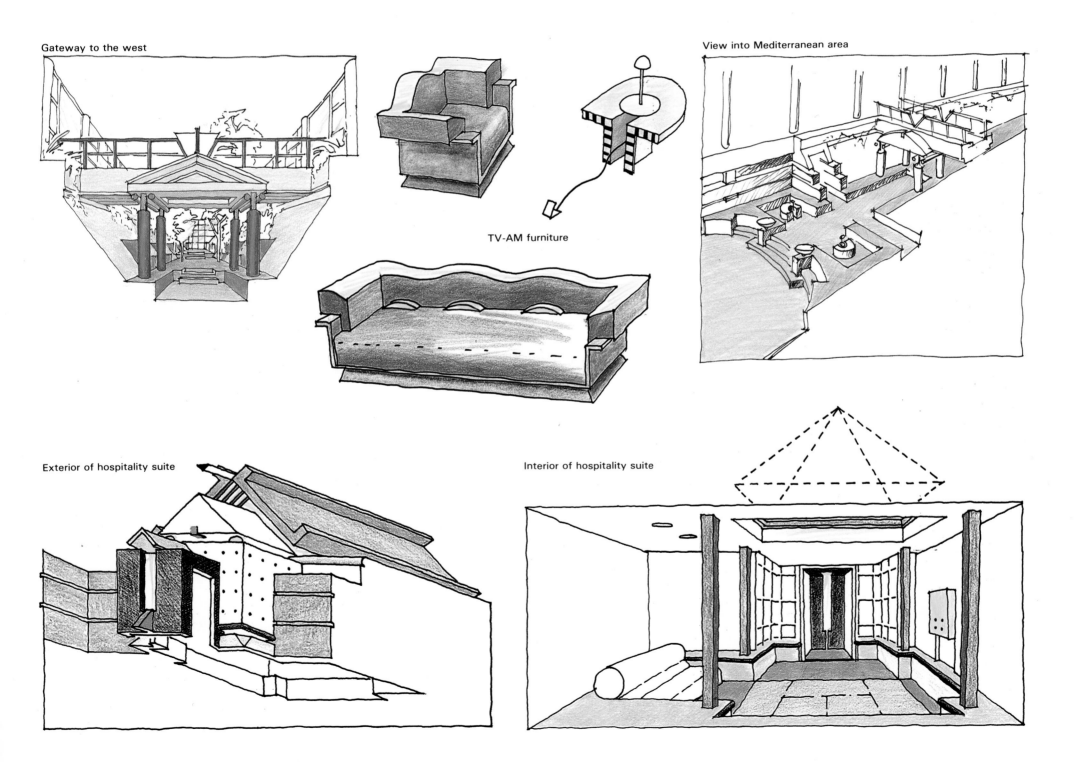

Gateway to the west

View into Mediterranean area

TV-AM furniture

Exterior of hospitality suite

Interior of hospitality suite

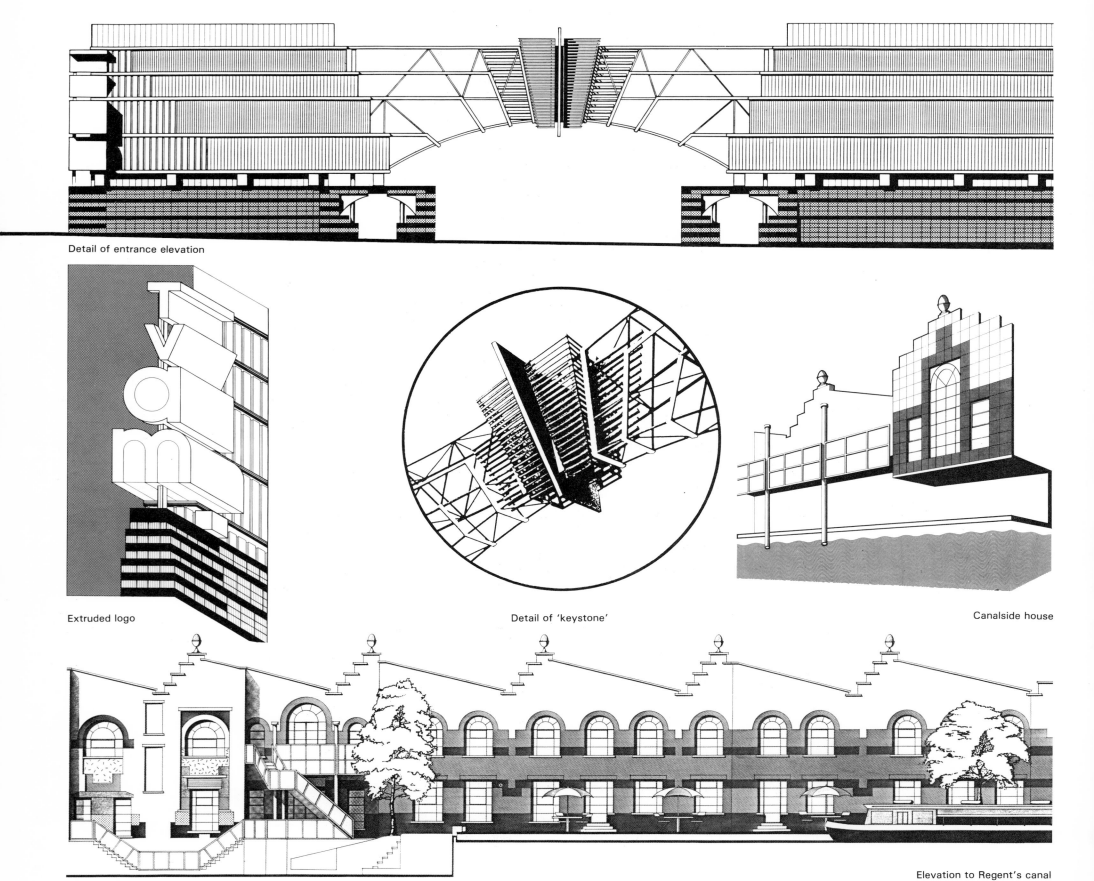

Detail of entrance elevation

Extruded logo

Detail of 'keystone'

Canalside house

Elevation to Regent's canal

THE TWA OPERATIONS BUILDING rests on top of a concrete purification tank and main pump hall which is part of a larger civil engineering contract for TWA. The H-plan was determined by two main factors. First, the Operations Building rests on top of a monolithic tank structure which is sunk 5 metres into the ground. Due to the prevailing water table conditions the structure essentially floats in the ground, with the control building balanced on top like a catamaran. The 1 m-deep layer of soil in the courtyards adds additional stabilising weight. Secondly, the H-plan sectionalises the building conveniently into three areas. The shorter south wings contain offices, laboratories and the operative areas. The longer north wing contains stores, operations equipment and workshops.

The planners required that the exterior of the building would relate to the landscape and the client wanted a low maintenance outer wall which would need little alteration in the future. Our response was to use a highly-controlled glazed cladding system which in appearance would relate to the sky. The reflective glazing reflects the clouds and apparently doubles the number of trees in the area. The curves naturally relate to water.

Another particular requirement was for a pedestrian route to be established for the public to connect various points of interest throughout the building. This also segregates the public from the operation areas. Different elements were placed along the path to signify separate zones. For instance, the entrance ramp is easily identified by the overscaled steps on either side. The pattern on the doorway signifies the sun and water and provides clues to the inside. The circular mullions on the mezzanine wall frame the River Kennet, Fobney's source of water. The lighting columns at the end of the vaults frame the raised observation platform overlooking the operation areas around the building.

PROJECT TEAM: Andrew Cowan, Michael Glass
ENGINEERS: Peter Brett Associates
QUANTITY SURVEYORS: Michael Edwards Associates
M + E ENGINEERS: Ronald Hurst Associates

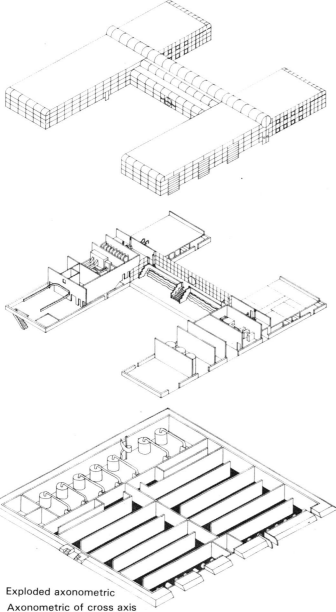

Exploded axonometric
Axonometric of cross axis

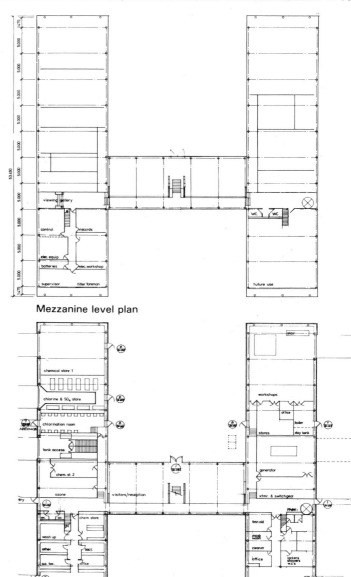

Mezzanine level plan

Ground floor plan

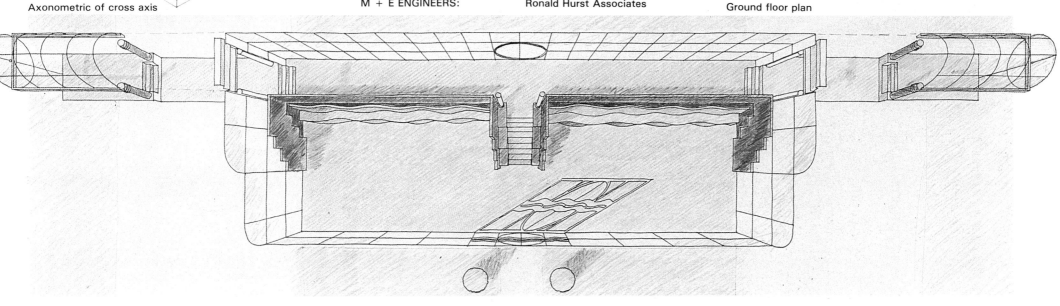

Exterior detail (ph Richard Bryant)

Axial view of entrance and courtyard (ph Richard Bryant)

View of top of staircase to mezzanine level (ph Richard Bryant)
Mezzanine level of cross axis (ph Richard Bryant)

Charles Jencks
FARRELL MOVES TOWARDS SYMBOLISM

ONE OF THE LESS QUOTED aphorisms of Mies was 'Build Don't Talk', a little known saying perhaps because it didn't encourage the very medium by which it might be repeated. In Chicago this command amounted to something like censorship. Since there was so much opportunity to build, conversation about architecture never developed much beyond the appreciative grunt or the censorious groan. At least until Stanley Tigerman and The Chicago 7-11-18 appeared on the scene. In England, Leon Krier has made a new tradition (and modest trade) from the dictum 'Draw Don't Build', and the best architects such as James Stirling seem doomed to make a profession from the meagre average of one finished building per year. This paucity of British building leads, no doubt, to more and more elevated chat, a talk which is positively rococo in its intricate and obscure subtlety; and at the AA it can also lead to such drawing. It's all very beautiful, but it hasn't resulted yet in much exemplary building. Mainstream practice is largely unaffected. The best architects continue to miss the best commissions, a dolorous state of affairs which must be continuously deplored at every possible opportunity.

Against this cultural breakdown, to which I have alluded elsewhere in this issue, the work of Terry Farrell gains in stature because it manages to bridge conventional stereotypes and traditional work patterns. He is an architect in the Chicago mould more given to building than verbalisation, but he has remained responsive to a changing theory while developing his own particular approach. This 'learning by doing' is perhaps more American than English, indebted to the pragmatic philosophy of John Dewey more than empiricism, just as Farrell's architecture develops from the Americans Kahn, Venturi, Stern and Graves. And this pragmatic approach has led to the accretion of practical knowledge: how to use new technologies in an expressive and economical way; how to exploit the best design talent in a medium-sized office; and how to knit together old and new buildings within a limited budget.

The approach might be partly summarised by the term 'Expedient Tech'—a phrase which has the advantage of being so ungainly that it is unlikely to be repeated. Expedient Tech was the earlier style of the Farrell/Grimshaw partnership. Not quite the transcendental High Tech of Foster (which they criticised for being inflexible) nor the sleek packaging of mirrorplate builders, it obviously related

to both approaches. Some obvious high points come to mind: the GRP bathroom pods of 1968, a built version of an Archigram speculation; the Park Road aluminium cladding which gave a new industrial image to housing in 1970 (now sadly aged without the compensating patina that might have formed on brick, copper or stone). More recently there is the doubly-curved polycarbonate sheeting used at Clifton Nurseries I—that wandering, undulating arch of green 'glass' that slithers over green plants—and the Teflon-coated, glass-reinforced fibre roof used at Clifton Nurseries II—a kind of buttoned-down-sail-boat-tent with wire cables stretching taut to a green steel frame. It's a finely strung, post-tensioned Tuscan temple.

All of this Clever-Tech might be applauded, and it certainly appeals to Martin Pawley and a host of born-again Modernists. When combined with fragments of the classical language it becomes canonic Post-Modernism, that is doubly-coded and consciously aimed at different taste cultures. Yet the pragmatic approach to technique, organisation and city context does not in itself constitute an architecture, which must be a self-reflexive language, a discourse focused on the expressive plane itself. This is now in the process of formation.

The Non-Anxiety of Influence or Transformational Eclecticism

The sources of Farrell's Post-Modern Classicism are clear, and he is as candid as Robert Stern in admitting them. The Vauxhall project has the top and plinth of Graves' Portland building, transformed in certain ways to which we will return. Clifton Nurseries II modifies Stern's fat columns and rusticated projects—notably the Llewelyn Park Poolhouse. The TVAM scheme mixes Venturian billboard with my own derivation of the Serliana, the ABA arch in the shape of a face with a stagger below. This flexible motif is used as both a major gateway for cars and two side doors for pedestrians, a formula adapted, perhaps, not only from my own house but also Guimard's wonderful entrance to the Castel Béranger (which also has columns smashing into the springing area of the arch). The Art-Deco Classicism of Wall Street and the Chrysler Building, Streamline Moderne and Hollywood Deco are also apparent on the facade and plaza of TVAM.

But what of British influence? Aside from the Expedient

Tech already mentioned there is little that Farrell finds of inspiration in the current scene. Mackintosh and Lutyens are, for him, the last great British masters from whom he can learn a free variation of classicism. The 'light' columns of his office show a Lutyensesque wit in their combination of column, quoin, lighting globe and heating duct. The influence of Mackintosh is apparent in the abstract rectilinear ornament, the flat horizontal, stepped mouldings, the set-backs and grids played against each other (as on the inside and outside of TVAM).

Admitting sources of inspiration is contrary to the Modernists' notion of creation *ex nihilo* and while creativity may indeed depend on intelligent theft inventively transformed, there is usually a taboo about admitting what an

1 Hector Guimard, Castel Béranger, Paris, 1894-8. The arch above the stepped-in rectangle sets curve against straight line This flexible motif, allowing variation in height and width is here intersected by columns at the extrados, the weak point. A formula which I developed into the 'face motif' and used to suggest eight different characters in a house, is turned by Farrell at TVAM back towards its source at the Castel Béranger. (ph: C Jencks)

2 Michelozzo, Pallazzo Medici-Riccardi, Florence, 1444-64. Then gradation of stonework from heavy bottom to light top was formulated in this building and established the typical code of the rusticated facade. A feeling of greater height is created by gradation; each floor is accentuated and the symbolism of usage is underscored (public base, piano nobile, private attic etc). Farrell's rustication of TVAM also observes the basic heavy/light distinction while adding a sun symbolism (ph: C Jencks)

3 Henri Labrouste, Bibliothèque Sainte-Geneviève, Paris, 1838-50). Stone swags partly used to soften an austere image, partly meant to symbolise an ancient ritual celebration –decorating buildings with garlands during feast days, marriages, spring festivals and so on. (ph: C Jencks)

4 Thomas Jefferson, 'Academical Village', University of Virginia, Charlottesville, Va, 1816-26. A subtle interlocking of ten pavilions for professors, student rooms (along the colonnade), gardens and 'hotels' (for eating) in back and a network of services and smaller buildings. The careful variations on a simple theme, both in elevation and section, produce a controlled layout which is always full of surprise. (ph: C Jencks)

5 Terry Farrell Partnership, Vauxhall Bridge competition entry, 1982.

1

2

3

4

5

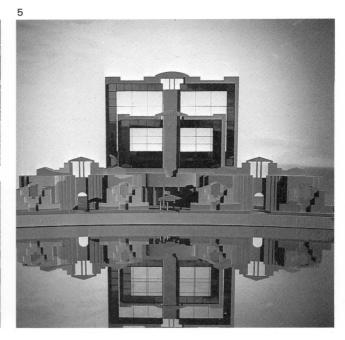

older generation considers a crime. Harold Bloom discusses this in a book which has itself influenced Vincent Scully and the American Post-Modernists (*The Anxiety of Influence, A Theory of Poetry*, 1973), and from this clarification we can understand more clearly the transfer of ideas and forms that is taking place. To quote Scully: *'... Bloom's "strong poet", inevitably fastens on the work of his chosen precursor, purposely "misreads" it, and finally "swerves" from it to create a new field of action for his own design'.*[1]

This 'swerving' from influence may be true when looked at from a psychological point of view, and it may help explain today's Mannerism, but in terms of the classical theory, it underscores the difference between imitating and copying. Imitation, the transformation of an idea and form through systematic recombination with other patterns, has always been encouraged by the classical tradition in opposition to replication, and this distinction finds an echo in TS Eliot's epigram: 'the bad poet borrows, the good poet steals'. Basically it's transformational eclecticism versus straight revivalism.

Note the way Farrell modifies several existing ideas on the facade of TVAM. Essentially a classical vocabulary of rustication and string courses is combined with an industrial vocabulary of corrugated metal, and Art-Deco streamlines in polychromy. The base 'plinth' is in dark grey and black signifying night time and dawn, while the lighter top in reds, yellows and oranges denotes the morning of breakfast television. The rusticated masonry and corrugated metal do not graduate in predictable diminution as in the classical palazzo (Michelozzo's Medici Palace, 1444, established this code). Rather they syncopate at the top, ABAB. This sets the viewer on edge. A further tension is created by the illuminated 'keystone', a giant billboard which will become the logo for TVAM (and the letters can be faintly discerned in the trusswork).

This keystone seems straightforward at first: it has a normal proportion of splay and sides. But on further inspection it turns out to be a distorted and transformed motif, combined first with a lightweight truss (to lower wind loads), secondly with a cathode tube (to light up the bisected centre), thirdly with 'organ-pipe' decoration, and fourthly with side string courses or streamlines. In effect it becomes still a fifth thing, the morning sunburst. The facade is then a creative transformation of several influences combined for the symbolic role of advertising breakfast television, as well as a welcoming sign, an archway for the car. As a whole it oscillates between one context and the next, always avoiding the cliché that the replication promotes. But for this very reason it may cause offence to some people. Traditionalists might term it a pastiche, as they tend to term a transformation of classical masonry into steel and glass; Modernists will be annoyed by the recognisable keystone, Purists by the hybrid language. Farrell may then have to pay the price which creative transformation and crossing traditions often entail: the accusations of ugliness and vulgarity. One might recall in this respect 19th-century cases—JJ Lequeu, William Burges, Robert Kerr, JC Loudon—where a symbolic architecture has also led to such censure, and remark that then it was defended as having 'muscularity', 'character' and 'truthfulness'. With time I presume Farrell's archway will be appreciated as an imaginative synthesis in a Free-Style Classicism.

Abstraction and Representation

One of the reasons why the facade has its openwork configuration is cost. The front wall, originally in glass, came in at a bid of £240,000 and more than £100,000 had to be trimmed from this figure. The solution was a lightweight truss to avoid wind loads, a cheaper material—corrugated metal—and a Venturian 'Billdingboard', a thin facade that shows its true nature at both ends (where further symbols occur). Economy often forces an architect to concentrate his mind on essentials: it made Graves simplify the facade and interior of his Portland Building so that it came in six million dollars cheaper than his competitors, and here it has focused Farrell's mind in simplifying details and re-using as much of the pre-existing building as possible. On the expressive plane it may force the architect from representation to abstraction. On the interior of TVAM, for instance, two grey grids are used on the ceiling at the same height, a very simple, cheap abstraction which pulls together the different spaces and gives a cool grey indirect light.

There is another, more important way in which representational imagery is made abstract: by multivalence, ambiguity and by interweaving several images at once so they afford multiple meanings. We have just touched on this in the TVAM archway, the multiple image which avoids its easy unities, its 'flash' qualities, by displacing them with further meaning, above all technical ones. One problem with Art Deco has always been its glitsy ease, its playing to the crowd. One can sense such a populist streak in Farrell's work but it is, by and large, overcome by the multivalence of images.

A negative case where this may not be true is the back of TVAM, where breakfast TV 'eggs' will decorate a syncopation of arches and staggers; the success or otherwise of this back elevation may depend on the final complexity and synthesis of motifs. An ambiguous case, which seems to work out in part, is the swag motif on the Clifton Nurseries II: here real, natural swags are suspended between decorative 'ears'. They recall Labrouste's garlands at the Bibliothèque Sainte-Geneviève, as well as Peter Smithson and David van Zanten's recent comments on swaggery (as stemming from a ritual application of nature turned into symbolic decoration). At Clifton II the game consists in reversing history since the swags are real garlands. This clever reinterpretation does a lot to displace the explicit imagery, but one may still have doubts as to whether the 'ears' and 'diglyphs' are not too stressed.

Such extreme representation stems from iconic architecture, again Lequeu, and Pop art. Whether it is appropriate in Covent Garden is arguable. The Tuscan temple of Inigo Jones, St Pauls, which acted as the major pretext for Farrell's Tuscan half-temple, is of course a sober affair with its plain heavy proportions and vernacular roof. Before the Clifton Nurseries were decorated with ears, swags and the rest, it had a quiet dignity, the abstraction which gave its simple message a weight and *gravitas*. The presence of the Teflon roof and green steel structure added seriousness to the building. Now it has been transformed in a picturesque and whimsical direction, a direction which may have always been intended if one judges by the earliest drawings. Nonetheless I find it a loss, the ascendancy of representation over abstraction. The difficulty and challenge of symbolism is in the careful balance of implicit and explicit sign; and this can be achieved by making explicit meanings multivalent, and thereby abstract.

The Return to a New Tradition

No doubt Post-Modern Classicism, in its first years of life, has all the teething problems of early Modernism: diagrammatic exaggeration, awkwardness, leaky roofs, naivety. Perhaps freshness mitigates these drawbacks, if it doesn't altogether excuse them. On the inside of TVAM, Farrell will attempt a symbolic ordering which may seem a trifle ingenuous: to the East of the plaza will be a Japanese temple, in the Near East a ziggurat stair will be built, and to the West some Dallas mirrorplate and Hollywood palms.

Undoubtedly this will go down rather well with Peter Jay, David Frost and those producers who see their message as having global implications, but one might ask whether the imagery might not have more complex ramifications. Perhaps it will when finally built.

In any case, it seems to me that the most mature statement of Farrell's work is his Vauxhall scheme, a proposition which won't be built. This was conceived in March 1982 when Farrell was locked up in a hospital, with a collapsed lung, far away from the hustle and bustle of his office. It resulted from a competition, called by the Minister of the Environment, to overcome the problem of the 'Green Giant', a commercial leviathan originally proposed for the site south of Vauxhall Bridge. Farrell's scheme reached the last stage of the competition only to be displaced, under the developer's influence, Arunbridge, in favour of a scheme rather like a late sixties megastructure. The introduction of public opinion, if not participation, turned out to be farcical. After voting on their favourite (either the Lacey or Farrell design) they were cheated of knowing their choice. Whatever the final outcome of this low comedy, the Farrell entry shows a competent authority, a sure transformation of classical themes, including those of Michael Graves. In this sense it represents a return to a tradition which is, paradoxically, new.

There are four basic transformations of a single idea. The smallest, riverside flats are given a four-square volume rather like Ledoux's masterful solution to the same problem type (the *Grange parée*) Ledoux cuts a centre void between two towers and supports this with a gentle pitched roof. Farrell adds wings to his version and thus defines garden paths to each side.

Behind these low-rise high-cost flats is a palace of apartments with a U-shape plan and a luxury penthouse—also with a pitched roof. Thus the unidirectional block in front is transformed into a more complex chateau type of plan. Finally, in the office blocks, the U-shape becomes two slabs connected by a bridge—or an H-shape block squashed down so that, as elsewhere, almost every room has a view of the river.

One of the hidden aspects of the Thames is that it suggests a front and back to any nearby building. Farrell accepts this latent rule and turns it into an image. His model shows row upon row of theatre goers gazing over each others shoulders to watch the world float by, an explicit celebration of the Thames in a rather Venetian manner. The directionality of the 'faces' is imposed by the broken pediments and the volumes which are sometimes staggered like theatre seats. The four different broken or set-back pediments (containing boardrooms or double-height living space) correspond to the four variations on a theme.

What gives the proposal strength, and I would even say brilliance, is the interlocking manner in which these parts are slotted together. The result is a pulsating, urban space of variety, a complex pattern of positive and negative volume which is repetitive and ambiguous at the same time. Like a geometric quilt which has been programmed with three or four conflicting patterns at once, the invention sparks off various readings. They are reminiscent of current contextual work, of Krier's urbanism, of Bofill's palaces; more to the point, they are reminiscent of Thomas Jefferson's 'academical village' in Charlottesville Virginia. Farrell's intention was to evolve a new village/city typology by varying a basic building block in plan and scale. Unfortunately it won't be realised at Vauxhall; but it is unlikely to remain lost for long, given the deep concern in this office for getting ideas built.

Notes
1 Vincent Scully, *The Shingle Style Today or the Historian's Revenge*, New York, 1974, p2.

YRM International
QABOOS UNIVERSITY, SULTANATE OF OMAN

THE NEW UNIVERSITY will provide teaching, residential, sports and support accommodation for an eventual total of over 5,000 students. After extensive analysis, a site, generally surrounded by low hills, was selected within a 14,400 hectare designated area. The site, which lies about 40 km west of Muscat, the capital of Oman, is close to the sea and has a spectacular backdrop of mountainous terrain.

The master plan, recently completed and approved, provides for a central academic area, separate male and female students residences, a staff housing complex, library, conference centre, administration block, a mosque, sports and recreational facilities and a 3,000 seat amphitheatre. The first phase will have faculties of Education and Islamic studies, Science, Agriculture, Medicine and Engineering, and provides full residential accommodation for over 2,000 of the 3,000 student population, plus some 600 academic and support staff.

The academic area will be designed on a central axis aligned towards Mecca with courtyard faculty buildings flanking common teaching blocks. A system of pedestrian circulation provides a network of two level streets and bridges, permitting the necessary separation of men and women. This system feeds into a central pedestrian mall which extends throughout the length of the academic area from the main entrance to the east, to the Mosque at the west. This linear form of development anticipates expansion in the future with the addition of seven new faculties. Self-contained student residences, each housing 144 students, extend from the central academic area. University staff will be accommodated in a village of 560 houses and flats, arranged around community facilities. Careful consideration is to be given to orientation and shading.

The contract for the project, worth over £200m was awarded to Cementation International with YRM International as architects, in March 1982. The team is committed to a very fast programme with the start on site planned for November 1982, and the first buildings scheduled to be complete for the 1986/87 academic year.

CLIENT: Cementation International Ltd for the Sultanate of Oman
CIVIL & STRUCTURAL ENGINEERS: Trafalgar House Engineering Services
QUANTITY SURVEYORS: Cementation International Ltd
BUILDING SERVICES CONSULTATION: YRM Engineers

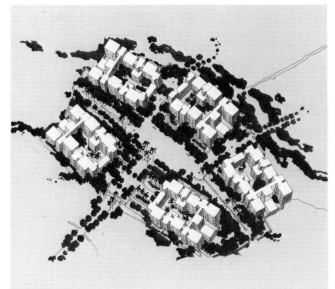
Perspective of staff housing

Interior walkway

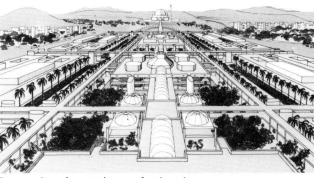
Perspective of central area of university

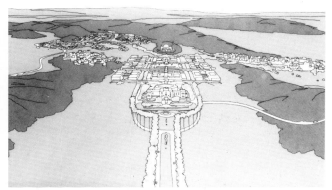
Aerial perspective, view from east
Overhead view of model

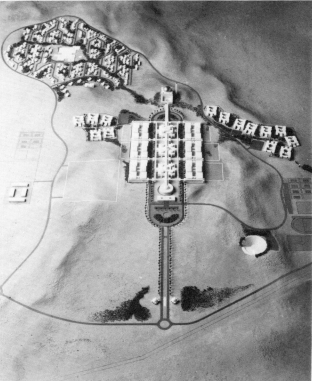

Central area, first floor plan

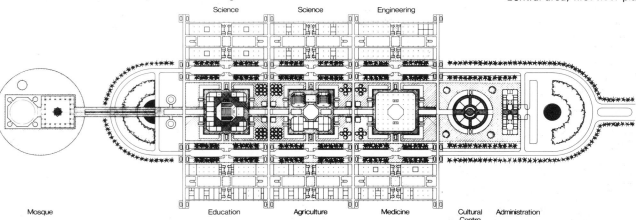

Mosque   Education   Agriculture   Medicine   Cultural   Administration
                                              Centre

Science   Science   Engineering

Model of student residence

Overhead view of Medical College

FOLLOWING a limited international competition YRM International were commissioned to design a new medical college for the University of Basrah, Iraq. The brief was to provide a College with medical teaching and research facilities for some 3,000 students and staff, together with residential accommodation for 1,300 students. The site is adjacent to the existing teaching hospital and overlooks an attractive canal near the Shatt al Arab waterway in the south of Basrah.

Academic and social activities, including a sports hall, student centre and library, are planned on the ground floor of the main building, with teaching and research laboratories around the courtyards above. The residential accommodation, designed with single aspect to preserve privacy and provide pleasant views across the canal, is parallel to the main building.

A covered pedestrian street between the housing and the main building will be the focus of the college life, linking together all the major activities. The complex will be fully air-conditioned and services to the upper laboratory floors will be standardised to provide flexibility for the future.

In designing the new college, the consultant team were aware of the need to establish a visual imagery that is sympathetic to the local environment and reinforces the importance of Islamic culture. This has been achieved in both the form of the building and the materials used. The central covered street, landscaped courtyards, and water gardens provide continuity between external and internal spaces. The use of brick and ceramic tiles establishes a cultural link with other major buildings in Southern Iraq, which is emphasised in a distinctive manner by the intricate geometry of the lightweight sunshades.

CLIENT: State Organisation of Buildings
ARCHITECTS: YRM in association with Mahmood Al-Ali & Ptnrs, Baghdad
STRUCTURAL ENGINEERS: FJS International
QUANTITY SURVEYORS: Widnell & Trollope
M & E ENGINEERS: DSSR

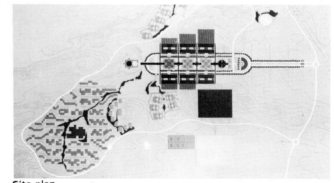
Site plan
Detail of grid above entrance

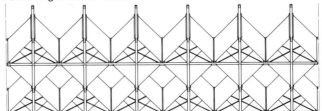

Douglas Stephen & Partners
CAERGYBI (HOLYHEAD) STATION AND FERRY TERMINAL

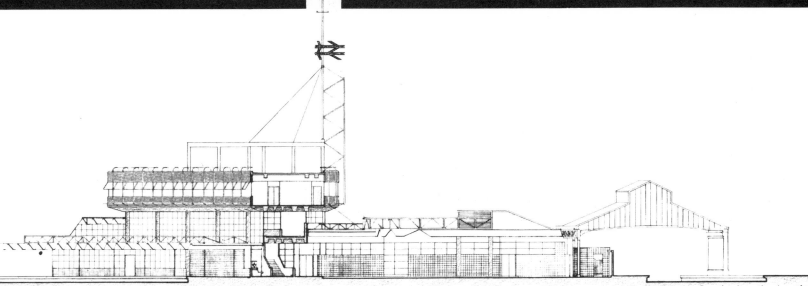

South elevation/section

THE VERY RESTRICTED SITE for this inter-change building for British Rail at their Holyhead ferry terminal is sandwiched between the convex curves of two sets of railway lines. At one extreme, a single loop links to a road bridge crossing the railway lines, at the other, the site expands to the broad reach of the harbour basin. Contextually, the site is isolated from the town, while the programme is dominated by physical systems, transit movement of people and services—typically a Modern Movement programme. In addition, because of the need to provide a turning circle for coaches and adequate waiting space for road vehicles, the amount of site which could be built over was very severely limited. Moreover, the procedural requirements of British Rail made this a very complex empirical programme, not one which could be dealt with by one single act of symbolic order-making.

From these constraints the main elements and their relationship were determined. Administration was the only function which could be raised up above the main public level, and this is held over to the side of the site adjoining the existing main line arrivals, where its structure could be assimilated in the platform structures. The turning circle necessarily gouges out even this location, but happily this loss of structure can be made to coincide neatly with the location of the main typing pool. The covered concourse requires a systematic roof structure which defines the rest of the accommodation, its diagonally offset curves defining road arrival and sea basin at either end.

The office block, the gouged indentation which it displays, and the regular ripples of the top lighting structure of the concourse, set up between them a counterpoint which both accommodates the varied functions of the site and orders them. The original clock tower from the old Holyhead hotel is re-sited at the hub of the entrance, and is echoed by the new British Rail logo on its scaffold tower.

The major element of accommodation at platform level is the waiting area of the concourse and this is subject to intermittent use, principally when delays occur in ferry sailings. To maintain this space at normal indoor comfort levels was not necessary, but a very quick response heating system was required to provide acceptable conditions during long delays. This was achieved by the use of overhead hot air radiant tubes, a system frequently used in industrial warehouse buildings as it is inexpensive and almost instantaneous in its effect. The design of the roof sections evolved about the distribution of these tubes and the requirements for insulating the upper surfaces. The rooflight sections incorporated a permanent finish top and bottom and all the drainage ways and artificial lighting, in addition to the heating and insulation role. The roof units were to be hoisted from below into the structural hollow section main support trusses, and each section was capable of being individually placed in case of damage.

The character of the building, in its isolation in the railway yards, relates primarily to the adjoining customs shed, but makes reference to the imposing influence of the goliath cranes and the occasional massive presence of the ferry.

This scheme was developed through to full contract drawings when arbitrary financial cuts left it, complete and buildable, on its own individual shelf.

CLIENT: The Regional Architect, BR London Midland Region, Chief Architects Department
QUANTITY SURVEYORS: BR Regional Architects Department
ENGINEERS: Chief Civil Engineer, BR London Midland Region

View of model towards the south

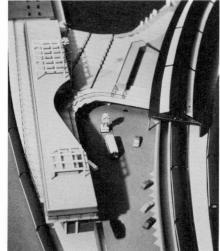

Roof plan

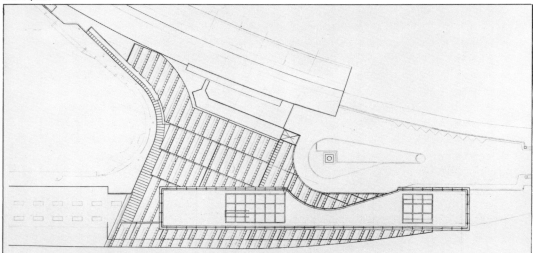

View of model towards the north

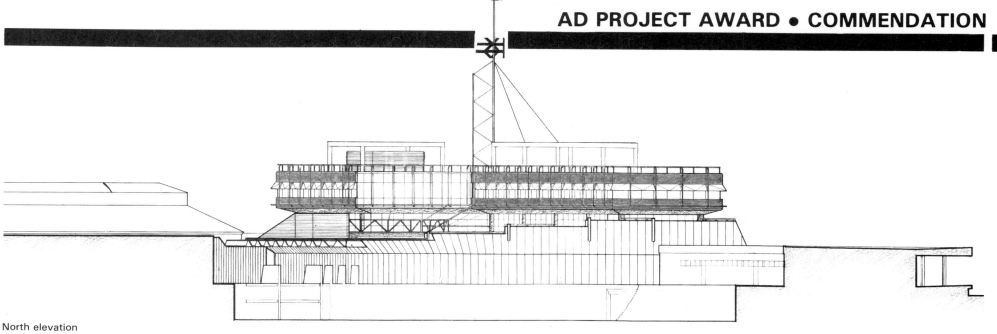

North elevation

HAMPSTEAD CENTRAL REDEVELOPMENT, 'SITE C'

THE BRIEF CALLED FOR offices to provide a commercial impetus and allow planning gain in the provision of residential and workshop units, with a few shops and an entrance to the adjoining British Rail station.

Two major considerations form the basis for these proposals: first, to relate positively to the existing street context; second within the constraints thus imposed to provide the best possible environment for workers and residents, in order to realise the full potential of the site.

The strategy adopted for fitting the development on the site aims to reinforce existing patterns of use and the urban structure. The offices are placed in the mainly commercial Finchley Road frontage, and along the railway, where larger bulk can be tolerated. They are stepped in section to relate to the existing frontages in Finchley Road and to the proposed new housing in Dresden Close.

The external faces will be clad in stainless steel and glass, with some areas of ceramic tile—all materials will reflect light and are easily maintained, so that the building can appear luminous even in overcast and fume-laden conditions.

We see this design as reconciling modern building forms and efficient internal planning, with the requirements of the existing urban structure and the need to represent and reinforce what is socially considered appropriate. This project won an open Architect/Developer competition, arranged by Camden Borough Council.

DEVELOPER: Co-Partnership Property Developments
QUANTITY SURVEYORS: Davis Belfield & Everest
COMMERCIAL CONSULTANTS: Montagu Evans

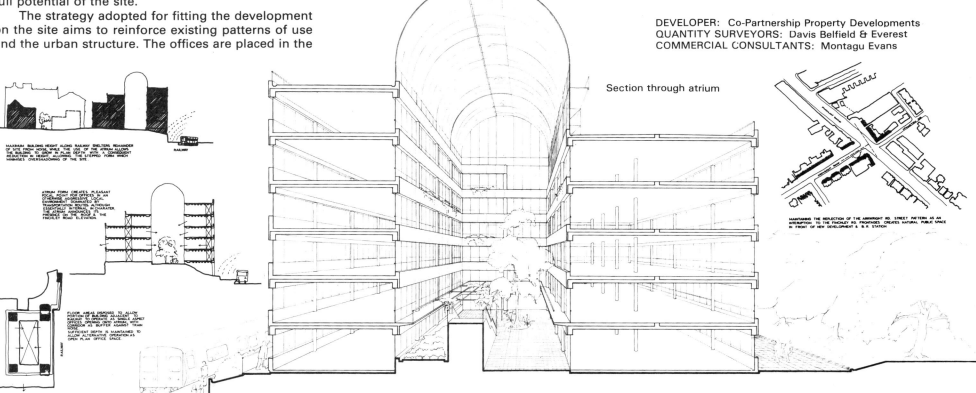

Section through atrium

Quinlan Terry
THE SALUTE BIRDCAGE

THIS BIRDCAGE is made in stainless steel mesh and faced with mouldings, balustrades, columns, pinnacles and pediments in limewood. The Corinthian capitals and cherubs are in polished brass. The rusticated base and steps are also in limewood, and the pedestal is mahogany.

The size was determined from the brass Corinthian columns for the major and minor order which are obtainable from catalogues. Thus the top diameter of the columns and pilasters are fixed; which in turn governs the sizes of the bottom diameter of the columns, entablature and all the other parts of the orders. The result is ten foot high including the pedestal.

This is not a model of a building, it is a piece of classical architecture with obvious associations; the association being Longhena's church of Santa Maria della Salute in Venice. The architectural game is to simplify the mouldings while reducing the scale and changing the materials. Thus an eight foot high main entablature in Travertine, in section is like this.

The architects had to produce 24 large drawings giving all the full-size details of all the parts. This was necessary because there are two types of portico, two large domes, three types of lanterns, campaniles as well as balustrades at several levels complete with finials, scrolled buttresses and other adornments.

STAINLESS STEEL & BRASSWORK: FW Hall (Norwich)
WOODCARVERS & JOINERS: Mabbitt (Colchester)
Front elevation of model

Front

'NEWFIELD', NORTH YORKSHIRE

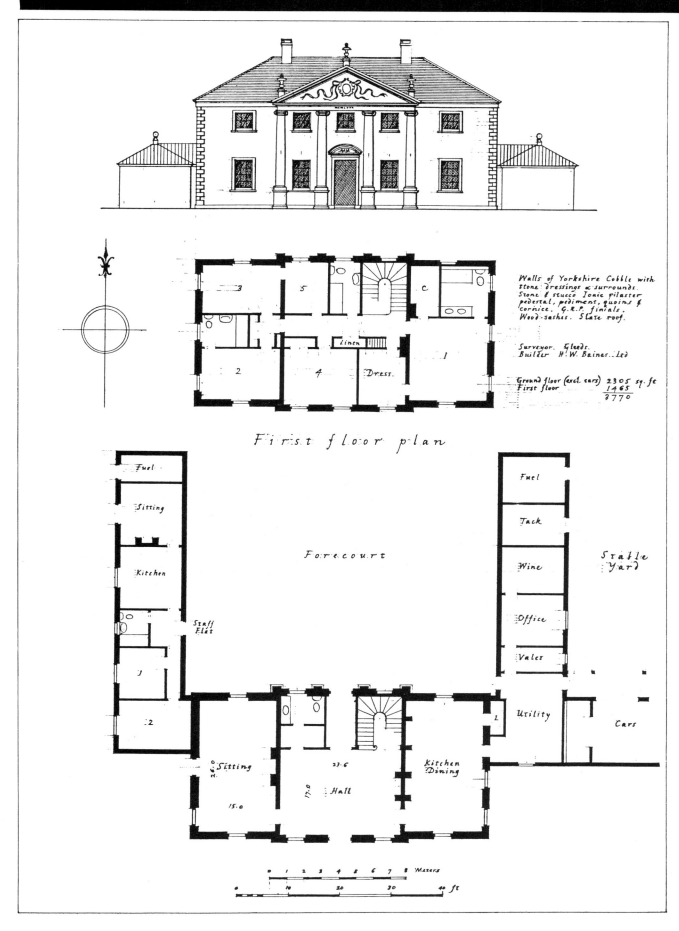

First floor plan

Walls of Yorkshire Cobble with stone dressings & surrounds. Stone & stucco Ionic pilaster pedestal, pediment, quoins & cornice. G.R.P. finials. Wood-sashes. Slate roof.

Surveyor. Gleeds.
Builder H.W. Baines. Ltd

Ground floor (excl. cars) 2305 sq. ft
First floor 1465
3770

Fuel · Sitting · Kitchen · Staff Flat · Forecourt · Stable Yard · Fuel · Tack · Wine · Office · Valet · Utility · Cars · Sitting · Hall · Kitchen Dining

AT NEWFIELD I WAS FORTUNATE in having a client who felt that a true country house is not an isolated building in the landscape but an obvious centre of a self sufficient and well organised farm.

Newfield is therefore the centre piece of a group of buildings arranged symmetrically on either side of its main axis. The walls of the house are made of Yorkshire cobbles (gathered out of the fields and fence walls around the site) and backed with an inner skin for insulation. The giant Ionic order on pedestals on the north front is in Portland stone and stucco; as are the central doors with a segmental pediment on the north, and with carved consoles on the south. The sash windows are set in reveals with wide glazing bars and reconstructed stone surrounds. The pediments and finials are in stucco and stone. The ground floor is solid, the first floor and roof are of a traditional timber construction. The slates are Welsh Bangor heavy blues.

The effect of scale is interesting when the house is seen from the road, as it stands in a commanding position against the dark background of a wood on the other side of the valley. As one approaches along the drive the symmetry of the wings and the barns add to this effect of importance. However, it is only when one stands close to the front door that the scale is reduced and one realises that this is in fact quite a small house.

MAIN CONTRACTOR: HW Baines

North front

Stables
Hay Barn

CHRISTMAS STEPS is a product of the medieval frontage type system characterised by an irregular frontage line lined now by pleasant 18th and early 19th-century traditional scale houses with ground floor shops.

Planning policy has been directed to repairing the derelict buildings at the top and bottom including, where appropriate, new buildings, in an attempt to revive the prosperity of the shops in Christmas Steps, which is thought to have considerable tourist potential.

A group of houses at the bottom of Christmas Steps, which originally closed the view down the steps, was removed when Rupert Street was transformed into a dual carriageway. Planning policy is now to close the view down the steps again with *new* traditional scale buildings.

The general improvement of Christmas Steps, generated by the concentration of effort at the top and bottom of the steps, is expected to transform the area into an important tourist attraction when completed. The competition brief suggests that an overall scheme for their improvement would be of great advantage to the area. It is also felt that the particular character of the steps could be considerably enlivened by colour and possibly by features above the pedestrian way.

Definitions
The problem of Christmas Steps is one of conservation, and the problem of conservation is one of definition. The case for the preservation of the historically evolved habitat was put quite clearly in a paper given by David Smith on the *Preservation of Historic Towns*, and which won the TPI Summer School Award for 1967. His arguments, developed from the Sittesque spatial model, were that old buildings, their spacing or groupings, and landscape are often so attractive that, regardless of the architectural merit of individual buildings, this character should be preserved; that the functional fitness of old towns can be argued to be superior to that of any built today; that on economic grounds, the conservation of resources represented by an existing development is desirable, and he went on to reiterate the British Travel Association's argument that Britain's international tourist trade is dependent on the country's *unique historical attractions*. But his final, and most important point was that the preservation of historic areas was necessary in order to provide a setting for important old buildings whose value would be lost if left in the midst of a new development. This is a widely held view and, to a certain extent, the planning policy as outlined for Christmas Steps follows suit. Why else re-enclose the Steps in *traditional scale* buildings implying from recent precedent, replicating the traditional *style* as well as scale.

The main problem of conservation is its very complexity. It is the preservation from destructive influences, natural decay and waste, and the preservation in being, life, health and perfection. The problem with the preservation of the historically evolved habitat is that much interest, whilst appearing to be concerned with *history*, is really concerned with *tradition* to the extent that we get *dead history*—a kind of environmental taxidermy. Why always *retain* when, by *transformation* we can often make such things more understandable by their very accentuation?

Ways of Seeing
Attitudes to conservation in both Britain and Europe are essentially pragmatic. And the inner failing of pragmatism, as Bruner argues in his book *On Knowing*, is that it may help us to pick the right machine to do the job but it will not tell us if the job is worth doing.

As Professor Robert Vickery has pointed out pragmatism is the *philosophy of practicality*. It grew out of the Industrial Revolution where the value of an idea was measured by its *utility*. It did not, however, raise the moral and philosophic question of whether the idea was of sufficient worth to warrant the setting in motion of the machinery necessary for its development.

In short, pragmatism defeats the conservationist because it does not give him sufficient nor proper values by which to judge the concept of preservation in any particular case. Pragmatism has become not so much a philosophy as an attitude or method.

Through the changing ideals of conservation in the 20th century the *image of the city* has become, in a sense, a work of art as complete and as protected as a Mona Lisa. As John Berger points out in *Ways of Seeing*, fear of the present leads to mystification of the past. The past is not for living in, it is a well of conclusions from which we draw in order to act. Cultural mystification of the past entails a double loss. Works of art are made unnecessarily remote. And the past offers us fewer conclusions to complete in action.

The archetypal problem, as represented by Christmas Steps, is that of the cultural mystification that goes on when a street, like this, which clearly belongs to one tradition is treated, by its very segregation, as if it actually belonged to another tradition. It's like the king's *new clothes*. Whilst he, in his mind's eye, sees this ceremonial gear, all we can see is his birthday suit. What we see here is an *ordinary* medieval street, made extraordinary, I'll grant you, by its rarity now, but clearly nothing monumental and grand yet, like the king's *new clothes* it is presented to us *now* as if it were, but all we see is what it was. Is it possible that some transformation is necessary, something more substantive and corporate than the planning policies suggested in the brief?

History v Tradition
Reconstruction of the past inevitably postpones the more necessary enrichment of the present. And, it can be argued, the appropriate architectural form for present needs can well enhance the built forms of the historically evolved habitat. But it would seem that many architects and planners today are bent on suppressing any notion of a *history* of architecture in preference for a *tradition* of architecture. History is about an ability to transform, to innovate; tradition is merely an ability to replicate. The latter is seen in a predilection for neo-vernacular. The former can be illustrated by reference to the work of Alberti—in particular his re-modelling of the church of S Maria Novella, Florence, in 1456. One can imagine the church fathers asking Alberti to redesign their Florentine church in the *new* Renaissance style. How to make the front facade appear as one unified whole instead of a high nave and two lower side aisles must have bothered Alberti until he came up with the idea of using a geometric curved form, the volute, to make a graceful transition from high to low. An original solution and so perfectly in harmony with Renaissance thought.

The Cultural Mystification
In order to understand the problem we should look at two extremes, as represented by Court Street, Faversham, and the Royal Crescent, Bath. Now Christmas Steps belongs to the additive fabric of the former yet ideologically it is said, by its very act of preservation, to belong, somehow, to the

latter. It is as if Low Art has been catapulted into the super world of High Art. Whilst it obviously retains overtones of its source and origin the wholly new impact it is meant to gain by such an apparent shift in context is non-existent for, as we perceive, the changed context (art gallery/museum/frame/pedestal) has not happened. All that we have is the idea, not the reality. Could we here, like the pop painter Oldenburg tries to do, reconcile *art* with *reality*? Could we not make the *new aesthetic* of Christmas Steps, whatever that might be, a reality? What our attitude to Christmas Steps implies is that the vernacular tradition as presented here (Court Street, Faversham) is ideologically now more a part of the Grand Design Tradition (Royal Crescent, Bath).

The former (Faversham) represents the life and activities of people directly whereas the latter (Bath) is more influenced and concerned with theories of architecture, fashions, impressiveness and the like, reflecting the pomp and ceremony of public occasions. The vernacular tradition is represented by tight, intricate spaces of high visual complexity and with hidden views. The Grand Design Tradition is associated more with vast open spaces, long vistas, grand axes and continuous frontages of excessive regularity.

Low Definition v High Definition
The first has a richly modelled fabric and less clearly defined structure, whilst the second has a clearly structured and highly defined image. There is here a code. On one hand a diffused image, and on the other a highly defined one. For the sake of argument I would like to call one LOW DEFINITION and the other HIGH DEFINITION. Low Definition is where the distinctness in the outline of an object or image is less ritualistic and acute, where it is humble and unpretending and a reflection of everyday social life. High Definition is where the distinctness in the outline of an object is intense, extreme, great, aloft or abstract; where it is acute or detached, a reflection of corporate mindedness. The image of Low Definition is mosaic in form in that it consists of an overall design composed of individual elements related to a common ground—the twisting frontage of street or path. The image of High Definition is where the arrangement of elements, the manner of their organisation, is clearly defined along a predominantly undeviating street or edge. The properties of Low Definition is that it is multi-form, disordered, non-linear, multi-coloured, non-repetitive and involving. The properties of High Definition is that it is clearly structured, ordered, monochrome, linear, uniform,

repetitive, continuous and non-involving. Ideologically the image of Christmas Steps is seen as an inversion of reality. But in order to de-mystify such a cultural cock-up we need to render the invisible visible by heightening the definition—in other words by rendering the void (street) more intense, extreme, ritualistic, acute and corporate. It is not necessary to make such an inversion complete, only partial. Such a hybrid already exists in Bristol which has elements of both, but with an overtone of the grand design. Perhaps in Christmas Steps the High Definition element needs to be an applied undertone.

Bristol / Hybrid of Grand Design + vernacular tradition

References
There are, of course, numerous references of the kinds of transformations that can occur in order to render a particular element/s with a renewed perspective. For the pop artists the strategy was to re-assemble (often visually inflated) low art artefacts in a wholly different context (art gallery/museum, etc).

For Michelangelo to transform the Campidoglio as the civic heart of 16th-century Rome, he had to radically restructure (render) the space (void) itself. To do this he radically re-mapped the Palazzo Senatore, applied a more boldly articulated facade to the Palazzo dei Conservatori (using for the first time in a secular building a giant order) and mirrored this opposite as well as appropriately marking the ground plane and reinforcing the axiality of the whole ensemble by a magnificent flight of steps. He shifted our way of perceiving this collection of buildings by acknowledging that it was no longer a part of old medieval Rome but of the new 16th-century Rome. In order to re-present these things in the perspective in which conceptually they desired to be, he radically changed the context. Whilst recollecting source and origin he allows us to enjoy the innovations in this *new perspective*.

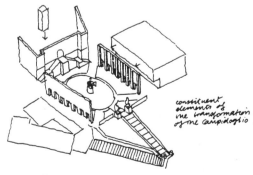

constituent elements of the transformation of the Campidoglio

The Street as Picture
The particular language of Townscape to which Christmas Steps belongs is clearly the inverse of the totalitarianism of the neo-classical. The particular language of Townscape here is about the visual impression of scenes accidentally encountered, such works (Port Grimaud/Costa Smeralda) are frankly and deliberately stamped with the spontaneous

character of sketches. The problem here is one of moving, like Cubism, in an opposite direction to Impressionism whilst retaining overtones of source and origin. What we want to do is to suggest perceptually that the street is highly defined whilst accommodating the Low Definition elements of the medieval frontage type system of what exists.

As various authorities have told us the task confronting a cartoonist is to represent in black and white some more or less familiar part of our visual world in a recognisable form. The cartoonist reduces complexity (of the photograph) without loss of vital features. Expressions are conveyed by eye-brows, shape of eyes and mouth etc. With this simple equipment a skilled cartoonist may convey a vast range of facial expressions. The emphasis is on the economy of line—much is omitted by the artist in such a way that they are perceptually present as the sections actually drawn. The image is so structured that the viewer is obliged to supply the missing parts. What we need to do here is to provide the *gestalt* completion picture of this new order.

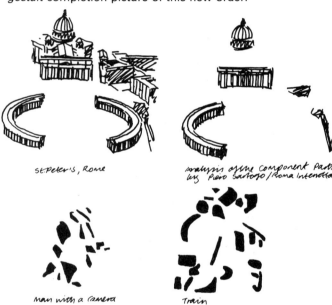

St Peter's, Rome

analysis of the component parts by Piero Sartogo / Roma Interrotta

man with a camera

Train

Transformations
There are a number of ways in which the definition of the street could be heightened. The street itself could be *closed* as a thing complete in its own right, like Sicilian Avenue, London. The void (street) could be rendered (articulated) by some kind of applied element, much as in the Station, Bristol. Or one could take a series of elements and, via the tension set up by the particular relationship between one element and another, establish a seminal (line of) force that would be sufficiently powerful to *carry* the idea of this new order whilst avoiding a radical transformation of the physical fabric.

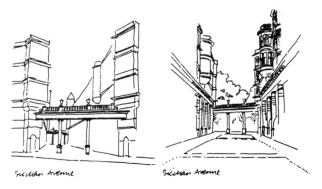

Sicilian Avenue.

Sicilian Avenue

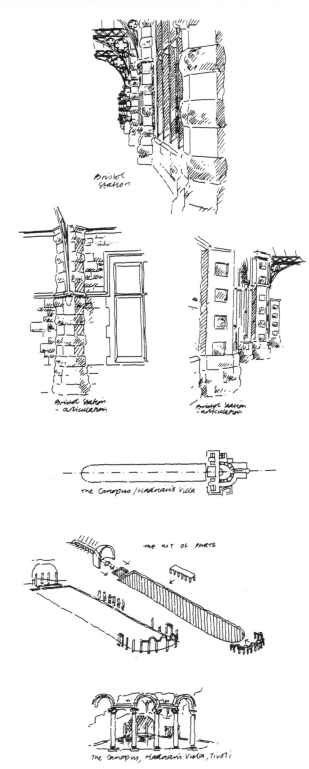

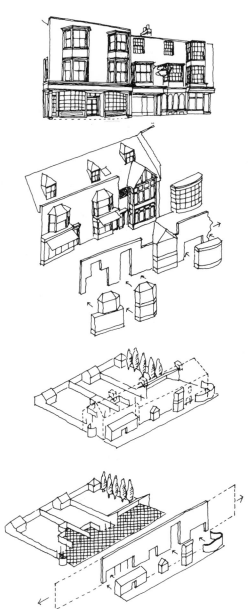

human actions within a certain framework, of how a house or living unit becomes a dwelling the moment the occupant begins to *possess* it by the very act of transforming it. However, the transformations that have already taken place in the archetypal medieval frontage type system are such that the outside of the individual house is now, with its neighbours, the architecture of the street and no longer merely that of the individual house. The facade/s in fact have now become the mediator between the public and private realm.

make the necessary transformation? Such elements are the ways the ground line is articulated by a rendered plinth, by the relationship of ground line to shop front or string course; by the stucco dressing to door and window surrounds.

The Additive Fabric

Neo-vernacular is obviously wrong in making a jelly mould of the Regionalist tradition. Form as a goal, as Mies van der Rohe pointed out, always ends in Formalism. Such striving is directed not towards an inside but towards an outside. He said that only a living inside has a living outside. But NJ Habraken has more recently pointed out that old houses left to us from the past have more often than not been transformed—of how each generation, each occupant, changed what he found. He sees DWELLING as the sum of

The Rendering of the Void

Christmas Steps, as a street, is a street in name only. It has not, as yet, been possessed. It is not a *real* street, only the *idea* of a street in city scale terms. It is a *local street* masquerading as something grander. But until the city's civic presence *possesses* the street and, by that very act, transforms it, it will never be what it aspires to be, only what it seems to be. What is needed is the articulation of this new way of seeing the street.

Already there is a language special to Christmas Steps. Can the elements of this language, coherently articulated,

Abstraction

If we abstract the elements of the street picture we can still perceptually *read* the street picture by the *gestalt* elements of such an abstraction. We can use the elements of the shops only, to render the message. But such a corporate identity, however, would inevitably kill the individualism that makes such a street attractive in the first place. What is needed is an order that creates this corporate identity of civicness whilst accommodating the existing (and future) personal enrichment and extension of shop fronts and entrances etc. What we need is to create the street wall, (an applied stucco band) that accommodates the individual shop fronts, articulates the street as a *street picture*, (as complete as a work of art in its own right) whilst allowing the upper stories, above the rendered band, to have their own personal and special character.

The Possible Strategy

The carved void (street) is articulated by a rendered band (partial wall/frame) which treats the shops as something inserted or breaking through. The void is *closed* at either end, the elements of entrance portico and apsidal-ended arch containing fountain/pool and flanked by sheltered seating are explicit in their own right. The apsidal arch is open to the street, but closed to the dual carriage way. Like the remains of some triumphal arch left over from the ancient classical world, it is half submerged by a grassy bank and planting. Christmas Steps metaphorically speaking, ends here, but the pedestrian can follow the dog legs sidestepping past the arch.

The subliminal insertion of grand design elements is treating the existence of such a concept merely as an idea. It is essentially an existentialist concept which says, as Louis Kahn said, something like *'The sun never knew how great it was until it struck the side of a building'* or *'I asked the brick what it wanted to be and it wanted to be an arch.'*

It would seem that what this street has become ideologically, but not perceptually, is *street as picture*. But such a fact is not visible. Certain spaces and forms say quite clearly what it is can be done with them. There are seminal forces within them that can control future creative acts.

What is proposed here is that the *gestalt* elements of the existing rendered more coherent can make the invisible visible. For the street to be seen as *picture*, it needs a new way of seeing, a new perspective. Change in perspective can come about through a shift or transformation of context. The hot dog is visually inflated by the pop painter and housed in a wholly new context where its new meaning becomes understandable. For the street it has to be done *in-situ*. To understand the *street as picture* you need some kind of frame, and that is what is proposed via the rendered band, the entrance portico, arch, grassy bank and the seminal force such elements set in motion.

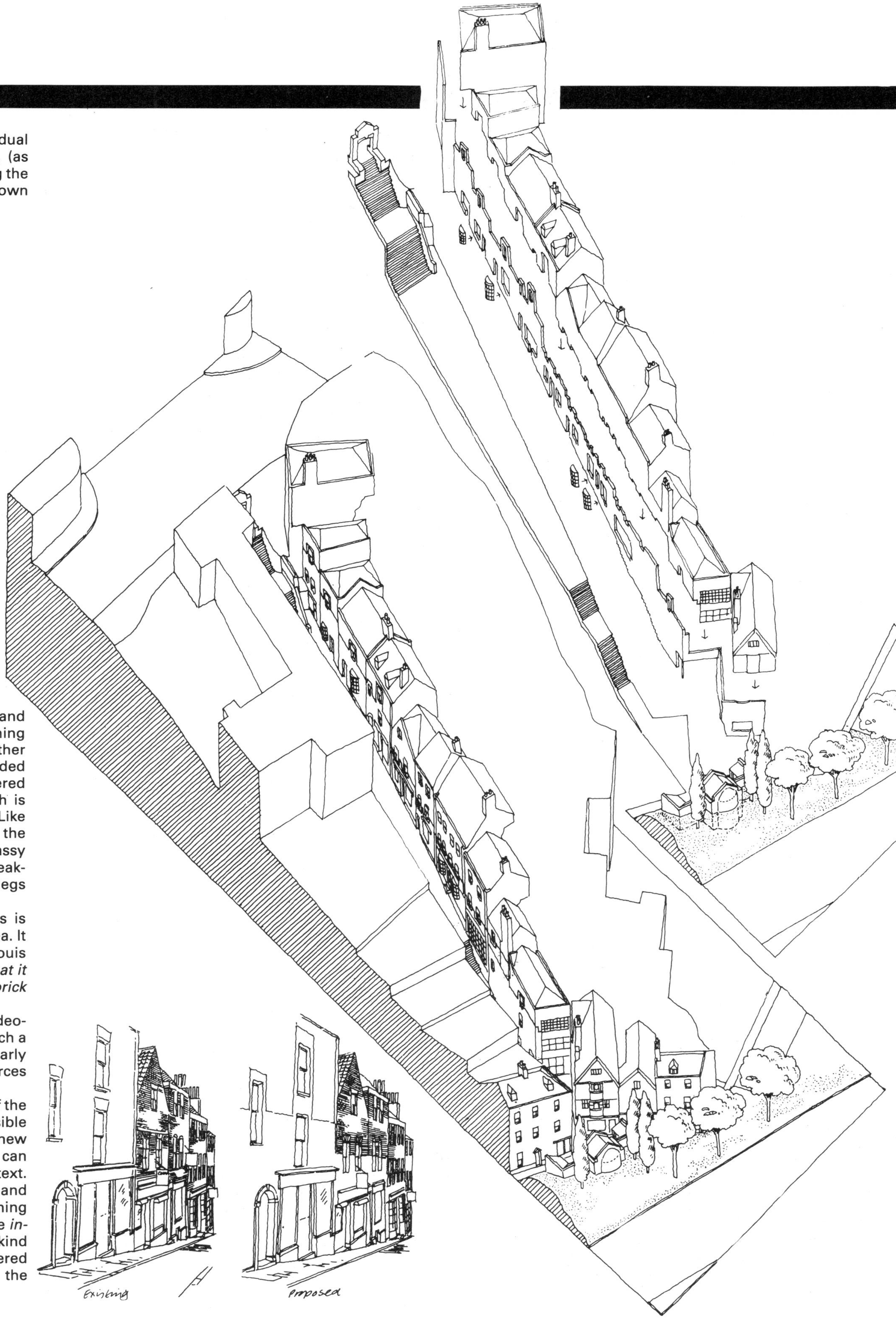

Existing

Proposed

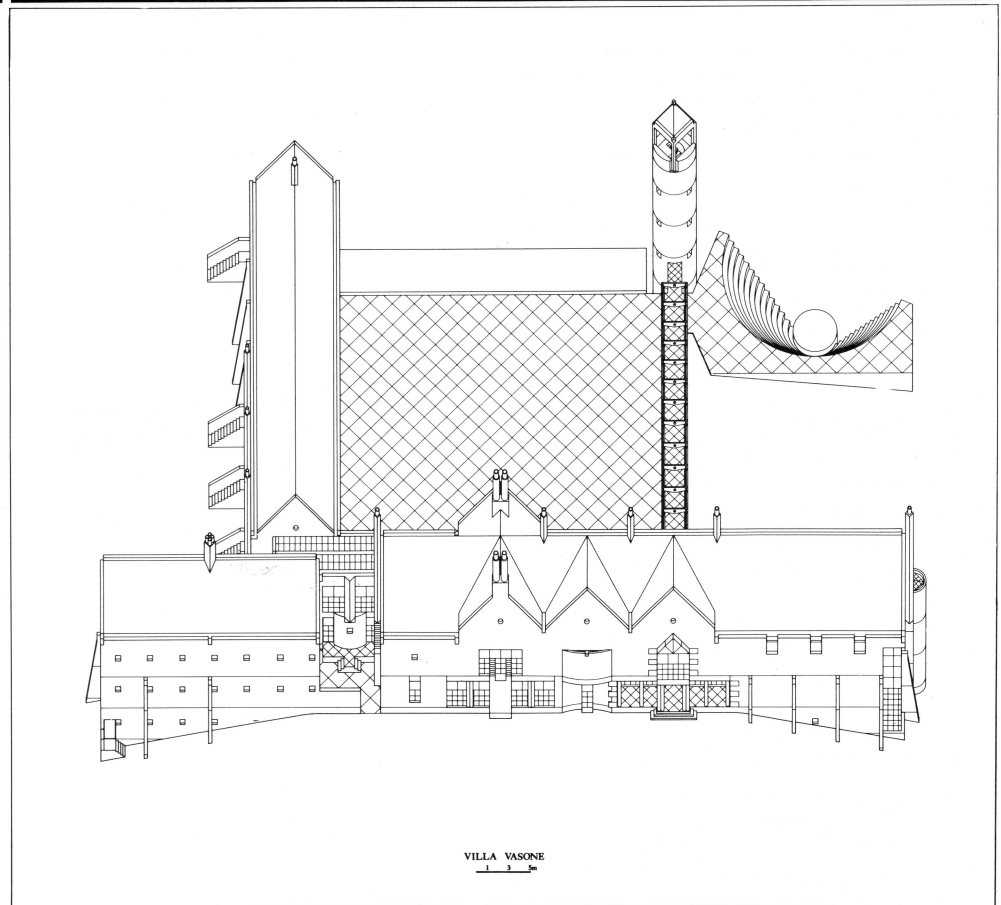

VILLA VASONE

1 3 5m

DEAR MR VASONE,

Since we met last December to discuss the house you wished to build on your mountain top site, we have been investigating the nature of such a house, the possible strategies to be employed in accommodating the various elements of the programme harmoniously, and the kinds of building and architectural traditions the kind of home we believe you seek might conceivably belong to. The following is a brief description of the kinds of experiences encountered on a visit to the proposed house and garden.

A narrow road winds in a series of dog legs up the northern side of the mountain. To the right the ground drops sharply away. For sometime, the road runs under an umbrella of trees and then begins to level out and finally arrives in a spacious clearing to the west of the mountain. To one side is a high, thick boundary wall, the centre of which is punctuated by a gate house. The gate house is articulated by two plain gables springing from the top of the boundary wall. To the left is the gate and arch; behind the gable to the right lies a small house, the living room window pushed into a boldly articulated bay through the boundary wall. There is a suggestion of a tradition going back to the gatehouses found in the English countryside. It is a prelude of things to come, in both space and time, perhaps a hint of something more heroic.

A drive, springing from the clearing, passes through the gate and climbs gently up through a fan vault of trees. The ground, thickly wooded here, rises steeply to the left. A path, running from the gate, climbs up this bank in a series of sharp zig-zags to what appears to be a terrace above, carved out of the trees. A curving balustrade, perhaps a suggestion from the Italian Renaissance garden, forms a belvedere.

The tree lined drive climbs higher before finally flattening out. The trees gradually recede and the drive runs out into a great crescent of gravel in front of a large gabled facade, an echo of the gate house but on a grander scale. The gabled centre here, drawn from several distinct traditions, is the statement of Architecture. Behind you, on axis with the main entrance to the house, is a broad avenue of lawn designed to tie the house to the site. This lawn stretches out to the curving belvedere which you saw rising above you when passing by the gate house.

No architecture can be free of influences from the past and the design of the facade is intended to portray this. Certain connections with late medieval architecture in England have been welcomed and exploited. The overall effect is of a building added to over a period of time. There is a pleasant disturbed symmetry, the necessary coherence and balance being provided by a uniform frontage line, a predominantly two storey facade, use of parapet walls, chimneys articulating the side gables of the principal block and a rendered ground plinth drawn across both the main block and the service wing. The first floor is defined by a string course drawn throughout the front facade. Boldly canted buttresses support the ends of both the service wing and the principal block. The ground line here falls sharply away revealing both a basement storey in the service wing, and the lofty proportions of the living room and library to the west of the principal block. The principal block itself is clearly differentiated from the service wing by a small recessed court, separating the two. Like Knole House, Sevenoaks, Kent, it has all the appearance of an older house re-modelled and extensively enlarged along a single frontage line.

There are no mouldings on the facade here to enliven the undecorated surfaces; the walls continue up as parapets beyond the point where the roof begins and are cut off square at the top, ending in gables on the narrow side of the service wing. The controlled, yet irregular nature of the front facade has all the hallmarks of Ruskin's analysis of Gothic out of which sprang his concept of changefulness. Gothic was, he urged, the only rational architecture for it could fit itself to every function. And he went on to show how '... *whenever it finds occasion for change in its form or purpose, it submits to it without the slightest sense of loss to its unity or majesty.*' In this facade each room is expressed on the outside. In Standen, Sussex, (1891–94) Philip Webb did exactly this. The rambling, additive nature of Standen is articulated by the use of different local materials, rough-cast, clapboarding, brick and stone, each material emphasising a different function. Even the windows are carefully differentiated, with leaded lights to show circulation spaces and big sash windows to indicate the nature of the room. The garden facade of Standen, with its formal landscape, has a multiplicity of boarded gables jettied slightly out from the main plane. This is the principal mediator between house and garden. Drawn across the main block and treated much like a separate element, almost as if added later, as with the Jacobean facade of Knole House and our proposal here, it appears to carry, single handed, the collage of parts behind.

The facade of the main living-room, to the right of the entrance porch, consists of a large and austere expanse of buttressed wall. The lofty interior is expressed by the tall corner window with its small panes and the stepped section exposed by the sharply falling ground line and enriched by the canted buttresses. This section of the building has all the boldness and simplicity of medieval England. It is what John Ruskin would have described as savage, a kind of unthinking primitiveness full of poetry, something elementary and genuine, a kind of fragment of rustic architecture. It is as if part of the Great Coxwell Barn,

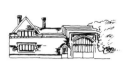

Mid 19th century gatehouse, south-east England.

Drive up to the proposed house.

The main entrance.

View to the gabled entrance from the front lawn.

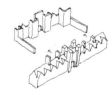

Jacobean facade added to Knole House, Sevenoaks, Kent

The epitome of Ruskinian changefulness. The Red House, Bexleyheath, designed 1859–60 by Philip Webb.

Standen, Sussex, designed 1891–1894 by Philip Webb.

Gloucestershire, which William Morris thought '... *unapproachable in its dignity, as beautiful as a cathedral, yet with no ostentation of the builders' art,*' had been attached at the end of the main house. High in the wall are three small, square windows. The parapet wall immediately above each is cut, suggesting crenellation.

In the most general sense, the entire facade is an intriguing hybrid between the vernacular tradition and the Grand Design tradition (a combination of changeful pictur-esqueness and Georgian regularity and uniformity). Whilst there are certain qualities, as Voysey pointed out, that are essential to all classes of homes, there are certain other qualities, like grandeur, splendour, pomp, majesty and exuberance, which are suitable only to comparatively few. If one can accept that the ends, the service wing and living-room, are primarily concerned with building, albeit on an heroic scale (ie the Old Tithe Barn, Bradford-on-Avon or even a Voysey house) the centre, with its three tall gables, is the statement of Architecture in the great expanse of wall.

The specific strategy is to have three separate yet related facades below each gable. The twin columned entrance porch stands on a stylobate and projects in front of the long recessed entrance loggia. Surmounting the porch is a glazed, gabled bay giving light to the reading room of the library above. The ends of the loggia are defined by quoins. The central gable has a concave ground storey, the centre of which is pierced by a projecting glazed bay. Surmounting it is a one storey convex bay with a clerestory light above. These two inverted elements express the double height withdrawing or reception room; the preponderance of solid wall to window provides the necessary privacy. The gable on the left is over the principal dining space. The facade here is composed of a two storey panel of mullioned window with the lower half filled centrally by the chimney breast. This is corbelled at the upper level back into the room, to reappear once more, crowning the gable with twin chimneys. These are repeated axially on the other side of the dining room.

The house here is intended to look as if it had always been there, sympathetic in the landscape and rooted to the site. In order to do that, as with the English houses built between 1860–1914, it is important to find a more accommodating strategy than that employed for the grand houses of the Palladian tradition of the 18th century, with their predilection for an extremely formal and symmetrical geometry.

There are numerous precedents for making the kind of facade as suggested here—irregular elements beneath regular gables—within the history and tradition of the English House. Interesting recent examples are Chigwell Hall or The Three Gables by Norman Shaw; Redcourt, Haslemere, by Ernest Newton; Avon Tyrell, Hampshire by Lethaby etc. The site for Chigwell Hall, for instance, was on open, rising ground, and something rather compact was needed to crown the height and control the drive. Contradicting tradition, Shaw brought the reception rooms round to the front, articulating them with bracketed windows and a projecting window bay surmounted by an open balcony. Three symmetri-cal gables crown the asymmetrical facade. The sides were given balancing window bays and a giant chimney piece. To the right of the large hipped roof is a third chimney, continuing the asymmetry of the front facade. Such irregularity and apparent informality was carried to extremes in Ernest Barnsley's design for Rodmarton Manor, Gloucester-shire. It is a large, meandering house with mullioned windows and multiple gables. Built in the strictest Cotswold tradition, it has all the aura of a medieval house, built with medieval craftsmanship. In re-using elements imbued with the associational values of the English House, it is important to avoid indulging in the kinds of replica men such as Barnsley were concerned with. And so the elements of Englishness here are not copies of those belonging to an English vernacular tradition, but instead are comments on the reinterpre-tation of such elements, as developed in the hands of Shaw, Voysey or Lutyens.

But this is to be both grand house as well as cosy home, an inherent contradiction that few country house architects were ever able to solve, with the exception of Lutyens. He saw, as we see, the need to combine both building and architecture. In his design of 1899 for Homewood, Knebworth, one finds boarded gables and symmetrical elevations combined with overtly classical detailing. It is as if the core of the house and design of the walls are classical whilst the generous roof and gables are vernacular. In his design for Tigbourne Court, Witley, Surrey, the formal ideas hidden in Homewood are more clearly expressed—there are projecting wings, recessed entrance loggia with columns and grand, Jacobean style gabled facade. It is a kind of scenographic architecture with the principal facades masking the often asymmetrical plan behind. This was not a new idea, it had already been utilised by Webb at Standen and Shaw at Chesters.

In the hands of Lutyens, the country house was transformed by an ingenious strategy combining the best of both worlds—the warm inglenooked snugness of early Shaw with the symmetry of the Georgian. An innovation of these plans, however, was that the right angle and, even the continuity of axes, were no longer sacred—if necessary they could be broken to suit both the topographical considerations and programmatic requirements. Such planning ideas have their origin in the classic Roman villas of the ancient world, such as the Villa Jovis, built by Tiberius, on Capri in the early 1st century.

Elements of such a scenographic strategy are employed in our proposal. In our proposed plan, the axial line of the entrance loggia is reinforced by the long broad lawn running out to the belvedere to the north. To the south from the Great Hall this line

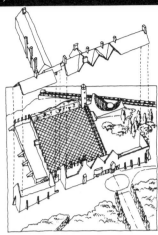

Diagram of the gabled front facade of the proposal, and showing the arrangement of elements added to the rear.

Left, the Old Tithe Barn, Bradford-on-Avon, 1350, and right Great Coxwell Barn, Gloucestershire.

The vernacular tradition—19th century Danish farmstead.

Two houses by C.F.A. Voysey. Left, proposed house on the Hogs Back, 1896 and right Broadleys, Windermere, 1896.

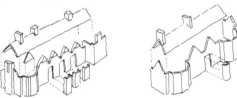

Fragments of the facades only as Architecture. Left, Avon Tyrell, Hampshire by Lethaby, 1893 and right, Redcourt, Haslemere, Surrey by Ernest Newton, 1895.

The Barn, Exmouth, Devon designed 1896 by Prior.

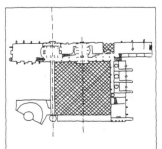

Plan of the proposed house.

continues along a pergola and is terminated by a round tower. The courtyard is centred on a second axis. This line is established by the projecting dining room bay and reinforced by the coupled chimneys which crown the gables, both at the front and back.

Up the steps, through the twin columned projecting porch and across the generous recessed loggia, you enter the Great Hall. Part of the loggia floor projects into the hall. From here you step up into the hall itself. In front of you are a row of coupled columns defining the connecting corridor which runs laterally across the house. Carried above these columns is the Long Gallery (memories of Elizabethan England). The hall facade of the gallery is enlivened by a generous opening. There is a large staircase in the left hand corner, at right angles to the hall, which ascends to the Long Gallery. The hall itself is open to the roof. The great timber trusses of this roof spring from the coupled columns on the entrance and Long Gallery sides of the Great Hall. Flanking the hall are two big fireplaces. The chimneys exposed within the hall soar upwards to the timber roof above creating a sense of loftiness. Beside the fireplace to the left is an entrance opening into the reception room. There is another big fireplace in here, but tucked in a more welcoming and less ceremonial manner, into the far corner, diagonally opposite this entrance. From this reception room another opening gives access to the dining room beyond.

Back in the Great Hall is a second fireplace. On either side of this are two large openings giving access to a curving balcony which springs out from the rear of the fireplace and projects into the spacious living room. In many ways the Great Hall proposed here, reminds one of the hall designed by Norman Shaw in 1877 for Adcote in Shropshire, a house which has all the trappings of the Old English style. This style, as developed by Shaw, has a simple additive vocabulary of great flexibility. Here, unlike the more restrictive planning of the Palladian or picturesque Italianate, large often irregular elements, such as the hall at Adcote, are quite easily accommodated. Built above the entrance loggia on our plan, is the reading room of the library. The Great Hall itself is portrayed as a ceremonial space opening out onto the connecting Long Gallery and corridor. Beyond the hall, arranged axially with the entrance, a pergola runs out to the round tower on the edge of the terrace.

A band of mullioned windows runs around the corridors edging the courtyard. Moving onto the corridor itself you get a clearer picture of the house and its relationship to the courtyard. The house has all the elements of the great Elizabethan or Jacobean mansions. Common to both was the Great Hall (generally covered by an open timber roof and connecting the various parts of the house); the grand staircase, adjacent to the hall; the Long Gallery (which was usually a spacious corridor or picture gallery with large mullioned windows and decorative plaster ceilings), and the withdrawing-room (often with projecting bays, large windows, panelled walls and carved chimney pieces). There are similarities in our proposal, except that here the elements are arranged with the principal rooms and circulation route articulated by free standing columns.

A long flight of steps descends from the corridor to the great living room. The steps widen as they go down, heightening the sense of grandeur. Projecting out of the wall to your left are three cosy inglenooks. Opposite the grand staircase is a small corkscrew stair which is built in a turret projecting out on the gabled end of the living room. This staircase gives access to the library gallery. This gallery encircles the living room on the upper level, adjoining the Long Gallery. The living room, like the hall, is open to the roof. The great roof trusses spring from the buttresses which project into the room like pilasters. There is a bar tucked beneath the convex balcony.

Leaving the living room, with the one storey high inglenooks to your right, the grand staircase narrows as you ascend. Its false perspective is intended to create an elegant vista reinforced by the long glazed corridor with its free-standing columns. From the corridor (a kind of glazed cloister walk), you have a clear field of vision out to the central courtyard as well as magnificent views across to the valley beyond. Passing the Great Hall, on your left there is a broad flight of steps to the Long Gallery. This also narrows as it ascends in emulation of the grand living-room staircase. The wall below the stair is cut back in line with the outer line of the staircase, continuing the angled plane which opens out into the dining room beyond. In the flange of the wall is carved a deep semicircular niche, with a font standing inside. The dining room may be reached in two ways; either from an opening cut by the angled staircase wall or by the north facing access corridor leading off the reception room. The dining room itself is a lofty cube of space, open to the timber roof above. The quality of the room is accentuated by tall, coupled columns and two large niches. Behind the convex niche to the west side is a long servery with counters and warming plates for dishes. The dining room is partially screened from the corridor by a big fireplace. There is another fireplace directly opposite at the other end of the room. There is a glazed bay, containing seating and doors to the courtyard, projecting from the south side of the corridor. This bay window is arranged axially with the courtyard and the dining room.

The feeling of the courtyard here is an amalgam of many things. There is an element of the Roman garden peristyle of Horace's Sabine Farm (fragmented as in the Villa of Sette Bassi with the buildings attached to one side). There is also a hint of an Elizabethan or Jacobean plan, as at Montacute House but the forecourt becoming here the private

Combination of symmetrical gables and asymmetrical fenestration. Left, the Three Gables, London by Shaw, 1881 and right Chigwell Hall, by Shaw, 1870's.

Left, Rodmarton Manor, Gloucestershire, by Ernest Barnsley, 1909-1929 and right Carr Manor, Leeds, by Prior, 1879-1882.

Homewood, Knebworth, Hertfordshire. Designed 1899 by Lutyens, it shows combination of vernacular and classical elements.

Papillon Court, Market Harborough, designed 1903 by Lutyens. Now destroyed, it had classical entrance loggias inserted into a vernacular house.

Chesters, Northumberland, designed 1889-91 by Shaw. It shows the beginnings of a scenographic architecture in the modern English house.

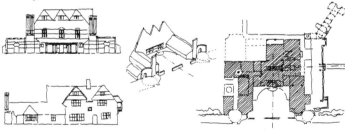

Tigbourne Court, Witley, Surrey, designed 1899 by Lutyens.

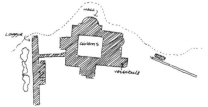

Villa Jovis, Capri. Designed by Tiberius in 14-37 AD.

Hardwick Hall, 1590-97   *Leyswood, designed in 1870 by Shaw.*

enclosure. On the east side of the courtyard are the bedrooms. These are built almost like the detached cells of a Charterhouse plan (such as Buxheim) with each bedroom suite having direct access via a projecting forestair, into the garden enclosure behind. The children's rooms are reached by secondary stairs contained in the double height glazed space which joins the three wings of the building together. The round tower in the south-west corner adds an element of asymmetry to the design as it does at Cloverley Hall or Cragside. The far edge of the courtyard dissolves in the mirror or water which reflects the perspective of mountains and sky beyond. This long rectangle of water, arranged laterally across the edge of the courtyard, is level with the courtyard. On the far side it runs, but only just, over a shallow surround before cascading down a flight of steps, in the Italian Renaissance tradition, to collect in an irregular shaped pool below. From here a path runs down to a lower terrace walk which is angled away from the house. This walk, cut into the mountain side, is terminated by an elegant gazebo, conceived as a place for rest and contemplation in the garden walk. The idea of placing elements according to topographical considerations goes back to the villas of the ancient classical world. As the terrace walk passes by the house, steps ascend to the orchestra of the amphitheatre.

The amphitheatre would be angled in plan to take best advantage of orientation as well as to fit as expediently as possible the topographical nature of the site. An irregular shaped terrace engages pergola, round tower and cavea of the theatre. The undulating ground wedged between these elements and the living room to the west of the main block, would have the aura of a Greek sanctuary, with lush planting, garden walks and statuary. Whilst there is a certain changefulness about the architecture of the house, the landscape elements of which the courtyard and amphitheatre are an integral part, are organised differently. The angles and awkward corners which undoubtedly bring such a plan alive would be the result of topographical considerations rather than design, for such a garden in the best of English traditions, needs to be formal. A degree of order has to counterbalance the wild naturalness of the mountain site. As Prior pointed out '... *the formality of the enclosures gives indeed the true garden motive, that of a plot separated for a man's fancy ...*' made to be another chamber of a man's house.

Even the Arts and Crafts gardens were remarkably formal with pergolaed walks, box hedging and terracing often aligned axially. As Muthesius pointed out in *Das Englische Haus*, 1904, the Arts and Crafts architects (and in a sense, this building, is in that tradition), considered the plan of the house more than its elevation. They were concerned with aspect, circulation and above all with the distinctive shape and character of each single room, its position in the house and its relation to the garden. The gardens here should have just such a relationship to the house. In siting this house it should be related as closely as possible to the terrain by (as at Deanery Gardens, etc) extending the architectonic ideas of the house out into the surrounding landscape in the form of terraces, flower-beds, pools, box hedges and pergolas.

There are many values here that are also found in the traditional English house, values, as Muthesius pointed out in 1904, that had '... *grown out of the revival of the traditions of early vernacular building and the modern Arts and Crafts movement ... it clings to the primitive and the vernacular and in this it closely follows the type of traditional country house.*'

The success of the English house as developed in the work of architects such as Norman Shaw, George Devey, Edward Schroder Prior, WR Lethaby, Charles Annesley Voysey and Sir Edwin Lutyens, was that they invariably used traditional forms but were rarely constrained by them. Whilst the references they chose from traditional English buildings were often quite specific, they were able nevertheless, to take liberties with them. Whilst they were able to learn from the traditional buildings of the countryside, they never made the mistake of assuming that they were replicating them. Traditionalism was not the answer, as Prior pointed out for '... the styles are dead ... such things are gone.' He urged a return to the principles underlying the style, of going back to the simple necessities of Building and finding in them the power of beauty, a poetry without rhetoric. He threw a great roof of thatch over his design for The Barn, Exmouth of 1896, but it was not like any roof he had seen on a traditional English house. When Ernest Gimson built Stoneywell Cottage, Leicester in 1898, he did in fact think of it as the real thing—a simple cottage built in the traditional way. It has an irregular thatched roof, with thick rugged walls pierced by small windows, but despite such characterfulness it was not like traditional cottages built in the traditional way, this cottage was carefully composed as a design on paper. Like Detmar Blow's design for Happisburgh Manor, Cromer, Norfolk of 1900 or Prior's The Barn, the major characteristics of such houses were irregular walls, projecting eaves, occasionally projecting parapet walls, gabled ends, porches and, quite often, elaborate barge boards over the gable roofs. The architects made reference to traditional building but were not, in fact, building traditionally.

Whilst most country house architects were quite clear about the kinds of references they were making to traditional building, they found it necessary to reinterpret them in order to avoid producing pastiches. Lethaby had warned that '... *the modern way of building must be flexible and vigorous, even smart and hard. We must give up designing the broken-down picturesque which is part of the ideal of make believe*'. Yet innovative as

Adcote, Shropshire, designed 1877–80 by Shaw. To the right is a diagram of the ceremonial hall.

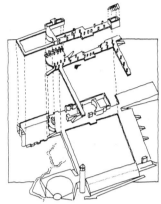

Diagram of circulation on ground floor and Long Gallery floor.

View from the living room towards the hall.

Left, Charterhouse, Buxheim; centre, sanctuary of Asclepios, Pergamon, c140–75; right, Horace's Sabine Farm, Licenza.

Left, Villa of Sette Bassi, Via Latina, Rome c140–60; right, Montacute House, Somerset, 1580–99.

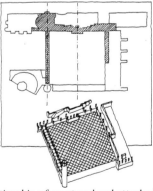

Diagram showing relationship of courtyard and attached elements in proposed house.

Left, stable tower, Cloverley Hall, designed by Nesfield in 1866–8; right, Cragside, Northumberland, designed 1870–1885 by Shaw.

the new architecture should be '... *no art that is only one man deep is worth much; it should be a thousand men deep. We cannot forget our historical knowledge, nor would we if we might*'.

Voysey considered the cottage as the ideal, even when building houses of a size and luxuriousness more appropriate to a palace than a cottage. His architecture was characterised by clearly articulated floors (often by jettying the upper storey), windows in mullioned bands crammed up against the jettied floor above, eaves or projecting gables. There were huge, enclosing, sweeping roofs almost reaching to the ground, white rough cast walls (strongly horizontal in design) relieved by massive chimneys, whilst entrance doors were designed generously wide to suggest welcome.

The important thing about such houses, despite their often large size, was that the architects, in devising a strategy which would hold the various parts of the programme together, invariably avoided the pretentious. As Muthesius saw in his studies '... *the English house lies in the midst of flower-gardens, facing far away from the street looking onto broad green lawns which radiate the energy and peace of nature; the house lies long and low, a shelter and refuge rather than an essay in pomp and architectonic virtuosity*'.

WR Lethaby despised paper architecture depending upon historical styles, and admired architects who made something new out of good tradition, such as Butterfield and Webb. In his design for Melsetter House, Holy Island, Orkney of 1892–1902, Lethaby modelled the exterior closely on the local vernacular with rough-cast walls, crow-stepped gables and Caithness flags on the steeply pitched roofs. But despite its resemblance to the traditional buildings of 18th-century Scotland it was, nevertheless, a modern house too. More importantly, however, it was also a home. As a guest at Melsetter pointed out it was, for all its finesse and dignity a '... *place full of homeliness and the spirit of welcome, a very loveable place. And surely this is the test of an architect's genius: he built for home life as well as dignity.*'

The programme that you discussed with us has a set of needs that are remarkably commensurate with the archetypal English house—great hall, partially enclosed court-yard, withdrawing room, library, long gallery, recessed loggia or porticoed entrance and a tower (a memory of the detached gatehouses of Elizabethan England). An additional ingredient, reminiscent of the ancient classical world, is an amphitheatre to be carved in the land to the edge of the courtyard and oriented along the cardinal points. Such a programme would appear to call for a hybrid in which the elements of the classical are combined with the less formal requirements of the traditional English house. It would seem to us that what you seek is both HOUSE and HOME, something with a degree of grandness, as well as a spirit of welcome and homeliness. It is possible to reconcile such diverse objectives by a synthesis of both building (reference to the medieval barn and the English vernacular house), and architecture (reference to the Elizabethan and Jacobean house and the classical villas of ancient Rome). But equally important, the house we have sketched out for you we believe, whilst in the spirit of our age, speaks about the past, a past rooted in the history and tradition of European housing particularly the English House which, one foreign critic once observed has '... *the subtle and intimate charm which makes so strong an appeal to the love of the home as well as to the love of beauty*'.

Yours sincerely,

[signatures]

Ralph Lerner and Richard Reid.
January 15th 1981.

Bibliography
Brandon-Jones, John; *CFA Voysey, Architect and Designer 1857–1941*; Lund Humphries, London 1978
Butler, ASG; *The Architecture of Sir Edwin Lutyens*; Country Life, London 1950
Davey, Peter; *Arts and Crafts Architecture the Search for Earthly Paradise*; The Architectural Press, London 1980
Downes, Kerry; *English Baroque Architecture*; A Zwemmer Ltd, London 1966
Girouard, Mark; *The Victorian Country House*; Yale University Press, New Haven 1979
Girouard, Mark; *Sweetness and Light: the Queen Anne Movement 1860–1900*; Clarendon Press, Oxford 1977
Howarth, Thomas; *Charles Rennie Mackintosh and the Modern Movement*; Routledge and Kegan Paul, London 1977
Inskip, Peter; *Edwin Lutyens*; Architectural Monograph 6, Academy Editions, London1979
Mawson, Thomas; *The Art and Craft of Garden Making*; Batsford, London 1907
Muthesius, Hermann; *The English Home*; Crosby, Lockwood, Staples, London 1979
Mercer, Eric; *English Vernacular Houses*; HMSO, London
Saint, Andrew: *Richard Norman Shaw*; Yale, 1976
Stamp, Gavin; *The English House 1860–1914*; Co-published by *International Architect* and the Building Centre Trust, London 1980

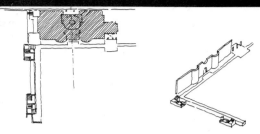

Relationship of house to garden—Nashdom, Taplow, Buckinghamshire designed 1905–09 by Lutyens.

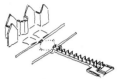

Little Thakeham, Thakeham, Surrey, designed 1902 by Lutyens.

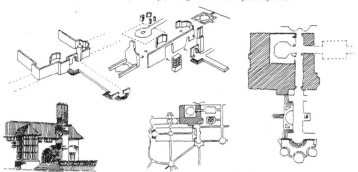

Scenographic architecture acting as a mediator between house and garden as seen in Deanery Garden, Sonning, Berkshire, designed 1901 by Lutyens.

Diagram showing relationship between house and garden in proposed scheme.

The Vernacular Tradition. Left, thatched cottages, Great Tew, near Banbury; right, cottages, East Lulworth, Dorset.

Re-interpretation of the vernacular. Left, Stoneywell Cottage, Leicester designed 1898 by Ernest Gimson; right Happisburgh Manor, Cromer, Norfolk, designed 1900 by Detmar Blow.

THE NEW HEADQUARTERS will honour the men of the past by embodying associations with tradition, so as to stand as a permanent memorial, and it will keep faith with them by ensuring that the crews of the future are provided with the best possible all-round support for the job. It will be a constant reminder of the foundations and vital principles upon which a successful future must continue to be based.

The building is thus seen as symbolic, utilitarian and memorial.

Richard Portchmouth
NEW HEADQUARTERS FOR THE ROYAL NATIONAL LIFEBOAT INSTITUTION, GREENWICH

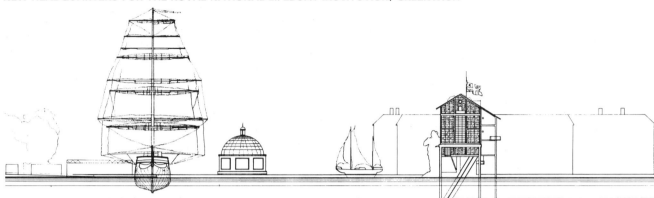

Elevation from the river Thames

The approach to Greenwich Pier Head

Exploded axonometric

Bartlett School of Architecture and Planning
UNIVERSITY COLLEGE, LONDON
AD STUDENT PROJECT AWARD

THE DIN OF GORDON STREET divides the Bartlett from the heart of University College London, and over 150 years separates the present College from its defiant foundation. Yet the ethos of our Benthamite founders still pervades the place: a moral commitment to social usefulness; an intellectual belief in reason and the benefits of humanely applied science, technology and creative imagination; and an aesthetic taste for the severe and the cerebral. Hardly a sparkling brew, but addictive and nourishing.

Bartlett Third Year projects are executed in this spirit. The programme is paramount: the briefing documents are long, detailed and doggedly mundane. For the struggle to accommodate the unforgiving demands of *everyday use* is the surest inspiration of architecture.

This should not be narrowly interpreted. Every work of architecture generates a mood, what pre-war writers called character, which has always been principally determined by structure and construction. So studio criticism stresses the *indivisibility of technique and aesthetic*.

Humane architecture, finally, is achieved not on paper but on the earth: the achievement is as much scientific as aesthetic, and is experienced as much on the small, touchable scale as on the larger scale of layout. So Bartlett student schemes typically illustrate the central importance of *technological realisation* and of *detail*.   *Philip Tabor, Year 3 coordinator*

Peter St John
DANCE HALL, HACKNEY

View of model

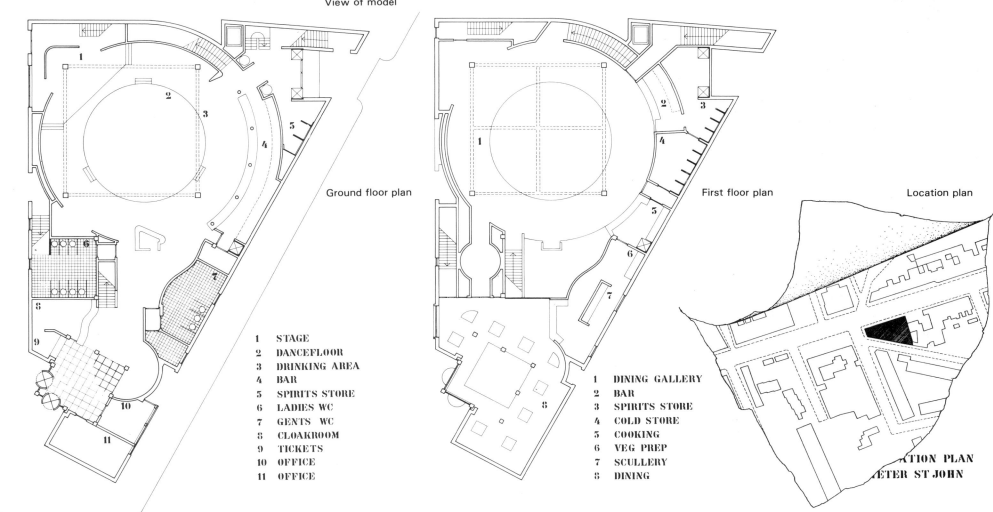

Ground floor plan

First floor plan

Location plan

1 STAGE
2 DANCEFLOOR
3 DRINKING AREA
4 BAR
5 SPIRITS STORE
6 LADIES WC
7 GENTS WC
8 CLOAKROOM
9 TICKETS
10 OFFICE
11 OFFICE

1 DINING GALLERY
2 BAR
3 SPIRITS STORE
4 COLD STORE
5 COOKING
6 VEG PREP
7 SCULLERY
8 DINING

ATION PLAN
ETER ST JOHN

Robert Mull
CHURCH AND COMMUNITY CENTRE, KENNINGTON

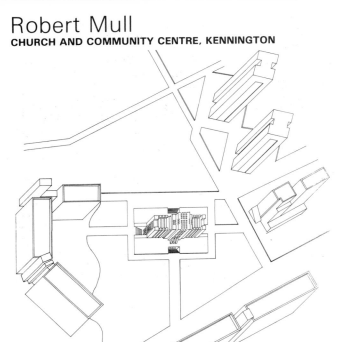

Richard Paul
OFFICE FOR A DESIGN CO-OPERATIVE, TOPPINGS WHARF

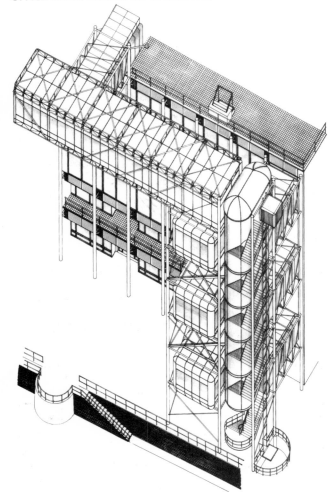

Kathryn Piotrowska
OFFICE FOR A DESIGN CO-OPERATIVE, TOPPINGS WHARF

Simon Barker
**HOTEL AND CONFERENCE CENTRE,
COVENT GARDEN**

Brian Ma Siy
CAMDEN TOWN

Marc Hacker
DANCE HALL, HACKNEY

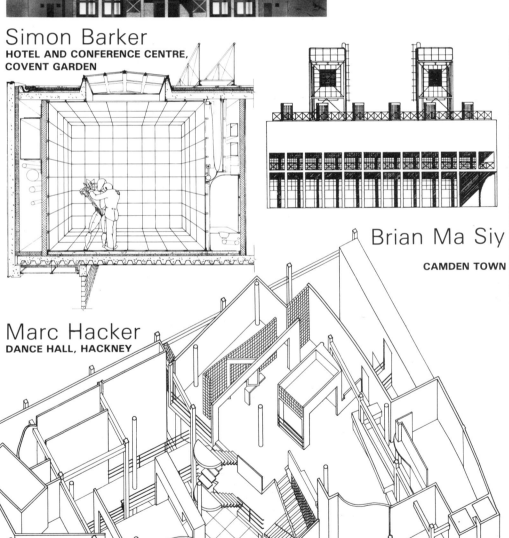

Polytechnic of Central London
ARCHITECTURE UNIT, SCHOOL OF ENVIRONMENT

Simon Lanyon-Hogg
THE HOUSE PROJECT

FROM EEYORE AT POOH CORNER to Robinson Crusoe on his island, the house has provided a home for an individual in all settings. How the house is placed on the urban scene is no longer a matter of choice, but where no site exists free intuitive design must be allowed to run its course and then returned to the urban setting to free the restrictions.

Reading the house should be like reading the detective story where clues are given: the framed facade pulled down to reveal the entrance like the portcullis, the line of the break defining the size of the courtyard and introducing the geometry of the whole. Elsewhere the facade indicates areas of use and how they're linked, broad banked lighting setting off the common areas and slivers of vertical linking the passive private corners of our world, small square set into applied frames indicate a small part of the whole.

It is a play of geometry where the 'broken' facade retains its own character and that of the interior allowing the inside-outside, public-private worlds to merge and a depth to co-exist. The geometry, emanating from the plan, carried through to the facades, extended in all directions, maintains integrity of the whole and the rivalry of each finished space to the whole.

Alan P Smith
HEADQUARTERS FOR TV FOUR, TRAFALGAR SQUARE

THE VACANT CAR PARK SITE to the west of the National Gallery, at the junction of Pall Mall and Trafalgar Square, was the site proposed for the administrative centre for the new Television Channel TV4. The centre would provide offices for staff and technicians, facilities for reprographics, studio work and limited on-air presentation, and substantial technical facilities.

The scheme attempts to employ formal means to organise a typological framework which is intended to speak of the true meaning of the programme. The architecture produced by these formal means attempts this critical expression and is also intended to sustain a level of poetic experience through which the building may be approached from positions other than the academic or ideological.

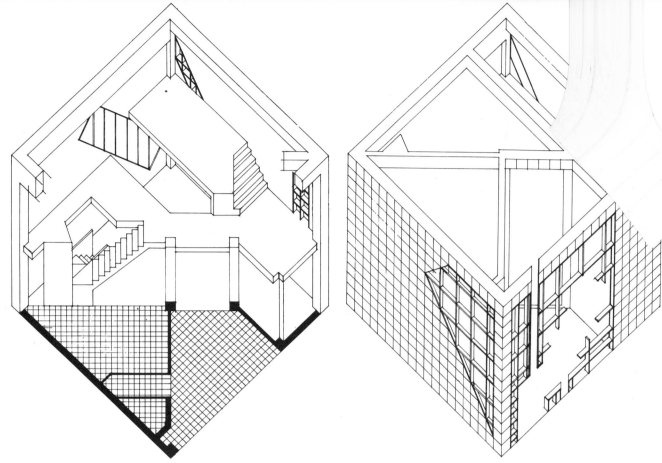

Library/theatre section

Court perspective

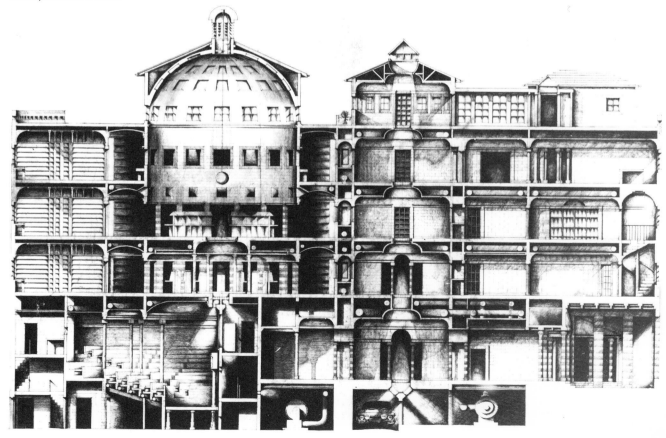

Elevation to forum

Bath House axonometric

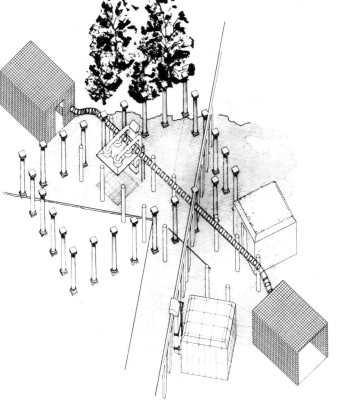

Michael Stiff
THE ROMAN FORUM

BY STUDYING THE ROMAN FORUM this project attempts to reconcile the relationship between the modern and the antique city. It thus engages the issues of archaeology, town planning, and the theories of modern architecture, all of which have shaped and influenced the present condition of the Forum.

The Forum is beyond the boundaries of everyday Rome, and this is emphasised by the way the Vittorio Emanuele monument and the Campidoglio both seem to turn their backs on the excavated areas. However this has not always been the case, before the excavations of the last century began and even until the 1930s this area was densely populated, it is only during these last 50 years of its 2500-year history that the Forum has been unoccupied. Excavation has laid waste a whole area of Rome that is no longer of archaeological interest to the experts and further excavation is planned. This will create more problems, less coherence and an even sharper contrast between the living and the dead city and the living and dead cultures.

These issues are approached at several levels within this project:
— to look at a large area of the city without relying on zoning diagrams;
— to create a dialogue between the Forum and the living city through the Campidoglio;
— by exploring the archetypal constituents of the urban schema—the street, the block, the house and the garden
— and to take one of the above, the house, and examine the language and the hierarchies within it.

Consequently this is not an attempt at total planning but an exercise in establishing a balance between a minimal framework and the optimum ways of handling some key areas as generating points.

Michael Lyons
DESIGN FOR A BATH HOUSE

THE BATH-HOUSE DESIGN consists of a set of experiences, encompassing a simple cleansing route and the more indulgent and pleasurable aspects of bathing. Each part has its own expression and character whilst being held in a total composition. It does not reduce to pure mechanism or get lost in romantic imagery but attempts to achieve a respect and balance of the individual parts.

Royal College of Art
SCHOOL OF ENVIRONMENTAL DESIGN, LONDON

Vakis Hadjikyriacou
NEAL STREET THEATRE, COVENT GARDEN

THE BRIEF CALLED FOR THE DESIGN OF AN INFILL THEATRE in Neal Street Covent Garden which could accommodate modern, Greek, round and manifesto performances. My solution provides a superstructure of a temple for all the types of performance. The dimensions beyond reality house the unreal world of theatre, while the inner chamber is uninterrupted from the 'under and in' street entrances.

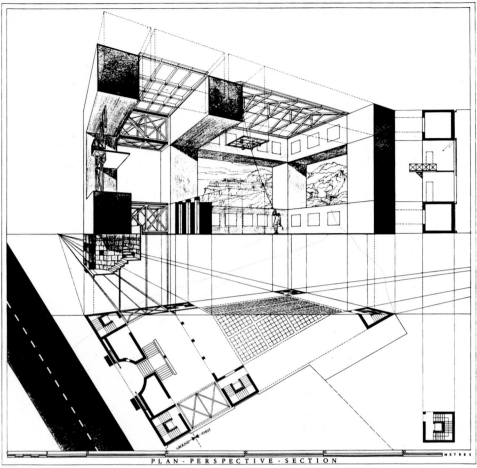

PLAN · PERSPECTIVE · SECTION

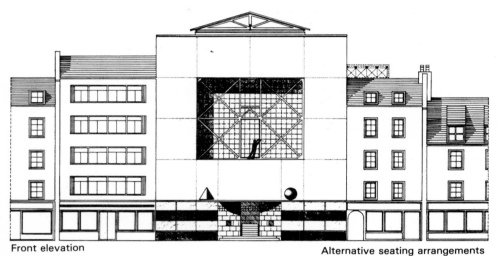

Front elevation

Alternative seating arrangements

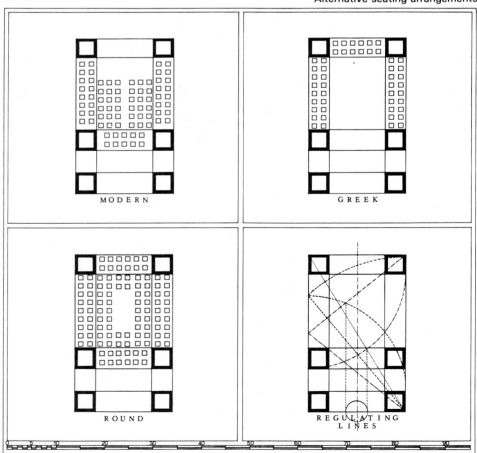

MODERN

GREEK

ROUND

REGULATING LINES

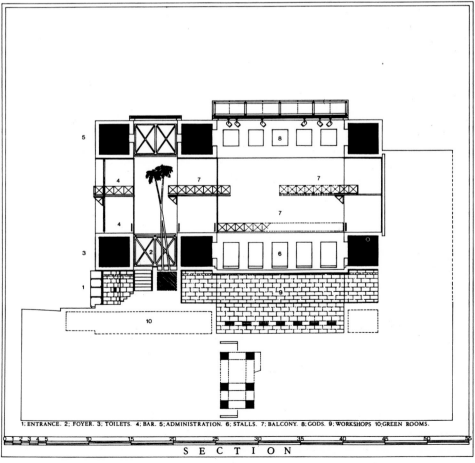

1: ENTRANCE. 2: FOYER. 3: TOILETS. 4: BAR. 5: ADMINISTRATION. 6: STALLS. 7: BALCONY. 8: GODS. 9: WORKSHOPS 10: GREEN ROOMS.

SECTION

Diana Hope
HOUSE FOR SELF

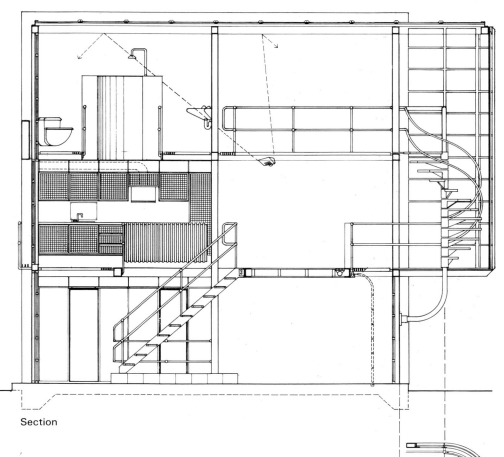

Section

First floor plan

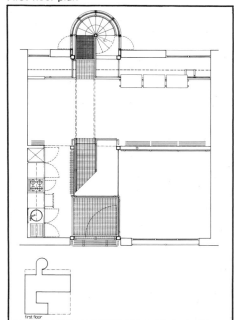

Second floor plan

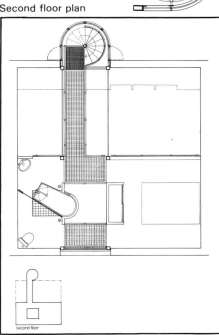

Taseer
THE URBAN VILLA

AS THE 'HÔTEL PARTICULIER' IN PARIS in the 17th century represented the idea of the country manor brought to the city, so the urban villa is its later and complementary Anglo-Saxon equivalent.

The first part of this work, described in the drawings is an investigation of the generic or prototypical villa (to have multi-occupancy—in this case six apartments) to be followed by a scheme for the whole site which will involve accommodating the Finchley Road existing public buildings.

The house is split into two halves at its ground floor. One half is then able to accommodate a 'through' apartment while the other half contains the hall and a fragment of each of two other apartments.

The hall has primary importance on the ground floor and then diminishes vertically within the villas. Three apartments are entered from the ground floor, two from the first and one from the second.

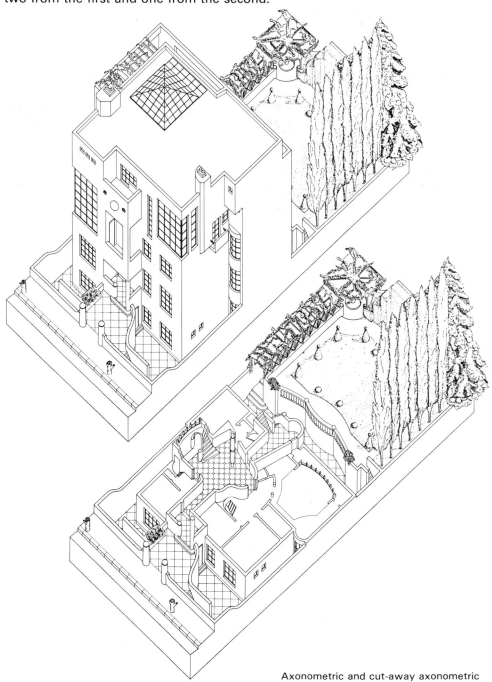

Axonometric and cut-away axonometric

Architectural Association

SCHOOL OF ARCHITECTURE, LONDON

AD STUDENT PROJECT AWARD

Amarjit Kalsi
PORCHESTER BATHS

IN THE BRIEF, PORCHESTER BATHS was to accommodate public as well as private bathing facilities together with shops, a club and a public library. The site, on which still stands the original building has a prominent street corner and overlooks Porchester Square.

The flow of the water initiates the disposition and form of the new baths. The water cycle begins as a public spectacle; a water fall crashes down from a corner tower, then cascades diagonally through a series of crystal troughs in the winter gardens, and finally ripples down a curved ramp to give birth to the main pool.

A canal runs tangentially to this swimming pool, breaking into tributaries that fragment the building into a labyrinth of increasingly private and exclusive rooms.

Axonometric

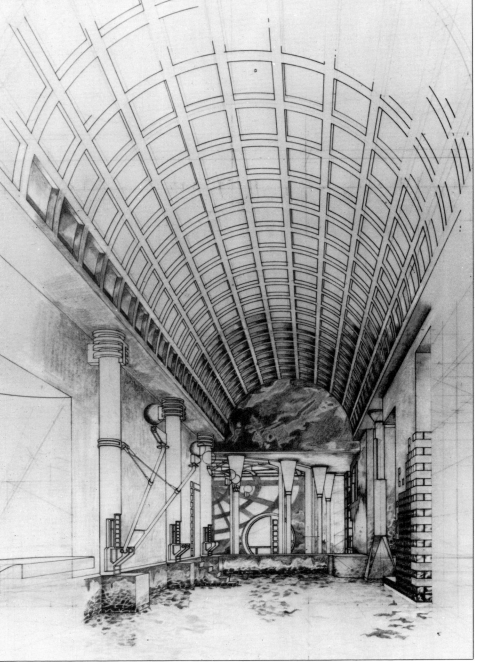

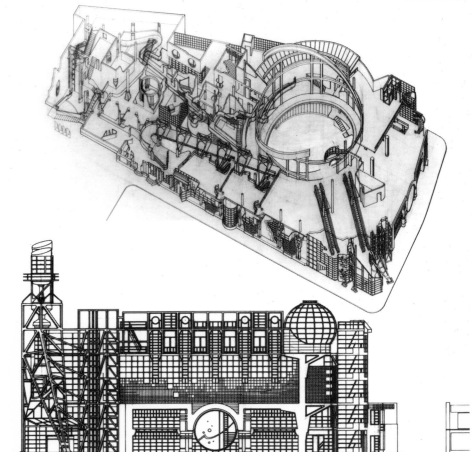

Porchester Road elevation

Perspective (looking towards dipping pool room)

Queensway elevation

Gregory Penoyre
NEW BUILDINGS IN THE PIAZZA ROVETTA, BRESCIA, ITALY

THE PIAZZA ROVETTA is one of five open spaces in the centre of Brescia. The space created was 'accidental' in the sense that it was formed by demolition and wartime destruction. It is bounded by five and six-storey buildings with shops and cafes at ground level with apartments above.

The project is based on proposals by the Comune de Brescia to develop the Piazza Rovetta with new offices as an extension of the Palazzo Loggia. In addition, a new council chamber accommodating 100 people, a new covered market of 40 stalls and an auditorium seating 500 people for use as a concert and public meeting hall are also planned. This latter building is linked to a large existing exhibition space in the Palazzo Loggia forming a public arts centre. A major requirement of the design is to maintain and enhance the social value of the Piazza Rovetta as a major external space.

Various elements in the brief form several separate buildings placed on the site. The auditorium is located adjacent to the Palazzo Loggia with foyers facing onto a new, smaller Piazza Rovetta. These foyers provide access both to the auditorium itself and the Palazzo Loggia via the existing annex which includes the main staircase. Alongside the auditorium and dominating the new Piazza Rovetta is the council chamber, accessible both from the street and from the council offices by means of an overhead passageway. Conversely, the market hall is 'hidden' within the main bulk of the council office accommodation and is an internal volume rather than a building in its own right. The market follows traditional patterns with stalls situated in the hall itself as well as surrounding arcades.

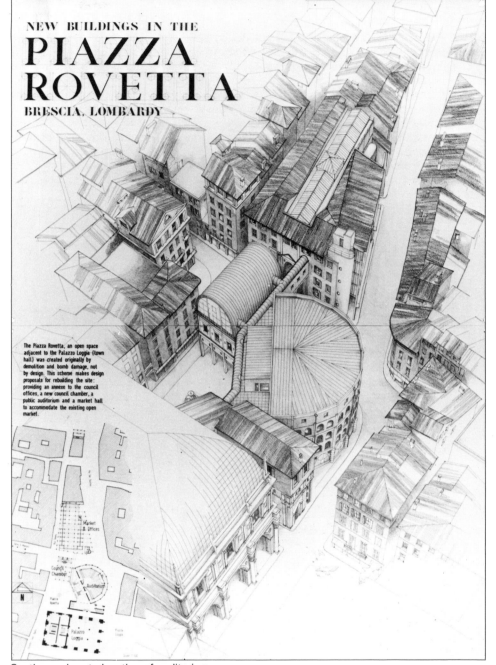

NEW BUILDINGS IN THE
PIAZZA ROVETTA
BRESCIA, LOMBARDY

The Piazza Rovetta, an open space adjacent to the Palazzo Loggia (town hall) was created originally by demolition and bomb damage, not by design. This scheme makes design proposals for rebuilding the site: providing an annexe to the council offices, a new council chamber, a public auditorium and a market hall to accommodate the existing open market.

View along Corso G Mameli

Section of covered market and offices

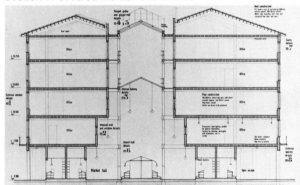

Section and front elevation of new Council Chamber

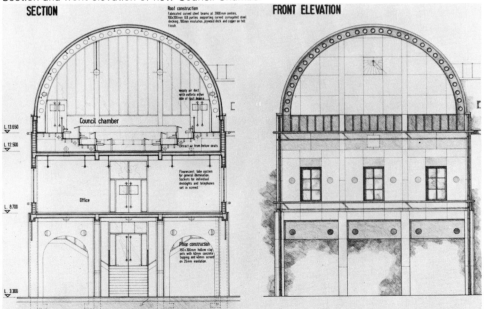

Section and part elevation of auditorium

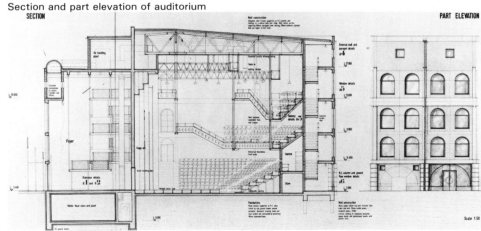

Mackintosh School
SCHOOL OF ARCHITECTURE, GLASGOW

Laurence Bain
MUSEUM FOR THE AGES OF GLASGOW

THE BUILDING IS LOCATED AT GLASGOW'S OLDEST CROSSROADS and everything from hanging to toll collecting took place at the Cross. These events are recalled by three monuments: the Iron Steeple, the Toll Booth Steeple and the Convenanter's Memorial all surrounding the site.

The museum is organised as a route entering through the 'Building of the Present' and then crossing the railway line by means of a link bridge to the 'Building of the Past'. The galleries are arranged to give a chronological picture of the history of Glasgow. The 'Building of the Future', of which a detailed study is made, is linked by an underpass that leads to the island on which it is erected. Its mausoleum represents the notion of death on the exterior—in sharp contrast to the interior which is full of imagination and ideas for the future.

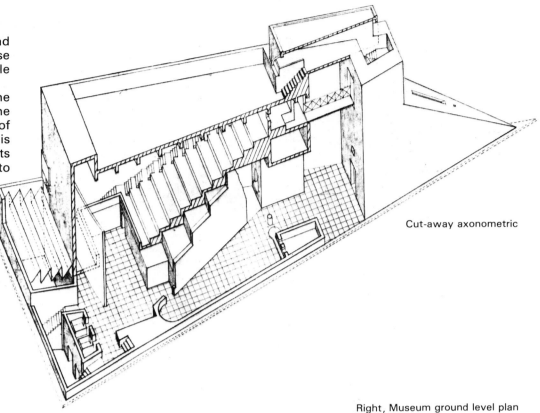

Cut-away axonometric

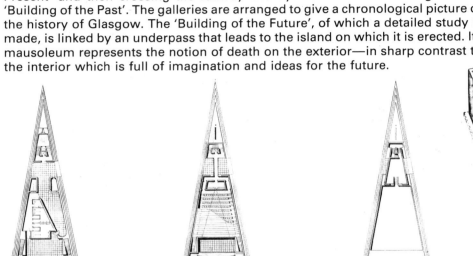

Part of detailed study of 'The Building of the Future' — plans

Right, Museum ground level plan

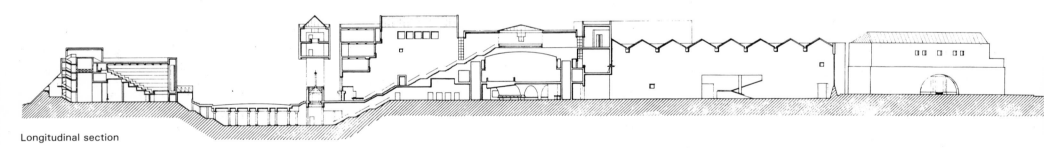

Longitudinal section

Part of detailed study of 'The Building of the Future' — sections

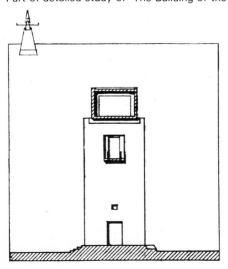
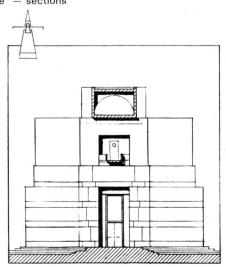
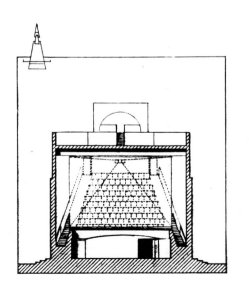
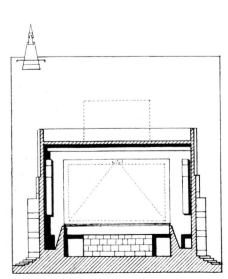

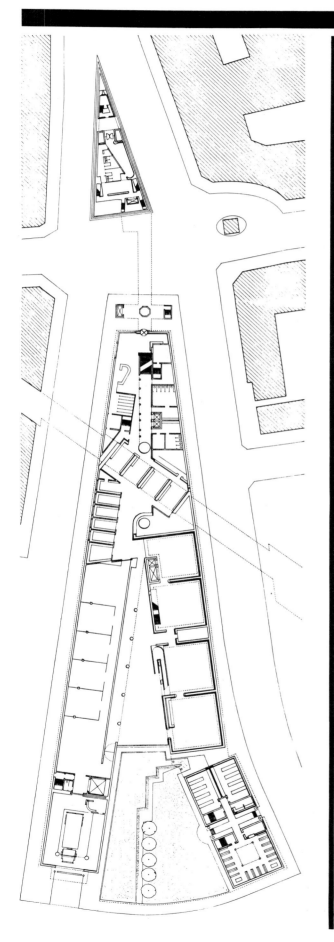

Guy Vaughan
ADULT EDUCTION CENTRE, SPANDAU, BERLIN

THE COMPETITION PROGRAMME asked for an adult education centre, including library, music school and kindergarten while retaining certain existing buildings. The site is an area of parkland which acts as a bridge between the towns of Old and New Spandau.

The project fronts onto existing buildings and is introduced by the *porte cochère* element, below which the entry stairs lead to the primary space, the first level concourse, opening the building towards the river. The hard fingers of the adult education building protect the single-storey kindergarten spaces nestling within.

The existing roundabout is transformed into a spiral parking mound, and the foundations of a church bombed during the war are excavated to form a pool marked by a water tower, a metaphor for the park's constant historical change between land and water.

Site axonometric

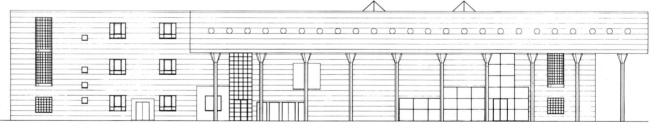

Entrance elevation

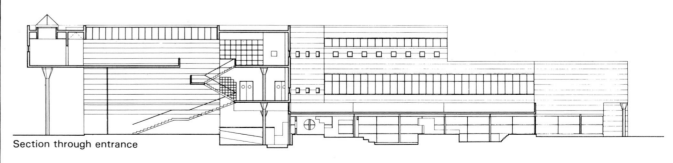

Section through entrance

Section through auditorium

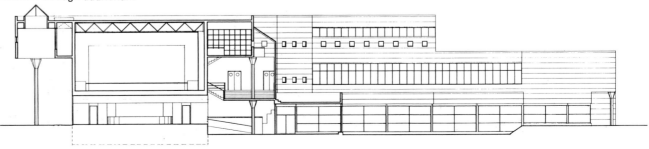

Portsmouth Polytechnic
SCHOOL OF ARCHITECTURE

View of model

Section through lecture theatre

Mark Taylor

CENTRE FOR ARCHITECTURAL STUDIES. The project explores an image for a centre of involvement in design which goes beyond the idea of a closed place for learning and invites, as well, participation from the local and the regional community. Deliberate emphasis is placed on the highly organised circulation routes and on the central 'workshop' courtyard. Attached to these circulation areas are a series of pavilion spaces each exploring a design theme relevant to architecture in the 1980s. The contrast between the formal circulation and the variety of spaces of individual character are intended to provide a stimulating experience and to encourage a better interaction between the building and its users.

Nick Woolfenden

EXTENSION TO AN ART COLLEGE. A major generator of the building plan was the need to provide a direct pedestrian link with the existing buildings. This pedestrian route evolves into a covered concourse containing communal facilities with ground floor and gallery access to the workshops arranged along the back wall. Each of the workshop wings is designed as a double height space for the more flexible and variable activities, with a two storey support zone down on side containing the fixed functions which require closer environmental control. Access can be obtained directly to any part of the workshop floor by means of the first floor gallery which in turn links back to the social concourse area.

Mary Weguelin

BOTANICAL EXHIBITION CENTRE. The building is designed to provide an exhibition facility for the display of a sample collection of arid, tropical, subtropical and temperate plants. Public routes through the natural settings of plants are organised to be as enjoyable and informative as possible. The focus of public access is a core containing lecture theatre, exhibition area, and a tea room which overlooks the main planted areas. The orientation and form of the building were carefully studied to ensure optimum conditions over the diverse range of environmental zones required. In particular, the avoidance of dripping condensation was a major factor in determining the form of the glazed structure.

Interior

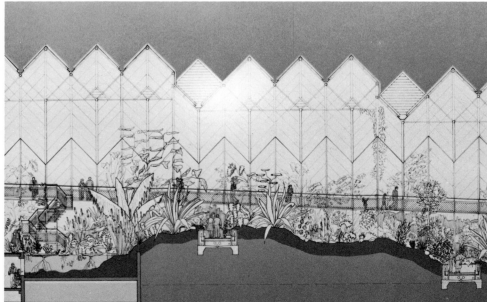

Interior landscape

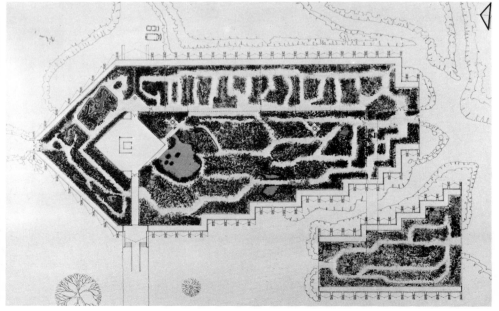

Canterbury College of Art
SCHOOL OF ARCHITECTURE

Peter Baynes
A NEW BUILDING FOR THE BRITISH FILM INSTITUTE

THE OBJECTIVES OF THE SCHEME fall into three categories. Those which concern the club and its members; the public and their everyday life in the surrounding streets, gardens and courtyards and, those which concern the building's users. The brief consists of the following departments:

— Administration, headed by a Director and Deputy Director;
— National Film Archive, this includes Acquisitions, Cataloguing, Viewing Service and the Production Library;
— Distribution Division, this consists of the Film Library and Publicity Unit, Programming Unit and Projects Unit. This division acquires and distributes films and television programmes and provides funds, advice and services for film and video activity around the country;
— Production Division, which exists to finance and supervise the production of independent films and video tapes;
— Publications Department, responsible for written material and editorial functions for the magazine 'Sight and Sound' plus NFT programmes and members' newsletters;
— National Film Theatre, consisting of two theatres NFT 1 (capacity 450–500) and NFT 2 (capacity 160–200), a clubroom, bar, restaurant, bookshop and exhibition. It is this section of the building which will annually host the London Film Festival.

The Institute is intended to be a new source of lively activity in the area whilst preserving those aspects of the Soho life which make it so distinguishable. Its status as the headquarters for a national institution must also be reflected. In short the building should appeal to the emotions of film lovers by being a monumental representation of the medium.

Section

Dean Street elevation of model

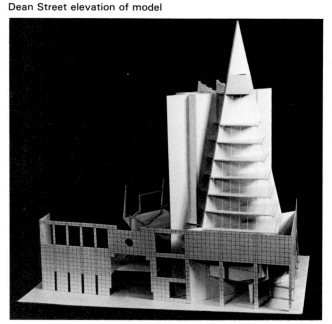

Level 1 plan

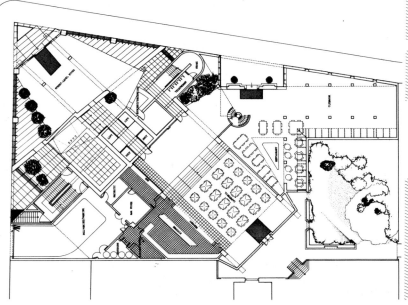

Site plan

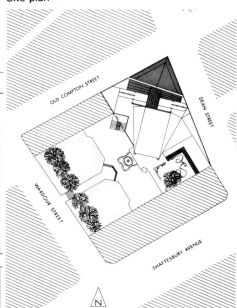

SOME ISSUES FOR THE FUTURE OF UK ARCHITECTURAL EDUCATION

Michael Bedford & Steven Groák

MANY ARCHITECTURAL SCHOOLS IN THE UK are faced with the prospect of an abrupt reduction in their activities, amounting in some cases to a crisis. Many of the ideas which seem likely to define the nature of consequent changes have been common currency for some time. As a result, we fear, they may now be enlisted uncritically or without sufficient regard for their significance to today's context. Nonetheless, these changes must also be exciting to anyone involved with architectural education—not only in the UK, but perhaps also in other countries. In this note we wish briefly to explore some of these ideas and, in particular, to ask if the difficulties can be turned at all to advantage.[1]

The direct pressure for reductions arises in two ways. First, the diminishing job prospects in architects' offices, as the construction industries' workload subsides, have led to concern about the number of prospective architects emerging from our schools. Second, as part of the wider public sector cuts, recently, in higher education, architecture has been singled out as a subject with a shrinking future. In practice, these have meant cuts in the monies allocated to some schools of architecture at the same time as requiring a reduction in the intake of 'home' students to the courses. Thus, the question of what might or should happen to the schools—individually and collectively—has suddenly become urgent.

This focus on architecture was at its most baleful in the 1981 allocations to universities by the University Grants Committee (UGC) and prompted an excellent letter to *The Times* by the President of the Royal Institute of British Architects (RIBA), Mr Owen Luder[2]. Three of the issues he raises are of special relevance here. First, the professional and academic institutions involved had not been consulted. Second, he suggests, there is no coherent policy on what national resources should flow into architectural education—witness the piecemeal approach to the cuts. Third, it had been assumed that the construction workload was the principal means for determining the scale of architectural education—which ignores arguments about the intrinsic quality of an architectural course as an education in its own right. To this, perhaps, we should add contrariwise that for some time practitioners have been uneasy about the objectives of contemporary architectural education and the relationship to professional competence. On occasion, this is construed as 'education *versus* training'.

We would add two other considerations. The UK construction industries have undergone significant changes in recent decades, technologically and organisationally, and have created a new professional context. (The recent decision by the RIBA to modify its Code of Professional Conduct, extending the range of work an architect may undertake, is a reflection both of these changes and of tougher economic circumstances.) Moreover, ideas for the future are generated from within the schools themselves. For us, the most critical 'internal' questions are: does architecture have a real future as an academic discipline in UK higher education? Can postgraduate architectural education sensibly develop in the manner that has characterised the science and science-based subjects? What funded research can be developed in current circumstances?

For many the most critical issue is the quality of architectural design. We suggest that this cannot be resolved at the level of educational organisation; it is essentially an issue for the profession at large. We recognise that many issues relate also to the social responsibilities of the schools[3], but we propose to limit ourselves to the areas identified above. To do this, we first set out some general background information for those—in the UK and elsewhere—who are not familiar with the detailed structure of our education system.

In passing, we should perhaps declare an interest. It is our view that many of the arguments for the development of architectural education set out at the 1958 RIBA Conference at Oxford and explained below, in principle are still useful today. However, that programme, we suggest, failed in its immediate purpose on three counts. It failed to seek retention and integration of the very real merits of traditional methods of education and training. It failed to develop adequate teaching methods for the new educational ideas. The proliferation of schools meant that virtually none today are sufficiently large to make possible the variety envisaged in each school. Today, the dilemma is that with the scale and timing of cuts, it may be impossible to achieve either the 'Oxford programme' or any other coherent pattern except that of survival.

Background

In the UK, the title 'architect' is protected by law and may only be used by someone registered with the Architects' Registration Council of the United Kingdom (ARCUK). The matter of detailed assessment of a person's competence and suitability to be registered has, *de facto*, been delegated by ARCUK to the RIBA. Over the years, the RIBA has evolved a three-stage procedure for determining professional qualification—known as RIBA Parts 1, 2 and 3—all of which must be passed in sequence by any intending architect. The RIBA itself conducts examinations for all three parts. It also 'recognises' schools of architecture in the sense that it accepts certain *academic* qualifications (eg BSc degree with specified options, Diplomas in Architecture, etc) as giving exemption from Part 1 and/or Part 2. Schools may also conduct Part 3 examinations on behalf of the RIBA.[4] The continued improvement of standards in practical training and Part 3 are very much a live issue at present within the RIBA.

The RIBA requires any intending architect to have undertaken at least five years of full-time academic experience (or the equivalent in part-time education) and at least two years of professional practice. Typically, RIBA Part 1 exemption will be gained after three years full-time education, coinciding with an undergraduate qualification, and RIBA Part 2 after a further two years study.[5]

To determine that a particular academic programme should continue to receive RIBA recognition, or that a new programme should be granted recognition, the RIBA has developed a system of Visiting Boards (drawn from academic and professional sources) which review each school every five years or so. Academic standards of the schools are scrutinised by various means, according to the nature of the host institution, but typically will involve some system of External Examiners meeting at the end of each academic year.

The educational responsibility of the RIBA, which is discharged through its Education and Professional Development (EPD) Committee, is additional to its role as a learned society and professional institution. Any architect may join the RIBA, but membership is not a condition of calling oneself an architect. In this respect, it is worth drawing attention to the Charter of the RIBA[6] and to its Code of Professional Conduct[7].

In passing, note RIBA stands for Royal Institute of British *Architects*, not *Architecture*; its ordinary membership have to be architects. It may be that in the future the scope of membership will be extended. This is a matter for the RIBA membership itself, but it may be helpful to explore some of the possibilities.

Numbers and Finance

At the time of writing (May 1982), there are 37 recognised schools of architecture in the United Kingdom, of which 16 are in universities, 16 are in polytechnics, and 5 are in other educational establishments[8]. These schools house some 7,250 students in their vocational academic programmes[9]. Each year, around 1000 students proceed from them into the profession to attempt full professional qualification—and there are about 28,000 registered architects in a UK population of around 56 million.

The financing of the schools depends on the nature of the host institution. For instance, universities are financed principally through central government funding, administered through the Department of Education and Science (DES). The total UK university grant is allocated by the University Grants Commission (UGC), a body with substantial academic membership. Polytechnics are also publicly financed, but their allocation is administered on a local basis, by the local authority.

An assumption is made for income from students' fees, which are distinct for 'home' and overseas students. Overseas students' fees have substantially increased in the last few years, on the argument that they should pay the notional 'full cost' of their places. The counter arguments include that which suggests that overseas students should pay the marginal costs of their place—ie the cost of teaching another student, given that certain fixed costs have already been incurred to set up a course in the first place for 'home' students. It remains to be seen whether the nett revenue from overseas students increases or decreases. It does seem however that the resulting uncertainty for individual teaching programmes is highly problematic. Wider questions of the social responsibilities of institutions of higher education, whether to students from the UK or elsewhere, seem not to have loomed large in these discussions.

Unlike some countries, UK full-time higher education is typically organised on the assumption that its students will either have a financial grant or their own or family money to contribute to fees and living expenses. Such courses are not arranged so that students can 'work their way' through college; students who do are, we believe, assumed to take part-time courses. (There are of course other good reasons for taking courses on a part-time basis.)

'Home' students who gain a place on an undergraduate degree course, or other similar programme, are entitled to a mandatory grant from their local authority if it is their first degree. This grant allows both for fees for the educational institution and for the student's maintenance (accommodation, food, etc), and is assessed according to the parental circumstances and the student's personal situation. This mandatory grant is available for the whole period of the degree, typically three years in the UK. In the case of architecture, however, because of the special requirements of its full-time education, the mandatory grant is available for five years. For 'home' students taking postgraduate degrees—and this includes postgraduate architectural studies courses not directly associated with gaining exemption from RIBA Part 2 examinations—central government grants are sought on a competitive basis. These State Studentships are administered by the Research Councils and are increasingly in short supply.

For students who already have a first degree in another subject and wish to change to architecture, local authority grants may be available on a discretionary basis. But, again, with public sector cuts, these are in practice hardly ever now possible. For such students, the remaining option is to finance themselves—the option also for those who do not gain a State Studentship or, in the cases of overseas students, who do not gain other forms of government finance or scholarship.

Recently, a query has been raised against the future of the five-year basis of architecture mandatory grants[10]. It can be seen as questioning whether in future all architecture students will receive public financial support to RIBA Part 2, provided they meet academic standards, or whether there might be a restriction upon those proceeding from first degree course or equivalent. More broadly, the question is raised as to what differentiates postgraduate courses in architecture from undergraduate programmes, other than 'more of the same only bigger.'

In dealing with aspects of financing UK higher education, a brief note on research funding might be helpful. The sources of research funds for schools of architecture are limited. Some work comes in the form of consultancy projects, in which some specialist ability of the school is hired for a specific task. Architectural research, in the more traditional sense, is mostly funded by government, directly or indirectly. A certain proportion is implicit in the general funding of institutions by UGC etc. Some comes from research councils—notably the Science and Engineering Research Council (SERC), which has in recent years given special attention to computer-aided design and to energy utilisation studies. The rest comes from research associations and government departments, such as the DES, the Department of the Environment (DOE), Department of Health and Social Security (DHSS) etc. Within this, perhaps special attention should be given to research contracts for the Building Research Establishment (BRE) of the DOE, which is itself a major research organisation with a world-wide reputation[11]. The RIBA and ARCUK provide small amounts of research funding, but they are essentially 'pump priming' in character.

Expansion and Contraction

The present structure of UK architectural education owes much to various post-War initiatives, notably the 1958 RIBA Annual Conference, held at Oxford[12]. That conference determined that architecture should seek to become a graduate profession and that, to this end, all schools not in universities should join them. Part-time education should be phased out altogether. In the event, many schools entered other institutions of higher education—16 now being in polytechnics—and a number of part-time courses have survived. Today, however, some argue that it was a mistake to try and eliminate part-time education in architecture; others have argued that polytechnics, with their bias towards industrial training, are in any case a more suitable home than universities for architecture[13]. (In passing, for foreign readers, we should say that the distinction between universities and polytechnics is not the same as that prevailing, say, in continental Europe or the USA. In the UK, the institutions have been plagued with that differentiation between 'intellectual' and 'manual' skills which infests much of our education system and which is particularly unfortunate in relation to architecture.)

At the time of the Oxford Conference, there were around 6,000 architecture students, of which only 4,000 or so were in recognised schools. The rest were prepared in a number of ways for the RIBA's own examinations. There were less than 19,000 registered architects. The substantial growth in numbers of architectural students—and hence, eventually, in architects—was part of a more general expansion of UK higher education, following the Robbins Report[14] and related initiatives.

This expansion suffered its first real reversal in 1981, when the UGC identified architecture and planning as university subjects which should reduce their intake over the next few years[15]. In the context of general public sector cuts in education, the justification was that these courses were essentially vocational and that the professions they supplied were suffering a diminishing workload, a trend which seemed likely to continue for some time.

It is worth noting that these changes have taken place during a period in which there appears to be increasing public concern about the quality of the built environment generally and architectural design in particular. This is emphasised by the apparent likelihood of failure of certain constructional methods. Although, we suggest, the nature, scale and responsibility for post-war construction failures is considerably more complicated than is recognised in the media—including many technical journals—it does appear that the public debate assumes as its starting-point a degree of failure in design and construction hitherto unknown. Moreover, within the more detailed arguments throughout the construction industries, professions, etc, it sometimes appears that the schools of architecture are regarded as carrying much of the blame for failing to maintain an adequate level of building competence. We regard this attitude as mistaken (although schools must obviously be responsible for the standards they inculcate) and fear it may prejudice a fruitful discussion on the educational future. Such issues may be explored in terms of the points identified above.

Consultation with Institutions

The nature and execution of the recent UGC cuts, consequent upon government policy, has raised questions about the quality of information available to the UGC members—and, by extension, to the government departments concerned. In respect of architecture cuts, it is unclear as to what the schools, the RIBA or even ARCUK would have wished to say. Clearly, the first response would have been likely to be one of resistance and this may have affected the UGC's general approach. What is more problematic in the UGC policy is that they did not limit themselves to broad resource allocations, but sought to influence detailed cuts on the basis of what appears to have been inadequate information. If we ask what might have informed any response by schools or the RIBA, in effect we ask whether any national policy exists on architectural education.

National Policy?

At the broadest level, policies do exist for the country's schools, in terms of the periods of full-time education in relation to pre-qualification experience, the implications for the *curricula* of the RIBA's own examination syllabus, the pattern of student grants and so on. Moreover, following the Oxford Conference, one can point to the situating of schools in universities and polytechnics, with the resulting increased use of 'A' levels as a control on entry and the diminution of part-time courses.

It is highly problematic whether in the short term major changes can be made to the organisation of UK architectural education; yet this is what in effect is being asked. With the lack of work for architectural offices, moreover, it is difficult to argue that the transition might be made by restructuring the relative proportions of experience between schools and offices. With these pressures it raises the spectre—already in the land—that whole schools of architecture might be closed rather than deplete many schools to the point of debility.

There are other factors to consider in defining intelligent options for a smaller provision of architectural education. Some are locational. Should there be a system of regional schools? Should schools be deliberately maintained in accordance with population distribution? Should they be preferred if they are close to major resources? For instance, schools in the large conurbations draw crucial part-time staff from nearby specialist consultants; this might be regarded as strength (ie providing high-quality diversity), or as weakness (ie making a school vulnerable since part-time staff are the most easily reduced, administratively, with financial cuts).

A review of academic resources will reappraise standards and patterns of teaching and learning. It may be that the concern with professional competence—as much of an issue *in* the schools as outside—will come to dominate strategic decisions on the schools. We expect that mid-career training, Continuing Professional Development (CPD)[16] could be associated with a reawakening of part-time education. The consequences for the remaining full-time courses is unclear, as is what in future might be the most suitable balance of academic and practical experience *prior* to qualification.

Other propositions from the Oxford Conference have seemed somewhat vague. For instance, joint education of different building disciplines remains a piety, following much urging in the 1960s, although some successes do exist. It continues to inhabit the agenda of most architectural education debates, but has been increasingly problematic when confronted with the demands upon students of even the most basic vocational programme in architecture. More effective, perhaps, has been the cross-fertilisation achieved by locating the schools in institutions large enough to have good departments in related subjects.

Another important argument from Oxford was that of the necessity for a 'critical mass', that a school needed to be of a certain size in order that specialist staff and, hence, research would be possible as there would be sufficient work for them to do. Despite the attempt at national coordination, diversity in architectural education was thought crucial[17]. Today, it is worth asking whether this is better obtained by diversity *within* schools rather than *between* schools. The former proposal further reinforces the case for fewer larger schools. (Interestingly, recent reports for London University argue a similar case in respect of some of their subjects[18].) Given that schools are facing cuts in student intake *and* in available resources, such judgements will crucially affect their future structure.

Competence[19]

One might expect ordinary practitioners to take the view that the benefits of higher education should be immediately apparent, although they can tolerate ineffectiveness where the experienced eye can pick up the fault fairly quickly and/or where the office is not likely to be sued if the fault is not picked up.

This raises the whole question—and perhaps this is a matter for policy—of whether the schools' vocational responsibility is seen to be the inculcating of established good building practice or to be essentially the teaching of new ideas which will complement and be honed by those in the practices. Moreover, at a pedagogical level, these two objectives may entail

conflicting approaches or require more time than is available to do each of them properly. Essentially this is a question of the extent to which design projects in the schools seek to mimic the typical project to be found in the professional office.

It has been our experience that students' work is often criticised along the lines of : 'Well, of course, you couldn't do that in the real world.' We suggest that the students live in a real world; and part of that real world involves projects whose explicit intention is to be different from those in offices. This is not to suggest that students should never confront the practical problems of building. It is simply that if the sole objective of the school were to replicate the office, we would be better off abolishing the schools and apprenticing everyone in offices. We recognise that for some people this conclusion is not entirely unpalatable.

Industrial Context

Since the War, the real output of the UK construction industries has grown steadily until the early 1970s, with a slight hiccough following the 1967 devaluation. Much has been made of the difficulties experienced with 'stop-go' economic policies, but the major effect of these would appear to have been within sub-sectors of construction—eg fluctuations in road building—rather than at the national level of aggregation. Nonetheless, there have been some extremely volatile characteristics to the context in which building professions have worked. These have included changes in the size and nature of contracts, trends towards sub-contracting (in particular, labour-only sub-contracting), more complex legal constraints and liabilities upon designers, greater demands to specify in detail as skilled craftsmen were seen to be less easily obtained, difficulties in defining 'conventional' or 'traditional' construction, introduction of computer-aided design, changes in the Codes of Conduct and so on. More recently, we have seen that repair and maintenance work is taking up an increasing proportion of all building work—itself something which might well affect assumptions about how and what design should be taught. In addition, we have an increasing standard of performance demanded of our buildings—improved energy efficiency being only the latest and most dramatic. And this occurs at a time when the range of new materials and methods for their assembly continues to expand.

Within the schools, this changing industrial context—and virtual explosion of technological processes—has itself presented a major pedagogical problem: what is the future of technological teaching? Neither the practices nor the schools can now separately cover the necessary range.

During the 1960s, with the work of the Tavistock Institute[20] etc, considerable attention was given to questions of communication in the construction industries. A particular consequence was interest in joint education for graduates seeking a variety of eventual professional and industrial roles—eg the urgings of the Noel Hall Committee[21]. Some of these ideas have been worked through in many schools—

eg informal relationships with Departments of Civil Engineering, etc, and some more formal integrations such as that at the University of Bath. Until recently, the prospect of professional recognition for someone who had not followed an established route to one of the building professions was non-existent. It would appear that there is renewed interest in a wider set of roles and this must surely be encouraged by the recent decision to change the ARCUK and RIBA Codes of Professional Conduct to allow architects to work as developers etc. Taken with these points we would suggest that clarifications in the legal responsibilities of building designers, problems of obtaining insurance and increased problems of quality control on site—with implications for the amount of supervision necessary today—mean a significant restructuring of the architect's industrial role.

Postgraduate Education and Research

Our survey which follows[22] gives particular attention to three concerns identified by the Oxford Conference: first, postgraduate degree courses; second, externally-funded research and, third, specialist courses either within a department or through collaboration with other more specialised departments within the university, polytechnic, etc. Whilst the intervening years have witnessed a growth in the direction indicated by the Oxford Conference, it is not clear that architecture and building have established themselves in higher education (in this country) as research-based disciplines with postgraduate work extending their limits.

It may be noted from our survey that the externally-funded research activity is dominated by two broad areas of work: computer-aided design and environmental science (especially in respect of energy utilisation). A separate survey suggests that 'private' research—eg doctoral theses, personal research by full-time academics—has a rather different character. Much of it reflects the trend of the last decade or so towards a greater interest in and awareness of historical/cultural studies in architecture, often encouraged by major advances in other academic disciplines.

Twenty-five years ago, the Oxford Conference confidently asserted the value of the new architecture which could be developed on the basis of scientific research; their problem was one of how to accomplish it within our professional/educational systems. Today's response is more disenchanted: the argument for research *at all* has now to be conducted. The Trench Committee has recently forcefully argued the need for independent, long-term research in construction as the basis of its case for retaining BRE[23]. However, even for some who accept the argument for a research activity in our subject, a question remains: are the schools of architecture competent to undertake it? If we take research to connote some basic theoretical exploration, in the scientific sense, then the question can be examined on two counts.

First, is architecture a body of knowledge, with a sufficiently clear theoretical framework to develop (in part at least) through research activity? And, second, if it is so constituted, are the schools the appropriate place for research to be conducted? We would argue their interdependence. Organisations such as BRE have pioneered research into building on the scientific paradigm; a number of distinguished professional practices have long records of development work associated with their areas of special interest. We would argue that a scientific basis should contribute to the development of the subject. And we would argue further that the fruits of research—as opposed to development associated with particular problems of practice—are best related to practice through teaching. (Such teaching may be in institutions of higher education or through CPD etc).

Our survey suggests that a good proportion of schools have a programme of externally-funded research—much of it in science-based investigations. We do not know how many students gain direct experience of research—its nature and, indeed, its excitements. But if, as we suspect, it is only a small proportion, then one of the important potentials of the investment in research will have been limited: students direct experience is important in order to develop a researching mentality—we would argue this as perhaps today's most crucial enhancement of traditional vocational study. (This was surely one of the fundamental purposes of the Oxford Conference in seeking development of the profession as a whole.) The development of a mutual sympathy between research and practice has been severely hampered by the inability of researchers to participate as members in the professional institute's activities. This owes its origin in architecture (in the UK) to the fact that much research is initiated and conducted by people trained in other disciplines. We suggest an urgent priority for the RIBA to consider a membership structure which recognises the contribution of its research strength. This could be modelled perhaps on membership of the Civil Engineering profession, where a research qualification can give entry to the chartered institution without necessarily giving a licence to design.

This matter of professional recognition may be related closely to postgraduate work generally. Apart from the main programmes leading to RIBA Part 2, it appears that schools have not developed specialist postgraduate courses to the same extent as their main research areas. For the architectural graduate, the length of time already committed to academic study and the difficulty of obtaining financial support must surely affect the attraction of such courses.

Today, however, the pressure of public sector cuts, and the 'rules' applying to costs charged to overseas students, encourages the non-vocational postgraduate courses to attempt a strong campaign for students from other countries. Higher education in the UK has a long and honourable tradition of educating overseas students, but in the past one of the main pedagogical arguments has been the mutual benefit for home and overseas students of studying together. It remains to be seen whether this persists as the mark of our postgraduate programmes.

Architecture as a General Non-Vocational Education
The notion that architecture might form the basis of a general undergraduate education—architectural studies—not necessarily leading to a vocational qualification, has been canvassed at various times in the last 25 years. The current crisis, with its projected decrease in the need for professional activities, has brought renewed calls for such a programme as a means of salvaging higher education in architecture at something like its present level. We believe that it is necessary to untangle three possibilities in this argument:
— There is a role in the construction industry and the architectural profession in particular for people who have not completed the full five-year programme to RIBA Part 2. (The latter could be reserved for a restricted group of talented designers.)
— An undergraduate education in architecture, basically as it exists, provides a way of thinking and an approach to problem-solving which finds applications in diverse situations and roles.
— 'Architectural studies' constitute an academic discipline in their own right, over and above or even distinct from the design activity, and could be constructed as an undergraduate education on a par with, say, history or geography.

We believe that there is a strong case to be made for the first possibility and to a certain extent for the second, although this is a subject for further research. The last option, however, is unrealistic in terms of both the level of academic teaching resources available and the constitution of the subject as presently conceived. Experience from other countries, especially where courses are less directly vocational, would be of great interest.

This argument in practice has been taken a step further. A number of non-vocational *postgraduate* courses in architectural studies have been successfully mounted in recent years, courses for which students will have already obtained at least one previous degree (or equivalent) not always in architecture. It would be interesting to know whether in general those with a previous *design* qualification show any special insight in such courses.

If it were possible for the RIBA substantially to restructure its forms of membership, without compromising the spirit of its charter, then one option is to give some professional status to people with Part 1 only (perhaps in a slightly revised form) plus supervised office experience. This implies that postgraduate architecture courses might then be of three forms. First, advanced design studies. Second, advanced professional studies—eg exploring project management or architect/planner roles. Third, advanced architectural studies as discussed above. In all three cases, it could then be argued, postgraduate grants would not be mandatory but would be competitive, as is the case with most other UK postgraduate subjects.

The combination of a first degree plus experience leading to final professional exams is of course familiar in other building professions. If architecture were able to encompass such a combination, the RIBA recognition of those other professions could be made that much easier. This might even have a reciprocal effect, in terms of some joint education, back to the schools. (It is worth noting that in some countries the full-time formal education in other building disciplines takes as long as that for architecture. Again, such experience would be of great interest to us.)

If the RIBA were able to develop in his way—and this might even involve the recasting of its Charter—then, as has been pointed out by Robert Fisher,[24] it becomes possible to differentiate quite properly the functions of the RIBA and of ARCUK. The ARCUK responsibility would relate specifically to the recognition of professional architects. The RIBA responsibility would take in the broader range of all those concerned with the production of architecture.

Financial Cuts
Reverting to the impetus for this paper, namely the urgent cuts, we can see that financial pressure on architecture in universities—and soon by implication on other institutions—is exerted directly in four ways. First, fees for overseas students have been drastically increased and it is yet unclear as to the long-term effect on revenue and cost-effective expenditure. Second, the number of home students is being restricted in many universities. Third, the resources available to university departments are also being cut. Finally, and perhaps most problematically, these changes in circumstance have been exerted in a very short space of time. There is some reason to suppose that similar constraints may soon be exercised in the polytechnic sector.

A fifth pressure is more indirect, namely the drop in architectural workload. The availability of good, early professional experience for many students has diminished alarmingly, throwing back onto the schools an increasing—and understandable—demand for them to provide more practical training.

Some possible consequences of these pressures can be suggested. Many schools depend on part-time teachers for a range of contributions. Some are 'permanent' specialist teachers who wish to retain substantial involvement in practice. Some cover essentially the same areas as full-time teachers, but are released to do other academic work as well—course development, research, lecturing, etc. Some are junior teachers gaining professional experience in teaching.

If cuts are taken in the short-term on 'windfall' retirements of full-time staff and, more generally, on part-time staff, then many schools will suffer. We suggest, with the modern technologies, generalist 'core' teachers with a practice background cannot alone cover the material with which today's and tomorrow's students should be familiar. The effects will fall on those schools which concentrate on vocational courses as much as on those which give more emphasis to research/postgraduate diversification.

Design practice is being revolutionised by micro-electronic hardware. Some schools—notably in Scotland—have pioneered the applications of computer-aided design and simulations in their teaching. Cuts in equipment grants etc will make it more difficult for schools to develop both pedagogic and professional applications.

An important hope of the Oxford Conference was that traditional academic skills would become more widespread in architecture—encouraging more diverse reading and the ability to prepare research reports. This, as many of their intentions, was associated with its inherent educational benefit and its eventual professional utility. But now the cuts are already affecting the books and journals budgets—items which in any case have been inflating substantially in price over recent years. (We imagine that the RIBA Library—one of the Institute's most precious assets—itself is feeling the cold winds.)

The 15% of our students from overseas may decide in the long-term to go elsewhere, which would significantly diminish the quality of experience for all students in our schools.

The broad point is that it seems unlikely that we can prevent serious damage even to those educational programmes we might all agree must survive.

Conclusions

Two broad lines of enquiry can inform the immediate debate. The first is perhaps to invoke the intentions of the Oxford Conference. The second is to explore a more straightforwardly vocational emphasis in the schools. We believe that both might be accomplished but certainly not in every school.

According to our survey there are, on average, 190 students per school in the full-time courses leading to RIBA Parts 1 and 2. The Oxford Conference envisaged much larger schools; indeed, the RIBA in 1965 foresaw a pattern of around 25 schools at a time when the real workload of construction was expected to grow considerably. That is, the programme involved a picture of UK architectural education with fewer (but much larger) schools than our 37 today.

We believe that it was a correct analysis 20 years ago and that it would be better now to have fewer, larger schools. This 'quantum' argument[25] would have allowed us to sustain the main traditional vocational courses while developing a proper research base. Today, this no longer appears to be an available option. Even if schools are closed rather than slimmed down, there is no reason to suppose that it will lead to a more effective remnant, as the context and pace of change are not construed in these terms. Moreover, for staff and students concerned in any closure, it will often mean sad and even stupid wastage.

In passing, we should say that it is manifestly unfair to blame the Oxford Conference and its effects for general environmental planning and building failures, on the grounds that well-established traditional training was destroyed and should now be re-established. It is only in the last few years that cohorts which experienced the new courses are coming into positions of responsibility[26]. The damage was done by previous cohorts—perhaps trained in the methods we are now urged to re-install?

The interest in resurrecting a more vocational—perhaps part-time—programme is also of great interest. But the profession is in no financial position to help in this way at the moment. It is notable that, of

the six part-time courses in the UK, four are in London. To set up a proper countrywide programme when schools are in such throes is exceedingly difficult, as the pedagogic issues are not straightforward.

Associated with this concern, in our view, are two areas for further study, on which the view of the RIBA membership and other registered architects would be welcome. The first is to explore how the professional practice period of qualification (pre-Part 3) can be systematically improved. We are not convinced that architects invariably know how to train 'apprentices'—they could learn much, for instance, from building contractors. The second is to extend the basis of RIBA membership, for reasons we have indicated above, which in turn we believe would encourage greater diversity amongst students.

Today, the immediate need is for a wide and much better-informed discussion of architectural education[27]. The RIBA itself has, in papers for its specialist committees and the reports of the Visiting Boards, a body of distinguished work which should rapidly be published as a contribution to that debate. The schools, too, in the last few years, have failed to make their cases clear and a range of position papers from different educational groups is now urgent.

We would suggest that a number of short studies[28], perhaps based on existing work by the RIBA and others, should be published to provide the basic information and range of options for discussion on:
— relationships between future professional roles and educational programmes;
— necessities and possibilities of in-office training and education;
— futher work on the curriculum for mid-career training and Continuing Professional Development;
— the range of jobs for which an architectural education has proved to be suitable (and perhaps the implications of new technologies thereon);
— the relationship between architectural and technical education;
— the range of viable specialist courses—both more academic (eg architectural studies) and more practice-oriented (eg building design studies on the basis of 'types'—by end-use and/or by technology);
— the basic numerical descriptions of the profession and the schools—already part of the RIBA's service.

It is our belief that the background information and definition of real possibilities is an urgent necessary preliminary to prevent the eventual debates degenerating into acrimony, banality or anecdote.

Notes

1 We should acknowledge the benefit of discussions with many colleagues, notably D Bishop, R Fisher, M Koudra, E Leopold and N Watson. We would mention also the paper on 'Architectural Education—A Personal View', Part 1—1981, Part 2—1982, by Professor JN Tarn, which seems to us a crucial contribution to the debate and one which we hope will soon be published. The views expressed here are those of the authors alone and do not necessarily reflect those of any institution with which either author has been associated.

2 The Times, 'Architects' share in education grants', correspondence column, 26 July, 1981.

3 Perhaps the most consistent exponent of one such position is Brian Anson—see, for instance, his 'Grand design that should go back to the drawing board', Times Higher Education Supplement, 17 April, 1981.

4 See: Guide to Good Practice at Part 3 Examinations in Professional Practice and Experience Held at Recognised Schools of Architecture, RIBA, 1976.

5 See also: RIBA, Architectural Education in the UK, mimeo leaflet, September, 1981.

6 The Charter, Supplemental Charter 1971 and Byelaws, RIBA, 1971.

7 Code of Professional Conduct, RIBA, July, 1982.

8 Schools of Architecture Recognised by the RIBA, RIBA, 1981.

9 M Koudra, The size of the profession—a framework for debate, mimeo, RIBA, January, 1982.

10 The Scottish Education Department considered imposing a quota of postgraduates in all subjects, not excluding architecture. Their intention was to support a student until he/she obtains their first qualification—in Scotland often after four years, with RIBA Part 1 being gained after three years. See, for example, letter to the schools by Mr P Gibbs-Kennet, RIBA Director of Education and Professional Development, dated 9 March, 1982, on this topic.

11 See, for example, Research Programme, BRE, DOE, annually.

12 'Report of the Committee on the Oxford Architectural Education Conference', RIBA Journal, November, 1959; and L Martin, 'Report of the Oxford Conference', RIBA Journal, June, 1958.

13 For descriptions and assessments of post-Oxford developments, see: R Gardner, 'The development of architectural education in the UK', Architects Journal, 9 October, 1974; A Cox, 'Where are we?', paper to the Schools of Architecture Council (SAC) Conference on The Making of an Architect, University of York, 1978; M MacEwen, 'New directions in architectural education', RIBA Journal, February, 1970; 'Education Year', the Cambridge Conference, special issue, RIBA Journal, May, 1970; Board of Architectural Education, 'Report on the Cambridge Conference, 1970', mimeo, RIBA, 1970; 'Educating the Architect', special issue on the Birmingham Conference, RIBA Journal, September, 1970.

14 Committee on Higher Education, Higher Education: Report of the Committee appointed by the Prime Minister under the Chairmanship of Lord Robbins, 1961–63, Cmnd 2154, HMSO: London, 1963.

15 The UGC general letter to the universities, 1 July, 1981.

16 'Green Report on Continuing Professional Development', RIBA Journal, October, 1979; J Carter 'Continuing Education', Architects Journal, 26 April, 1978.

17 See, for instance, Diversification, Report to the Board of Architectural Education, RIBA, December, 1964.

18 Reports of the Subject Area Review Committees for Social Studies, Engineering, Languages, Biological Sciences and Physical Sciences, University of London, January, 1982.

19 The general concern about the level of professional competence manifest in architectural graduates was a particularly public issue in 1975, witness: 'Professional Competence', Report of the Professional Competence Group of the RIBA, RIBA Journal, September, 1975; 'Beyond the Competence Debate' (articles by G Broadbent, T Markus and M Quantrill), RIBA Journal, November/December, 1975; M MacEwen 'What can be done about competence?', Architects Journal, 19 November, 1975; P Bartlett 'Can competence be monitored?', Architects Journal, August, 1975.

20 M Higgin and N Jessop, Communications in the Building Industry, Tavistock Institute of Human Relations, 1965; Tavistock Institute of Human Relations, Interdependence and Uncertainty, Tavistock Publications, 1966.

21 Sir Noel Hall, Report of the Joint Committee on Training in the Building Industry, published jointly by IOB, RIBA, RICS and IStrucE, November, 1964. A more general discussion is in DA Turin, 'Building as a Process', Transactions of the Bartlett Society, Vol 6, University College London, 1967–68.

22 M Bedford and S Groak '1982 Survey of Academic/Vocational Programmes in UK Schools of Architecture', April 1982. This survey can be found on the following pages of this issue of AD.

23 Report of the Research Working Party (Chairman: Sir Peter Trench) to the Building and Civil Engineering EDC, National Economic Development Office, London, February, 1982.

24 We are indebted to Mr Fisher, of the Bartlett School, for his very clear explication of this point.

25 See also: 'The future pattern of architectural education', paper to the University Grants Committee, RIBA, February, 1965.

26 A similar point is made in: T Markus, 'How do we get there?', SAC, op cit.

27 Some reflections may be garnered from R Llewelyn-Davies and Lionel Esher, 'The architect in 1988', RIBA Journal, October, 1968. Other points of interest are in: J Carter, 'Ten Years On', Architects Journal, 16 August, 1978 (Report on the PSA Training Office); J Musgrove and S Hunt, 'Schools of Architecture and the Profession', Architects Journal, 14 June, 1978; earlier, in the work of Dr Jane Abercrombie, at the Bartlett School; and the work of Notts CC in its 'Research into Site Management' programme. More recently, important issues for UK postgraduate education generally are raised in: Report of the Working Party on Postgraduate Education (Chairman: Sir Peter Swinnerton-Dyer), Advisory Board for the Research Councils, London, HMSO, April, 1982.

28 An example of the sort of report we might eventually hope for is V Wigfall and R Fisher, Follow up of ex-students of architecture, Final Report, ARCUK Research Report, University College London, April, 1975.

1982 SURVEY OF ACADEMIC/VOCATIONAL PROGRAMMES IN UK SCHOOLS OF ARCHITECTURE

Michael Bedford & Steven Groák

NOTES

1　This matrix summarises certain information about all 37 Recognised Schools of Architecture in the UK. The categories have been selected to give particular prominence to postgraduate and reseach work, ie. that which extends beyond the typical requirements for 'mainstream' professional architectural qualification.

2　We would emphasise that, where a school is shown not to have extensive postgraduate research programmes, this in no way is intended as a criticism. to concentrate their programmes.

3　We wish to thank all those schools (virtually 100%) who helped for their prompt responses on earlier draft information. We would particularly mention those academics who had some reservations about the categories used but nonetheless were prepared to assist us.

4　The categories selected are our responsibility, as is the amount of information included in them. Whilst every attempt has been made to ensure the accuracy of the information, we cannot accept responsibility for that accuracy; any intending student should contact directly any school whose programme appears to be of interest for the full up-to-date information.

5　Research projects listed have been restricted to those with external funding, as it did not prove possible on this occasion to compile a comprehensive account of personal research, etc. Some further information will be available in the forthcoming RIBA *Survey of Research in the Schools of Architecture.*

6　In Category (5)a, 'higher degrees' means MPhil and PhD by research and does not include MA, MSc, etc.

7　Nothing in this report should be seen as necessarily implying approval by any organisation or institution with which the authors have been associated.

8　Where no information is recorded in a category or subcategory, this means that either there was nothing to report or that reliable information was not available at the time of compilation.

Michael Bedford, Research Section, RIBA
Steven Groák, Bartlett School of Architecture and Planning

1 Name and Address, Telephone Number, Head of School	2 Full-time Architectural Vocational Courses: a RIBA Part One (title and length) b RIBA Part Two (title and length) c Number of students (approx.)	3 Part-time Architectural Vocational Course: a RIBA Part One b RIBA Part Two c Number of students	4 Postgraduate courses offered in the Department (other than columns 2 or 3)	5 Research information: a Number of students registered for Higher Degrees 1981-82 b Research Units in the Department c Current Externally-Funded Research Projects	6 Notes: a General Remarks b Specialist Courses/Options offered in the Vocational Architecture Programme c Joint Courses/Options with other disciplines in the University/Polytechnic/College d Building-related disciplines offered in the University/Polytechnic/College
Scott Sutherland School of Architecture, Robert Gordon's Institute of Technology, Garthdee, Aberdeen AB9 2QB / 0224-33247 / Professor S Wilkinson	a BSc (Hons) in Architecture, 4 years b Diploma in Advanced Architectural Studies, 1 year c 200	None	MSc in Rural and Regional Resources Planning, 2 years, full-time. Diploma in Urban Design, 1 year, full-time. MLitt in Historical Studies, 1 year, full-time or 2 years part-time	a 6 b Computer aided architectural design unit; Energy conservation unit c Influence of environmental and architectural form on the design and thermal performance of a flat plate solar collection system; House design systems and methodology for computer-aided design; Machine refinement of raw graphic data input for translation into a low level data base for a CAAD decision matrix; Passive solar space heating in housing with particular reference to the Scottish climate	b Computer-aided architectural design, energy studies, urban design c Rural and regional resources planning course run jointly with University of Aberdeen d Civil engineering, mechanical engineering, urban design
School of Architecture and Building Engineering, University of Bath, Claverton Down, Bath BA2 7AY / 0225-61244 / Professor M Brawne	a BSc (Hons) in Architectural Studies, 4 years (sandwich course) b BArch (Hons), 2 years (sandwich course) c 150	None	None	a 20 b None c Development of a decision model for energy conservation planning in existing NHS buildings; Investigation of possible techniques of measuring ventilation in occupied spaces; Development of a range of surface stressed flexible structures; Evaluation of a solar heated school at Port Isaac; The visual effect of various types of cladding materials on large dome structures; Solar energy measuring project; Investigations of internal environments of air supported structures	a The sandwich course operates on a six-year cycle with fourteen terms spent in the university interspaced with four terms in practical training b Computer-aided architectural design, conservation studies, energy studies, urban design c The first two years of the architecture course are integrated with those in civil/structural engineering and building services engineering d Civil/structural engineering, building services engineering
Department of Architecture, The Queen's University of Belfast, Belfast BT7 1NN / 0232-661111 / Professor W J Kidd	a BSc (Hons) in Architecture, 3 years b Diploma in Advanced Architectural Studies, 2 years c 131	None			d Civil engineering, mechanical engineering, urban and regional planning
Birmingham School of Architecture, City of Birmingham Polytechnic, Perry Barr, Birmingham B42 2SU / 021-356 6911 / Mr A D Collier	a BA (Hons) in Architecture, 3 years b Diploma in Architecture, 2 years c 150	None	None	a 1 b None c Energy efficient schools; Energy improvement kits; Social and behavioural aspects of energy conservation and consumption; Microprocessor control of preheating of buildings	d Civil engineering, mechanical engineering, urban and regional planning, interior/3-dimensional design, landscape design, quantity surveying, estate management
School of Architecture and Interior Design, Brighton Polytechnic, Mithras House, Lewes Road, Brighton BN2 4AT / 0273-693655 / Dr J P Lomax	a BA (Hons) in Architecture, 3 years b Diploma in Architecture, 2 years c 156	None	None	a 5 b Research unit c None at present	b Computer-aided architectural design, conservation studies, energy studies, tropical/third world design studies c The first year of the architecture course is run jointly with the interior design course. Joint projects are organised in subsequent years with interior design and building students d Building, civil engineering, mechanical engineering, interior/3-dimensional design, landscape design, history of design

1 Name and Address Telephone Number Head of School	2 Full-time Architectural Vocational Courses: a RIBA Part One (title and length) b RIBA Part Two (title and length) c Number of students (approx.)	3 Part-time Architectural Vocational Course: a RIBA Part One b RIBA Part Two c Number of students	4 Postgraduate courses offered in the Department (other than columns 2 or 3)	5 Research information: a Number of students registered for Higher Degrees 1981-82 b Research Units in the Department c Current Externally-Funded Research Projects	6 Notes: a General Remarks b Specialist Courses/Options offered in the Vocational Architecture Programme c Joint Courses/Options with other disciplines in the University/Polytechnic/College d Building-related disciplines offered in the University/Polytechnic/College
Department of Architecture University of Bristol Bristol BS1 5RA 0272-24161 Mr M Burton	a BA (Hons) in Architecture, 3 years b Diploma in Architecture, 2 years c 180	None	MSc in Advanced Functional Design for Buildings, 1 year, full-time or 3 years part-time Certificate course in Conservation, 2 years, part-time	a 2 b None c Acoustic scale modelling techniques An integrated approach to communications within the building design team Application of a hybrid computer to dynamic thermal modelling Vapour transfer through building materials Data base aspects of CAD systems The Computer in the early stages of design The history of the RIBA The history of the Modern Movement	a At the time of preparation a Committee of the Court is considering the future of the department b Elective system in year 3 and an option system in year 5 gives students the opportunity to engage with the wide variety of research interests of the staff c None d Civil engineering, mechanical engineering, urban studies, history of art
University of Cambridge School of Architecture 1 Scroope Terrace Cambridge 0223-69501 Professor C St.J Wilson	a BA (Hons) in Architecture, 3 years b Diploma in Architecture, 2 years c 170	None	None	a 17 b Martin Centre for Architectural and Urban Studies c A selective approach to energy conservation in schools Passive solar energy and non-domestic buildings Acoustic survey of British auditoria Advanced passive solar gain and housing design The human contribution to energy conservation in buildings Acoustic model studies of large spaces Vulnerability of low-income housing in earthquake areas	b Computer-aided architectural design, conservation studies, energy studies, land use built form and transportation studies, third world/tropical design d Civil engineering, mechanical engineering
School of Architecture Canterbury College of Art New Dover Road Canterbury Kent 0227-69371 Mr M Crux	a BA (Hons) in Architecture, 3 years b Diploma in Architecture, 2 years c 145	None	None	a 0 b Vernacular research unit c None at present	b Vernacular studies c Joint options with students in painting, sculpture, photography, graphics, 3-dimensional design, practical building crafts d Building, art and design
The Welsh School of Architecture University of Wales Institute of Science and Technology King Edward VII Avenue Cardiff CF1 3NU 0222-42522 Professor J Eynon	a BSc (Hons) in Architectural Studies, 3 years b BArch (Hons), 2 years (the first year of which is spent in supervised practical training) c 240	None	None	a 6 b Welsh School of Architecture Research and Development 1 Architectural science 2 Human studies 3 History and housing studies 4 Project office c Monitoring the human response to the introduction of microprocessor control of energy consumption in a non-housing local authority Energy conservation in foundries – use of waste process heat for building heating Low-energy design in school building Interaction between thermal properties, heating systems, patterns of occupation, and energy use in domestic-scale buildings A finite-difference thermal model for housing Effective use of incidental heat gains in dwellings Energy conservation in office lighting Frogmore School monitoring, Hants. C.C. Physical and subjective characteristics of impulse sound insulation measurements in buildings Energy conservation in advanced factories Disabled in the Welsh housing environment Area improvement/renewal policy Conservation and historical studies of listed buildings	a One of only two courses in the UK which requires 4 years at the university, with the other year undertaken as supervised practical training (cf. Bartlett School of Architecture and Planning) b Building science, human studies, housing, advanced building studies, contract administration c None d Civil engineering, mechanical engineering, urban and regional planning .
School of Architecture and Landscape Thames Polytechnic Oakfield Road Dartford Kent 32-21328 Dr J Paul	a BA (Hons) in Architecture, 3 years b Diploma (Hons) in Architecture, 2 years c 164	a BA in Architecture, 4 years b Diploma in Architecture, 3 years c 167	None	a 8 b None c None at present	b History, theory and criticism of architecture c Joint projects undertaken with landscape design students d Civil engineering, mechanical engineering, building surveying, landscape design, quantity surveying, estate management, environmental health
Department of Architecture University of Dundee Duncan of Jordanstone College of Art Perth Road Dundee DD1 4HT 0382-23261 Mr J Paul	a BSc in Architecture, 3 years b BArch (Hons), 2 years c 200	None	None	a 3 b Urban deprivation action unit c Housing in low-let and demand estates in Dundee Vernacular architecture of Gtr. Strathmore Scottish methods of meat and fish preservation and associated buildings Historical Greek construction	b Energy studies, urban studies, professional studies c Joint courses with students of building economics at Dundee College of Technology d Civil engineering, mechanical engineering, urban and regional planning, interior 3-dimensional design, quantity surveying

1 Name and Address Telephone Number Head of School	2 Full-time Architectural Vocational Courses: a RIBA Part One (title and length) b RIBA Part Two (title and length) c Number of students (approx.)	3 Part-time Architectural Vocational Course: a RIBA Part One b RIBA Part Two c Number of students	4 Postgraduate courses offered in the Department (other than columns 2 or 3)	5 Research information: a Number of students registered for Higher Degrees 1981-82 b Research Units in the Department c Current Externally-Funded Research Projects	6 Notes: a General Remarks b Specialist Courses/Options offered in the Vocational Architecture Programme c Joint Courses/Options with other disciplines in the University/Polytechnic/College d Building-related disciplines offered in the University/Polytechnic/College
Department of Architecture Heriot-Watt University Edinburgh College of Art Lauriston Place Edinburgh EH3 9DF 031-229 9311 Professor J D Dunbar-Nasmith	a BArch (Hons), 4 years (RIBA Part One after 3 years) b Diploma in Architecture, 1 year (for students who have completed a Scottish 4 year first degree course) or 2 years (for students who have completed a 3 year first degree programme elsewhere) c 180	None	Diploma in Urban Design, 1 year, full-time MSc in Urban Design, 1 (calendar) year, full-time Diploma in Architectural Conservation, 1 year, full-time MSc in Architectural Conservation, 1 (calendar) year, full-time	a 18 b Conservation unit Environmental science unit Architectural acoustics unit (in conjunction with Department of Building) c Subject preference design criteria for theatre acoustics The Soundfield Simulator – a design tool for theatre acoustics Music quality-subject preference design criteria Lightness discrimination Colour vision	b Computer-aided architectural design (starting), conservation studies, energy studies, third world design studies (with urban design course), housing studies, urban design, interior design, landscape design c Joint courses with urban design and town planning students (future) d Civil engineering, mechanical engineering, urban and regional planning, landscape design, quantity surveying, building, estate management
Department of Architecture University of Edinburgh 20 Chambers Street Edinburgh EH1 1JZ 031-667 1011 Mr E C Ruddock	Route One: a MA (Hons) in Architecture, 4 years (RIBA Part One after 3 years) b Diploma in Architecture, 1 year Route Two a BSc (Social Science) 3 years (principal subject: architecture) b Diploma in Architecture, 2 years c 180	None	MPhil in Landscape Architecture, 2 years, full-time	a 20 b Edinburgh computer-aided architectural design (EdCAAD) c Software techniques for mounting CAAD systems on small dedicated computers Investigation of techniques to support non-prescriptive mode CAAD systems A practical non-prescriptive tool for (CAAD) applications Early American timber bridges Textile fabrics in construction Cataloguing of archives The development of a framework for energy education for the building design professions Micro-climate, energy and built form A theory of performance-based descriptions of building/environment interactions	b Computer-aided architectural design, conservation studies, energy studies, landscape design, fire safety engineering c The Department organises a course in architectural science for engineering students and courses in architectural studies throughout the University. It is possible to take a non-vocational undergraduate degree in architectural studies. d Civil engineering, mechanical engineering, urban and regional planning, urban design, landscape design, fire safety engineering
The Mackintosh School Department of Architecture Glasgow University and Glasgow School of Art 177 Renfrew Street Glasgow G3 6RQ 041-332 9797 Professor A MacMillan	a BArch, 3 years or BArch (Hons), 4 years b Diploma in Architecture, 2 years c 160	a BArch, 4 years b Diploma in Architecture, 3 years c 141	MA in Urban Building	a 6 b History unit Built environment unit C.A.A.D. unit c None at present	b Computer-aided architectural design and energy studies (as part of architectural science course), conservation studies d Civil engineering, mechanical engineering, urban and regional planning, interior/3-dimensional design, urban design
Department of Architecture and Building Science University of Strathclyde 131 Rottenrow Glasgow G4 0NG 041-552 4400 Professor F N Morcos-Asäad	a BSc (Hons) in Architectural Studies, 4 years b BArch, 1 year c 194	None	MSc in Building Science (Computer-Aided Building Design), 1 year, full-time MSc in Building Science (Building Climate and Energy), 1 year, full-time	a 17 b ABACUS (computer-aided architectural design) ASSIST (Action research in urban renewal) c Computer-aided design appraisal Development of 2nd extensions to ESP (Environmental Systems Performance) Accuracy and accessibility to ESP Development of a CAAD curriculum Heat transfer processes in air-heating solar collectors The optimisation of the design of air-heating solar collectors The performance of air collectors with expanded aluminium mesh absorbers Timber joints with mechanical fasteners Climatic severity index Mineral underworking study Handbook of maintenance and repair of tenements Visual impact analysis	b Computer-aided architectural design, conservation studies, energy studies, experimental aesthetics d Civil engineering, mechanical engineering, urban and regional planning
Department of Architecture Studies Gloucester College of Arts and Technology Oxtalls Lane Gloucester GL2 9HW 0452-26321 Mr H G Powell	a and b Diploma in Architecture, 4 years (RIBA Part One after 2 years) –see notes in column (6) c New course – first year intake 1982 will be 36	None			a The DipArch course is a new one starting in August 1982 and intended for mature students who have practical experience or completed an arts foundation course b Community architecture, conservation studies, design and build, energy studies d Landscape design, urban and regional planning
School of Architecture Huddersfield Polytechnic Queensgate Huddersfield HD1 3DH 0484-22288 Dr A Forward	a BA in Architectural Studies, 3 years b Diploma in Architecture, 2 years c 130	b Diploma in Architecture, minimum 3 years	None	a 1 b None c Housing rehabilitation	b Computer-aided architectural design, conservation studies, energy studies d Mechanical engineering, building

234

1 Name and Address / Telephone Number / Head of School	2 Full-time Architectural Vocational Courses: a RIBA Part One (title and length) b RIBA Part Two (title and length) c Number of students (approx.)	3 Part-time Architectural Vocational Course: a RIBA Part One b RIBA Part Two c Number of students	4 Postgraduate courses offered in the Department (other than columns 2 or 3)	5 Research information: a Number of students registered for Higher Degrees 1981-82 b Research Units in the Department c Current Externally-Funded Research Projects	6 Notes: a General Remarks b Specialist Courses/Options offered in the Vocational Architecture Programme c Joint Courses/Options with other disciplines in the University/Polytechnic/College d Building-related disciplines offered in the University/Polytechnic/College
School of Architecture Hull College of Higher Education Brunswick Avenue Kingston Upon Hull HU2 9BT 0482-25938 Mr C Padamsee	a BA in Architecture, 3 years b Diploma in Architecture, 2 years c 183	None	None	a 0 b Buiding science unit; Energy studies unit c Low-energy housing project; Sociological implications of the low-energy housing programme; Solar heat pump design; Energy conservation in horticultural glasshouses; Building design for fishing communities in tropical regions of Third World countries; Technical education in Egypt; Continuing professional development in the architectural profession	a After a compulsory first introductory year, students join the workbase system selecting from the various options on offer. Participation in each workbase may be from one up to three terms and involves working with students from different years b Energy studies, computer-aided architectural design, third world/tropical studies, housing, alternative technology, rural planning c A joint course is run interior design with students from the School of Visual Communication/Design d Civil engineering, mechanical engineering, interior/3-dimensional design, landscape design, urban design, building
School of Architecture and Landscape Leeds Polytechnic Brunswick Terrace Leeds LS2 8BU 0532-462222 Mr W T Bradshaw	a BA (Hons) in Architecture, 3 years b Diploma in Architecture, 2 years c 180	None	Diploma in Architectural Science, 2 years, part-time MA in Town Planning (Urban Design Option)	a 2 b Computer unit; Architectural science unit; Smoke and fire unit; History unit c Solar water-heating in the textile industry; Low-cost microprocessor-based data logging; CAAD – 'AMTK' graphic systems for building design and appraisal; Oral history of architecture; Smoke flow in buildings; Hearing damage associated with pop music and other leisure-related activities	c The Interdisciplinary Studies Group includes students from landscape, town planning, quantity surveying and building d Mechanical engineering, urban and regional planning, interior/3-dimensional design, landscape design, urban design, building, quantity surveying
School of Architecture Leicester Polytechnic PO Box 143 Leicester LE1 9BH 0533-551551 Professor T Matoff	a BA (Hons) in Architecture, 3 years b Diploma in Architecture, 3 years (sandwich course of which one year is spent in practical training) c 185	a and b Diploma in Architecture, 7 years c 79	Diploma in Architectural Building Conservation, 2 years, part-time		c Building surveying, interior/3-dimensional design, mechanical engineering, history of design, urban processes problems and policies
Department of Architecture Liverpool Polytechnic 53 Victoria Street Liverpool L1 6EY 051-709 0571 Mr K E Martin	a BA (Hons) in Architectural Studies, 3 years b Diploma in Architecture, 2 years c 160	None	None	a 0 b None c A physical description of vernacular settlement patterns; Design theory teaching: computer programmes for problem identification and solution strategies; Conservation in Danish villages; Computer graphics systems – micro and mini-based	d Building, building surveying, civil engineering, estate management, quantity surveying, urban design
Liverpool School of Architecture University of Liverpool Abercromby Square Liverpool 7 051-709 6022 Professor J N Tarn	a BA (Hons) in Architecture, 3 years b BArch (Hons), 2 years c 230	None	Master of Design (M.Des), 2 years, part-time	a 11 b None c None at present	b Computer-aided architectural design, energy studies c Joint courses are organised in planning with civic design students and in building services and environmental issues with engineering students d Civil engineering, mechanical engineering, urban and regional planning, landscape design, urban design, building science
Architectural Association School of Architecture 36 Bedford Square London WC1B 3ES 01-636 0974 Mr A Boyarsky	a and b AADiploma, 5 years (RIBA Part One after 3 years) c 350	None	AA Graduate Diploma, 1 year, full-time; AA Graduate Diploma (Hons), 2 years, full time in one of the following areas: Energy; Housing; History and Theory. Diploma in Planning Studies, 1 year, full-time; Diploma in Planning Studies (Hons), 2 years, full-time; Diploma in Conservation, 2 years, part-time	a 3 b None c Energy systems and design of communities; Development of educational material on energy conservation for secondary schools; Evaluation and development of solar design aids; Energy conservation and solar systems in Athens; Approaches to contemporary architecture in Britain	a Students can be admitted either to the first year or to the intermediate school (years 2 and 3). Most work is organised on a unit structure b The AA offers a varying programme of specialised lecture series by visiting academics d Urban and regional planning
Architecture Unit School of Environment The Polytechnic of Central London 35 Marylebone Road London NW1 5LS 01-486 5811 Mr A Cunningham	a BSc (Hons) in Architecture, 3 years b Diploma in Architecture, 2 years c 270	None	Diploma in Urban Design, 2 years, part-time	a 5 b Built environment research group c Lighting in multi-purpose sports halls; PCL solar house at Milton Keynes; Group solar housing project; Design and cost-effectiveness of active solar space and water heating systems; Design and performance of low-cost solar heat stores; Computer modelling of solar heating systems and domestic hot water; Design of public buildings, spaces and transport for the visually handicapped	d Civil engineering, mechanical engineering, urban and regional planning, urban design, quantity surveying, estate management, building

1 Name and Address Telephone Number Head of School	2 Full-time Architectural Vocational Courses: a RIBA Part One (title and length) b RIBA Part Two (title and length) c Number of students (approx.)	3 Part-time Architectural Vocational Course: a RIBA Part One b RIBA Part Two c Number of students	4 Postgraduate courses offered in the Department (other than columns 2 or 3)	5 Research information: a Number of students registered for Higher Degrees 1981-82 b Research Units in the Department c Current Externally-Funded Research Projects	6 Notes: a General Remarks b Specialist Courses/Options offered in the Vocational Architecture Programme c Joint Courses/Options with other disciplines in the University/Polytechnic/College d Building-related disciplines offered in the University/Polytechnic/College
Bartlett School of Architecture and Planning University College London Wates House 22 Gordon Street London WC1H 0QB 01-387 7050 Professor J Musgrove	a BSc (Hons) in Architecture, Planning, Building and Environmental Studies, 3 years b Route One: Diploma in Architecture + Pre-Diploma course (field experience), 2 years Route Two: Diploma in Architecture + Pre-Diploma course (architectural studies), 2 years Route Three: Diploma in Architecture (1 year full time) + one of the MSc in architecture subjects listed in column (4) c 216	None	MSc in Architecture, 1 year full-time or 2 years part-time, in the following subjects: · Advanced architectural studies · Building economics and management · Environmental design and engineering · History of modern architecture · Production of the built environment (planned) MPhil in Town Planning, 2 year, full-time Diploma in Development Planning, 1 year, full-time MSc in Urban development Planning, 1 year, full-time	a 31 b Unit for architectural studies Building economics research unit Joint unit for planning research c Morphology of building complexes The interaction of task illumination and luminaire luminance on lighting adequacy Decision-making for rural areas Policies for labour market adjustment Party political linkages between the centre and the locality An investigation of the costs of construction site accidents Aspects of the growth of owner occupation, 1890-1939 Evaluation of training in the DHSS Study of the provision of housing assistance to migrant employees Evaluation of the determinants of training provision in the construction industry Land prices and builders' profits Teaching through case studies of architecture in its social context	a Route one of the part 2 vocational course (column 2) involves only 4 years of full-time study at the university. The other year is a supervised practical year (cf School 9) The Bartlett School is a single department of architecture, building and planning and includes the Development Planning Unit b Conservation studies, energy studies, third world planning studies, research methods c The undergraduate programme is a single integrated degree within the UCL course-unit system. Exemptions from RIBA, CIOB exams etc. are gained by passing specified courses. The degree thus may also be taken without any professional exemptions accruing. d Civil and municipal engineering, mechanical engineering, urban and regional planning, photogrammetry and surveying
School of Architecture Kingston Polytechnic Knights Park Kingston-Upon-Thames Surrey KT1 2QJ 01-549 6151 Mr D Berry	a BA (Hons) in Architecture, 3 years b Diploma in Architecture, 2 years c 262	None	None	a 1 b Architectural psychology research unit c None at present	b Conservation studies, energy studies, computer-aided architectural design, architectural psychology, research methodology, cultural history (in total the department offers 82 optional courses). c All the optional courses are run in conjunction with the School of Three-Dimensional Design and the School of Complementary Studies d Civil engineering, mechanical engineering, interior/3-dimensional design, quantity surveying and estate management
School of Architecture Faculty of Arts North-East London Polytechnic Forest Road London E17 4JB 01-590 7722 Mr N Silver	a BSc in Architecture, 3 years b Diploma in Architecture, 2 years c 141	a BSc in Architecture, 4 years b Diploma in Architecture, 3 years c 132	None	a 0 b None c None at present	d Civil engineering, mechanical engineering, quantity surveying, estate management
Department of Environmental Design Polytechnic of North London Holloway Road London N7 8DB 01-607 2789 Mr W Briscoe	a BSc (Hons) in Architecture, 3 years b Diploma in Architecture, 2 years c 164	a BSc in Architecture, 4 years b Diploma in Architecture, 3 years c 242	Diploma in Health Facility Planning, 1 year, full-time MA in Health Facility Planning, 1 year, full-time Diploma in Urban and Rural Conservation (proposed)	a 6 b Medical architecture research unit Structural geometry research unit Computer-aided design research unit Urban planning research unit Construction development research unit c Space utilisation Study of nurse staffing in relation to ward design Ward analysis package Use of medical gases, suction and space in accident and emergency departments Building notes/space utilisation - research assistance Evaluation of Cumbernauld Infirmary Health facility provision in the third world Housing associations in London 1920-80 Local authority housing in London 1920-1950 Teaching packages for architectural technology	b Urban design c Joint courses with planning and interior design d Urban and regional planning, interior/3-dimensional design, leisure planning
Department of Architecture Polytechnic of the South Bank Faculty of the Built Environment Wandsworth Road London SW8 2JZ 01-928 8989 Mr H Haenlein	a BA (Hons) in Architecture, 3 years b (Post-graduate) Diploma in Architecture, 2 years c 220	a (Graduate) Diploma in Architecture, 4 years b (Post-graduate) Diploma in Architecture, 3 years c 150	None	a 2 b Design research and development unit c Theory teaching in schools of architecture	b Conservation studies, computer-aided architectural design, energy studies, third world/tropical design urban design c Joint courses with all other disciplines within the Built Environment Faculty d Civil engineering, mechanical engineering, urban and regional planning, interior/3-dimensional design, building, building surveying, quantity surveying, estate management
School of Architecture Department of Architecture and Landscape Faculty of Art and Design Manchester Polytechnic Cavendish Street All Saints Manchester M15 6BR 061-228 6171 Mr M Darke	a BA (Hons) in Architecture, 4 years (sandwich course) b Graduate Diploma in Architecture, 2 years c 192	None	None	a 2 b Institute of Advanced Studies (incorporating the Centre for Environmental Interpretation) c A microprocessor-based building and planning system Urban regeneration	b Conservation studies, computer-aided architectural design, energy studies, third world/tropical design, urban design c Joint courses with landscape students and options in 3-dimensional design d Mechanical engineering, interior/3-dimensional design, landscape design, environmental health, history of design

1 Name and Address Telephone Number Head of School	2 Full-time Architectural Vocational Courses: a RIBA Part One (title and length) b RIBA Part Two (title and length) c Number of students (approx.)	3 Part-time Architectural Vocational Courses: a RIBA Part One b RIBA Part Two c Number of students	4 Postgraduate courses offered in the Department (other than columns 2 or 3)	5 Research information: a Number of students registered for Higher Degrees 1981-82 b Research Units in the Department c Current Externally-Funded Research Projects	6 Notes: a General Remarks b Specialist Courses/Options offered in the Vocational Architecture Programme c Joint Courses/Options with other disciplines in the University/Polytechnic/College d Building-related disciplines offered in the University/Polytechnic/College
School of Architecture University of Manchester Manchester M13 9PL 061-273 3333 Professor J A M Bell	a BA (Hons) in Architecture, 3 years b BArch, 2 years c 200	None	MA in Urban Design, 1 year, full-time MA in Conservation, Vernacular and Historical Studies, 1 year, full-time	a 22 b Design theory unit Vernacular architecture research group Architecture for industry unit c Furniture design unit	b History of art, urban design, conservation design, building performance design, computer-aided design, architecture for industry, buildings in landscape c Joint working with Departments of Building (UMIST) and civil engineering (UMIST and Owens) d Civil engineering
School of Architecture The University Newcastle-Upon-Tyne NE1 7RU 0632-28511 Professor B Farmer	a BA (Hons) in Architectural Studies, 3 years b BArch (Hons), 2 years c 142	None	MPhil in Housing for Developing Countries, 2 years, full-time	a 7 b Building science section c An investigation of the seasonal performance of domestic heat pump systems Investigation of the relationship between materials and thermal behaviour in traditional and pre-fabricated building systems in Iraq Rationalisation of traditional building materials and techniques in house construction with special reference to Zambia	b Conservation studies, computer-aided architectural design, energy studies, third world/tropical design (all integrated with main architecture programme) d Civil engineering, mechanical engineering, urban and regional planning, landscape design, urban design, land surveying
Department of Architecture University of Nottingham University Park Nottingham NG7 2RD 0602-56101 Professor C Riley	a BA (Hons) in Architecture, 3 years b BArch (Hons), 2 years c 120	None	None	a 8 b None c Adaptability of space in housing Illumination in buildings from cloudy skies	b Energy studies, computer-aided architectural design c The department runs a course in 'Architects and Society' in the Faculty of Law and Social Sciences d Civil engineering, mechanical engineering, urban and regional planning
Department of Architecture Oxford Polytechnic Headington Oxford OX3 0BP 0865-64777 Mr R Maguire	a BA (Hons) in Architectural Studies, 3 years b Diploma in Architecture, 2 years c 340	None	Diploma in Urban Design, 1 year, full-time or 2 years discontinuous study MA in Urban Design, 1⅓ years, full-time	a 19 b Social services buildings research team Building research team Disasters and settlements unit Energy research unit c Brief formulation and the initial design of buildings Briefing and appraisal of small factory buildings Survey and appraisal of housing estates with innovatory roads and footpath systems Post-disaster shelter and housing provision The social, cultural and economic aspects of housing improvement programmes in seismic zones Energy conservation design parameter measurement and the treatment of existing school buildings	b Convervation studies, energy studies, third world/tropical design, management of existing built resources, urban design; also simultaneous study for first year of the Diploma in Urban Design (discontinuous study mode) c Joint option with departments of town planning and estate management d Civil engineering, mechanical engineering, urban and regional planning, urban design, estate management, history of art
School of Architecture Plymouth Polytechnic The Hoe Centre Notte Street Plymouth PL1 2AR 0752-264645	a BA in Architecture, 3 years b Diploma in Architecture, 2 years c 203	None	None	a 2 b Computer-aided architectural design unit Community architecture workshop c Control and prevention of condensation and mould growth in local authority housing Low thermal capacity floor-heating systems Computer-aided visual impact analysis Socio/spatial structure of small towns	b Computer-aided architectural design, energy studies, urban and regional studies, professional management and law c Environmental services d Civil engineering, mechanical engineering
School of Architecture Portsmouth Polytechnic King Henry 1st Street Portsmouth PO1 2DY 0705-827681 Professor G Broadbent	a BA (Hons) in Architecture, 3 years b Diploma in Architecture, 2 years c 200	None	None	a 7 b Housing association research team School design research group Semiotic research group c Energy conservation behaviour in primary schools Energy-conserving design through computer-managed learning Learning styles of information and needs of architects and engineers 'Hassle' (an education and management tool in the context of housing associations)	b Computer-aided architectural design, energy studies, conservation studies c Joint options with departments of civil engineering, surveying, and the College of Art as a whole d Civil engineering, mechanical engineering, quantity surveying, urban land administration
Department of Architecture University of Sheffield Sheffield S10 2TN 0742-78555 Professor K Murta	a BA (Hons) in Architecture, 3 years b Diploma in Architecture or MA in Architecture, 2 years (entry to MA course subject to degree classification) c 255	None	None	a 11 b Ecotecture group Computer-aided architectural design unit c GABLE Computer-Aided Architectural Design System Solar-heated experimental dwelling Design methods of low-energy and passive solar building design Shopping facilities and urban design	b Computer-aided architectural design, energy studies, urban design, conservation, housing studies c Construction and technological studies d Civil engineering, mechanical engineering, urban and regional planning, landscape design, building science, urban studies, computer-aided design

THIS IS PROBABLY THE ONLY TIME YOU'LL SEE ONE OF TV-am's BIGGEST STARS ON T.V.

This is what Terry Farrell would look like on TV if he ever made it.

Instead, you'll have to make do with David Frost, Angela Rippon, Robert Kee, Michael Parkinson and Anna Ford. You'll be able to see all these famous faces, along with some not so famous ones, (not yet anyway), on your screens from February 1983.

And what about Terry Farrell? Well his company are responsible for TV-am's outstanding new studio and office complex alongside the Regent's Park Canal in London. TV-am is a new kind of Television Company; our programmes will be different and innovative; we're broadcasting at a new time of day, and apart from the stars, we've got some of the most imaginative and 'able' bodies in the business working for us.

Within days of the announcement that we had been awarded the franchise, we were inundated with architects offering their services. Big firms. Small firms. You name them – they probably approached us. After a painstaking selection process, we chose the Terry Farrell Partnership. And we're glad we did. Terry and his Company have produced a building which is practical, yet exciting, progressive and more advanced than any other Television Studio anywhere. In fact just the way we want our Company to be.

So you could say that one of TV-am's biggest stars will never make it on TV.

And it could be said, that without him, we wouldn't have made it on TV either.

tv-am
BREAKFAST TELEVISION CENTRE
HAWLEY CRESCENT, LONDON NW1 8EF

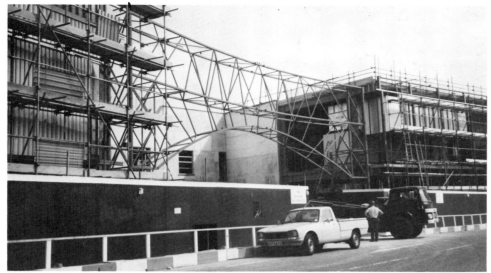

Hawley Crescent, entrance showing the new studio extension on the right of the entrance. June 1982.

General view of structural steel for new studio extension. December 1981.

THE CONSTRUCTION of the new TV-am Headquarters and Studios at Hawley Lock is an outstanding example of the broad scope and functional advantages of the 'Wiltshier Single Source Responsibility Service' in present-day building and development processes: as Peter Jay so accurately puts it, 'One head to pat and one butt to kick'.

The very nature of the project and the pressures imposed by TV-am's anticipated 'On Air' dates, demanded a full commitment and acute awareness of the requirements of the client by the whole project team throughout the construction process.

Wiltshier Management Ltd. were appointed by the client to undertake the leadership and overall co-ordination of the project from initial site finding and analysis, through design and general construction to the technical fitting-out and the specialist works with the Studios. Close co-operation with the client was maintained at all times in the preparation and development of the overall brief and technical operational feasibility of the project.

In the latter part of August 1981, Wiltshier London Ltd. were appointed to undertake all of the construction works on site. It became clear that the tight completion programme would necessitate the design and construction operations being carried out on a 'East Track' basis, with the ongoing requirements of the client being translated by the design team and effected by the contractor on an almost parallel basis.

Construction works commenced on site in October 1981 when the specialist mechanical, electrical and architectural designs were just emerging from the embryo stage. Pre-ordering of the majority of the major plant and long-term delivery items was also undertaken at that time.

The Wiltshier London Construction Team were then joined by their principal subcontractor, Ellis Mechanical Services Ltd. and site works of approximately £5 million, to be completed in just twelve months, got off to a flying start.

Trying to undertake construction works during the worst winter since records were kept does not facilitate fast-track working. Also the client's decision to substantially increase the work content of the project without extending the programme time, whilst being most welcome in many respects, added to the fast-track burden.

Despite these challenges the client, from only six months into the project, has been progressively occupying various parts of the building to commence the technical studio installations and other works necessary to meet the operational dates.

Thus by employing a single organisation, responsible for the overall co-ordination of the project from the earliest briefing to occupation of the building, the completion dates originally promised will be achieved.

Rear view of administration building from Regents Canal. June 1982.

WILTSHIER

WILTSHIER LIMITED
Nepicar House, London Road,
Wrotham Heath, Sevenoaks,
Kent TN15 7TB
Tel: (0732) 882477
Telex: 95426 WILCON G

Rear view of administration building from Regents Canal. March 1982.

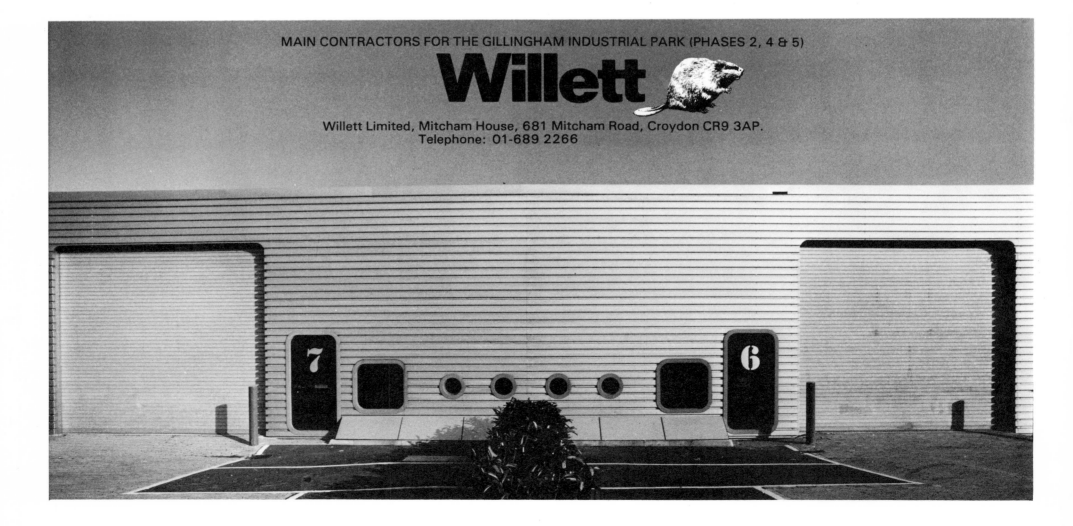

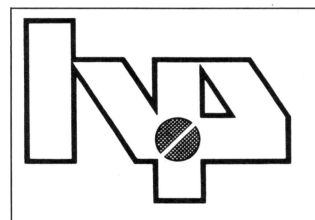
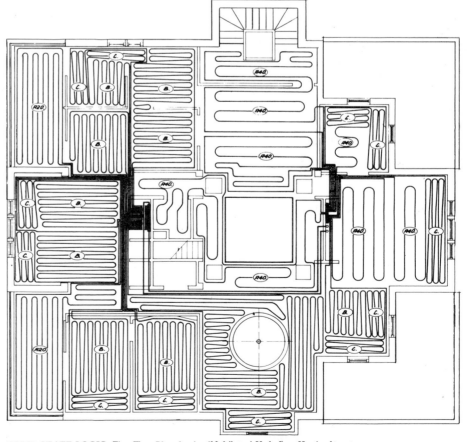

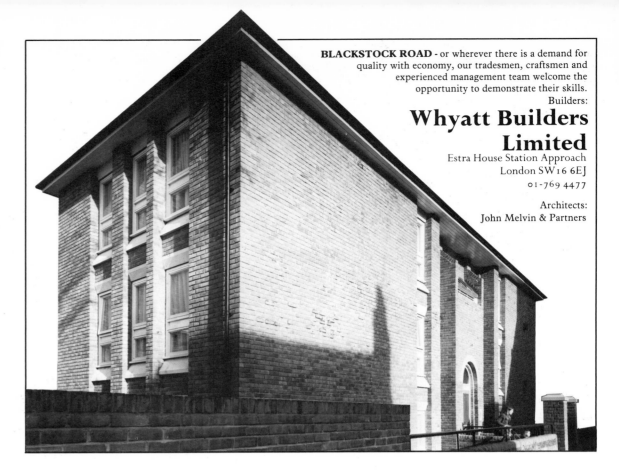

ARCHITECTURAL DESIGN
would like to thank the following for their kind contributions to this issue of BRITISH ARCHITECTURE

Solid State Logic, Stonesfield, Oxfordshire.

Ibstock Building Products Ltd., Ibstock, Leicester LE6 1HS Tel: Ibstock 60531

Sadolin (UK) Ltd., Tower Close, St. Peter's Industrial Park, Huntingdon,
  Cambridgeshire PE18 7DR. Tel: (0480) 50041

Skansen Windows, Market Harborough Joinery Co. Ltd., Riverside, Market Harborough,
  Leicestershire LE16 7PT. Tel: (0858) 65376

■243■

Project Awards 1983

The jury for the **1983 AD PROJECT AWARDS FOR BRITISH ARCHITECTURE** will meet in Febuary under the Chairmanship of Derek Walker. Prospective candidates are requested to submit their entries by **Monday January 31st 1983.**

In accordance with the recommendations of last year's jury the following categories have been proposed:
1 **Built projects** completed after August 1981 (including urban schemes and interiors)
2 **Unbuilt projects**
3 **Student awards**

We hope to announce two Project Awards in each category, though the exact number of Grand Project Awards, Project Awards, and Commendations will be decided at the discretion of the jury. In addition to submitted projects the jury may nominate for the Project Awards.

Submissions should comprise:
Visual material in the form of prints and photographs (maximum size A3). No original drawings, mounted panels, models etc should be sent.
Written material providing details of architect, design team, client, project, and location, together with a description of the brief, the conceptual and technical solutions, totalling not more than 1000 words, and a note of the entry category.

Submission of any project allows AD publication rights.

All submissions, clearly marked **'AD Project Awards'**,
should be sent to **Architectural Design, 42 Leinster Gardens, London W2.**

AS ONE OF THE LEADING English-language architectural magazines in the world, *Architectural Design* brings you up to date on the latest buildings, projects, and ideas within architectural theory and production drawn from a wide range of schools and practices throughout the world. AD has a policy of active participation in architectural discourse, and as well as commissioning special profiles with the aim of furthering the architectural debate on topical issues such as the role of classicism within contemporary practice, the magazine also sponsors lectures, such as the annual series at the Polytechnic of Central London, symposia, competitions such as the increasingly influential annual Project Awards and recent popular Doll's House competition, and exhibitions held at AD's private gallery to promote and stimulate architectural thinking and practice. AD subscribers are entitled to participate in any of the events organized by the magazine, and receive free of charge the AD News Supplement which gives news of recent exhibitions or events of current interest. The imaginative commissioning and continued high standards of editorial selection and production make subscription to AD essential for architects, students and their teachers.

A.D. ARCHITECTURAL DESIGN SUBSCRIPTIONS

RATES

	UK & O'seas	USA & N America (Airspeeded)
Full annual subscription	£39.50	$75.00
Special annual student rate	£35.00	$65.00

NOTE   Subscriptions can be backdated and include AD News.

AD 'AGENTS' collect five new subscriptions to get their own free - enclose five subscription orders with payments, we will send one year free.

To start your subscription now, please complete the panel on the right and send this form together with your payment/credit card authority/bank draft, direct to:-

Subscription Department,
ARCHITECTURAL DESIGN,
7/8 Holland Street,
London, W.8.

☐ I wish to subscribe to AD at the full rate.
☐ I wish to subscribe to AD at the student rate, and enclose proof of student status. (College . . . . Year . . . .)
☐ I claim a free subscription to AD, and enclose five new subscription orders (please attach names and addresses) and payments.
Starting date : Issue No . . . . Year . . . .
☐ Payment enclosed by : cheque/postal order/draft,
VALUE £/$ . . . .
☐ Please charge £/$ . . . . . . to my credit card.
Account No.

☐ AMERICAN EXPRESS
☐ DINERS CLUB
☐ ACCESS/MASTER CHARGE/EUROCARD
☐ BARCLAYCARD / VISA

Signature . . . .
Name . . . .
Address . . . .
. . . .

Books from
ACADEMY EDITIONS

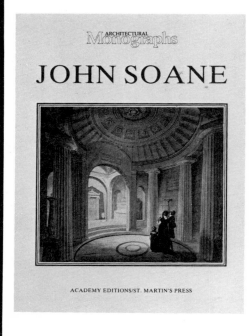

ACADEMY EDITIONS/ST. MARTIN'S PRESS

ARCHITECTURAL
Monographs

SIR JOHN SOANE
Contributors Sir John Summerson,
David Watkin and G. Tilman
Mellinghoff

This issue on the distinguished English architect Sir John Soane contains three essays by leading historians in addition to a pictorial description of the architect's own house at 13 Lincoln's Inn Fields, London. Sir John Summerson of the Soane Museum writes about the man and his style, David Watkin describes Soane and his contemporaries and G. Tilman Mellinghoff discusses the Dulwich Picture Gallery and Mausoleum. London buildings featured include alterations and new buildings for the Royal Hospital, Chelsea; Pitzhanger Manor, Ealing; the Soane family tomb, St Pancras and a number of churches and houses. Numerous pages in colour feature paintings never before published and, in particular, panoramas of all Soane's built and unbuilt projects. There is also a full list of buildings and projects 1780–1831, together with an extensive bibliography.

ISBN 0 85670 805 4 Paperback £9.50
29.2x21.6cm 128 pages over 200 illustrations including 58 in colour and 6 colour gatefolds

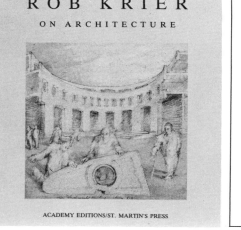

ROB KRIER
On Architecture

This easily accessible introduction to the theory and practice of one of the most influential figures in today's architectural discourse presents over 100 of the distinctive drawings which have become a trademark of Krier's style, accompanied by a highly readable commentary by the architect on his work.

ISBN 0 85670 797 X Hardback £12.50
ISBN 0 85670 692 2 Paperback £9.50
24 × 21.6 cm 96 pages 156 illustrations including 93 in colour

Tom Heinz

FRANK LLOYD WRIGHT

Thomas A. Heinz, editor of the Frank Lloyd Wright Newsletter, provides an insight into the incredible diversity of plan, structure and texture within Wright's work from the standpoint of his own intimate knowledge of the 50 carefully selected buildings featured. Illustrated with 80 specially commissioned colour photographs which include many previously unpublished views, this modestly priced book is a perfect introduction to the cultural legacy of Wright's built work.

ISBN 0 85670 796 1 Hardback £9.95
ISBN 0 85670 693 0 Paperback £6.95
24 × 21.6 cm 96 pages 106 illustrations including 80 in colour

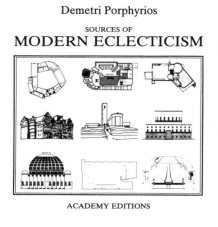

Demetri Porphyrios

SOURCES OF
MODERN ECLECTICISM
Studies on Alvar Aalto

This timely and well-researched reassessment of Aalto's work provides a reinterpretation of his production within the context of the Scandinavian versions of national Romanticism, Arts and Crafts, Neoclassicism and Modernism, and thus a new critical understanding of 20th century architecture and more specifically of the sources of Modern Eclecticism. Divided into two parts, the first comprising a formal analysis of Aalto's work and the second situating his design strategies within their ideological context, Porphyrios' scholarly study contains a wealth of new historiographic information illustrated with numerous photographs of the work of Aalto and his contemporaries.

'Porphyrios provides not only a convincing rereading of Aalto's work, but also a thorough and well-constructed account of the phenomenon of modern eclecticism from the Enlightenment to the present. In this, the book is exemplary: an excellent case-study whose implications will have a serious impact on all future interpretations of Modernism.'
Anthony Vidler

'Not only is this study one of the most perceptive analyses of Aalto's architecture, but it is also a theoretical work of the highest calibre ... This is, without doubt, one of the most important studies made in recent years. It should be read by the widest possible audience, by architects, historians, and the general public alike.' Kenneth Frampton

ISBN 0 85670 766 X Hardback £15.95
ISBN 0 85670 684 1 Paperback £12.50
24 × 22.5 cm 160 pages 307 illustrations 1982

Academy Editions/St. Martin's Press

JAMES STIRLING

A detailed presentation of Stirling's major recent projects and catalogue of selected work produced in collaboration with the architect to commemorate his receipt of two of architecture's premier awards—the Royal Gold Medal and Pritzker Prize. Addresses given at both ceremonies are reproduced in full, together with critical evaluations of Stirling's work by Robert Maxwell, Charles Jencks, Paul Goldberger and Ada Louise Huxtable.

From the Contents: The Pursuit of the Art of Architecture by Robert Maxwell; The Royal Gold Medal—Introduction by Norman Foster, Acceptance by James Stirling, Concluding Address by Mark Girouard; The Pritzker Prize—The Pritzker Prize in Architecture 1981, Pritzker Price Acceptance Speech by James Stirling; Buildings and Projects—Complete List of Buildings and Projects, Selected Work 1950–1980, Dresdner Bank Marburg, Bayer AG PF Zentrum Monheim, Staatsgalerie New Theatre Building and Chamber Stuttgart—A Note on the Drawings by Charles Jencks, Topping Out Ceremony 1982, Luxury Houses Manhattan, Science Centre Berlin, Rice University Houston—Buildings in Context by Paul Goldberger, Fogg Art Museum New Building Harvard—A Style Crystallized by Ada Louise Huxtable, The Clore Gallery London—Literal Eclecticism by Charles Jencks.

ISBN 0 85670 770 8 £7.50
104 pages 237 illustrations including 40 in colour